# Strategic Issues
# Management

*Robert L. Heath*
*and Associates*

# Strategic Issues Management

*How Organizations
Influence and Respond
to Public Interests and Policies*

**Jossey-Bass Publishers**
San Francisco  •  London  •  1988

STRATEGIC ISSUES MANAGEMENT
*How Organizations Influence and Respond to Public Interests and Policies*
  by Robert L. Heath and Associates

Copyright © 1988 by: Jossey-Bass Inc., Publishers
                     350 Sansome Street
                     San Francisco, California 94104
                          &
                     Jossey-Bass Limited
                     28 Banner Street
                     London EC1Y 8QE

Chapter Three reprinted, with modifications, from *Planning Review*,
published by the Planning Forum, 5500 College Corner Pike, Oxford, OH
45056.

Chapter Four reprinted with modifications, with permission, from *Futures
Research Quarterly*, published by the World Future Society, 4916 St. Elmo
Ave., Bethesda, Maryland 20814.

Credits continued on page 415.

**Library of Congress Cataloging-in-Publication Data**

Strategic issues management.

  (The Jossey-Bass management series)
  Bibliography: p.
  Includes index.
  1. Issues management.   2. Corporate planning.
3. Strategic planning.   I. Heath, Robert L.
(Robert Lawrence), 1941–     .  II. Series.
HD59.5.S76  1988        658.4′012        87-46335
ISBN 1-55542-083-4

Manufactured in the United States of America

The paper in this book meets the guidelines for permanence and
durability of the Committee on Production Guidelines for Book Longevity
of the Council on Library Resources.

JACKET DESIGN BY WILLI BAUM

FIRST EDITION

*Code 8808*

# The Jossey-Bass Management Series

Consulting Editors
Organizations and Management

Warren Bennis
*University of Southern California*

Richard O. Mason
*Southern Methodist University*

Ian I. Mitroff
*University of Southern California*

# Contents

ix

# Preface

In the mid 1970s, an atmosphere of increased hostility toward private-sector practices led business communicators such as W. Howard Chase and John O'Toole to rethink the role of corporate communication. Chase and O'Toole coined the terms *issue(s) management* and *advocacy advertising* to define the strategies they thought companies needed to become more involved with in shaping public policy and in countering efforts by activist groups to pressure legislators and regulators for stricter control of business activities.

In its infancy, issues management was little more than advocacy advertising and complex discussions of corporate social responsibility. For example, Chase articulated a rationale for issues management that made it a form of external communication. Many writers were trying to capture in abstract terms the ethical responsibilities companies have to their neighbors; employees and consultants charged with being the consciences of companies set forth codes of conduct to show enterprises how to become good citizens. Much of this discussion led in circles. Nevertheless, several valuable themes have persisted and matured.

Realizing that adopting performance standards is the first step toward managing issues, several leading companies implemented a kind of preventive maintenance to guide operations and assure employee ethics. A good example of a company that took corrective measures is Dow Chemical, which was broadly criticized in the 1960s. Having heard that Dow had implemented rigid codes of operating standards, I asked about them. A long-time Dow employee told me, "The bottom line is, we do not pollute; as an employee, I know that I have no excuse for allowing or causing pollution."

In the spirit of helping companies lessen the friction between themselves and their sociopolitical neighbors, this book is intended to be practical, without losing its comprehensiveness and thoroughness or abandoning its theoretical and conceptual underpinnings. Despite the many common threads that run through the chapters that follow, some heated debates would occur if these contributors were pressed to agree on all the particulars of issues management.

The selection of authors and materials for this book reflects a spirit and a fond hope. The spirit comes from what seems to be an increased willingness by corporate leaders to act constructively and sensitively in behalf of the public interest. They seem to show a genuine desire to improve the public images of companies and to change the ways they are being treated by the media and activist groups. These battles are less frequently characterized by the narrow, self-serving stridency and outrage typical of those of the 1960s and 1970s. Instead one finds careful, calculated efforts to be sensitive to public opinion, without bowing to it or dealing with its manifestations behind closed doors of legislative halls or in company-owned sporting lodges. Many major companies have chosen to openly debate key public policy issues in the spirit implicit in First Amendment rights and responsibilities. Even though few campaigns are as sizable and aggressive as Mobil's, the end of the low profile has come. Many corporate leaders are convinced that the public needs and wants to understand the business point of view. More and more companies have become willing to help correct the problems of ill-informed and narrow public policy discussions.

In addition to spirit, this book demonstrates a hope that corporate leaders will become more willing to include issues management in their strategic planning. People intimately involved in the discussions of issues management have been sensitive to the need to define what it can do for companies, particularly in helping them deliver goods and services in a manner consistent with public expectations. Gone is the time when whims alone led company executives to implement and fund issues management. Indeed, some critics believe that issues management is a fad whose time has passed. In the face of this opposition, the people who contributed to this book — and others who should be in it — will continue to play instrumental roles in convincing managements across this country that public policy is vital to the balance sheet. These advocates can persuade executives to take positive steps to maximize the advantages that come their way by understanding how public policy interacts with performance in the marketplace. Without doubt, some companies will accomplish superior public policy adjustments and thereby produce better-than-average performance records. For other companies, mismanagement of public policy will lead to a fight for survival.

Recently it has become apparent that critics of the corporation have gained the status of an institution and will be of continuing importance. Corporations have responded in many ways to this agitational, post-Vietnam operating environment. Vague complaints from corporations about media bias and angry rebuttals to the claims and studies mounted by organizations critical of some business practices have not been effective counterweights to the gains made by "public interest" advocates. Such groups often attract substantial media and donor support, represent a loyal following, are well organized, and employ refined pressure strategies. Some receive federal and state funding.

One response to the institutionalization of corporate critics has been the creation of the Issues Management Association. Founded in 1981, it was designed to bring together interested practitioners and scholars "who work in or significantly contribute to the fields of foresight, policy development and issues management in business and industry, government, education, trade and professional associations." Its membership growth parallels the fact that at least half of all *Fortune* 500 companies have instituted issues management programs, and many universities are integrating such studies into their curricula.

Because issues management is beginning to claim its rightful place in corporate activities, the opportunity to read the essays collected here should be valuable for operations managers, strategic planners, corporate communication practitioners, faculty members, students, and others concerned about understanding, planning for, and managing corporations' place in sociopolitical change. In coming years, issues management studies can further help the private sector do its job even more effectively and responsibly. If we are right in our vision of what companies can and should do, we will see a future of increased partnership between the public and private sectors.

Issues management is maturing as an academic discipline. Many books and articles have been written recently to define the boundaries of this vital corporate activity. In this regard, this book is an extension of work I did with Richard Alan Nelson in *Issues Management: Corporate Public Policymaking in an Information Society* (1986). When we began that project, we had no idea how much related work had been done, because it was so scattered. Other writers had focused on what to us seemed to be pieces of the whole fabric of issues management. But none had gathered all aspects of issues management and packaged them between two covers. Attempting a comprehensive definition of issues management, we sought to distinguish it from related disciplines such as public affairs, public relations, and one of its primary means of communication, issues advertising. Although we saw issues communication as a vital part of the total process, we were convinced that issues management was more than old-hat communication practices typical of traditional public relations or public affairs departments. So we discussed the history and contemporary practice of corporate public policy efforts, issues monitoring, and efforts to create and implement codes of corporate social responsibility. We recognized that special-interest agitation is more than a communication breakdown; the stark reality is that the battle between companies and special-interest groups is a contest of power resource management that can best be described by a game-theory approach. This power struggle translates into varied ground rules that are ostensibly designed to bring accuracy and balance to the public discussion of key issues. These rules are implemented through the Internal Revenue Service, the Federal Communications Commission, and the Federal Trade Commission. Convinced that television and other media had helped create a negative view of corporate America, we analyzed the problems of access to television, constrained by the fairness doctrine, and suggested many alternative uses of television and various new communication technologies.

The chapters that follow are arranged in five groups. Part One discusses the relationship between issues management and strategic planning. Part Two centers on the identification and analysis of public policy issues and explores strategies for bringing issues management into play in day-to-day activities. Part Three shows how the issues identified can become part of a company's communication and power positioning strategies. Some key roles of trade associations and public information organizations are the theme of Part Four. Part Five looks to the future by discussing how issues management may mature, especially in conjunction with public affairs and emerging public policy issues.

The author wishes to acknowledge the help of Richard Alan Nelson at several vital points in the creation and development of this book. Laura Lerond offered valuable suggestions for improving the manuscript. Jane Work, of the National Association of Manufacturers, provided information about NAM's NAMNET system. I thank the dozens of issues experts who offered insights and constructive criticism during the development of this manuscript.

*Houston, Texas*                                    Robert L. Heath
*March 1988*

# The Authors

Robert L. Heath is a professor of communication and director of the Institute for the Study of Issues Management at the University of Houston. He received his bachelor's degree in communication from Western State College of Colorado (1963), his master's degree from the University of New Mexico (1965), and his Ph.D. degree from the University of Illinois (1971).

Heath's academic interests include research on the communication and planning activities that companies use to adjust to public policy changes. He has examined how the fairness doctrine affects corporate communication practices and has studied the cognitive processes and media effects associated with audience responses to issue advertising. Much of his work has been in defense of corporate efforts to take public policy stances through public debate. He has studied the roles that activist groups play in the public policy process. Heath's research has been published in many professional journals, including the *Journal of Marketing, Public Affairs Review, Public Relations Review, Public Relations Quarterly,* and *Journal of Communication.* In 1986, with Richard A. Nelson, he published *Issues Management: Corporate Public Policymaking in an Information Society.*

Heath's current research efforts concentrate on helping trade associations understand how consumer issues mature into public policy issues. Through the Institute for the Study of Issues Management, he is examining the roles of public relations practitioners in corporate efforts to create and implement codes of conduct. He is analyzing which monitoring techniques are most useful in helping companies calculate the content and depth of opinions held by various key publics.

Edward L. Aduss is vice-president, advertising, U.S. Committee for Energy Awareness, Washington, D.C.

Herbert E. Alexander is director, Citizens' Research Foundation, and professor of political science, University of Southern California.

Charles B. Arrington, Jr., is vice-president of Newmyer Associates, Inc., Washington, D.C. He is former director of public affairs issues and planning for Atlantic Richfield Company, Los Angeles.

Rogene A. Buchholz is professor of business and public policy in the School of Management at the University of Texas, Dallas. He is the author of several books on corporate behavior and public policy.

Abraham M. Buchman has been legal counsel to the American Beverage Alcohol Association since 1963. He has been counsel to the Vermouth Institute, Inc., the International Vermouth Institute, Inc., the New Jersey Vintners Association, the Wine Conference of America, Federazione Italiana Industriali, and the American Wine Association.

Phil Cates is regional coordinator in the Governmental Affairs Department of Tenneco Inc. He served four terms in the House of Representatives of Texas, including a term on the Appropriations Committee.

Joseph F. Coates is president, J. F. Coates Inc., an issues-monitoring and public affairs consulting company in Washington, D.C. He is adjunct professor in the School of Public and International Affairs at George Washington University.

Fritz M. Elmendorf is director of communications and public relations, Consumer Bankers Association, in Washington, D.C. He was assistant manager of public relations with the American Bankers Association during the 10 percent withholding controversy.

Jennifer Jarratt is a staff member at J. F. Coates Inc., a Washington, D.C., firm specializing in futures research and policy analysis.

Stephen J. Kasser is an account executive with E. J. Hughes Company in St. Petersburg, Florida. Until the fall of 1986, he was issues management administrator for Tampa Electric Company, Tampa, Florida.

Patricia C. Kelley is research associate, Public Affairs Research Program, School of Management, Boston University.

O. W. Markley is associate professor, studies of the future, University of Houston, Clear Lake.

Richard Alan Nelson is associate professor of communication at the University of Houston.

Mary Ann Pires is principal, The Pires Group, which she founded in March 1986. She held managerial positions with Combustion Engineering, Texaco Inc., and the John Hancock Mutual Life Insurance Company. She joined Combustion Engineering after seven years with Texaco, where she developed a prototype constituency relations program.

James E. Post is professor of management and public policy at Boston University.

Matthew C. Ross is vice-president, Ogilvy & Mather Advertising.

Richard N. Sawaya is director of government and tax affairs for Atlantic Richfield in Washington, D.C.

Herb Schmertz is vice-president for public affairs, Mobil Oil Corporation.

Margaret A. Stroup is director, Department of Planning, Monsanto Chemical Company.

Greg Truax is manager of public and employee communications for Tampa Electric Company, Tampa, Florida.

# Strategic Issues
# Management

# Introduction:
# Issues Management:
# Developing Corporate
# Survival Strategies

*Robert L. Heath*

The past two decades have been particularly troublesome for business leaders. They have been charged and
convicted for failing to adopt Japanese management styles.
Corporate executives are faced with what seems an inexorable
shift from a "smokestack economy" to an "information society."
Business strategists plead for increased productivity. And companies have been buffeted by militant consumers, angry neighbors, hostile activist groups, employees worried about their
health and safety, and media reporters who specialize in sensa-
tional accounts of corporate irresponsibility, no matter how
atypical.

We are at one of those rare turning points in history where
elemental structures of society and economy shift — impercepti-
bly at first, then with increasing vigor — from the certain to the
uncertain. As we move into an information-based service economy, the need to plan proactively for new, uncharted public
policy considerations becomes urgent. The domestic marketplace is giving way to the dynamics of an unprecedented and
uncharted global marketplace. The recent turbulence in the
New York and other stock exchanges may result from basic shifts
in the value structure that surrounds businesses as they seek to

1

maximize their interests while maintaining harmony with the interests of others in their operating environments.

Those who guide businesses should not forget that marketplace forces are mingled with regulation. In the midst of apparent corporate prosperity, compliance with federal, state, and local regulations costs the private sector billions of dollars each year. Though enjoying some respite during the Reagan administration, companies have never been more politicized. Any moment of peace should not lull them, because public policy battles are cyclical. To protect their interests and work harmoniously with their various stakeholders, companies need principles and strategies to survive in a dynamic and increasingly demanding public policy environment. Policy debate centers on the quality of operations, products, and services. Even the amount of profit a company expects from its investments can become a public policy issue, and public policy can result in misinvestments if dollars are channeled into unproductive or socially unpopular projects. A good business plan can turn sour if the public policy environment changes. Companies do not succeed or fail only because of their ability to compete in the marketplace; survival also depends on how they position themselves in the public policy arena.

This exacting level of performance has developed since the mid 1960s, when activist groups started to become permanent fixtures in the legislative and regulatory process. The growth of issues management as a corporate and trade association activity has corresponded to increasing awareness by savvy executives and managers that any business planning scenario must recognize that activist groups have become highly skilled in their tactics, well funded, and firmly institutionalized (Bennett and DiLorenzo, 1985). For example, the Council on Economic Priorities recently published a 500-page book evaluating companies' corporate consciences. The book is a buyers' guide that, the council hopes, consumers will use to impose corporate conscience by purchasing products from the most responsible companies (Lydenberg and others, 1986). The public has learned that it no longer needs to suffer in silence in the face of what it believes to be outrageous corporate behavior. And it knows that it can have a voice in defining the standards of that behavior.

As a countermeasure to unwarranted regulation, the growth of issues management is recognition that the private sector does not have to be held hostage by dramatic public policy changes that can harm the bottom line. During the decade since its conception, issues management has become more than just public relations, public affairs, or the creative use of advertising. It requires expertise in business planning and sensitivity to how public policy can interrupt business planning. It is the one corporate function that brings together those persons who plan and guide corporate activities and ethics, those who manage operations, those who market products and services, those who monitor the corporation's sociopolitical environment, and those who communicate with key audiences. Effective issues management integrates these components into a holistic combination of attitudes and activities: listening, analyzing, planning, controlling, and communicating. Combined, these can become part of each company's culture.

What is public policy? In Chapter One, Rogene A. Buchholz argues that it refers, not to public opinions, but to actions that governmental or other bodies take to guide business operations. These actions result when legislatures, regulatory bodies, or courts create standards that impose or remove boundaries on business planning and operations. Buchholz's definition of public policy does not deny the potency of public opinion; it acknowledges how public policy can grow from public opinion. Often, influentials, whether intellectuals or special-interest activists, alter key publics' perception of what constitutes acceptable corporate behavior or expose corporate actions that conflict with established standards of acceptable behavior.

Effective strategic planning and management demand that all variables instrumental in a company's success *or* failure be identified and controlled. This task is not easy, because public policy can rise from many springheads, such as lawsuits, as well as public dialogue by special-interest advocates, legislators, or critics in the media. These voices can lead "the public" to want to impose its will on corporate behavior. And issues arise when intra- and interindustry advocates seek such measures as tax reform, regulation, deregulation, or protective tariffs.

Some public policy issues are extremely technical and arise because of advances in knowledge. For example, the health impact of chemicals such as benzene, vinyl chloride, and formaldehyde is being carefully examined. Always a candidate for scare tactics as well as legitimate concern, this kind of issue is debated in courts and hearing rooms where company experts clash with representatives of activist groups. In 1986 benzene made a major step toward becoming a public policy issue when a $108 million judgment went against Monsanto because the plaintiff successfully argued that the chemical causes leukemia. Monsanto's defense was that benzene does not cause the kind of cancer fatal to the family member involved in the case. As a result of the case, the Occupational Safety and Health Administration considered whether to strengthen its benzene standard to 1 part per million—a major public policy stance. Sometimes advances in public policy result from new instrumentation that allows even more precise measurement or from long-term medical research that links chemicals and health.

Other public policy issues arise from economic changes. For example, the electrical generating industry has been hard hit and has many tumultuous years ahead. Typical of this crisis, Gulf States Utilities and Middle South Utilities considered bankruptcy because of the resistance they encountered when trying to recover the costs of building nuclear generating plants. These companies were caught with high construction debts at a time when state agencies became reluctant to grant rate relief and when stagnation of local economies lowered the demand for electricity-generating capacity.

Public policy issues can also result when companies are discovered to be violating accepted public standards of responsible business behavior. For this reason, the chemical industry is being watched to determine whether groundwater is being polluted in ways that pose substantial health hazards. The historic Pure Food and Drug Act did not result from a massive change in public values but from public awareness that some companies were producing unsanitary and unhealthful food products or unsafe drugs and cosmetics.

A few public policy issues appear without warning and mature with blinding speed to the point where crisis management is required. For example, the Food and Drug Administration carefully orchestrated a public outburst against Procter & Gamble over the toxic shock syndrome scare involving Rely tampons several years ago. But extensive and scrupulous research coupled with a skillful crisis communication campaign averted disaster for this company.

Other public policy changes result from evolving attitudes and values. For example, the beer, wine, and spirits industry has seen public opinion shift to the point where product liability cases related to alcoholism and product misuse (drunk driving) might dramatically affect the industry. Only the most prophetic planners can predict which product or industry will suffer in coming years, but the vigilant will be the more likely to survive.

### The Public Policy Battleground: Two Case Studies

For readers who doubt the power public policy can have over companies' destinies, two brief case studies — A. H. Robins and Manville — may be instructive. They underscore how failure to *read shifts* in the policy environment and *make appropriate adjustments* can bring companies to the brink of financial disaster. Both cases originated from product liability disputes, typically a personal matter between plaintiff and company. However, in both instances, the issue did not stop in court. The A. H. Robins Dalkon Shield case involved Food and Drug Administration policies, and the asbestos crisis produced new standards promulgated through the Occupational Safety and Health Administration and the Environmental Protection Agency. A. H. Robins and the members of the asbestos industry sought federal protection—a clear case of public policy. Robins led in the creation of a political action committee (PAC) serving the Product Liability Alliance and the Coalition for Uniform Product

Liability Law. PAC funds have been spent in an attempt to pass legislation that would limit product liability. These cases reveal what can happen when companies do not manage an issue but allow it to manage them.

*A. H. Robins and the Dalkon Shield.* A. H. Robins Company manufactured and sold the Dalkon Shield, an intrauterine device (IUD), in the United States from 1971 to 1974. Acting on evidence that the shield was unsatisfactorily designed and consequently harmful to users, the Food and Drug Administration asked Robins to stop sales in the United States, a major public policy decision.

Even though the product was removed from sale, the floodgate of lawsuits had been opened. As of June 30, 1985, A. H. Robins and its insurer, Aetna Insurance Company, had spent $378 million to dispose of liability cases (Mintz, 1985). Legal fees added several million dollars more to the cost. A decade after suspension of sales, hundreds of thousands of cases were pending. Because the company's future was uncertain, it became a highly speculative investment and was courted by several suitors seeking a takeover.

The trouble began, plaintiffs alleged, because the string attached to the IUD served as a wick to transmit bacteria into its users. Side effects included severe pelvic inflammatory disease, unwanted pregnancies, birth defects, and infertility. Even when reputable physicians complained about these effects, executives at Robins were slow to respond and apparently turned a deaf ear to these complaints. After several liability cases had been decided against Robins, the company undertook a $4 million advertising campaign warning women of the danger and advising them to have the device removed.

Over the years that it sold the shield, the company was in a position to receive enough independent, reputable complaints to warrant a full-scale internal investigation; however, if such studies were conducted, they were not used proactively to mitigate the harm done by the public outcry. One of the battles waged by plaintiffs' lawyers centered on cover-ups of damaging reports that had warned Robins's executives of the dangers. Vital documents and entire files had disappeared. Robins appears to have been extremely reluctant to alter its strategic plan and operating style even in the face of public outrage and its inability to defend against lawsuits.

The range of choices available to Robins narrowed in 1983 when several judges increased their pressure and the National Women's Health Network worked to stop international sales. Robins adopted two major ploys: to call for federal laws limiting the amount of product liability that could be imposed on a company and to seek protection by reorganizing under Chapter 11 of the Federal Bankruptcy Act, which Robins hoped would protect its interests from creditors, particularly the persons who were seeking redress because they had been harmed by the product. Under pressure, the company established a reserve of $615 million to pay compensatory damages and legal fees.

Massive product liability problems and the attendant unfavorable public policy decisions had a detrimental effect on A. H. Robins's balance sheet, even making the company vulnerable for a takeover. However, suitors such as American Home Products were cautious in their takeover efforts because the magnitude of liability was so great.

*The Asbestos Industry: Failure to Warn.* The asbestos industry was wrecked by the discovery that the product it manufactured and installed played havoc with the health of the population. Myriad public policy decisions have arisen regarding what levels of asbestos are safe and who is responsible for removing asbestos from living and working environments. The crisis, though synonymous with Johns Manville, affected many other companies, including Owens-Corning Fiberglas, Pittsburgh Corning, Pittsburgh Plate Glass Company, Raybestos-Manhattan, Eagle-Picher, and UNARCO Industries. In 1986 Manville was required, as part of its bankruptcy proceedings and in response to litigants' claims, to establish a trust indefinitely binding some $2.5 billion to meet the needs of persons who suffer from asbestos-related illnesses. Whatever the major asbestos companies did to protect workers and users of their product, courts have decided that the measures were inadequate — constituting a failure to warn.

In 1982 Manville Corporation filed for reorganization

under Chapter 11. Experts estimated at that time that Manville could face as many as 120,000 liability suits totaling $5 billion. This leader in the manufacturing of asbestos had learned a very tough lesson about changes of opinion that had occurred during the 1960s. The public was outraged to learn that it could not trust an industry. By the 1970s, when the number of suits was swelling, the crisis had been reached. But it was too late to "manage" the issue — the industry could only hope to minimize its losses. Inadequate early warning systems and a weak sense of ethical responsibility allowed the industry to suffer financial disaster. In January 1985, *Fortune*'s poll on corporate image ranked Manville last among 250 companies in terms of community and environmental responsibility and 248th as least admired. In 1987, the same poll discovered that Manville continued to be one of the least admired (296th of 300).

The asbestos story is one of mixed results. Thousands of lives have been saved because of asbestos's flame-resistant characteristics; homes, commercial establishments, public buildings, and World War II military equipment enjoyed state-of-the-art technology. But asbestos is also extremely hazardous to the health of those who handle and live with it.

Brodeur (1985) claims the asbestos industry had reason to know of the health hazards associated with its product. Industry studies and those by independent physicians established health problems as early as the 1920s. Manville had settled health claim cases as early as the 1930s. In 1942 Dr. Irving Selikoff of the Mount Sinai School of Medicine in New York began a research project on 632 members of the International Association of Heat and Frost Insulators and Asbestos Workers. The research lasted for twenty years and concluded that these workers suffered higher-than-normal levels of health disorders. After this study, Manville placed warnings on asbestos products in 1964. It bragged in 1973 that it was developing state-of-the-art techniques for ensuring employee safety. In their defense, asbestos companies point out that the effects take decades to appear. Determining the safe level of asbestos in the working and living environment will take a long time.

Efforts had been made to have asbestos workers use protective respirators, but the health hazards were not fully and dramatically explained to the workers until they began to come out through several major product liability cases. The landmark case, *Borel* v. *Fibreboard* (1973), concluded that companies that manufactured the product were liable for damages because they had not sufficiently warned those who bought and used it. This case laid the foundation for a warning label stating that asbestos could cause health problems. Cognizant that asbestos had been linked to cancer, Manville worked with public officials to develop standards for employee and public safety. But why did the industry not initiate extensive and disciplined studies to confirm or disconfirm the connection of asbestos with the health hazards that had long been linked to it, a connection that employee health records seemed to confirm?

Manville and other companies have tried to use the federal government as a buffer, arguing, for instance, that since workers in shipyards were technically federal employees, the government is responsible for their health benefits and liability claims. The companies encouraged then-Senator Gary Hart to introduce legislation that would have had the federal government use tax dollars to pay the victims. Hart failed to get the legislation out of committee.

Were the companies as socially responsible as they should have been? Did they show concern for the lives their products would harm? Did the war effort create such a national emergency that people would have used asbestos even if they had known of its dangers? The companies that could have helped society address these issues apparently did not.

This classic case demonstrates how a narrow vision toward a business activity can mushroom into a major public policy crisis involving liability to employees and the public. Sparks fly in all directions when a company's performance does not match established public expectations about the kinds and qualities of products and services that corporations must provide. In the Dalkon Shield and asbestos cases, issues communication may have helped the companies, but the real solution was an honest effort to change corporate policies to realistically face the harm caused by products. Another point: If companies cannot decide what constitutes corporate ethical responsibility, the courts can.

## Not All Is Bad News

Public opinion and policy shifts can mean bad news for companies—but they do not have to. In fact, companies often promote policy changes, and enterprising business leaders look for policies that offer opportunities to increase profit, change operations, and enhance revenue. Public policy sometimes affects operating conditions for the better. The real challenge is foreseeing opportunities so that they can be planned for and the alternatives maximized.

*Successful Adaptation in the Tobacco Industry.* Whereas Robins and Manville responded with too little too late to adjust to their public policy environments, the tobacco industry is a good example of how comprehensive planning increases the likelihood of survival. This industry appears to be managing its product mix and, through diversification, becoming less dependent on unpopular product lines. R. J. Reynolds changed its name to RJR Nabisco Inc. to soften the company image, claiming that this new name more accurately portrayed its product mix. It has discussed creating a limited partnership as a way of protecting most of the company's assets from liability claims.

The tobacco industry, in 1986, was jolted by many events. One of the most interesting occurred when Patrick Reynolds, an heir to the R. J. Reynolds fortune, publicly turned thumbs down on cigarette smoking. He appeared as an actor in an advertisement for the American Lung Association, announcing that he had sold his tobacco stock because he believed that the product had contributed to the death of his father, who had suffered from emphysema.

Recently, the status of smoking has changed significantly. In fact and myth, tobacco is as old as this country, a vital part of Americana. Inseparable from American Indian folklore, it was vital to the colonial period of our country's history when it was introduced into Europe. Eventually a major economic force, this plant helped endow institutions of higher education and served as economic mainstay for many workers and entire regions. Smoking has been identified with physical attractiveness and maturity. It has been associated with the liberation of women.

But, more important, it is criticized for what many medical groups and a growing number of legislators contend are its health hazards. Cigarette packs and ads are required to carry health warnings. The product cannot be advertised on television. A move is afoot to ban its advertising entirely. Smoking is no longer assumed a right that smokers can exercise at will. City ordinances across the nation now prescribe where people may smoke. Companies have become "smoke free." The army has taken steps to curb smoking. New York's mayor has supported a tough antismoking law. The American Medical Association increased its campaign to ban cigarette advertising. The Federal Trade Commission accused RJR Nabisco of misrepresenting the hazards of smoking in its advertisements. To this list of landmark occurrences was added a liability case that received national attention because the plaintiff alleged that smoking had caused a death; in another case the allegation was made that smokeless tobacco had caused cancer of the mouth.

The tobacco issue is not easy to solve. The industry is economically vital to sections of the country and to segments of the economy. Millions of dollars are invested in facilities for raising tobacco and for making, transporting, and selling cigarettes. Thousands depend on tobacco as a primary source of income, from farmers to truckers to clerks in retail sales outlets. Magazines and newspapers draw advertising dollars. More important, the people in the tobacco industry realize that 55 million people are regular smokers and resist giving up their habit. This is a very stable and lucrative market. Is this issue manageable? Can it be influenced by issues communication?

*The Bright Side of Public Policy.* Some public policy changes create markets and give companies incentives to change their product lines. In the midst of the pollution battle in the 1960s, Ethyl Corporation suffered a blow because lead was associated with high levels of pollution. Some observers predicted the demise of this company, which drew 90 percent of its operating profits from this one additive; the prevalence of the labels "unleaded" and "use unleaded gasoline only" testifies to the degree to which this company took a public policy body punch. But twenty years later, the company has shown dramatic growth, not bad for a company once destined for the public policy bone pile. Its new additives have been accompanied by strategic diversification. This company learned a public policy lesson. Its tuition was well spent.

Public policy not only takes away—it also offers opportunities. As it changed the clothing industry, requiring that flame retardants be added to children's clothing, public policy created a new market and, along with it, new jobs. Some companies prospered because they produced flame-retardant materials. Similar changes resulted from the pollution battles. For every company that had its operating systems altered, new jobs were created and new companies came into being to help solve the pollution crisis. Rollins Environmental Services, created in 1982, has become an industry leader in hazardous-waste treatment and water disposal. Though sometimes embattled in very technical regulatory disputes, this closely scrutinized company is one of many that came about because of public policy.

Public policy produces a mixture of outcomes, some good and some bad. Savvy companies understand public policy and the people who work to form it; these companies realize that public policy, like any other operating condition, can produce profit or dampen income. Public policy should be treated like any other dominant variable in strategic planning—the process of laying out a company's long-term profit objectives. Just ask General Motors, as large and powerful as it is, why it no longer produces Corvairs.

So the record on public policy battles is mixed. Some companies have been hurt by confronting public opinion in ways that have led to legal battles and increased public policy legislation and regulation. Other companies have been helped. Some have made a transition from the wounded to the well. The overall conclusion is that if a company is unready to manage an issue, it is likely to find itself in a reactive, rather than a proactive, position. Of course, companies cannot always avoid trouble no matter how sophisticated their issues management systems, just as they cannot predict the success of every business venture.

Willing to take the chance that it could minimize public policy impact, General Electric early in the 1970s decided that it was not serving the interests of its employees, customers, industry associates, neighbors, and shareholders if it did not do its best to monitor issues and incorporate the findings into its strategic planning. GE was one of the first companies to use strategic planning and public policy monitoring to become more responsive to changing standards of corporate behavior. It developed a planning/operating matrix consisting of four variables that interface operations, planning, and public policy issues: technological, economic, social, and political. Economic forecasting and planning consider the financial and marketing environments that will affect the company's future. Technological forecasting attempts to determine what innovations are likely to challenge the directions of the markets in which GE participates. Its social monitoring looks for changes in values, life-styles, and demographics that will affect its operating environment or its marketing plan. The political arena concentrates on the legislation, regulatory agencies, and special-interest groups that may rise to change GE's operating environment. This complex of efforts cannot ensure that GE will always be totally prepared to predict and forestall crises. But it increases the likelihood that GE will minimize its operating surprises and stay in a leadership position in technical, political, and social areas where it has the greatest opportunity to influence and adapt to its environment.

Does socially responsible management increase profitability? This issue continues to be debated. Aupperle, Carroll, and Hatfield (1985) contend that corporate social responsibility is not correlated with profitability. The Council on Economic Priorities challenges this view by citing studies to prove that responsible, "progressive" companies are at least as profitable as less responsible ones and sometimes more so (Lydenberg and others, 1986, pp. 7–15). The verdict is not in, but a case can be made that profits are hurt if a company is overregulated, fined, or otherwise punished for irresponsible activities. In highly competitive markets, the most savvy companies will prosper best. And public policy variables are an inextricable part of the planning and operating environment.

### Survival Principles: Public Policy Partnerships

What can we learn from this review of the mixed blessings of public policy for corporate survival? It seems clear that companies must be ever vigilant to avoid the pitfalls and take advantage of the opportunities that public policy brings. But this stance does not fully address the issue of corporate ethics. Is it possible to balance economic, public, and social performance? The discussion is maturing toward a principle that will properly balance the three (Wartick and Cochran, 1985). Perhaps the best term is *corporate responsibility*, which incorporates economic, public, *and* social concerns.

Over the years a heated debate has been waged to define the requirements and boundaries of what is often called corporate social responsibility. Some discussants have abandoned the term *responsibility* in favor of *responsiveness*, which is alleged to require proactive efforts to meet community needs beyond avoiding being in conflict with community standards (see, for instance, Buchholz, Evans, and Wagley, 1985). Some scholars and corporate leaders complain that both terms, *responsiveness* and *responsibility*, imply that companies will not act ethically unless pushed to do so by their critics. They bristle at the charge that companies are irresponsible or unresponsive to customers and other stakeholders. Moreover, *responsive* seems reactive, not proactive, and *responsible* may sound defensive.

Stressing the economic side of the equation, Milton Friedman (1962, 1970) argues that companies' only responsibilities are to produce goods and services and to provide jobs and dividends. Another view of this requirement is expressed by Peter F. Drucker (1984): "The proper 'social responsibility' of business is to tame the dragon, that is, to turn a social problem into economic opportunity and economic benefit, into productive capacity, into human competence, into well-paid jobs, and into wealth" (p. 62).

But the economic side may not stand alone. The need for careful monitoring and strategic change was reinforced by the unanticipated consequences that Nestlé Corporation faced as a result of its controversial decision to market baby formula in developing nations. A key player in this effort, Rafael D. Pagan, Jr. (1983), stresses two points he had learned: "For business, the cost of social awareness programs is great, but the cost of ignoring the outside world is greater." He proposes, "Issues managers can help instill social awareness into a business." With issues management, corporations can realize the cost savings of monitoring and managing issues before they become explosive. Early response can be fiscally astute as well as ethical and responsible.

The external community is a reality that company leaders cannot ignore. Jones (1985) helps us understand this fact by enumerating the forces that bound corporate autonomy: shareholders as litigants, labor unions, special-interest groups, market forces, regulatory agencies, stock exchange regulations, creditors, proponents of ethical norms, statutory law, case law, foreign policy edicts, and shareholders as investors. Issues management, to be comprehensive, must be sensitive to these internal and external constraints because they form vital parts of the sociopolitical environment.

The problem of corporate responsibility is made greater by the imprecision of ethical standards. What constitutes responsible business behavior is far less precise than a 55-mile-per-hour speed limit. A leading writer on the topic, William C. Frederick (1986), pinpoints the crux of the issue: "Ethical problems arise precisely at these normative junctures, where alterations of interests occur and norms come under stress" (p. 127). Decisions related to issues monitoring and the reformulation of company operating values are not cast in absolute, static terms. Such standards are fluid and can even be capricious. The goal, Frederick argues, is to achieve *corporate social rectitude*, which "embodies the notion of moral correctness in actions taken and policies formulated" (p. 135).

In the absence of absolute standards, issues managers must constantly monitor subtle trends and recognize their implications for company operations. When values shift, the effect ripples throughout related standards of performance. Changes in values and norms produce stress points between public and corporate interests. Skilled analysts look for stress points in much the same way a physician does. Where is the pain? How long has it been there? What remedy (realignment) is necessary?

The fluctuation characteristic of public issues perspectives requires constant monitoring, corporate strategic planning adjustments, and communication to blunt unwarranted criticism and to exploit opportunities. Companies are unwise to approach such decision points with a defensive stance; rather, these should be viewed as opportunities to make valuable changes in corporate operations or to take advantage of new market possibilities. Change is marketable, whether the innovation is a product or a service or the company image.

Even those persons who bristle at the assumption that companies will not be responsible unless critics tell them to be admit that some companies have deservedly better reputations than others. Most companies do their best to understand and meet the standards of ethical behavior that key publics hold. However, such standards are always subject to interpretation; business critics are quick to seek ever new and more demanding standards. Companies must be prepared to discuss the topics candidly and in terms of their audiences' self-interests.

To make the concept of corporate responsibility more proactive, the key term should be *concern*. Whether to foster a candid and realistic sense of values or in response to power politics, each company should be concerned about the interests of its stakeholders—those who consume its products, use its services, share its products, earn its wages, and share its environment. The goal is *corporate social partnership* whereby a company makes a commitment to achieve harmony with each of its stakeholders (Freeman, 1984). Several principles can guide a company's sense of corporate social partnership.

1.  Business profits and public policy are inseparable.
2.  The public is indifferent to fine distinctions between law and ethics. The latter will guide condemnation; the anger will be greater if the law is used to avoid what vital publics

consider ethical behavior. Remember that those who are outraged can bring about changes in the law.

3. The public is unimpressed by the needs of a company if they conflict with the public interest. But likewise, the public seems willing to learn about and understand corporations' points of view, especially when they foster the public interest.

4. In the mind of the public, an attack on one company or industry is not a challenge to capitalism.

5. If a choice is required between company interests and family security, the latter will win.

6. The public can distinguish facts and values. It wants to be informed and assumes companies that are not open are not truthful.

7. If companies do not inform the public on public policy issues, someone else will.

8. If companies do not establish realistic codes of operating ethics, someone else will.

9. All these principles can be used to the advantage of companies.

The message to corporate leaders: Be realistic. If you think you are correct, enter the debate and let the judgment of public opinion prevail. Integrate ethics into strategic planning and operations. Make corporate responsibility basic to employee appraisal and reward. Look for opportunities for new processes, products, and services. Announce your corporate mission and performance standards and demonstrate to employees that they are inseparable. Tell your stakeholders how your operations are better than those of your competitors. Responsiveness is a marketable and valuable aspect of company image.

## Vitality of Issues Management to Strategic Planning

During its short history, issues management has been characterized in many ways. Some consider it nothing more than one aspect of corporate communication, advocacy advertising (O'Toole, 1975; Sethi, 1977). In this vein, a plethora of issue ads flooded the print media in the 1970s, the result of companies' desire to tell the public how business interests were being hurt. Because most of these ad campaigns were unsuccessful, the narrow advocacy advertising orientation was short-lived. Another common view of issues management is expressed by such writers as Ehling and Hesse (1983), who contend that it is nothing but a new name for standard public relations practices.

Recently, a gradual evolution has led many to believe that issues management is more than monitoring issues and communicating with various publics. As will be argued here and in Part One, issues management can support corporate strategic planning. Figure 1 shows how issues management fits into the total strategic planning and strategic management process. As a counterpart to operations and marketing, issues management is designed to maximize a corporation's fit with its sociopolitical environment in the same way the other two activities are used to position the company in its economic and market environments.

Integrating the public policy planning aspect of issues management into strategic planning puts even more burden on strategic planning, which itself is not universally accepted. Corporate strategic planning is being buffeted, Gray (1986) says, by those who debunk rational planning in favor of more intuitive, less data-intensive analysis. Challenging this tendency, Gray concludes: "Strategic management . . . treats strategic thinking as a pervasive aspect of running a business and regards strategic planning as an instrument around which other control systems—budgeting, information, compensation, organization—can be integrated" (p. 89).

Not all is hopeless for those who prefer systematic strategic planning and support comprehensive issues management. Studying the status of strategic planning, Paul and Taylor (1986) found that 95 percent of all *Fortune* 500 companies use strategic planning (33 percent a great deal; 62 percent somewhat). As evidence of how difficult the planning process is, respondents lacked confidence in any business plan projected beyond five years. Many respondents (62 percent) believed that strategic

**Figure 1. Issues Management in the Strategic Planning
and Strategic Management Process.**

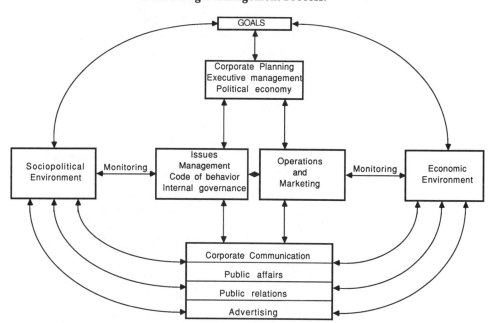

planning had its greatest impact on resource allocation, acquisitions and divestitures, new-product development, and similar decisions. Although corporate communication activity was improved because of strategic planning, only 4 percent of the companies believed that strategic planning helped meet external threats. (Whether those were public policy threats was unclear.) Strategic planning, portrayed in this discussion as essentially economic planning, is experiencing "growing pains." The impact of issues management was not evident in this study. Thus, an argument can be made that one reason business plans produce uncertain results is that public policy, a major part of each company's operating environment, is often omitted from strategic planning.

What is strategic planning? It has matured from its origins in the budgeting process to now propose what the budget must achieve and how. It assumes that effective forecasts and careful allocation of funds can position a company better than traditional budgeting processes did. Typically, strategic planning derives from a budgeting model designed to establish a viable business plan prepared to create and implement the operations necessary to generate revenue. Strategic management is the integrated complex of coordinated philosophies and tactical activities designed to operationalize the strategic plan.

Marrus (1984) proposes that the planning process be governed by five separate but interrelated elements: situation analysis, statements of objectives, strategy development, tactical planning, and means for control. Situation analysis involves internal and external environmental scanning. Its purpose is candid assessment of the full range of resources and obstacles relevant to achieving the corporate plan. Objective statements express what the company wants to accomplish, such as "Increase market share in X product line"; such a statement would be supported by goal statements that specify the exact amount of share desired and the targeted time frame for achieving the objective. Strategy statements encompass the general efforts needed to achieve the goals and objectives. These statements propose the steps and expenditures necessary to meet the objectives. Tactics are the specific means for implementing the strategies; statements of tactics are designed to help each support and operating unit know what its responsibilities are for implementing the strategic plan. And control entails the means for monitoring progress toward achieving the objectives.

Traditional approaches to strategic planning (see Hax and Majluf, 1984a, 1984b; Marrus, 1984) recommend a hierarchy of types of plans. In this hierarchy, corporate planning is at the top, supported by strategic and tactical planning. Together, these plans constitute the business plan. In this hierarchy of plans, the corporate plan is global, expressing the company's philosophy, values, and mission. Means for achieving this plan are developed through strategic planning, typically designed by an executive committee with input from staff and operations personnel. This strategic plan uses data generated by various forecasts, including econometrics, and should include public policy/opinion monitoring. These forecasts supply vital information that can be used to reexamine the premises on which the plan is based. They offer a vision of the future, including favorable and unfavorable conditions, especially in terms of market share, financial resources, demand for products and services, and public policy constraints and opportunities. Strategic planning represents the culmination of executive decisions on efforts to change external market share and internal service/product mix. This plan focuses top-management attention on a company's businesses, on asset acquisition and disposal, and on marketing strategies. Carefully assessing the internal human, financial, and structural resources and the external environments, strategic planning is typically divided into long-range, three to five years, and short-term, one to two years.

Strategic planning is translated into action by means of strategic management, which constitutes the operating philosophy a company uses to execute its tactical plan. This plan should consist of the business and public policy plans. The corporate strategic plan should be supported by business plans developed by individual departments, such as the market plan, the financial plan, the production plan, or the operations plan. How each department will control and marshal its material resources and coordinate and reward employees is essential to its business plan.

Effective strategic planning requires constant reassessment of the total market(s) in which a company is involved, with special attention to specific shares and to potential markets (and shares) in which the company might engage. It includes the company's capabilities to maintain or increase market share (or open new markets) given its human, material, financial, and policy resources (Paul and Taylor, 1986). Moreover, estimates are needed of the external human and material resources available to the company and the relative skills and resources of its competitors. This approach enables a company to predict how it will fare in competition with others in the market and thus to refine its decisions on what it wants to be and what it can be.

Strategic planning begins by conducting market-share

analysis to determine how the company can best generate revenue. To estimate the company's market-share position, the planner should conceive of the market as a whole that is segmented
by competitor. Similar analysis can be applied internally to
ascertain what proportion of the company's total revenue is
achieved by each major product or service. Such diagnosis helps
to paint a picture of the company's strengths and weaknesses
(Hax and Majluf, 1984a).

The Forecasting can be improved by applying similar analysis
to the image of the company and its industry. Like the product
or service market, public policy and public opinion constitute a
kind of whole. Companies and industries share an image; they
are blessed or plagued by the whole of opinion toward their
kind of company and industry (such as chemical, financial,
automotive, or pharmaceutical). For instance, the image of General Motors, along with those of Ford and Chrysler, is governed
by the public's opinion of the automobile industry in general
and the domestic car industry in particular. Each company can
estimate how much of the negative and the positive in its image
is generated by itself as opposed to others in the industry.
Polling to determine the comparative images of companies in a
market is not difficult. In this way, a company can determine
what changes are needed and how such efforts should be coordinated industrywide, perhaps through trade associations. Legislative and regulative requirements, by definition, are general;
they apply to the responsible as well as the irresponsible. In most
cases, irresponsibility by a few companies generalizes to many
others, in general and by industry.

The part of planning sensitive to public opinion must
take into consideration not only what the particular company
wants to do, vis-à-vis its economic market location, but also how
it fits with other companies into the particular public policy
arena. This realization should discourage each company from
thinking of itself as an island; each is part of a public policy/
public opinion whole that it and other companies contribute to
negatively and positively. Awareness of this whole is a further
rationale for trade associations that can help industries be self-
regulating and join in a common public policy effort.

Sociopolitical forecasts concentrate on estimates of how public opinion and public policy trends are developing in the legal and governmental environment. Such forecasts attempt to determine why public opinion is shifting and what persons and groups influence these trends. The objective of issues forecasting is not only to monitor opinions and public policy developments but also to calculate the impact of these factors on the strategic business plan and its management strategies.

Despite the platitudes of forecasting and planning, even the casual observer of industry fortunes realizes how quickly the best-laid plans and the most carefully prepared forecasts can be discredited if they fail to foretell dramatic market swings. An excellent example is the oil industry (and those businesses that depend on it), which based plans in the early 1980s on crude-oil price projections that ranged from $35 to $105 per barrel. When crude prices dipped below $15, the oil industry that had forecasted halcyon days entered a depression threatening the fortunes of many well-established companies and oil baron families. Coupled to this faulty planning was that by utility companies dependent on oil-related activities as well as state budget officers reliant on the oil industry. Errors of faulty forecasts rippled through oil-dependent states, affecting individuals, universities, small businesses, shareholders, and state and local governments. The amalgam of plans and planning mistakes underscores the necessity of a complete analysis of each company's operating environment. Because forecasting deals with an uncertain future, it is extraordinarily problematic. For this reason it is easily discredited. (But as is argued in Part Two, a company without monitoring and forecasting can only stagger along blindly.)

Forecasting as an issues management function is less interested in market trends than in shifts in public opinion, public policy, and the dynamics of power politics. Not all shifts in opinion are crucial to strategic planning; the goal is to determine which ones are. To be effective, foresight needs to estimate the likelihood that an emerging public policy issue will affect company plans, operations, and profit. It should also estimate the extent of that impact. With this information, public policy impact statements can be developed; contingency plans can be adopted. Eventually the company can decide what it is going to do to try to obviate or take advantage of the situation.

The gains that can be derived by vigilance outweigh the liabilities of making false predictions. A company is better off for having the attitude that its employees (in addition to the issues management staff) must be vigilant for changes that may affect how it does business. This attitude makes the company sensitive to its sociopolitical operating environment. Without effective forecasting, a company cannot plan because it does not know what it is planning for; nor can it examine the premises on which it is operating. *A company's stance on any policy issue is integral, not incidental, to its strategic planning.*

Listing the typical kinds of decisions made through strategic planning can help demonstrate what it does. Some decisions are driven primarily by the economy, whereas others are sensitive to the sociopolitical environment. Examples of typical options are as follows.

*Market-Driven Decisions in Strategic Planning* (decisions that are made primarily to adapt to changing market conditions and competitor activities):

- Undertake a product/service
- Abandon a product/service
- Target new markets for product/service
- Increase quality of product/service
- Downscale quality of product/service
- Diversify operations or holdings
- Consolidate operations or holdings
- Change operations or holdings
- Change methods for financing
- Change resource utilization
- Change resource allocation

*Policy-Driven Decisions in Strategic Planning* (decisions that are made primarily to adapt to changing public policy conditions that can affect market conditions and competitor activities):

- Take a public communication stance on key policy issues
- Change operations to adapt to public policy issues
- Change mission to adapt to public policy issues
- Change operating standards to adapt to public policy issues
- Change product/service lines or mix to adapt to public policy issues

Issues management can make a company plan more sensitive to sociopolitical trends, variables, and assumptions. It can help strategic management avoid operating philosophies and tactics that spark public outbursts which eventually lead to changes in public opinion with the ever-present possibility of becoming public policy battles. And issues management can help integrate public policy concerns into a company's operating system; for instance, employee appraisals can be used to evaluate how well workers understand issues implications and take corrective action.

### Toward an Integrated View of Issues Management

Even as some writers criticize the effort to make strategic planning more quantitative and precise, issues management is being indicted for being too subjective and imprecise to be useful in coping with the sociopolitical environment. Whereas many companies now have only rudimentary issues management programs and rely heavily on subjectivity, intuition, and luck, this vital corporate activity should increase in importance over the years. As social scientists explain the variables involved in public policy change, issues management will become more precise but will also allow for common sense and intuition, as any planning strategy does.

Issues management offers a company a matrix of executive, staff, and line personnel to work systematically to establish a platform of understanding and partnership with various stakeholder publics. In addition, it coordinates forecasting and communication activities that executive, staff, and line personnel need to develop and execute the public policy plan. When fully implemented, issues management functions include the following:

- Integrating public opinion/policy issues analysis into corporate strategic planning.
- Monitoring internal and external standards of corporate social performance to discover opinions and values stakeholders hold that can affect how the corporation may and should operate.
- Developing and implementing codes of corporate ethics.
- Assisting senior management decision making, particularly in readjusting corporate goals and operating policies to maximize wins and minimize losses vis-à-vis public interest critics.
- Forecasting, identifying, analyzing, monitoring, and prioritizing issues to assess their likely operational, economic, and political significance to the organization.
- Creating multidimensional proactive and reactive response plans from among the available issue change strategies.
- Communicating on issues important to various key publics to shape internal and external opinion, motivate grass-roots involvement, and stall, mitigate, or promote development of legislation and regulation.

The purpose of issues management is to locate and create *opportunities* for advancing the interest of the company (maximizing wins) while identifying and responding to *stress points* (minimizing losses). To do this, a major function required of issues management groups is to communicate public policy information to the key managers for use in planning.

Sharing a perspective gained through their experience in Atlantic Richfield's public affairs department, Arrington and Sawaya (1984b) claim issues management can be used to ensure that the strategic plan is consistent with major developments in a company's sociopolitical environment and among its tactical operations. It does this, they argue, because it adds three activities to strategic planning: forecasting, policy development, and advocacy communication. Arrington and Sawaya view foresight as "planning-intensive," the means by which public issues are identified, monitored, and analyzed for their impact on the strategic plan. The goal of issues management is prevention of, or at least early entrance into, the public policy contest (Chase, 1984; Crable and Vibbert, 1985). Effective foresight gives a company time for policy development that allows adjustments of the strategic plan to meet external conditions.

Using forecasts, executives must decide at what point to become involved in the issues process. Early actions offer the most uncertainty but the greatest flexibility. At that point, voluntary changes in company operations may eliminate the public concern that feeds special-interest agitation. Up to the time issues become written into legislation, campaigns can be used to make targeted publics aware of how companies are meeting public expectations or to show that those standards are unrealistic or irrelevant. As an issue matures in the legislative process, companies have a better idea of how they can influence the policy outcome, but they also lose many of their options. Moreover, the costs of grass-roots efforts are often greater because the Internal Revenue Service typically denies them as operating expenses and the fairness doctrine precludes use of the electronic media except in referendum or initiative campaigns (Heath and Nelson, 1986, chap. 4).

An ongoing communication campaign can reach beyond company image and product publicity to help key publics understand the operating requirements of a company and its industry as well as the benefits offered by its products and services. Such a campaign can convince audiences that steps should be taken to enhance the business potential of the company and its industry. Effective communication can help vital publics make informed judgments about the criticism being launched at a company. This goal does not deny the reality that at times companies are wrong, but it acknowledges that they may be correct. Examples are legion where media and special-interest claims simply are untrue or ignore a valid competing perspective to explain why a company or industry operates as it does. Serving as liaisons between departments responsible for the corporate communication function, issues managers can help

executives formulate a public policy plan that reflects the decision to communicate in an effort to create a more favorable
public opinion environment or to alter corporate practice in
light of new public expectations of the quality of products,
services, or operating procedures. (Parts Three and Four examine topics related to timing, strategies, and tone of issues
communication.)

A corporate stance on public policy trends is likely to fail
if it does not grow from a realistic assessment of what can be
done to influence the public opinion and policy environments.
Effective planning requires an accurate view of one's corporation, its mission, and its position in its economic and sociopolitical environments. It should calculate the human and
material resources required to alter, as well as adapt to, changing
conditions. Issues management as a control system can help
each company adjust to its public policy environment in ways
that advance its well-being.

To achieve this end, issues management should be integrated into strategic planning as shown in Figure 2. The model
features planning at three levels (corporate, staff support functions, and operations that generate revenue) and emphasizes
that each has responsibilities related to the management of
issues. Corporate-level planning activities focus on setting the
company mission and making broad plans, in light of various
key assumptions, needed to achieve that mission. The second
level, support functions, consists of activities that assist executive management and revenue-generating operations (those that
directly produce and deliver the goods or services used to
generate income).

Each level should be involved in the strategic plan, which
is segmented into five integrated processes: environment/posi-
tion assessment, strategy formulation, tactical programming,
budgeting, and strategy assessment, which entails control. The
first category uses data generated by assessment (quantitative
and qualitative) and forecasting to refine mission statements for
all three levels — corporate, support staff, and revenue-
generating operations. The planning process requires that the
executive level create a corporate mission statement that ad-

# Figure 2. Integration of Issues Management into Strategic Planning.

| | Environment/Position Assessment | Strategy Formulation | Tactical Programming | Budgeting | Strategy Assessment |
|---|---|---|---|---|---|
| **Corporate** | 1 a / c | 4 d / f | | 11 k | 10 j |
| **Support** | 2 b / 3 c / 6 c | 4 d / e | 7 g / h / i | 11 k | 9 j / i |
| **Operations** | 5 c | 4 d | 8 i | 11 k | 9 j |

**Business Plan**

1 Create Corporate Plan: Philosophy and Mission
2 Forecast Economic/Market Conditions
3 State Mission of Support Function
4 Formulate Business Plan
5 State Mission of Revenue Functions
6 Assess Human/Economic Resources
7 Develop Support Tactical Plan
8 Develop Revenue Tactical Plan
9 Create Control Measures for Operations
10 Assess Business Plan
11 Budget for Business Plan

**Public Policy Plan**

a Formulate Code of Operating Standards
b Forecast Sociopolitical Issues
c Assess Issues Impact on Goals: Corporate, Business, Function
d Formulate Public Policy Plan: Corporate, Support, Revenue
e Identify Stakeholders and Coalitions
f Assess Human/Sociopolitical Resources
g Create Governmental/Grass-Roots Tactical Plan
h Develop Communication/Message Tactical Plan
i Set Control Measures for Internal Issues Implementation
j Assess Public Policy Plan
k Budget for Public Policy Plan

dresses the following kinds of concerns: market share, financial planning, operational philosophy, and public policy stance. Production of this statement requires staff support to develop and refine internal and external market-related and public policy decisions. Given the missions, the resources available, and external conditions, strategies can be formulated to achieve the missions by applying the resources in light of the conditions. Strategy formulation is followed by tactical planning to develop specific activities needed to implement the strategies. All these tactics are budgeted. Built into the strategic plan are the means to assess the effectiveness of the business and public policy plans and control the implementation of the tactics.

As a support function, a primary role of issues management is to ensure that all three levels participate in developing the public policy plan and perform within its guidelines, in keeping with the company's vision of its social partnership. The model suggests that issues management guide the planning function at all three levels. Groups at each level must consider how their activity corresponds to the public policy arena. The model attempts to capture the longitudinal nature of the business and public policy plans as well as the way both are integrated into the corporate hierarchy. It underscores the need to calculate as carefully as possible the impact public policy changes can have on the strategies needed to actualize the business plan.

This planning model operationalizes the fact that public policy can affect a company at each stage of operations. Costs of items used in the manufacturing process, for instance, can be raised or lowered by public policy decisions. The same is true of throughput costs required to transform the materials into products. And the cost of the final product may be influenced by public policies that prescribe its quality, as in the food and drug industries. For instance, the electric utility industry must meet requirements specifying the quality and abundance of its product. It is affected by regulations regarding input, such as fuel cost. The cost of the final product, the kilowatt-hour, is subject to throughput decisions that affect plant efficiency, construction costs, and cogeneration. Legislation and regulation affect the cost of producing the product, as in pollution control and operating safety.

The model treats issues management as an attitude and as a complex of activities. Public policy planning requires that all levels in a company have well-defined roles and responsibilities needed to manage issues. Issues management is most likely to achieve success when it is integrated into planning and tactical activities at all levels.

In addition to endorsing the process, executives are responsible for defining the corporate mission, establishing guidelines necessary to achieve socially responsible operations, involving line personnel in the development and execution of issues strategies, and implementing a reward system that reinforces the overall effort to bring harmony between the company and its many stakeholders. Corporate executives need to communicate with many key publics, such as employees, special-interest groups, media, regulators, and legislators. These discussions must candidly and informatively seek agreement. Although much of the day-to-day issues communication is done by others in the company, executives must periodically address key publics to establish the credibility that is impossible for staff personnel to achieve. Executives need to be sensitive to public policy trends, but it is not their responsibility to monitor them closely. They should assess the short- and long-term impact that key issues will have on corporate operations. Management must set the tone for the issues activities to be implemented by others throughout the company.

As a staff-level activity, formal and systematic issues monitoring is performed, and communication activities are executed, typically through public affairs and public relations. But elsewhere in the company, issues management requires key personnel to be constantly alert to observe issues trends, assess their implications, and assist in adjusting the strategic plan to achieve harmony with the external environments in keeping with the corporate vision. The issues management staff collects and assesses the data generated by this process.

Line personnel should be trained to execute the issues management effort, with guidance from management and consultative assistance from issues specialists. Line and service managers are vital to issues management because they have an excellent vantage point from which to observe issues as they are emerging and to know their implications for current operating procedures and philosophy. Whereas executive management can give scope and purpose to monitoring and setting issues priorities, staff members and operations managers are in the best position to know what problems and costs are involved in coping with emerging issues.

The effort to manage issues should be integral to the planning and operations of individual departments. Departments such as finance, budgeting, engineering, research, construction, production, and marketing should not work in a public policy plan vacuum. They should know the contents of the company public policy plan and be expected to contribute to it and follow it in their daily activities. Unless department-level personnel have input into the issues management system and understand its strictures, the corporate public policy effort will fail, because most decisions and actions that produce public outbursts occur at department and division levels. The public policy plan can help individual department managers be alert for operating standards that need reevaluation. Such plans make the managers aware that they are jointly responsible for attending to the delicate issues that can grow into major public policy battles. For instance, financial specialists have to be sensitive to the ways they raise money and the stands they take on corporate tax positions. Construction engineers must be responsible for constantly monitoring standards to avoid collision with public expectations. This limited list of the many issues responsibilities that must be central to department planning and management indicates how the public policy plan is vital to creation and execution of the business plan.

*The Public Policy Plan.* How a company responds to its market forces is decided through the business plan; how it seeks to accommodate the strains and exploit the advantages of its sociopolitical environment is stated in its public policy plan. Public policy planning is an outgrowth of skills often found in sophisticated public relations or public affairs departments. But it may draw on outside consultants to help monitor, analyze issues impact, set issues priorities, and conduct issues communication. It must draw on the expertise of operations personnel who best understand how public policy proposals can affect operations. This complex of activities is designed to serve the company internally to plan for and manage subtle issues changes, preferably before they grow into public policy battles. If this plan is successfully executed, it can preclude the need for intervention to prevent or mitigate legislation and regulation.

The public policy plan is a comprehensive statement that includes the company's public policy objectives, its internal and external tactics to achieve these objectives, and the criteria for evaluating the plan's success. The plan specifies what individuals and groups are responsible for monitoring, forecasting, and isolating key issues for special attention. This team includes not only the issues management group but also key executive, staff, and operations personnel who work at vantage points that allow them to spot issues trends. Incorporated into the plan are the criteria a company uses to appraise employee performance to ensure compliance with operating standards relevant to public policies, such as those promulgated by the Occupational Safety and Health Administration and the Environmental Protection Agency. This document helps departments be sensitive to how public policy relates to their operations. This integration is enhanced when individual departments participate in developing the public policy impact statements that calculate the impact of public policy on operations and profits.

The public policy plan can help company personnel know and appreciate their issues management responsibilities, which include planning, monitoring, and assessing the implications of issues for operating policy and practices. Without a public policy plan, issues managers cannot help executive management and line personnel gather data needed to stay abreast of emerging issues. The plan provides a comprehensive study of what issues are developing and how they will affect revenue, profits, and operations. Issues managers should conduct risk analysis to determine the consequences of not responding to stress points and of missing opportunities. Issues planning in-

volves the calculated allocation of material and human resources to produce carefully identified results.

Each key department must know what issues messages are
being developed so that it can ensure their accuracy. The plan
coordinates communication activities so that key personnel
know who is saying what to whom and with what intended effect.
Without a public policy plan, corporate communicators will not
be fully prepared to discuss the substance of the stance they are
taking, and key personnel will be unaware of the corporate
position.

*The Communication Plan.* As a part of the strategic planning process, companies need a communication plan that begins by assessing which public policy battles can and cannot be
won by strategic communication tactics. Moreover, the plan
makes operations personnel aware of how their activities will be
supported by communication but also alerts them to the reality
that communication cannot solve all problems that result when
operations conflict with accepted public standards. This effort
increases the likelihood that company activities will correspond
to the claims being made by corporate communicators. In
conjunction with the public policy plan, the communication
plan is designed to achieve understanding and agreement
among internal and external stakeholders. The messages communicated and the objectives targeted are based on short- and
long-term public policy projections. Such communication
efforts may have better long-term success if they are guided by a
genuine desire to create a partnership with the stakeholders
who affect the success of the company. Communication planners should never naively believe that their primary goal is
bringing audiences to understand their issue position. The
experience of the past two decades should be sufficient to show
that the communication effort must recognize that the company
may need to play power politics, which may include acknowledging a need for change in its own policy.

Most issues communication will be undertaken by corporate and staff personnel. But from this hub, messages must be
filtered outward to other personnel. Staff personnel typically
associated with public relations and public affairs participate in

the design and execution of corporate communication efforts. Staff personnel are likely to be in liaison with industry trade associations and lobbying efforts, which include strategic communication as well as legislative tracking. A comprehensive issues management program makes sure that someone scrutinizes the content of all corporate communications, such as those issued by public relations, public affairs, investor relations, and product or service advertising. This monitoring process seeks to ensure that messages from different groups do not conflict with one another or with the corporate mission and operating philosophy.

Because policy responses may demand advocacy communication, the issues management function needs to be closely allied with communication specialists. But issues managers need not be communication experts. Perhaps, as Schmertz (1986) suggests, their best training is in politics. This stance does not negate the use of issues management to help each company harmonize its operations with the interests of its community of stakeholders. The key: This harmony should not be one-sided, leaning too far toward the perspective advocated either by media or by special-interest advocates; nor should the stance be skewed too self-interestedly toward the interests of financial stakeholders. The goal of effective issues management is to create a balance, a partnership, among all interests, and this goal may require that companies assert their rights rather than allow those rights to be defined by special-interest and media critics. The stance adopted and the personnel needed to execute the communication effort must be part of the strategic plan. The success of any strategic plan rests with the ability to implement it; issues communication is vital to that implementation.

## Organizing for Issues Management

Strategic planning and management should consider how the issues management function will be organized and integrated into the company. Reading and discussions with company personnel indicate that three models are being used for organizing for issues management: *centralized, diffused,* and *inte-*

*grated.* Each model assumes some matrix interaction among staff, executives, and operating managers, but in each the locus of authority and responsibility is quite different. Some work toward understanding the different kinds of organizational structures and means for integrating activities is beginning (Wartick and Rude, 1986). But extensive research using surveys and case studies is needed to compare the weaknesses and strengths of the various arrangements. Such study can explore the rich mix of variables, including executive personality, type of industry, public policy performance record, sophistication, and business operation structural type and philosophy. This kind of study must acknowledge that what works in one company or industry may be quite ineffective in another.

*Centralized.* The centralized model concentrates responsibility and authority for issues management in one key executive officer of the company. This person is responsible for creating the corporate public policy mission and deciding on the company's issues priorities and positions. Usually in this arrangement a close-knit advisory group assists corporate management in the discovery, analysis, and development of issues response priorities. The major tasks conducted in behalf of the company's public policy agenda are closely coordinated with the CEO or president. Assignments flow downward from this pinnacle; employees are directed to participate in various ways in support of public relations and public affairs activities. Issues monitoring, whether internal or by consultants, is performed at the direction of executive management, which analyzes the data and estimates the likelihood that legislation and its concomitant regulation will result. Relatively little issues input is expected from the operating levels.

Companies that successfully use this method are those whose executives are prone to take high-profile public policy positions. Such officers and their public policy assistants must be extremely familiar with the technical side of the company and be capable of sophisticated issues communication. Without this knowledge, a substantial gap exists between a company's statements on complex issues and the facts about how the company operates. A centralized issues management structure is not recommended for companies just beginning issues management unless they have an extremely capable public relations/affairs group and an executive management willing to personalize and aggressively conduct the management of issues. Worked effectively, such strategies can be quite successful. Employed by less capable staff members who support executives unwilling to take bold public policy stances, the centralized style of issues management will result in a downward spiral. Long lists of issues may be analyzed to the point of boredom but never be effectively addressed by changing operations or by communicating to disarm and challenge media and special-interest detractors.

Although the public affairs or public relations personnel act in an advisory capacity in this organizational arrangement, they must receive their authorization from the key executive for the goals and budgeting of campaign efforts. Operating personnel may not be directly involved in the issues management process; the assumption is that these personnel are doing their job according to prescribed standards. Typically, operations personnel will not participate in the development of a public policy plan; executives may asume that such personnel do not need to know what the plan is but must carry out their functions in support of the company's business plan, leaving issues management to key people at the top. Operating and financial disciplines, according to this model, must have a clear understanding of how their function produces income while complying with prescribed standards of performance.

*Diffused.* The diffused approach works on a shared-responsibility paradigm whereby each president of a division or major operating manager is responsible for identifying issues, estimating their impact, and developing internal and external market and policy adaptation strategies. This organizational type seems to work best in companies that are clearly segmented into major operating units, each capable of generating its own cash flow. Although executive management is ultimately responsible for approving and carrying out the public policy plan for the whole company, key operating personnel can be charged with the bulk of the responsibility for creating and implementing the plan. As with the budget, each major unit is required to develop and execute a public policy plan that integrates with and supports the plan developed by the corporate executives. The executive public policy plan is a product of lower-level plans amalgamated into one coherent effort. Corporate mission and operating philosophy are affirmed by management, but not without careful and thorough input from below.

Companies can be successful with this organizational arrangement when they have a clearly defined public policy mission, when operating personnel are highly sensitive to public policy implications of operating philosophies and activities, and when these personnel are schooled in public policy response strategies. Failing those conditions, companies that employ diffused issues management strategies will likely find their business and public policy efforts fragmented and poorly executed. Great effort will be needed to ensure that operating units are not at odds with one another over some major public policy stance. Anothe drawback is the tendency of operating personnel to stonewall or ignore issues rather than manage them. Concern for the financial bottom line can produce callous disregard for issues management until crises arise.

*Integrated.* The first model described above is oriented toward a top-down philosophy; the second assumes that the key personnel, whether closely associated with the CEO or scattered throughout the company, are in the best position to know what public criticism is being launched against the company and how to respond to it. The third model acknowledges the valuable contribution that an even broader array of employees can make in recognizing and responding to public policy changes, particularly internally and through contacts with key stakeholders.

The integrated model is designed to strike a balance between the other two. It places the responsibility for integrating and conducting issues management in the hands of key staff members who have the budget and the authority to conduct issues monitoring, analyze issues, and propose issue postures. These activities are performed in conjunction with key operating personnel who are expected, as in the diffused model, to understand the regulatory issues surrounding activities and to know that public policy efforts are to be integrated with staff and revenue-generating operations. The public policy plan becomes a means by which the operating units can share public policy concerns and strategies with one another and with issues management, public relations, and public affairs personnel.

Checkpoints are built into operating and staff activities because operating personnel are made responsible for helping to create and carry out the public policy plan. This arrangement fosters accountability between operations and issues management. Issues management personnel are responsible for reviewing operations to determine, with executive management, each operating unit's performance vis-à-vis the public policy plan. Likewise, the issues management team is established as liaison between management and business operations on public policy matters. This team serves in a consultative capacity to operating business units that need the knowledge of philosophies and strategies and the skills to conduct issues management, including monitoring and communication activities in support of the company's total effort.

The integrated approach requires that management set a public policy philosophy to guide operations and communication efforts. Managers must be actively involved beyond providing budgetary support; they must consider the public policy implications in preparing the strategic plan and serve as spokespersons in behalf of issues positions. Operations personnel are responsible for understanding the company's public policy philosophy and for being sensitive to emerging public policy positions that can affect implementation of the business plan. These personnel can help weigh the consequences of various issues response plans. An issues management staff helps monitor issues, estimates the power resources that special-interest groups are marshaling, develops communication response strategies, helps deploy these strategies, and helps assess the campaign's effectiveness.

*Arranging the Players.* Any company undertaking issues management must decide which activities it will handle and which will be undertaken by trade associations, by major public relations/advertising agencies, and by specialty firms. However, no matter what configuration of players emerges, the focal point will always be the company. The following assessment of the strengths and weaknesses of each option can help a company arrange its issues management effort. (Parts Three and Four further elaborate the relationships among the members of the communication team.)

*Company:* The company may develop its own extensive issues management system (often focused around public affairs, public relations, and issues management departments). But the question is: How much can the company do for itself more cost-effectively than outsiders could? Only the largest companies are likely to have a complete issues management group. Even those companies often seek support through trade associations and agencies.

Strengths:

- Company employees are intimately familiar with the operations of the company and the industry. Large public relations/advertising agencies often lack understanding of the company and its industry, particularly on public policy matters.
- This cadre of company employees offers continuity and focus to the public policy effort, especially strategic planning, which requires substantial understanding of the particular company's operations.
- Companies can uniquely feature their issues management efforts in behalf of their image and that of their products or services. This uniqueness is lost if a company must accept standards set by a trade association.

Weaknesses:

- Fixed costs for space and personnel are hard to justify when no major crisis is apparent or when the economy turns sour. For this reason, companies are prone to reduce their issues management groups to lower fixed costs.
- Myopia, blinders typical of persons in a company, may limit

the effectiveness of the effort because company personnel hate to acknowledge that the company is under fire.

*Trade associations*: Hundreds of trade associations have grown up as a result of efforts to broaden the political base, spread costs, and lessen the political visibility of individual companies. Many industries have more than one trade association, and some associations cut across more than one industry.

Strengths:

- Trade associations give a sense of industrywide uniformity.
- They offer an "outsider's" perspective that can increase candor and clarify vision.
- Their personnel understand the industry.
- They offer additional resources for monitoring.
- They mask the visibility of companies involved in the effort and spread costs.

Weaknesses:

- A byzantine system of political wrangling over priorities, budgets, and operating standards often frustrates associations and can lead to the spawning of new ones.
- Companies can lose flexibility and influence over how the campaign is executed.
- Gaining and maintaining constituent support for the association stance is often extremely difficult.

*Large public relations/advertising agencies:* Large agencies can help in polling as well as in designing and conducting issues communication.

Strengths:

- Large agencies increase flexibility by supplying communication specialists without fixed costs to the company.
- They are often geared to conduct target-audience impact analysis.
- They can help with communication media buy and mix.

- They offer a talent pool capable of helping to design messages.

Weaknesses:

- Large agencies usually lack understanding of operating and policy requirements of the company or industry.
- They can provide no input for strategic planning.
- They rarely offer a stable pool of personnel who handle an account and who are expert in an industry. Issues communication, unlike product, service, or image advertising, requires intimate understanding of key facts and issues.

*Specialty agencies:* Issues management has fostered a growth market for firms and agencies that specialize in one or more of the following activities: monitoring/forecasting, consulting for strategic planning, or highly specialized communication efforts such as direct mailing, grass-roots coalition building, or policy development. These agencies are usually small, with fewer than 100 persons, and often specialize by industry to provide a narrow range of in-depth services.

Strengths:

- Such agencies can specialize by industry, thereby lowering fixed costs without losing expertise.
- Some have the expertise and knowledge of the industry to assist in strategic planning.
- Some have more knowledge of specialty publication outlets than is typical of major firms.
- They can offer more focused assistance in designing and executing monitoring systems than large firms can.
- They increase flexibility by supplying communication specialists without fixed costs.
- Some can provide target-audience impact analysis.
- Some can assist with communication media buy and mix.
- Some can offer message design and placement assistance.
- They give an "outsider's" perspective that can increase candor and clarify vision.

- They can increase clients' awareness of the operating re-quirements of the industry.

Weaknesses:

- Personnel quality can be mediocre if the best people are employed directly by companies.
- Continuity will suffer if specialty agencies have difficulty surviving.

This list of considerations offers an issues manager many organizational options for drawing together the best combination of personnel and expertise needed for the complex processes of planning, monitoring, and advocating.

This overview of the issues management process gives scope and focus for the following sections, each of which concentrates on an aspect of the total effort. Part One is concerned with the public policy cycle and how companies can incorporate public policy into strategic planning. Part Two examines how companies organize to monitor issues and integrate issues awareness into operations. Parts Three and Four turn the process outward to convey the message to the proper audiences. Part Five looks at how issues management is progressing and the challenges it will face in coming decades.

# Integrating Issues Management and Strategic Planning

## Introduction by Robert L. Heath

Issues management can make a company an open system alert to its external environments, particularly the forces produced by public policy. To achieve its promise for any company, issues management requires the development of a public policy plan that is brought to bear on the assumptions involved in strategic planning. This effort begins with a candid assessment of the prevailing standards of corporate responsibility. As well as discussing the pitfalls of being inattentive to public policy, Part One emphasizes the positive side: Public policy can offer business opportunities. Strategic planning must acknowledge the relationship between market and public policy issues. This section presents three chapters to justify integrating issues management into company planning and operations.

Key people in companies that have implemented issues management note that their effort is incomplete until they have made issues management integral to executive management philosophy and day-to-day operations. If issues management cannot be integrated into the routine activities of a company, it will fail to bring harmony between the company and its stakeholders, particularly those vital to the public policy environment. Moreover, issues managers must have the correct philosophy and mechanisms for making employees aware of and involved in the issues management process.

**45**

Bringing issues management into a company is not easy. There are many pitfalls to be avoided, and certain internal conditions are necessary for success. Some issues management programs are introduced from the top down, when a president or CEO decides the company needs such a program. Often issues management is introduced by a staff-level individual who recognizes the need for a program and promotes it to executives. Some programs have been created anew, in addition to existing groups within the company, such as public relations, governmental affairs, or corporate communications. Other issues efforts have grown out of existing departments such as public relations, external affairs, legal affairs, or corporate planning.

However it originates, an issues management program will thrive only in an atmosphere committed to achieving systematic change. It requires recognition of the brutal reality that businesses do not live by market forces alone. Implementation of an effective issues management program requires several conditions.

• Management must be committed to issues management as an internal *and* external process. Executive support is not a foregone conclusion; some executives believe issues management is a fad. Therefore, issues managers have to continue to prove that they can make a difference.

• Executives must understand what issues management can and cannot do. False expectations will kill the effort. The biggest misunderstanding about issues management is that it can protect a company so that it never has to alter its business plan or operations. Limitations on what communication can accomplish should not scuttle the effort in its infancy. The fact is that sometimes the best issues management tactic is to change the way a company does business.

• Like executives, department managers must accept issues management as a constructive addition to their activities rather than a hindrance and a threat to their authority and responsibilities. Unless issues management becomes integral to the thinking and actions of mid-level managers, it will fail to meet its full potential.

- An issues management system is best when it helps generate standards of performance that are integrated into the company's performance appraisal system. Employees need to know that the company is serious in its commitment to corporate responsibility and that they are expected to watch for issues, to act in concert with company public policy positions, and to communicate the company's public policy stance.

- A successful program requires people who are articulate and politically savvy. Because issues specialists must work with operations and staff personnel to create and implement a public policy plan, they need to understand company and industry operations; to comprehend the complexities of public policy developments and discover leverage points; to be able to handle the communication and political aspects of public policy maneuvers; and to be shrewd communicators who can deal with public policy issues with candor rather than guile.

- The program must be objectives/goal-oriented — key people must be accountable for making appropriate moves in the public policy arena. Companies can create an issues apparatus and name people who are responsible for its functions, but unless the effort is targeted toward achieving specific objectives/goals, it will not succeed, unless by accident.

- An issues management program will fail if it becomes nothing more than a debating society devoted to generating a series of public policy statements.

Issues management will not succeed if its focus is misplaced on understanding policy rather than taking action for internal and external change. Companies can bog down while deciding what issues are important and how to manage them. The most serious challenge to issues management is to take the right actions, to make something happen.

A company's issues management effort needs to be adapted to the unique qualities of its age and the aggressiveness and effectiveness of the regulators that work with the company. Ungson, James, and Spicer (1985) have discovered that different types of industries need unique issues management systems. They found that the effects regulatory agencies have on a company vary with its age and its industry group. Companies are frustrated by the lack of predictability demonstrated by most regulatory agencies, and regulatory agencies are perceived to be more predictable in developing policies on some kinds of issues than on others. For instance, companies in extraction and timber use think policies relevant to their operations develop predictably whereas those relating to environmental impact are not predictable. The researchers also found that companies are frustrated by the overlap and conflict between regulatory agencies. The difficulty of predicting regulatory behavior also differs by department within a company. Some departments have relatively stable public policy environments, whereas others do not.

*Issues management begins with the determination to do something constructive in response to changes in public opinion and policy.* But this commitment will fail unless the company develops the internal tactics to bring public policy analysis to bear on planning and operations. Successful issues management depends on how effectively a company keeps track of issues and works to take corrective action. Savvy issues managers know that they cannot always tell which issues will have what effects on their business plan. But they constantly strive to keep track of changes in each issue and assess their impact. Moreover, not every issue can be changed through communication, grass-roots efforts, and governmental relations. Some issues are managed best by seeing that business operations do not cause unnecessary friction with accepted public standards.

Some companies lack faith in issues management because they got lost in the maze of deciding which issues to take stands on at a particular moment. This stance fails to note how capricious public policy development is. Instead of worrying through the process of deciding which few issues they can manage, many successful companies assume the greater risk is managing too few. Not every issue must or can be handled through a complex process that culminates in decisions and direct involvement by executive management. Many issues can be handled by competent staff and operations personnel who understand how their company must operate and know it must work in ways that are compatible with community standards.

In the first chapter that follows, Rogene A. Buchholz demonstrates the inextricability of market and public policy environments. He explains the stages in the life cycle of public policy issues and suggests strategies that can be used externally to react to public policy changes. Buchholz contends that management needs to understand and respond strategically to the stages of the public policy life cycle. He encourages managers to think to the future and weigh the consequences of their actions, considering both business and social values. His goal for the private sector is to help create a just and prosperous society.

In the second chapter, Richard N. Sawaya and Charles B. Arrington, Jr., draw on their experience at Atlantic Richfield to contend that strategic planning should constantly reexamine the premises that support planning models. The authors argue that strategic planners can increase their effectiveness by monitoring outside events, including public policy shifts, and using them to correct the planning model their company is using internally. They challenge executives to use information discovered through monitoring to steer their companies in directions that avoid the pitfalls, and make use of the opportunities, of public policy. Their analysis makes apparent why strategic planning requires more than econometrics and market forecasting. Moreover, they propose that companies should actively work to shape their public policy environments.

In the third chapter, Margaret A. Stroup of Monsanto Chemical Company explains how the Strategic Premises Program at Monsanto identifies planning assumptions that must be examined to determine where opportunities lie and which premises are false. She details the internal committee structure and review process by which Monsanto uses public policy issues analysis to decide which strategic planning premises are and are not valid in light of forecasted public policy trends.

In combination, these articles demonstrate that when issues management is more than a buzzword, it can help companies survive and prosper, because planning becomes sensitive to the many forces that constitute a company's environment.

1

# Adjusting Corporations to the Realities of Public Interests and Policy

*Rogene A. Buchholz*

Over the last two decades, public policy has become an ever more important determinant of corporate behavior, as market outcomes have been increasingly altered through the public policy process in the form of legislation and regulation to address issues of importance to society. Business operates within a statutory framework built by Congress over the past two decades to address social issues. It is increasingly clear that the environment in which business functions is composed of two major sociopolitical processes through which decisions are made about the allocation of corporate resources: the market system and the public policy process. Both of these are necessary to encompass the broad range of decisions that need to be made about the corporation and its operations. The market mechanism and public policy are both sources of operational guidelines and performance criteria for managers.

American business has not had to concern itself throughout most of its history with the public policy process, because it could assume with some confidence that the basic value system of Amerian society was economic and thus public policies were generally supportive of business interests. Throughout most of American history, public policy has, by and large, been designed to promote business rather than interfere with its functioning. With recent changes in American society, this situation has changed, and business can no longer assume that public policy will be supportive of its interests. In fact, most, if not all, of the social responsibilities of business that are now public policy measures interfere with normal business operations and result in nonproductive investments from a strictly economic point of view. Public policy measures directed toward pollution control, safety and health, and the like interfere with the ability of business to fulfill its basic economic mission.

The impact of public policy on business organizations, then, makes it important for management to understand the nature of public policy and how the public policy process functions. Management also needs to understand the role public policy plays in a market-oriented society and the interaction between the public policy process and the market system. The managerial task now includes a public policy dimension to go along with the technical, administrative, and human relations dimensions it has always had (Held, 1967). New organizational forms and functions have emerged in the last ten years to facilitate corporate involvement in the public policy process.

In corporations, management's participation in the public policy process is generally the responsibility of the public affairs department, and there is some evidence that these departments have become more important over the past several years in managing a corporation's response to a public issue (Public Affairs Research Group, 1981). What is not so well known is the extent to which the corporate community as a whole is using certain strategies to participate in the public policy process and how effectively its responses to public policy issues are being managed. It is not clear that corporations are engaged in strategic thinking when participating in the public policy process, as much of their activity seems on the surface to be short-run and reactive. Thus management may be overlooking important opportunities to influence the public policy environment by taking a more long-term strategic outlook on public policy and the issues that the public policy process addresses.

## Nature of Public Policy

In developing principles and strategies that will be helpful in navigating the complex environment in which business functions, one of the first tasks is to develop some working definitions of key terms and concepts. The term *public policy* itself is obviously a critical concept that must be understood before moving on to more strategically oriented concerns. What does *public policy* mean, and what are some of the important related terms that are important for a manager to know something about?

One way to define the term is simply to say that public policy is policy made by a public body, such as government, that is representative, at least to some extent, of the interests of the larger society. Government is the legitimate institution to make public policy, and therefore whatever policy is developed by the various branches of government in the form of legislation, regulation, executive orders, court decisions, and so forth is public policy. This definition, however, is too simple — it does not do justice to the complexity of government or society.

Some authors state that a useful definition of public policy interprets public policy as a pattern of governmental activity that concerns some topic and has a purpose or goal. Public policy is purposeful, goal-oriented behavior rather than random or chance behavior (Anderson, Brady, and Bullock, 1978, pp. 4–5). This definition does not make the mistake of equating decision making with policy or confuse the stated goal of action with what is actually done. Public policy consists of courses of action, according to these authors, rather than separate, discrete decisions or actions by government officials. Furthermore, public policy refers to what governments actually do about some public problem, not what they say they will do or what they intend to do.

Preston and Post (1975, p. 11) offer a quite different definition of public policy. They refer to policy, first of all, as principles guiding action, and they emphasize that this definition stresses the idea of generality, by referring to principles rather than specific rules, programs, or practices or the actions themselves. They also emphasize activity or behavior, as opposed to passive adherence. Public policy, then, refers to the principles that guide action relating to society as a whole. These principles may be made explicit in law and other formal acts of governmental bodies. But Preston and Post are quick to warn against a narrow and legalistic interpretation of the term *public policy*. Policies can be implemented without formal articulation of individual actions and decisions. These are called implicit policies.

The first definition is unnecessarily restrictive. Government need not engage in a formal action for public policies to be put into effect. Pressures have been developed outside government by stockholders and other groups, for example, to "encourage" American companies who have facilities in South Africa to sell off these holdings and withdraw from the country entirely. Preston and Post's definition, however, confuses principles and action. Principles can guide action, but the principles themselves are not necessarily the policy. *Policy* does more appropriately refer to a specific course of action with respect to a problem, but not to the principles that guide the action. Current monetary policy is a specific course of action taken by the Federal Reserve Board to either tighten or loosen the money supply. The principles that guided this action were derived from some kind of theory about the money supply and its effects on economic activity, but these principles do not constitute the policy itself.

For our purposes, public policy is a specific course of action taken collectively by society or by a legitimate representative of society, addressing a specific problem of public concern, that reflects the interests of society or particular segments of society. This definition emphasizes a course of action rather than principles. It does not restrict such action to government, it refers to the collective nature of such action, and it does not claim that each and every public policy represents the interests of society as a whole.

The specific course of action that is eventually taken is decided through the public policy process. The term *public policy process* refers to the various processes by which public policy is formed. There is no one single process (Anderson, Brady, and Bullock, 1978, p. 6). Even when public policy is formalized by government, there still is no single process that is always used. Public policy can be made through legislation passed by Congress, regulations issued in the *Federal Register*, executive orders issued by the president, or decisions handed down by the Supreme Court. Thus the term *public policy process*, when used in the singular, is not entirely accurate, but it will be used here to reduce confusion and for convenience.

The public policy agenda is that collection of topics and issues with respect to which public policy may be formulated (Preston and Post, 1975, p. 11). This is an important concept for management to understand, because the public policy agenda contains many issues that may involve corporate behavior. There are many problems and concerns that various people in society would like to be acted on, but only those that are important enough to receive serious attention from policy makers constitute the public policy agenda. Issues that find their way onto the public policy agenda are thus interjected into the public policy process, and eventually some kind of public policy may be formulated on those issues.

### Nature of Public Issues

From society's point of view, public issues are those that work their way into the public policy process because their extensive impacts and collective nature require society to develop a common course of action to deal with them. Public issues arise when there is a public with problems that demand some kind of collective action and when there is public disagreement over the best solutions to the problems (Eyestone, 1978, p. 3). Those issues that are important to enough people and affect enough interests in society are placed on the public policy agenda. The specific course of action that is eventually taken with respect to an issue is decided through the public policy process. Most public issues eventually result in some kind of public policy that seeks to address the issue and resolve it to the satisfaction of enough people or groups in society so that the policy will be accepted. Once accepted, a policy has to be implemented through some kind of compliance mechanism.

Public issues emerge in our society because values change or because corporations operate in ways that conflict with existing values. Either condition is sufficient to generate pressures on our institutions by causing a gap between public expectations and institutional performance. The things that people want, and think are good for themselves and their society, change over time because of various influences. Values change in response to advances in technology which make it possible to do things which could not have been done before but which may also have some adverse side effects. New information changes the way we think and feel about products and the goals we pursue in our society. Shifts in population affect the dominant value systems in society. Another factor influencing values is education. As people attain more formal education, they may question their desires and the things they were raised to believe were important. They may come to reject these traditional values appropriated from their families and adopt a new set of desires and goals to pursue.

Changes in basic institutions affect values, institutions such as the family and religion. These institutions are often crucial in the socialization of children and the transmitting of values from generation to generation. Finally, affluence causes values to change. As more and more people become affluent and fulfill their basic economic needs, other things may become important to them that were not within the range of possibility before. They may desire other goods and services and pursue other goals related to self-fulfillment or quality of life for themselves and others.

When a relatively homogeneous value system exists in a society over a period of time, that society is stable and experiences little social change. When a homogeneous value system begins to break up and large segments of society begin to express different values, social change of some kind seems inevitable. New issues are raised that find their way onto the public policy agenda so that they get the attention of government and corporations. Social change of this sort usually brings about changes in the major institutions of society to incorporate these new values and reduce the gap between public expectations and institutional performance.

The structure of the social/political process also has a great deal to do with the kinds of problems that get attention and the issues that find their way onto the public policy agenda. Ours is a pluralistic society, open to all sorts of influences and pressures from individuals and groups who are active in the public policy process. Many individuals join groups that can quite properly be called interest groups because they form around shared interests. People organize such groups and join or support them because they hold common attitudes and values on a particular problem or issue and believe they can advance their interests better by organizing themselves into a group than by pursuing their interests individually. These groups become political when they make claims on other groups or institutions in society.

Such interest groups are conveyers of certain kinds of demands that are fed into the public policy process. They fill a gap in the formal political process by representing interests that are beyond the capacities of individuals acting alone or representatives chosen by the people. At times they perform a watchdog function by sounding an alarm whenever policies of more formal institutions threaten the interests of their members. They generate ideas that may become formal policies of these institutions and help to place issues on the public policy agenda.

These interest groups may become part of broader and more comprehensive social movements that spread throughout the entire society. Social movements have been defined as large-scale, widespread, and continuing elementary collective action in pursuit of an objective that affects and shapes the social order in some fundamental aspect. These movements become the focal point for many groups and individuals interested in the same issue. There are four stages in the development of a social movement: (1) dissatisfaction of a group, (2) dramatic events, (3) strategies to obtain social change, and (4) emergence of strong leadership (Lang and Lang, 1961, p. 490).

In a pluralistic society, problems are identified and issues raised in a bottom-up fashion—concern about a problem may begin anywhere at the grass-roots level in society, and the problem may eventually grow into a major public issue that demands attention. Public policy reflects the interests of various groups in the policy-making process and results from a struggle of these groups to win public and institutional support. Management must be aware of how issues are raised in our society and understand something of the stages issues pass through on their way to affecting corporate behavior. Such knowledge is essential to anticipate the issues that will affect corporations and design corporate strategies that will be effective for both the corporation and society.

### Public Policy Life Cycle

The notion of a public policy agenda suggests that public issues have a life cycle—a problem goes through a series of stages as it evolves from an issue of little importance to one that receives major public attention. This concept is important for management to grasp, as the development of effective strategies to influence public policy depends on an accurate assessment of the stage an issue currently occupies.

The life cycle begins with changing public expectations that create a gap between corporate performance and what the public expects from its institutions. The seeds of a new public issue are sown when the gap becomes wide enough to affect significant numbers of people and cause extensive dissatisfaction with corporate performance. The issue begins to be discussed at grass-roots levels, and people begin to form opinions. These new expectations may then become successfully politicized. As the issue becomes widely discussed in the media and becomes a concern for activist-group discussion, it may be picked up by some politicians to be introduced into the formal public policy process. Thus the issue is brought before the public, so to speak, and is placed on the public policy agenda, where it will most likely be the subject of some kind of action.

The legislative phase is the period surrounding the enactment of legislation dealing with the issue and its implementation. The rules of the game for business are being changed in this phase as legislative and regulatory requirements are formally enacted. New legislation and regulations may require considerable debate and bargaining and even be the subject of court rulings. But at this stage, the issue has become institutionalized as society has changed the contract between business and society and expressed its expectations in formal legislation and regulation.

The last stage, the litigation phase, is one of implementing the new rules of the game. During this period, many negotiations may occur between government and business regarding enforcement standards and timetables for meeting the new requirements. If government agencies do not believe business is successfully meeting the new rules and negotiation breaks down, they may file suit in court to force compliance. In this stage, the adversarial relationship between business and government is most pronounced and the opportunities for cooperation to meet public expectations severely limited.

The particular model adopted and the number of stages involved are probably not as important as simply recognizing the importance of the public issues life cycle and keeping this notion in mind when developing strategies to influence public policy. In this chapter a three-stage model of the public policy life cycle is used as the basis for strategy development. This model is described in the following paragraphs.

*Public Opinion Formation.* The first stage of the public policy life cycle can be called the stage of public opinion formation. At this stage, the concern of the corporate strategist is with the emergence and development of public opinion. The focus is on emerging issues of concern to business. In this stage, the major strategic approach available to a corporation for influencing the public policy process is to communicate its view on public issues to the public at large. Participation in the public policy debate gives the company the opportunity to present alternatives that could obviate the need for specific regulation altogether. A good communication strategy reduces the need for more expensive and potentially troublesome strategic options further along in the public policy life cycle.

*Public Policy Formulation.* At the second stage of the public policy life cycle, public policy formulation, the concern is with some legislative proposal that has been introduced into Congress and will directly or indirectly affect the business firm. The issue has now become politicized and has taken on form and substance as a proposed legislative enactment. The primary strategic objective of the corporation at this stage is to oppose or support bills (depending on their impact) or try to get them changed so that they are more acceptable. Communication strategies are still useful at this stage, but a new element is introduced into the process: The focus is now on the officeholder who will be dealing with the issue as it evolves into a formal legislative or regulatory enactment.

*Public Policy Implementation.* The last stage of the public policy life cycle is called the stage of public policy implementation because at this point the statutory legislation has been enacted and regulations are being promulgated that will impose costs and changes in operations on the corporate community. Since the issues have become bureaucratized and the emphasis is therefore on administrative decision making, the primary objective of business is to obtain regulations it can live with and transfer the regulatory costs, to the extent possible, onto the consumer or other parties. A strategic option available to companies at this stage is to generate a new public policy issue, thereby forcing the problem back to the first stage of the public policy life cycle in hopes of changing public opinion with resultant changes in the enabling legislation and implementing regulations.

### Strategic Options

Figure 1, a strategic management model of the public policy life cycle, summarizes the strategic options that a firm might employ at each stage. The options open to business for responding to an issue are different at each stage, and corporations must therefore concern themselves with "goodness of fit" between the life cycle of a public issue and their response. Taking this life cycle into account is important for the development of corporate strategy. For the corporate strategist, the question is not whether to participate in the public policy process, but how to participate effectively and efficiently—that is, how to formulate, select, and implement public policy strategies.

Figure 2 lists the focus and the key actors at each stage of the public policy life cycle. In stage 1, the issue is an idea being discussed, of concern to some people, that may involve a change in corporate performance. The key actors in society in championing this issue are activist groups who seek to enlist broader

**Figure 1. Strategic Options Available by Stage of the Public Policy Life Cycle.**

| Public Policy Life Cycle | Strategic Options |
|---|---|
| Stage 1: Public opinion formation | Communication strategies<br>Advocacy advertising<br>Annual report<br>Corporate newsletters<br>Direct meetings<br>Economic education programs<br>Image advertising<br>Press releases<br>Public service announcements<br>Reports to government<br>Special media presentations<br>TV and radio talk shows |
| Stage 2: Public policy formulation | Participation strategies<br>Coalition building<br>Lobbying<br>Honoraria<br>PAC contributions<br>Political parties<br>Public affairs groups<br>Public service meetings<br>Trade associations |
| Stage 3: Public policy implementation | Compliance strategies<br>Cooperation with agencies<br>Creating a new issue<br>Legal resistance<br>Judicial proceedings<br>Noncompliance |

**Figure 2. Nature of Issue and Key Actors by Stage
of the Public Policy Life Cycle.**

| | Stage | | |
| --- | --- | --- | --- |
| | *1* | *2* | *3* |
| Nature of issue | Idea | Legislation | Law |
| Key actors in society | Activist groups | Officeholders | Regulators |

support for their interests. They can use various strategies—protests, boycotts, demonstrations, media coverage, and the like—to gain attention and have their concerns placed on the public policy agenda. If corporations want to participate at this stage, they must become involved in the discussion.

In the second stage, the issue has been translated into a proposal for legislation that is being considered to deal with the concerns raised in stage 1 by requiring a change in corporate behavior. The key actors at this stage are elected officeholders who introduce and debate the legislation and who eventually vote to support or defeat it. For corporations to be involved at this stage means they must relate to these officeholders and their staffs in some fashion.

The third stage focuses on implementation of legislation that has been enacted. The original issue has now become institutionalized, and the idea has been translated into legislation that has become the law of the land. The principal actors at this point are regulators in government agencies who are writing and enforcing rules to bring corporations into compliance with legislation. Corporations can choose to work with these regulators to write and interpret rules so as to take corporate interests into account, they can challenge particular rules in the courts, or they can adopt a strategy of noncompliance.

The actors at each stage of the public policy life cycle form what has come to be called the infamous iron triangle. The iron triangle consists of the activist groups that have a significant stake in a particular issue or issues, the regulatory agency that has responsibility for implementing the legislation on the issue, and the subcommittee or committee of Congress that had primary responsibility for shaping the legislation and continues to exercise an oversight function regarding the regulatory agency. Some commentators have held this iron triangle to be virtually impregnable, particularly if each of the three parties has the same interest in the issue. Consequently, it is important for business to recognize the significance of such triangles and their implications for the formation and implementation of public policy.

Managers at all levels of the organization need to recognize the public policy dimension of their jobs and the need for strategic thinking about public issues of importance to the corporation. The front office or boardroom should not be seen as the only place where public matters are considered, nor should the public affairs department try to insulate operating management from public policy concerns. The public policy dimension must be diffused throughout the organization and become a part of every manager's method of operation so that concern for public issues will become a routine and accepted part of business planning and operation.

### Legitimacy of Corporate Involvement in Public Policy

The foregoing comments about business involvement in the public policy process raise a most critical issue concerning the legitimacy of corporate involvement in the public policy process. Many critics of business would like to severely limit political activity by business because they believe business can wield too much political power and shape public policy in its own favor much more than other institutions and individuals in society. The economic power of the large corporation can readily be transformed into political power, it is believed, because business can raise huge sums for lobbying and for political contributions through political action committees (PACs). Thus it is feared that the public policy process will come to be dominated by business interests if corporate political activity is allowed to expand without limits, and business values will largely shape public policies to the detriment of society as a whole.

Lindblom (1977), for example, argues that business has a privileged position vis-à-vis the political system and therefore should not be viewed as just another interest group on more or less equal terms with all other such groups. Businesspeople are not representatives of a special interest, but are functionaries performing tasks that government officials regard as indispensable. Government officials, particularly elected ones, depend on a healthy and growing economy to remain in office, and they must collaborate with businesspeople to make the system work appropriately. But governments cannot command a certain level of business performance to provide more employment and growth in gross national product. Instead, they must offer inducements to business in the form of market and political benefits and must often defer to business leadership on matters pertaining to the economy. Collaboration and deference are at the heart of politics in a market-oriented system.

Such mutual adjustment between business and government does not usually take the form of an explicit agreement; rather, it is most often impersonal and distant. This adjustment operates through an unspoken deference of administrations, legislatures, and courts to the needs of business. And it relies on shared understanding between the two groups of leaders about the conditions under which enterprises can or cannot profitably operate. Because of this understanding, businesspeople need rarely threaten any collective action such as a concerted restriction of business activities. They usually need only point at the increased costs of doing business because of government interference, the state of the economy, and the dependence of economic growth and stability on their profits or sales prospects and simply predict that adverse consequences will follow on a refusal of their demands.

In summary, the nature of a market-oriented economy and the dependence of the political system on acceptable economic performance give business a disproportionate influence in the political system. To encourage and legitimize the further involvement of business in the public policy process will make an already serious problem worse from the point of view of society. If Lindblom's view is correct, what we should probably be doing is talking about limiting the involvement of business in the political process to prevent it from taking undue advantage of its privileged position.

It is also argued that business managers lack political legitimacy to participate in the public policy process beyond the participation open to an ordinary citizen. These executives are not duly elected representatives of the public, and to have them play a dominant role in public policy formulation is to make a mockery of representative democracy. Their competence in the public policy arena is also questioned. Business executives would be better off to stay at home and mind the store, so to speak, than to get involved in an area where not only their legitimacy but their competence as well is questionable.

There is some evidence that society or the public holds a rather negative view of business political activity. That is the conclusion of a *Harvard Business Review* study (Brenner, 1979) using data from a survey of executives and a national consumer opinion poll. Brenner states that while business has become better organized and more skillful at using the political process, society has shown substantial distaste for the growth of political muscle by corporations. The perceived propriety of various political activities, especially those that involve direct business-to-politician contact, is on a discernible downward trend (Brenner, 1979, p. 152). Whereas only 37 percent of the executives rate past corporate political activity as "extensive," 70 percent of the public does. And while 71 percent of executives want future corporate political activity to be "extensive," only 14 percent of the public sample shares this view (Brenner, 1979, p. 154).

Thus there is a clear divergence between executives and the public regarding past and future corporate political participation. Society does not seem to share business leaders' confidence in the benefits resulting from corporate political activities, and the gap between the societal and the executive viewpoints should be a cause of concern for business. Brenner reinforces this point: "Perhaps the most significant finding, the single result which business managers should not overlook, is that business and society have different views of corporate political activity. The former group believes it is necessary and proper for its view to be effectively and forcefully supported in the governmental process. The public seems less sure of and certainly less comfortable with corporate political activity. This divergent view has boiled down to the question of whether organized business involvement in the political process is legitimate participation or illegitimate infiltration" (p. 162).

The arguments in favor of political participation are based on the view that such participation is inevitable given the nature of our highly diverse and yet interdependent society, where many issues require collective action in order to be successfully resolved. Corporations have legitimate political concerns in such a society because they are affected by this collective action. Corporate interests should be placed on a par with other interests, and corporate institutions should be recognized as legitimate participants in the public policy process. Thus political participation by management and other employees of the corporation not only is inevitable but is as legitimate as any other form of representation within a pluralistic decision-making process, as Preston and Post (1975) conclude: "Managerial participation in the public policy process . . . is inevitable and legitimate; and, as public policy becomes an increasingly important consideration in the process of management, such participation can be expected to become widespread and significant. Our caveat is that such participation should be acknowledged for what it is . . . both with respect to source and with respect to purpose . . . and that it not be conducted in such a fashion as to exclude other views and interests from equal participation in the process itself" (p. 147).

Another argument in favor of business participation in the political process concerns the information and expertise that business can provide for the successful resolution of social and economic problems. Many issues that either are currently on the public policy agenda or will make their way to that agenda will affect business in some way. Resolution of these issues needs business participation. It is in society's interests to have business input, because of the technical and managerial expertise that business possesses. We would have better public policies today if more business input had been provided. According to Dunlop (1979), "The absence of effective leadership for the business community on many public policy questions — in consensus building and in dealing with other groups and governments — means that business enterprises forfeit almost entirely to politicians. The rapid expansion of government regulations in recent years and specifically government's penchant for rigid, bureaucratic 'command and control' regulations, even when ineffective or counterproductive, have arisen in part from a lack of coherence and consensus within the business community about more constructive choices for achieving social purposes" (p. 86).

The question whether corporations have a legitimate right to participate in the public policy process is an important one that cannot be avoided. The debate about further limiting the contributions of political action committees and continuing to deny corporations access to television for advocacy advertising must be seen in this context. The right to participate in the political process is not unlimited, and the limitations placed on business will depend on the public's view of the influence corporations are having in the political system.

## The Public Interest

If corporations are to attain a legitimacy in the public policy process that they do not now enjoy, they must take the public interest seriously and make a serious attempt to define their involvement in those terms. If corporations' participation in the public policy process is rationalized in terms of either blatant or disguised self-interest, the legitimacy of their participation will continue to be questioned, and that participation will no doubt be limited. This presents a serious challenge to corporations that has been defined by Sethi (1982) as follows: "The style and substance of corporate political involvement and the contributions of business to the public interest will largely determine the degree of public acceptance of the corporation as a political participant and whether or not the corporation

becomes a positive influence for social change. . . . Any inconsistencies in current corporate behavior and rhetoric, or the
perception that the corporation is not acting in the public
interest, will have a disproportionate impact on the future political role of the corporation and reinforce the negative perceptions created in the past" (p. 33).

The motivating principle in the public policy process is
the public interest rather than self-interest. This principle is
invoked by those who make decisions about public policy.
Elected public officials often claim to be acting in the interests of
the nation as a whole or of their state or congressional district.
Activist groups also claim to be devoted to the general or national welfare. These claims make some degree of sense. But they
present only part of the truth. When politicians decide how to
provide some public good or service, they cannot accurately
claim to be acting in the self-interest of everyone in their constituency. When goods and services are indivisible across large
numbers of people, it is impossible for individual preferences to
be matched. Nor can public policy makers claim to be acting in
their own self-interest — such a claim is not politically acceptable. Some more general principle such as the public interest
has to be invoked to justify the action.

Defining the public interest, however, is problematic. The
term can have at least four meanings. It can refer to the aggrega-
tion, weighing, and balancing of a number of special interests.
In this view the public interest results through the free and open
competition of interested parties who have to compromise their
differences to arrive at a common course of action. The public
interest is the sum total of all the private interests in the community that are balanced for the common good. This definition
allows for a diversity of interests.

The public interest can also refer to a common or universal interest that all or at least most of the members of a society
share. A decision is in the public interest if it serves the ends of
the whole public rather than those of some sector of the public,
if it incorporates all the interests and concepts of value that are
generally accepted in our society. Such a definition assumes a

great deal of commonality in basic wants and needs of the people who make up a society.

There is also an idealist perspective on the meaning of the public interest. Such a definition judges alternative courses of action in relation to some absolute standard of value that in many cases exists independently of the preferences of individual citizens. The public interest is more than the sum of private interests; it is something distinct and apart from basic needs and wants of human beings. Such a definition has a transcendent character and refers to such abstractions as "intelligent good will" or "elevated aspirations" or "the ultimate reality" that human beings should strive to attain. The difficulty with this definition is finding someone with a godlike character who can define these abstractions in an acceptable manner.

Another definition of the public interest focuses on the process by which decisions are made rather than the specification of some ideal outcome. This definition involves the acceptance of some process, such as majority rule, to resolve differences among people. If the rules of the game have been strictly followed, which in a democratic setting means that interested parties have had ample opportunity to express their views, then the outcome of the process has to be in the public interest by definition.

These definitions all have their problems, making an acceptable definition as difficult to arrive at as a specific public policy itself. Most public policies undoubtedly reflect all four definitions in some manner. But for business to be effective in responding to public issues, it must be motivated to look beyond its own immediate economic self-interest and at least recognize the public interest as a legitimate and worthy objective.

Thus far business has got by on largely economic grounds by raising questions about the cost of complying with regulations, the impact of regulation on economic growth, the economic constraints of being socially responsible, and similar arguments. It is unlikely that this strategy will be enough for business involvement in the future. Public policy issues involve questions of justice, rights, fairness, equity, goodness, and purpose—all ethical concepts. For business to participate meaningfully in the resolution of public policy issues, it must learn ethical language and concepts and deal explicitly with the ethical and moral dimensions of these arguments. Otherwise, business may lose the battle by default, as Williams and Houck (1982) conclude: "Executives today are living 'between the times'— that is, they are caught between the time when there was a strong social consensus that the market mechanism was the best way to control business activity and some possible future time when society has a clear consensus about just how business institutions ought to advance human welfare. We are now searching for a new consensus: Economic language, which has in the past often provided the sole rationale for corporate decisions, no longer, in itself, strikes a note of legitimacy for the American public. While corporate critics speak in ethical language employing terms such as fairness, justice, rights, and so on, corporate leadership often responds solely in economic language of profit and loss. Such discussion generates much heat but little light, and the disputing parties pass like ships in the night" (pp. 2–3).

What can emerge from ethical discourse and ethical analysis is a set of ethical principles that will guide management involvement in the public policy process, principles that relate to both the ends and the means of involvement. Corporations must be able to develop a cogent view of the public interest and then develop positions on public issues that embody this notion. In doing this, companies must think about how their products and processes contribute to the betterment of life, what cultural and social role their products and services play, and what difference they make to human welfare and the attainment of personal objectives. The corporate interest must then emanate from and be consistent with the broader public interest. As Sethi (1982) puts it, "The public interest must not be perceived, prescribed, or acted upon by the corporate community as if it were the secondary effect of corporate actions whose degree and magnitude depend on the extent to which corporate self-interest can conveniently accommodate the general interests of society" (p. 34).

Business must also adopt political strategies which are

supportive of the democratic process, which do not undermine our pluralistic structure, and which allow for maximum participation by all members of the corporate community, who may have diverse views on a given public issue. Business must not pursue worthy objectives by means that are regarded as unethical and illegitimate. Both ends and means must conform to ethical principles that are accepted by society at large in order for business to attain legitimacy in the public policy process.

### Business as an Ethical System

These comments suggest that one can view corporate organizations as ethical systems. In this perspective, management becomes the management of values rather than the management of people, machines, money, or something else more traditionally thought to be a manager's province. The management of values implies that corporations, as organizations, create values that are either consistent or out of step with the values of the society in which corporations function. To survive, corporations must adjust their internal values to the changing values and ethics of the larger society.

If ethics is understood as being concerned with actions that are directed toward improving people's welfare, the primary mission of business is to enhance the economic welfare of society by producing goods and services that make people's lives better and more meaningful. In this sense, business creates economic value by taking resources and combining them in such a way as to produce something that has utility and will sell in the marketplace. The traditional function of management is to manage these resources efficiently to create as much economic value as possible and in this way make a significant contribution to society.

But business is not just an economic institution that has to do only with economic value, it is also a social institution that creates or destroys social value. If business pollutes the environment in the process of creating economic value, it is destroying a social value of great significance for human life and survival. If business undermines the trust and confidence of the public through fraudulent and deceptive practices, it is destroying social value by violating ethical principles that form the basis of marketplace transactions.

For business to maintain legitimacy in the public policy process, it must think in terms of creating social value as well as economic value. Business can create social value that enhances people's welfare just as economic value does. When workplaces are made safer, this creates social value by protecting the lives of workers and making injuries less likely. When business reduces its pollution, it creates social value by protecting the quality of the environment, which is necessary for human life.

Management guidelines that emerge from this way of thinking have to do with a positive approach to public issues — viewing them as opportunities to contribute to the welfare of society in new and different ways, beyond producing goods and services. Such a positive approach would seem to be a much better way to deal with these issues than the negative approach of grousing about government intrusion and the costs imposed on business.

Thus, in the final analysis, issues management and strategic planning are not just methods of adjusting corporations to a changing environment as necessary for corporate survival. Issues management linked with strategic management can be a way of creating the future by identifying social problems that are important in society and working through the public policy process to resolve those problems effectively.

Involvement in the public policy process thus provides business with exciting challenges to contribute more to the betterment of society than it has in the past with a narrow focus on economic impacts and outputs. Through positive political strategies based on a broad concept of the public interest, business can become an initiator of public policy by identifying issues that will become agenda items and by developing positions that reflect public as well as corporate interests in creating a just and prosperous society. This initiator role stems from defining the business mission in both economic and social terms and seeing both of these involvements as important. Business initiates new products that it thinks will make a profit; it can also initiate public policy that it believes will benefit society.

The kind of thinking that is required to link environmental assessment with strategic planning could be called "strategic thinking." This kind of thinking is comprehensive and takes account of all factors that could affect the corporation, including social and political factors. Because strategic thinking is future-oriented and anticipatory, business need not merely react to events beyond its control and adjust to changing values that are being created elsewhere. Instead, it can have a positive influence in designing the future.

# 2

# Linking Corporate Planning with Strategic Issues

*Richard N. Sawaya*
*Charles B. Arrington, Jr.*

A decade ago, strategic planning held pride of place in many corporate hierarchies. Staff bureaucracies were built, and careers catapulted, on the strength of strategic planning as a process critical to making key decisions. Strategic planning was by nature long-term. Five-year plans, even ten-year plans, according to their promoters, could focus diverse expertise on the "real issues" so as to raise the chances of corporate success.

Then, conventional practices began to insulate planners, executives, and managers, making them ignorant of key facts. Some, without even the excuse of ignorance, have used conventions to evade the implications of facts. The fortune of strategic planning is a case in point.

Came the 1980s, the U.S. political economy changed. This disorder, of course, required forceful accommodation within corporate hierarchies. "Back to basics," "lean and mean," and "hunker down" ushered out the gaudy elaborations of five- and ten-year projections. Who, after all, is fool enough to prognosticate in the face of appalling discontinuity? Instead, the corporate sector devoted itself to intercorporate asset reshuffling ("Pac-Man") or intracorporate restructuring ("Transformers") or both. Staff bureaucracies were identified as corporate fat, fit for excision, in the interest of cost-cutting efficiency.

This chapter attempts to relate a practical notion of issues management to the practice of strategic planning overall in U.S.

corporations. Our experience has led us to conclude that it may be helpful to look critically at strategic planning and at how serious consideration of public issues fits within it to the benefit of the corporation internally and externally.

Let us start with language: The word *strategy* comes from the Greek *stratos* ("army") and *agein* ("to lead"): "to lead an army." The *stratos* component puts us on analogical grounds: Corporate organizations are like military organizations—both hierarchical and both, in the United States, systemically bureaucratic, put together by the numbers. *Stratos* is a collective noun, all but eliminating, as it were, the human factor. But the verb *agein*, "to lead," brings back the human by pointing to the idea of *someone* who decides. Strategic planning, etymologically, is bound up with leadership. Leaders make strategies; they decide things. However, we are talking about chief executive officers, heads of organizations that are systemically bureaucratic—an oxymoronic situation at best.

Passing from the semantic implications of *strategy*, what about its manifestation in corporations—the planning process? In its corporate heyday, strategic planning was an idea dimly understood at best, often honored mainly in organization charts and sometimes transformed from a qualitative means to critical judgments and difficult truthtelling into a bureaucratic exercise in numerical confirmation of decisions already made. It went like this: Corporate decision makers, executives at the top (leadership by group, another oxymoron), embraced strategic planning in the form of specialized staff, spawning other specialized staff in operating divisions. Soon a strategic planning "cycle" was in full force. Corporate strategic planners would develop key assumptions or scenarios, in the form of econometric forecasts, for division strategic planners. Using the forecasts, division planners would make up their plans and submit them to corporate planners for integration. Corporate planning and division planning would present The Plan to executives at the top for their review and decisions. Budgets (capital and operating expense) would then be carved out, based on (1) the key assumptions and (2) the persuasiveness of division plans. Next, the process would begin again.

As long as the internal and external environments of a corporation remained stable, strategic planning seemed an effective way to organize decisions. In too many cases, however, strategic planning was harmful because it masked the internal politics of decision making. For example, numbers could help avoid thought. Adopting quantitative key assumptions could shield decision makers from conscious conversations about qualitative factors in the external environment that might affect business operations. Key assumptions, expressed as numbers purporting to forecast GNP growth, capacity utilization, product demand, price inflation, and so forth, became reified and thus became conventions to avoid confronting the inherent messiness of the environment.

Another example: Strategic planning could work against itself. Division strategic planning, bound only by key assumptions, was by virtue of its reporting relationship the tool of division management. Division plans, therefore, easily became sales pitches to achieve capital allocation. Most often, they resembled, in their graphed iconography, a hockey stick — that is, great in the distant future. This was so no matter whether division profitability was good or bad.

Shorn of its rhetorical pretensions, that was often the strategic planning game. The human realities were that a corporate planning staff worked at the behest of corporate management — that is, with little if any independence of inquiry. Correspondingly, division planning staff did the bidding of division management in the intracorporate war for capital allocation, crunching numbers to substantiate preexisting conclusions. A plausible tour in division strategic planning lent luster to one's management career in a given division. The real thought processes informing key decisions remained largely the unarticulated, and therefore unassailable, perquisite of senior managers. Their authority was not to be challenged by facts beyond the conventions of the planning schemata. To put it another way, strategic planning was a gentleman's game on the playing fields of corporate bureaucracy.

Now, the external economic environment that influenced strategic planning to develop in such a way was, of course, inflationary. To paraphrase John F. Kennedy: A rising price level lifts all boats—and covers over a multitude of sins. Inflation lends itself to the iconography of hockey sticks.

The coincidence of Paul Volcker heading the Federal Reserve and Ronald Reagan heading the White House changed that external environment and, in due but abrupt course, the game of strategic planning. Disinflation and deficits (budget and trade) placed hockey-stick planning graphs in too ridiculous a light. A falling price level beached many boats, especially broad-bottomed ones. The financial arcana of Pac-Man and Transformers inexorably followed. And strategic planning was relegated to being a subject for corporate rhetoric, staff decimation, and gallows irony.

One irony, of course, is that strategic planning, by definition, was supposed to help anticipate just such a change in the external environment. In that vein, let us engage in a modest, speculative fiction—a small fable for our business times.

The management triumvirate of XYZ, Inc., are having a strategic planning meeting in the fall of 1981. Staff present are the manager of strategic planning, an economist (MSP), and the manager of public affairs, a generalist and politico (MPA). These two "hang out" together. The managing triumvirate are the chief executive officer and chairman of the board (Mr. Outside: CEO), the president and chief operating officer (Ms. Inside: COO), and the chief financial officer (Mr. Wall Street: CFO). Imagine the following:

*CEO:* I'm sure Ronald Reagan will be a two-term president. He's captured America. He's brilliant on television.

*MSP:* His fiscal policy is a disaster. The budget deficit is going to be astronomical, unprecedented.

*MPA:* It won't go away. The tax bill is a Roman circus. Breaks, breaks, breaks. For you, me, the company. Democrats trying to give away more than Republicans. The revenue loss will be enormous.

*MSP:* Exactly. More red ink.

*COO:* What's the bottom line for the company?

*CFO:* One thing—a nasty, tight-money recession. That's really Volcker. His anti-inflation agenda just fits inside Reagan's rhetoric. But he'll make it stick.

*CEO:* Does the deficit mean anything? How does it play with tight money?

*MSP:* Who knows? The tax bill is consumption. The deficit is consumption—defense and entitlements. Tight money and red ink will keep interest rates high. A recession will increase the red ink. It's all unbalanced. I don't know what it means, long-term.

*COO:* It means we're a sitting duck and the storm's coming. We're high-cost, fat, slow. We need to recapitalize, to research. And we need time.

*CEO:* You know, Ronald Reagan's not interested in the *Fortune* 500. We're the status quo. He wants change.

*CFO:* Tax breaks don't cut it for us. They're great if you're on a roll—they increase the take. If you're stuck, they're not relevant, except as aspirin and for takeovers.

*MPA:* The president wants guns. He can't get them with cuts in other programs. So his blank check is the deficit. It's also his club to slow the growth of government he doesn't like. It may not be voodoo, but it's a gamble.

*MSP:* It's a new playing field. Low inflation. High interest rates. The economy's going into the wringer. And if the red ink stays, some part of it will bounce back like gangbusters whenever Volcker eases up.

*CFO:* Tougher markets for us. No price increases, maybe decreases.

*COO:* It's time for XYZ to get into shape. Pronto.

*CEO:* All of us. Top down. And it's time for me to work the "loyal opposition" in Washington.

*MPA:* Daniel in the lion's den?

*CEO:* The lion's den is the name of our game.

Soapiness notwithstanding, the point of the fable so far is that strategic planning is a *shared* process (1) of criticizing assumptions and making judgments about precisely those "exogenous" phenomena (that is, events outside the corporation) that numerical analysis alone cannot capture and (2) of gaining knowledge and making decisions about "endogenous" phenomena, that is, controllables within corporate purview (recall the origins of *strategy*: "to lead an army"). In their laconic, disjointed conversation, the strategic planners at XYZ—the managing triumvirate plus the relevant "experts"—illustrated both.

In our example, the exogenous phenomena were the following: (1) A changed political landscape—seven years of a powerful president ahead, one whose interests are not necessarily those of the *Fortune* 500. (2) Policy imbalance resulting in structural fiscal imbalance. Consumption incentives, savings disincentives (spend now, pay later). (3) Recession followed by asymmetrical recovery; continuing disinflation. (4) Government growth, political party stalemate—the primacy of political logic. Endogenous phenomena were these: (1) Markets tell the tale; subsidies mask the real story (in spite of the CFO's previous career as a corporate tax specialist). (2) XYZ is facing hard times (in spite of the common management assumption that tomorrow is another day in which to muddle through). (3) Smaller is better (in spite of the COO's assumption throughout her entire career that big is best).

The leaders of XYZ, in fact, developed a plan in that meeting. Then, our fable continues, they executed it.

XYZ bought out 50 percent of its work force by means of targeted, generous severance/early retirement offers—working from the top down, negotiating optimal jobs with retained employees. Simultaneously, headquarters was moved to a new, "urban village" location (the prestigious in-town real estate was sold for a bundle). All remaining employees went on profit sharing. The COO spent most of her time integrating research, product development, marketing, and plant and equipment investment. Her primary tool was relentless "shirtsleeves" sessions. The CEO became recognized in the halls of Congress, to great effect later. His external calendar was almost exclusively "no frills" governmental. The CFO had present values on all capital investments calculated without regard to any tax incentives.

What were the consequences? When the trade deficit began to hit (the unknowable "X factor" in the Federal Reserve/ budget deficit/exchange rate equation), XYZ was positioned to stay competitive, lost no market share, and enjoyed a modest increase in profitability—and formidable equity appreciation in the bull market that also hit. A happy ending, indeed.

Is this story implausible? Only if one assumes that, by the process of corporate self-selection they undergo, corporate decision makers ignore the total environment in which they operate or become incapable of thinking and acting as disinterested stewards of the assets they manage and the equities they must adjudicate. (Although the insights that XYZ acted on were certainly not the accepted ones at the time, the external evidence important to our fable was easily available to corporate thinkers in the early 1980s.)

It ought to be clear from our speculative fiction that, to make a difference, strategic planning depends completely on the imagination, understanding, courage, and integrity of the decision makers at the top of any corporation and the degree to which they apply those qualities to both the external and internal environments. We all have "mental maps"—settled convictions, unconscious assumptions, key experiences—that determine how we think the world works and how our particular chink in it works. We are all conditioned, too, by the "rules of discourse" that determine how we say what we say in particular circumstances, such as the corporate conference room. It requires an act of supreme imagination to summon up a skepticism sufficient to subject our mental maps to criticism in plain, blunt, even corrosive terms. Yet imagination—the ability to get beyond ourselves, to have in our characters the will to suspend belief in the conventions that keep us comfortable—is required.

For decision makers to enjoy such skepticism and the discourse it engenders among themselves, they must call upon appropriate expertise within their ranks for facts. After all, they pay by the hour or year for people to attend, full-time, to sets of

exogenous and endogenous phenomena: government, technology, specific markets, plant operations. To get at the facts they
need in order to lead, decision makers have to use their imagina-
tions to persuade these people to use their own speech—to tell
the truth as they see it, unconditioned by preconceptions of
"what management wants to hear (so that I can get ahead—or
keep my head)." Not an easy task; perhaps the most difficult thing
not impossible in an organization systemically bureaucratic.

Put another way, corporate decision makers have to break
through the invisible shield that walls them off from those who
report to them. They have to display the courage "to hear it as it
is" that will convince their subordinates that truth is not only a
burden but a responsibility. They can do so by committing
themselves to self-scrutiny, scrutiny of one another, and (albeit
grudging) appreciation for the bearers of bad news. It seems
evident in our experience that their commitment must not only
exist but be seen to exist.

Such an effort, such a character, will enable decisions. The
decisions will be difficult to the degree that their rationale is not
apparent from the facts. But that is the burden of command—
that and the responsibility to follow through with the consequences of the decisions, to exercise integrity.

We now go back to our speculative fiction to sketch a
taxonomy of decision and implementation. Mr. Outside, the
CEO, leads the enterprise. He represents the corporation's interests exogenously. He sets the example, endogenously, through
his conduct, consciously or not. He is always building the character of the corporation. He spends his outside time—and he
has little of it—with those external phenomena that are important. If, as in our example, the halls of Congress are important,
he listens to his people on the scene. He realizes it is not enough
for him to say, "Politicians are important." He has to work those
politicians who are important to the interests of his corporation,
and he has to understand the logic and ideological conventions
that animate them.

Ms. Inside, the COO, may have an equally daunting task:
the care and deployment of the human beings who make up the
corporation. Necessarily, she shares this responsibility with the

rest of the leadership (indeed, with all "management"); but the buck should land on her desk. She has to know what is going on inside the corporation that might conceivably affect its viability. Are the right people in the right jobs? Are all the jobs being done correctly—for example, are all processes and practices safe and equitable? She cannot rely on the so-called chain of command looping up the ivory tower. She has to be in the field, with her troops, fostering a climate that allows them to tell the truth. Plant fatalities, pollution incidents, human incompetence—they are her beat.

Together, the COO and the CEO have to construct the right organization. All the maxims apply: promote the best; use as few people as possible consonant with responsible and competent operations; minimize hierarchal perks; enforce an ethic of mutual obligations.

The CFO, for his part, has to resist the blandishments of his own numbers. He has perhaps the most difficult balance to achieve—between taking the point position in the struggle for short-term performance and ensuring that long-term considerations are not lost in a sea of calculations. His mental map is necessarily schizophrenic.

The economist, too, has to work against the conventions of her discipline. She must not be seduced by the elegance of her quantitative projections—no matter how good the factual data. She must insist that those projections are mental constructions, no more or less worthy of credence than her qualitative intuitions. Moreover, she has to remain conscious in an increasingly international and public business world of the limitations that a focus on the domestic economic theater can create.

The public affairs politico is the quintessential "trusted outsider." He must understand the political and public relations logic behind the seeming inanities that occur in the public sector and sufficiently schooled in company operations to translate the implications of that sector for the company's fortunes. He has to be rigorous in analysis of how the activities of one will affect the other. And he must use the CEO to maximum effect in the public marketplace.

All the characters in our speculative fiction must recognize the partial nature of their judgments, the obduracy of reality, and the necessity of entertaining fact unadorned. They must know they cannot afford the luxury of ideology or the substitution of convention for imagination.

In summary, strategic planning as sketched includes an extraeconomic dimension. The leaders of XYZ, Inc., have marshaled resources to manage key issues: They have assessed the environment, set priorities and goals, developed an action plan, and executed it. They will have to evaluate results, of course, and make adjustments. But XYZ's actions illustrate how thinking about qualitative internal and external issues contributes critically to strategic planning for the enterprise.

Ah, exclaims the skeptical reader! Your historical synopsis of strategic planning as it has happened rings true—but your fiction about its putative value, in the face of that synopsis, is normative, self-evident, and circular. Able corporate decision makers will be strategic because they are able. Corporate decision makers who are not able will not be strategic because they are not able. No amount of profession to them about being what they are not will make them what they are not.

We quote Hebrews: "Now faith is the substance of things hoped for, the evidence of things not seen." And we speak from recent experience with the fortunes of one large corporation, Atlantic Richfield Company (ARCO).

Like many large corporations, ARCO had evolved a strategic planning process during the 1970s. Simultaneously, the corporation saw fit to develop a sizable public affairs division, including a planning-oriented issues group. (In 1984 we described the form and function of that group and its relation to strategic planning. See Arrington and Sawaya, 1984a.) In 1985, in comparatively early response to a very changed business environment, ARCO engaged in a massive corporate restructuring, including substantial personnel reduction in corporate staff groups such as public affairs. The restructuring was the consequence of strategic thinking by the decision makers of the corporation that yielded (1) a perception that oil prices were likely to tumble in the future, because of structural conditions in world oil markets, (2) a recognition that U.S. capital markets, regardless of future oil price behavior, would not tolerate business as usual in light of domestic exploration failures, and (3) a realization that the inflationary boom years of the 1970s had resulted in staffing levels, companywide, that were excessive and burdensome in the face of competitive realities of the 1980s. Having experienced such changes in their mental maps, ARCO's decision makers changed the asset and employee base of the corporation. They sold off nonperforming assets, including refining and marketing east of the Mississippi. They substantially reduced capital for, and redirected the intent of, hydrocarbon exploration. They offered voluntary, enhanced early retirement and severance companywide. They reviewed the entire corporate organization to eliminate job categories not judged essential to the future viability of the company.

Many corporate staff functions were ended—but not strategic planning. Much of public affairs was eliminated—but not a core issues group or the Washington, D.C., office.

These days, hindsight understandably is deeply discounted. But it does have the advantage of including a few facts. The fact is that ARCO's decision makers involved themselves in strategic planning at the normative level. For them, strategic planning in practice was more than a buzzword, with a vengeance. Nor did they shrink from the responsibilities of leading their subordinates through the humanly difficult consequences of strategic planning—the restructuring. The subsequent oil price collapse—even more precipitous than foreseen—has underscored the value of strategic planning in the company.

The fact is, too, that the actions of ARCO's decision makers show that they believe paying attention to exogenous phenomena like public policy making in Washington is important. They kept a functioning presence in Washington and a core analytical group in headquarters. And even during the restructuring of the company, they selectively prosecuted advocacies on those public issues of clear importance to the company. One vivid example was that they pursued, with extraordinary purposefulness, a company-developed resolution of a key federal public policy issue with implications for strategic planning, reauthorization of Superfund.

Superfund (the Comprehensive Environmental Response, Compensation and Liability Act) was first legislated in the 1980 lame duck session of the 96th Congress. Its proponents billed it as the means to ensure cleanup of abandoned hazardous-waste dump sites in the United States, in cases where responsible parties could not be identified and promptly brought to account. Authorized at $1.6 billion over five years, Superfund was paid for mostly by taxes on chemical feedstocks and crude oil, because abandoned dump sites were judged to be preponderantly "the fault" of these industries. ARCO and a select number of other oil and petrochemical companies bore the brunt of the tax in the amount of many millions of dollars a year.

The first years of Superfund's implementation were marked by apparent inaction and reports of administrative scandal at the Environmental Protection Agency (EPA). At the same time, the Superfund program became inflated, perhaps inevitably, into a de facto national public works program, as each state had to have its fair share of sites identified for priority cleanup. Not surprisingly, in 1984 Superfund's champions were laying the groundwork for reauthorization at much higher funding levels and with more draconian program provisions, threatening to magnify by five or six times the tax burden on just a handful of companies, including ARCO.

At the same time, the person in the issues group at ARCO responsible for environmental issues, James Ford, led the difficult negotiation of a proposed company strategy among the varied and sometimes conflicting operating and corporate interests in the company—including planners—for the decision of senior management. That strategy (1) recognized the political inevitability of an expanded Superfund despite Reagan administration opposition, (2) focused on the funding question as of strategic moment to ARCO, and (3) advocated a broad-based corporate tax as an alternative to the narrow base of chemical feedstocks and crude oil. Management decided to adopt the strategy and vigorously implement it at a point in the legislative cycle early enough to permit ARCO to become a real player in a complex political process.

ARCO commissioned an independent study by the Management Analysis Center concerning the feasibility and equity of a broad-based corporate tax as the principal funding mechanism for an expanded Superfund. At his own request and as luck would have it, Ford moved to Washington, D.C., as ARCO's representative on environmental issues in 1985, thereby personally assuring advocacy consistent with analysis. He and his colleagues in that office began the arduous task of "selling" the company position to other oil and chemical companies, to industry associations, and to Democratic and Republican legislators. They were joined in this effort, on an as-needed basis, by senior company management. They persevered, despite administration opposition to the idea of a broad-based corporate tax.

After almost two years of "in the trenches" advocacy, the ARCO position, initially scorned, was adopted in the Senate's version of Superfund reauthorization, though narrowly rejected in the House's version (despite a favorable Ways and Means Committee vote). In subsequent conference committee deliberations, a broad-based tax component was accepted by conferees, though with a major increase in the tax on crude oil. The House and Senate strongly endorsed the conference compromise. Finally, the administration, despite repeated veto threats, determined to accept the legislation for an expanded Superfund ($8.5 billion) with its mixed financing arrangements. It was signed into law on October 17, 1986.

Apart from the specifics of the laborious reauthorization of Superfund, a broad-based corporate tax was a major element in the debate. ARCO's efforts, though not alone, were integral to that accomplishment. On an issue that mattered—large dollar consequences to the enterprise and large public interests—the company acted constructively and effectively.

In other words, consideration of issues, in concert with strategic planning, can result in a useful public policy advocacy to external audiences as well as bring worthwhile public policy insight into the company. The ARCO examples demonstrate the importance of the public policy aspect of strategic planning, of company decision makers' involvement in the execution of a strategy, and, concomitantly, of having the right people in the right jobs.

Obviously, this discussion raises numerous questions about the nature of contemporary American culture. Any prescription about corporate management begs larger issues about ways in which our culture shapes the character of corporate activity. To mention just one, ours is a profoundly individualistic culture. Some say we idolize the self. Needless to say, primacy of the self is not conducive to the kind of organizational enterprise implied in our discussion of strategic planning. And yet, ours is no less profoundly a voluntaristic culture, able to produce exquisite teamwork when the dignity of individuals is maintained, goals are clearly defined, standards of conduct are observed without exception, and sacrifices and rewards are shared. Good strategic planning and the issues thinking integral to it depend on such teamwork.

The kind of teamwork subsumed under strategic planning is aptly summarized by the economist Donald McCloskey (1985). He cites the German word *Sprachethik* to capture the conversational norms appropriate to successful economic discourse and, we would add, to successful strategic planning: "Don't lie; pay attention; don't sneer; cooperate; don't shout; let other people talk; be open-minded; explain yourself when asked" (p. 24).

In addition, strategic planning needs to be informed by a recognition that as we approach the end of the twentieth century, the U.S. corporation, with its history of survival in commercial competition, must also compete in the broader arena of public decisions. As the late commentator Elmer Davis (1954) pointed out three decades ago, "This nation was conceived in liberty and dedicated to the principle—among others—that honest men may honestly disagree; that if they all say what they think, a majority of the people will be able to distinguish truth from error; that in the competition of the marketplace of ideas, the sounder ideas will in the long run win out" (p. 114).

# ⁙ 3

# Identifying Critical Issues for Better Corporate Planning

## Margaret A. Stroup

Since the earliest days of American corporations, the planning for new products, their manufacture, their introduction into the marketplace, and their hoped-for earnings has been an essential ingredient of the industrial scene. From early informal phases, planning has grown into functions and formal processes. It has not, however, always evolved into successful results.

Despite the introduction of computer models, consultant advice, and revolving-door ever-changing attempts to plan better, many companies annually repeat an increasingly frustrating exercise of numbers no one believes in and plans no one uses. Each year, planners carefully integrate products, cost of goods sold, marketplace tactics, and earnings results into superbly constructed plans. Then, false assumptions—or factors completely unthought of—intervene, making the plans worth less than the paper they are written on.

Unspoken assumptions have always been the nemesis of planners. Nowadays, the effects of those assumptions can be swift and powerful. One such assumption, that the future always holds greater opportunity and achievement, has prevailed in American business for most of the past 200 years. By the 1950s, the rate of change in the world, and the repercussions of such change on business, began to accelerate. The arrival of long-range planning represented a fundamental change in business management. It was the first flicker of recognition that business must forecast the future and plan for change. Successful answers to the problems planning was supposed to solve, however, remained elusive.

By the 1970s, the assumption of an ever-brighter tomorrow was clearly outdated. Complex political, social, and economic trends were wreaking havoc on business's forecasts and plans; the need to predict and prepare for the future was critical. Long-range planning was not providing management with the information it needed. Not only were its predictions of the future based on the past, but it virtually ignored nonmarket issues.

Since instituting long-range planning in 1972, Monsanto has been fine-tuning its system to cope with the problem of unplanned factors and silent assumptions. The system has never ignored assumptions entirely. For example, the planning process had traditionally used economic forecasts. Our economists provided answers to questions about interest rates, GNP growth, or demographic forecasts, and these were routinely incorporated into the long-range plans. It was clear by the early 1980s that these economic factors were not enough. With an overreliance on economic and market data and with the poor reliability of earnings forecasts, the long-range planning system was working with blinders. Traditional "number crunching" exercises were producing inadequate plans. The corporation needed to understand the external nonmarket issues that were profoundly affecting its businesses and its results. Specifically, management needed to focus attention on the underlying assumptions that formed the basis of the long-range plans. It needed a system to expand awareness of those assumptions and to provide a response mechanism in case the assumptions were inaccurate.

Monsanto now has such a system, a program called "Strategic Premises." The program was not born overnight. Nor was it implemented in a calculated, textbooklike fashion; we did not pick a model and rigidly impose it on our existing planning structures. Strategic Premises evolved slowly, through trial and error, and I believe that approach has much to do with its success. In this chapter I examine the evolution of the Strategic Premises Program from its issues identification beginning, through the nuts and bolts of its implementation, to, finally, its success as an integral part of Monsanto's planning system.

## Genesis of the Strategic Premises Program

Strategic Premises began in Monsanto's social responsibility program — an unusual beginning but a perfectly understandable one. As the Social Responsibility Committee dealt with societal expectations for business in general and Monsanto in particular, it felt that industry was always "playing catch-up." We were reacting to pressures that were full-blown and attitudes that were solidly entrenched before management could adjust company actions to those changed expectations. To alter our catch-up position, in 1978 the Social Responsibility Committee created an issue identification program to determine the trends of societal expectations. Early knowledge of these trends would give the company more time to change negative attitudes toward business or to adapt business practices proactively if attitudes and expectations could not be swayed from the identified path.

In those days the program was the responsibility of Monsanto's director of social responsibility. To facilitate the issue identification process, the best minds in the company were brought together to think about the societal factors in the external world that could affect Monsanto. It is not surprising that those minds soon began to consider issues beyond the original mandate.

When the first list of identified issues appeared in 1981, it included the growth of regulatory processes, increased control by state government, the increase in redundancy laws, changed employee expectations, and the dissatisfaction of the scientific community with its role at Monsanto. These issues could at least partly be labeled societal expectations. Other issues, including the movement of oil companies into traditional chemical businesses, the computer/electronic revolution, and the growing impact of biotechnology, were clearly beyond the realm of societal expectations. They were recognizable parts of Monsanto's strategy.

The issue identification group presented its list of issues to the eight vice-presidents who composed the Social Responsibility Committee. Most of these vice-presidents had traditional "line" responsibilities such as agricultural products, industrial chemicals, and textiles. They had expected a list of issues about day care and sheltered workshops; imagine their reaction when instead they received a list of issues affecting the corporation's overall strategy!

A void had clearly existed at Monsanto, and the issue identification process, still called "social responsibility," had moved to fill it. Fortunately, executive management recognized the critical nature of the void and was pleased with the outcome of issue identification, even if it was still labeled "social responsibility." As a result, in January 1983, the issue identification system and staff moved to Corporate Plans with the specific purpose of building external factors and their impact on Monsanto into the long-range planning process. As we became aware that the major problem of planning was that age-old nemesis of assumptions, issue identification quickly evolved into a review of Monsanto's assumptions in the long-range plans.

### Obstacles to Implementation

From the beginning, we knew there would be several major difficulties in implementing a program to review the assumptions (soon called "premises") on which the plans were based:

1. We could not begin to list all the assumptions underlying the plans. Even if that were possible, management's attention could be drawn to only a few issues because of time constraints. We therefore identified premises not only on the basis of their importance to the plans but also on the basis of our understanding of how well the assumptions had already been thought through by top management.

2. We had to deal with strategic, not tactical, assump-

tions. Monsanto's decentralized planning system and the result-ing focus of the top-management committee on corporate issues meant that individual factors for our various businesses must initially be ignored to bring proper attention to those few "corporation-moving" items.

3. Adoption of strategic premises by the organization would be slow and sometimes would seem impossible. We hoped to change top managers' thinking as they reviewed the long-range plans from the various operating units. In time, we hoped to widen our focus so that each of the operating units would become better at analyzing its own assumptions. We wanted the operating-unit managers to develop their skills in clearly delin-eating those factors that make the difference between hoped-for earnings and earnings that can really be counted on. But we knew that our first emphasis had to be at the top.

4. We would never convince all the top managers that review of assumptions was an important part of the long-range planning process. Of the ten members of the Executive Manage-ment Committee (the chief executive officer and the top nine individuals in the corporation), we would always have one or two who gave the whole process only cursory attention.

In spite of these foreseeable difficulties, we pressed on with the program. Fortunately, Monsanto's chief executive was struck immediately with the importance of the process. He endorsed it strongly and led the discussions throughout.

### Implementing the Strategic Premises Program

The program was implemented in three phases. Although the process appears orderly now, it did not seem so at the time. At any given point, we knew what our goals were and what the next step toward them should be, but we did not start with a road map of how to implement a strategic premises program. The absence of a formal plan freed us from preconceptions of how the implementation process should unfold and contributed to our creativity in tailoring the program to Monsanto.

In the first phase of implementation, we consulted people

both internal and external to Monsanto who knew what they were talking about. We again formed a committee of the best minds in the company, people who had both conceptual thinking and long and varied experience, and called it the Strategic Environment Group. We also gathered information from SRI International, the Institute for the Future, and the Center for Futures Research. We then narrowed, ranked, reranked, reworked, and rewrote premises, eventually producing six major strategic premises. Because the chief executive usually asks, "What just missed the cut?" we added the four "near misses" to the list.

The six strategic premises and the four near misses were presented to the Executive Management Committee. We told the committee that this was a fledgling process that would evolve and be perfected over the years. We also reiterated that the list was not comprehensive, stressing the criteria by which the premises had been selected. We obviously did not tell our top managers that we were trying to stretch their thinking and get some of their "unmentionable items" onto the table to be discussed in a nonthreatening environment. As we stood back and watched, however, we saw expanded thinking begin.

In the second phase of implementation, the Executive Management Committee met in four sessions to discuss the premises. It quickly decided that the near misses were too important to omit. The CEO added one more premise, bringing the list to eleven. We then gave the committee three choices to make about each premise.

The committee could say, Yes, we're going to accept the premise. The risk of its being incorrect is low, or we can live with the assumption if it is wrong.

Or the committee could ask, What action can we take to make sure the premise holds? What can we do to change the action of the company, or the factor itself, to maximize the likelihood that this assumption will develop as predicted?

The remaining response option was to ask, What will we do if the worst occurs? That question raises the specter of contingency plans. Contingency planning, however, can become a game in itself, a paper exercise to see how many versions of the same plan can be written in a specified period of time. We did not want written plans; we wanted contingency *thinking*. We wanted worst-case analyses that could be discussed with senior management. Since we did not choose to write plans for every possible outcome,we asked the Executive Management Committee to direct its "what if" questions to the managers running the businesses.

After reviewing the three response options, the committee decided which response was appropriate for each of the eleven premises. The premises that required proactive action then resulted in specific assignments to members of the committee.

In the third phase of implementing the Strategic Premises Program, we communicated to the writers of the long-range plans of all reporting units that the executives who would be reviewing them had gone through this exercise. This stimulated those planners to incorporate the spirit of Strategic Premises into their presentations.

### First-Year Results:
### Open Examination of Critical Assumptions

The results of the program surpassed our hopes for its first year. Strategic Premises questioned the forecasted earnings of certain of our businesses, the GNP growth, and the growth of the chemical industry. We questioned our assumptions about the productivity of our employees. We looked at the growing phenomenon of the litigious society and its possible impact on Monsanto, including a corporation-threatening settlement. We wondered whether genetically engineered products would be accepted complacently by a fearful public. Unfortunately, our fears on this premise were realized in 1986 as the first two genetically produced products were stalled in their regulatory reviews.

But Strategic Premises did more than examine issues; it prompted action. For example, one premise questioned the seven- to ten-year process of getting new products from research to market, asking whether the time frame could be shortened.

The result was almost a cultural change in our market approach from "technological push" to "customer pull." The change was reflected in Monsanto's organizational restructuring in January 1986, in which businesses were redefined from a consumer perspective. For example, the Plastics Division was reorganized into groups like Housing Plastics, Business Machines Plastics, and Auto Plastics rather than Plastics "A" and Plastics "B."

Another response to the issue of new-product cycles was a decentralization of research and development activities. Corporate Research and Development efforts were downsized, and researchers were moved to the operating units. Integrating the scientific community with commercial resources enabled new-product ideas to move considerably faster.

As the final step of the first-year process, the list of strategic premises was used as a basis for Monsanto's annual planning conference. The twenty-four vice-presidents who attended the conference further expanded on the premises, discussing their ramifications within the individual businesses.

### Second-Year Results: Improved Earnings Forecasts

The Strategic Premises Program underwent a distinct evolution in 1985, its second year. Early in the year it was obvious that the 1984 list was still a vibrant document that would continue to be applicable to the long-range plans slated for review in 1985. We toyed with the ideas of making minor modifications in the list and of simply waiting until 1986 to come up with revisions.

As we debated this, the attention of the Executive Management Committee turned to the unreliability of forecasted earnings. Since these forecasts form the basis of Monsanto's spending projections, particularly for long-term research and development projects, their lack of accuracy was becoming critical for the corporation. As a result, the 1985 long-range planning process emphasized bringing greater reliability to forecasted earnings. The manner in which this problem was addressed became an unnamed supplement to Strategic Premises.

The long-range planners had always asked the operating

units for a "most probable" forecast of earnings, a term that meant there was a 50 percent chance that actual earnings would be lower than the forecasted number. Because long-range plans were widely circulated and often used as motivational tools, the numbers generated upward from lower levels in the organization became highly optimistic, almost unattainable. Much of the unreality of the forecasts had evolved in response to the perception that optimism was desirable behavior. The long-term impact of resulting research and capital expenditures had demonstrated, however, that the company could no longer tolerate wildly optimistic forecasts.

What ensued looks deceptively simple in hindsight. First, for the 1985 plans, we asked the operating units to give us a "nearly certain" number, one that had a 90 percent probability of being achieved. That number obviously was much lower than the so-called most probable one.

Then the Corporate Plans Department made a critical proposal: We asked the head of each operating unit to structure the executive summary of his long-range plan around the *bridge* between the "most probable" and "nearly certain" numbers. When those writing the plans disciplined themselves to define the difference between the two numbers, suddenly the underlying assumptions, particularly the external, nonmarket issues, were thrown into high relief. Events such as products being banned, changes in the GNP rate, litigation, parity, and the strong dollar, as well as the traditional write-offs and competitor actions, began to receive direct attention from our business directors and their planners.

## Institutionalization

By bridging the gap between "nearly certain" and "most probable" forecasts, the Strategic Premises Program gained acceptability by the back door—and was on its way to institutionalization. At Monsanto, "institutionalization" refers to the stage at which a program becomes incorporated into every manager's thinking and activities. Strategic planning has often failed at this point. After well-intentioned corporate planners have spent much time and energy developing strategic planning programs, those programs are never integrated fully into operations and never produce the results they were designed to deliver.

The institutionalization of Strategic Premises was reinforced in the company's 1986 decentralization. In the chemical company's Planning Department, we are further institutionalizing Strategic Premises. Before the long-range plan process begins, the strategic premises are reviewed with the heads of the six divisions within the chemical company. Through discussion, the basis for each division's projections is tested and compared — with the projections of the other divisions, the chemical company overview, and the corporate initiatives. Then each division writes its plans, but the involvement of Strategic Premises does not end there.

As part of the review process for each division's plans, the strategic premises again play a role as the building blocks for the questioning and review. Then, when the six division plans are consolidated into one chemical company long-range plan to be sent to top corporate mangement, again the strategic premises are the final tests for our projected strategy changes, tactical maneuvers, and forecasted earnings.

Strategic Premises is a crucial support system for long-range planning. Reviewing assumptions can keep business plans on the right track. Using long-range planning alone, companies put themselves in the position of a driver with her foot on the accelerator and her eye on the rear-view mirror: She might be moving, but she won't get where she wants to go.

In implementing Strategic Premises there is much to be said for an incremental style of program growth. A complete road map is not required for success. In fact, a formal plan may even be detrimental, as it can limit creative thinking and the ability to respond quickly and appropriately to immediate circumstances. Gradual implementation also assists in integrating the program at all levels of operation. Certainly Strategic Premises is still not "final" at Monsanto, even though its institutionalization is well on its way in the chemical company. Each year we will use some process—but not always Strategic Premises—to ensure that we have examined the assumptions used in our plans and that we have not neglected the factors of importance to our company's long-term earnings and survival.

# Organizational Tactics for Effective Issues Management

## Introduction by Robert L. Heath

No company likes surprises, even favorable ones. For this reason an issues management program is unsuccessful if it cannot minimize the surprise of suddenly discovering that an issue has become unmanageable because activist groups and other advocates have established the conditions for its debate by legislators or regulators. Nor is an issues management program effective if it cannot help company operations conform to prevailing standards of corporate responsibility. These themes are central to Part Two, which examines the tactics needed for spotting and monitoring issues and for determining how aware a company is of issues and how prepared it is to respond to them. The three chapters presented here stress the importance of vigilance in avoiding unwinnable external battles and the need for sensitivity to public policy issues as a part of the corporate culture, involving all employees.

Supporting these themes, Joseph F. Coates and Jennifer Jarratt explain the difficulties encountered in determining what issues are emerging and when they have advanced to the point where they deserve systematic attention. They advise companies to avoid worrying about fine distinctions regarding the type of issue and expend their resources on creating permanent means for identifying and analyzing issues. O. W. Markley uses a case study to explain how to carry out a situation audit and how to determine when a company is capable of monitoring and using the audit data to adjust plans and operations in the face of environmental changes. Markley's discussion reveals that an understanding of employee networks and corporate climate will help managers isolate issues and integrate them into planning and operations. Stephen J. Kasser and Greg Truax explain how a corporate communication group can centralize and expedite the flow of information on issues stances by using a database system such as the one they helped develop for Tampa Electric, which provides those who work with issues on a day-to-day basis with easy access to the current company position.

To be surprised by changes in the operating and planning environment means that a surveillance system is not working properly. One of the greatest concerns felt by any responsible leader is that something totally unexpected will occur. A competitor will come out with a new product or process. A market will change with little warning. Fads come and go with blinding speed. A regulator changes a ground rule. An activist group comes into being or begins to exert more power than early estimates predicted. Some nut tampers with a product. A journalist writes a feature article that contains inaccuracies or, perhaps worse, is quite accurate and very embarrassing. In hopes of avoiding surprises or at least foreseeing possible responses, a company can conduct extensive surveillance only to discover that the results are based on unfounded market, economic, financial, or public policy premises. Such surprises upset the orderly execution of the strategic plan.

By the same token, a company can ill afford to become so bogged down in issues monitoring and analysis that it defaults in the public policy process. Horror stories abound of companies that spent hundreds of hours analyzing issues only to find that the issues had escalated or died without any direct intervention by the company. Perhaps for this reason, some management teams complain that they cannot do anything to prevent surprises. They whine that investigative reporters and special-interest advocates are a pack of unethical, un-American curs carping about a company that is merely trying to create jobs and make a profit. These sorts of "apple pie" arguments do not impress the public and often create an ostrich mentality that damages the company's ability to respond.

Because no organization can easily identify, track, and manage every issue, the company culture should make employees sensitive to the ways public policy can affect planning and operations. Weick (1987, p. 112) makes a similar point by arguing that "accidents occur because the humans who operate and manage complex systems are themselves not sufficiently complex to sense and anticipate the problems generated by those systems." This problem, what he calls *requisite variety*, results "because the variety that exists in the system to be managed exceeds the variety in the people who must regulate it. When people have less variety than is requisite to cope with the system, they miss important information, their diagnoses are incomplete, and their remedies are short-sighted and can magnify rather than reduce a problem." In similar fashion, keeping track of public policy concerns is a task too great for one person. A matrix is needed that is comprehensive while being flexible. But a matrix alone will not solve the problem. Extrapolating from Weick's analysis, corporate culture should clearly indicate that public policy issues are important to the company's well-being and that each employee has a part to play in the monitoring and response process. This tack can help personnel to know what an issue is and how it can affect planning and operations. Key employees must know the company is searching for issues that can affect planning and operations in order to know what they are looking for and that they will be rewarded for discovering and reporting emerging policy issues.

Some issues are easy to track. For instance, once issues have become institutionalized into the legislative or regulatory process, they are easy to monitor because formal communication channels exist. In fact, some issues are like a nuisance dog — constantly underfoot. Often issues that have become locked into the regulatory system are so complex and sophisticated that they have left the realm of public discussion and are debated in hearing chambers by experts representing companies or activist groups.

Knowing the kind of issue helps issues managers know

where to look to monitor its status. Issues can be divided into five types according to how far they have progressed in the governmental process: legal/administrative litigation, legislative, prelegislative, potential legislative, and emerging. The first four types are relatively easy to monitor because they are being discussed and debated in established media and governmental arenas. A tracking system is needed to keep a company abreast of any movement an issue makes within the various stages. Many consulting services and trade associations are available to assist, but by being constantly alert, companies can do a great deal to aid themselves in this process. Although subtle changes may occur quickly, issues mature slowly, sometimes taking decades to be resolved.

The toughest issues to identify and monitor are those that are emerging. Identifying relevant emerging issues is probably as much intuition and luck as science. Because it is so difficult, many companies fail to make the effort. They often rely on the fact that after an issue emerges, it takes ten to fifteen years to reach final legislative stages. Most never survive and die a natural death because public opinion changes or an activist group or interested legislator is unable to promote legislation or regulation.

The following guidelines assist in deciding what emerging issues warrant monitoring and impact assessment. Many potential issues might be put into a "watch" category, but an issue should enter the company issues management system only when it meets one or more of these criteria:

1.  It is listed in standard indexes — a sign that journalists have come to believe it is legitimate and worth general public discussion.
2.  A case can be made that if the issue matures, it will harm company operations or offer new market or public policy opportunities.
3.  It is being discussed by an activist group, leading spokesperson, or other company that has a track record of bringing issues into legislation or regulation or at least is capable of doing so.

4.  It is being defined and made a part of the public policy process by the acts of the judiciary. Most litigation occurs after an issue has worked its way into regulation. However, some public policy issues arise through the court system, as demonstrated by product and workplace liability cases.
5.  It is being discussed in scholarly literature with sufficient popularity that it may emerge into popular literature.

These criteria do not preclude the full deployment of early warning systems. Careful attention and strategic adjustments can prevent issues from "emerging." But the larger objective addressed here is how to operationalize the issues-monitoring and impact-assessment system in an orderly fashion.

The primary concern is spotting as early as possible those issues that are most likely to damage or foster the company mission. At a given time, any company or industry will have hundreds of pieces of federal, state, and local legislation—to say nothing of regulations by agencies—that will (or at least could) affect operations or mission. For each issue, potential impact can be estimated by applying four criteria: likelihood, impact, timing, and potential resolution. (Brown, 1979, pp. 31–32, has proposed placing the first of these items in a matrix that allows issues analysts to isolate the high-profile issues, those having high probability of occurrence and high impact. See also Coates and others, 1986, p. 102.)

What is the *likelihood* that an issue will mature into legislation or regulation? Aids in estimating the probability that an issue will gain momentum include the extent of its ties to the self-interest of key publics, its promotion by sophisticated activists who have established followings and effective communication networks, and the willingness of the press and legislators to discuss it because of its "story" value. These indicators suggest the extent to which the issue's proponents are sophisticated in their power tactics, funded for a campaign, and dedicated to waging a battle. Most issues that become topical in public opinion never go this far, but those that do must be identified as early as possible to prevent damage that could have been mitigated by proper communication and operating adjustments.

Issues monitors must also assess the *impact* the issue may have on company mission, operations, and profits if it matures into legislation or regulation. In the abstract, such discussions are difficult to imagine because impact is certainly a function of the type and severity of regulation, which in large part relate to likelihood. The more explosive the issue and the closer its ties to profit, the greater its likelihood and the more damaging its impact on the bottom line. The impact statement addresses the effect (with special attention to cost) an issue would have if brought into legislation or regulation.

Many monitoring models exist for calculating the *timing*, or evolution, of an issue along a continuum from emergence to legal/administrative litigation. Issues managers can assist in short- and long-range planning by estimating when an issue will begin to affect operations. With the current sensitivity to the public policy arena, many companies change operations in the prelegislative stages in order to blunt public criticism that can lead to legislation or regulation. In estimating timing, several variables interact: intensity and breadth of public concern, existing activist group/legislative structure, environment, self-interests, and potential that a communication campaign can blunt the emerging public concern.

Lastly, the analysis statement should assess the *potential for resolution*—the degree to which key audiences (internal and external), activist groups, legislators, or journalists are likely to receive and yield to the corporate message on the issue. Not all issues exhibit the same level of resistance. Any estimate of resistance must also take into account the difficulty and cost of changing the company mission or operations to resolve the issue.

By carefully weighing these dimensions, a company can begin to develop its strategic response and cost-effectiveness statements. The key element in the decision process is whether living with the legislation or regulation would be more costly than trying to oppose it.

Any discussion of monitoring brings up visions of thousands of dollars being spent on costly issues analysis and polling tactics. But in fact, companies sometimes have ample knowledge of a potentially explosive problem because key people perceive that company products or processes violate accepted standards, such as public safety or esthetics. Elaborate issues-monitoring schemes are unnecessary when a company or industry has evidence of such a problem.

Issues monitoring and analysis will be ineffective if executive management is unwilling to acknowledge that it may be in error. Some executives are angered by the prospect that others can "dictate" how they will operate their companies. Moreover, their reluctance to acknowledge that public policy issues are brewing discourages employees from waving a flag. They ask, why rock the boat when the boss doesn't want it rocked?

Effective issues analysis begins by asking what the chances are that the critics are correct, instead of assuming that they are meddling crackpots. All public criticism should prompt corporate leaders and operations managers to conduct studies to determine whether the charges are true and whether key publics are believing the allegations. A company is wise to institutionalize such distant early warning systems throughout its operations and staff functions. One of the primary motives for the creation of a social movement of activist agitation is a widely held and deeply felt belief that companies have been irresponsible. The companies involved must have had ample evidence that something needed to be done. What if asbestos, benzene, vinyl chloride, or formaldehyde creates health hazards? What if cigarette smoking is related to major illnesses? Asking "what if" questions can keep a company alert to danger zones.

Standards of corporate responsibility are often complex and difficult to resolve. In this endeavor, external focus groups including people representative of the general public can be used to determine whether company actions violate accepted standards of corporate responsibility. Expert panels can also help companies increase their sensitivity to those standards. Keep in mind: Even if you are not defining the ground rules of public policy performance, other people are.

Willingness to be open to outside criticism and set up

mechanisms to check the veracity of complaints is a major step toward issues monitoring, which obviously has vital links to marketing and corporate image management. If products are causing problems, early warning alerts can help the company develop new designs or create maintenance procedures that not only forestall a crisis but can translate into marketing strategies. Likewise, complaints about the company or industry can serve as incentives and guides for corrective behavior as well as image advertisements that favorably compare the sponsoring company with others in and outside the industry.

Trade associations are vital to issues monitoring and analysis because they can surface complaints within an industry. Besides monitoring public, regulatory, and legislative arenas, these associations can foster development of a public policy agenda based on members' complaints about the actions of other members. Industries have also established groups within trade associations to monitor issues and to regulate behavior industrywide. For instance, the Chemical Industry Institute of Toxicology is an independent, not-for-profit organization that receives contributions from its constituent companies to conduct and commission studies on toxicity. Institutes such as the Energy Production Research Institute and the Edison Electric Institute are designed to help sponsoring companies improve their performance, including the ability to understand and respond intelligently to technical, social, political, and economic issues.

As well as having several issues handed to them through "complaints," some companies know what the issues are because they periodically battle experts for the opposition. Pollution standards and working environment conditions brought about a new breed of expert. Believing that companies were too slow to respond to health and environmental problems, activist groups developed their own expertise to examine these issues. In the asbestos controversy, the National Cancer Institute for Occupational Safety and Health has studied potential carcinogens. It has provided expert testimony for liability cases. Companies and activist groups are in constant conversation over the latest findings on levels of toxicity, long-term health hazards of chemicals, and so on. The point: Any company that wants to spot problems early has plenty of opportunities.

This is easily said, but deciding how it can be done most effectively is much more difficult. Coates and his associates (1986, pp. 45–95) describe twenty-five means for gathering and making sense of data: networking, precursor (bellwether) analysis, media analysis, polls and surveys, juries of executive opinion, expert panels, scanning and monitoring, content analysis, legislative tracking, Delphi, conversational Delphi, consensor, cross-impact analysis, decision support systems, computer-assisted techniques, small-group process, scenario building, trend extrapolation, technological forecasting, decision analysis, factor analysis, sensitivity analysis, trigger event identification, key-player analysis, and correlation/regression. They evaluate each of these approaches in a complex analytical matrix that can help issues managers decide which methods to adopt (pp. 46–47). Turk (1986) argues that scanning, trend extrapolation, Delphi including cross-impact analysis, and scenario building combine into a "sequential" forecasting system.

Many of these methods can be expensive; some are very expensive. All have their problems, their limitations, and their strengths. Some overlap and complement each other. A few are merely statistical methods, whereas others require sophisticated subjective decision making. Issues managers face many difficult choices in selecting and implementing the means for gathering and analyzing data. Some issues monitors believe that the "news hole" technique is best. This approach assumes that only so much news can be disseminated on a given day. The trick is to caclulate the proportion of the whole each story contributes. In tracking the trends, one can estimate what the emerging and declining issues are by quantifying their shares of media attention. But this method assumes that media coverage is a true indicator of public sentiment and the conviction of special-interest advocates and key legislators. Several years will pass before the techniques are refined well enough that an issues manager can feel comfortable in selecting among this array of issues identification and monitoring techniques. Meanwhile, life goes on and each company must do its best.

Monitoring must take into consideration how issues originate. Three sources seem to predominate: (1) legal, (2) concerned advocates, whether special-interest, legislative, regulatory, employees, other companies, or media, (3) the company or the industry itself. Court decisions based on medical research, for instance, will determine whether benzene becomes more closely regulated. As shown in the cases involving Manville and A. H. Robins, product liability is not inherently a public policy issue. But it becomes one when enough people are harmed and when public policy issues and accompanying regulation grow from the legal issue. The activities surrounding Manville and A. H. Robins have substantial implications for various regulatory agencies, such as FDA and OSHA, for subsequent legislation, and for other companies in the same regulatory environment. Anger at one company or industry creates a hostile environment and a greater likelihood of lawsuits and additional regulatory control for other companies.

A second source of public policy issues is vested-interest advocates. The issues these advocates make salient become part of the conflict that companies need to manage. These issues entail efforts to communicate with the public and create stakeholder participation to prevent, mitigate, or promote legislation or regulation. Coupled to the difficulties of monitoring specific issues are decisions about what groups to monitor. Any issues-monitoring system worth its cost is based on the realization that issues do not foster and promote themselves. Their lifeblood is enthusiastic, dedicated, and articulate spokespersons. Many corporate leaders hate to admit that they have to listen to the Ralph Naders and the Sierra Clubs. But the fact is that no issue will reach a legislative assembly unless it is energetically sponsored. Some legislators have a public policy agenda. For instance, one chemical company is so intent on watching the efforts of Rep. Henry Waxman (D.–Calif.) that it has his picture on an office wall, set up as a dartboard.

Other issues originate because of efforts by an industry or a company. In 1986, for instance, the textile manufacturing industry called for protective tariffs. When issues are introduced this way, the company or industry, rather than reacting on terrain chosen by activist groups, legislators, or regulators, can more easily set the tone and select the territory for the battle. Activist groups and key legislators find their role reversed. This time they oppose the companies' efforts to define the issues, inform the public, and create the legislative agenda, including the wording of legislation and the securing of legislative support.

Issues are often virtually impossible to spot before they find their way into court or into the minds of key advocates or corporate leaders. Some issues begin in the laboratories and minds of highly specialized scholars. The first glimpse of these issues may come out in party conversations, lectures, dissertations, or scholarly papers. Professors who have discovered that fluorocarbons seem to be damaging the ozone layer around the earth have written scholarly papers and sent notices to companies and governmental officials. Are they crackpots? Some companies probably think so. But if they are not wrong and if they are energetic and dedicated, they will prevail. No company is hurt by opening a dialogue with such persons. In the case of fluorocarbons, even du Pont finally agreed that a major problem exists.

Building rapport with activists, critics, and scholars is a helpful way of monitoring. One soon separates key players from the nuts. Rather than fearing the presence of these players, working with them gives them less incentive to go to the press to gain attention for their findings. Similarly, effective media relations can use news reporters as issues watchers. When someone in the media calls, his or her questions signal the presence of an opinion or issue that could grow in consequence. The company's side of the story often kills the news item, because once the reporter understands what a company is doing, the story dies. But this issue should be flagged in the issues-monitoring system so that it can be watched.

Issues identification and monitoring boil down to the simplistic observation that issues managers want to know who is saying what to whom about what and with what effect. The success of issues identification, monitoring, and analysis depends greatly on the assumptions that support them. The methods for gathering and assessing the information are relatively straightforward. Data services will eventually provide almost instantaneous access to a great deal of information. Data-base systems are expanding at a phenomenal rate. Surveys and polls are routine.

Another refinement in monitoring can be achieved by distinguishing among kinds of issues and understanding the requirements for dealing with each. Issues can be defined by their substance: fact, value, and policy. *Issues of fact* concern either the accuracy of details or the interpretation of details. Deciding what issues of fact are crucial begins with deciding what facts are important to the company's mission, image, and policy stance. Issues managers need to distinguish between vital and trivial information in order to know which factual inaccuracies to ignore and which to challenge. Assuming that the company is trying to establish a platform of *vital* fact with stakeholders, the next decision is whether those publics have the needed facts and, if not, how they can be communicated. On December 29, 1973, leaders at Mobil Corporation were shocked to read on the front page of the *New York Times* a story that confirmed rumors that oil tankers were holding in New York's lower harbor until the price of oil went up. The papers obtained information from the Coast Guard that disconfirmed this rumor, and a representative of the oil industry denied the rumor. Nevertheless, a story was written. These were facts detrimental to the image and operating environment of the company because they made it likely that critics would falsely blame oil companies for the shortage and look to the government for regulation (Schmertz, 1986, pp. 33–34).

*Issues of value* relate to any evaluations or abstract ideals that are used as background rationale for deciding what regulatory measures are reasonable. The 1960s and 1970s produced many changes in values, usually originating on college campuses, in think tanks, and in nonmainstream publications. During the 1960s, environmental advocates made esthetics a major value that led, for instance, to regulation of strip mining. Changes in value are very difficult to monitor because one does not always know how they will affect regulatory efforts. Value

**Issues Matrix.**

| Stakeholders | Issue Type[a] | Dominant Motivator[b] | Consequences |
|---|---|---|---|
| Employees (unions) | | | |
| Consumers | | | |
| Neighbors | | | |
| Investors | | | |
| Intraindustry | | | |
| Interindustry | | | |
| Regulators/legislators | | | |
| Activist groups | | | |

[a] Issue types: fact, value, policy.
[b] Dominant motivators: equality, security, esthetics, fairness.

changes are vital to monitoring corporate behavior in regard to the business plan. The key questions are whether the values can be changed and, if not, what contingency plans the company has should those values become part of the prevailing operating standards.

*Issues of policy* come about only after changes in the platform of fact and value. The logic that the special-interest agitator applies is this: Companies are doing this act or using this standard (*fact*) which violates these *values*; therefore, they should be regulated in the following manner (*policy*). An effective issues analysis system focuses on where in this equation an issue is at the moment and what strategy allows the greatest leverage. Whereas value issues are relevant to standards of corporate responsibility and the business plan, issues of policy are contestable in public and through lobbying.

The issues matrix shown here is designed to help reduce all public policy issues to manageable terms. Issues impact analysis entails three tasks. The first is to identify the key stakeholders in the contest. They are senders of messages, receivers of messages, or both. Trying to understand the flow of communication can be valuable. The second task is to determine what kind of value underpins each issue. Public policy issues boil down to a few dominant values that motivate people to be disturbed by the situation. For instance, Buchholz (1982) identifies several dominant public policy issues: antitust, equality of economic opportunity, equality of results, equality of employment opportunity, occupational safety and health, consumerism, and the physical environment, including pollution issues. From this list, we can extract four dominant values that are central to most public policy decisions: equality, security, esthetics, and fairness. As an example to show how stakeholders and dominant values interact, security includes safety in the workplace (employee issue), safety in the environment (neighbor), safety of product use (consumer), limited liability and likelihood of regulation that would affect investment (investor), buying other manufacturers' parts that, in turn, could make one's own final products unsafe (interindustry), and the extent to which a "bad apple" product contaminates the marketplace (intraindustry). The third task of this analysis is to estimate the consequences of each issue so that the stress points and leverage points can be assessed. The issues matrix offers an issues manager a means to consider the relationships among stakeholders, issues, and consequences. The analysis of these issues can be linked with the key dimensions mentioned earlier: likelihood, impact, timing, and potential for resolution.

Even though a department such as issues management or public relations/affairs may have primary responsibility for issues monitoring, some issues are best monitored by other departments. Each department should understand its role and responsibility in the issues-monitoring process. Moreover, each major division or department should create issues impact analyses. For instance, Finance has to be sensitive to issues of fairness and security in regard to how it generates revenue. The operating section of a company can monitor three broad types of issues: input, output, and throughput. Input involves the source and quality of materials. This could entail all four kinds of issues: The materials must be safe, obtained in a way that does not offend standards of esthetics, obtained fairly without damaging others' interests, and obtained with equality. Throughput—methods and procedures, along with standards used to process the materials—could be subjected to similar analysis, as could output, which introduces issues of quality, value, and availability. (Production of gasoline exemplifies each of these three output issues.) Similar analysis could be generated for the technical, engineering side of the company and for explorations, acquisitions, marketing, quality control, customer contact, and many other departments. Although individual departments have a responsibility to monitor and analyze issues, this information must be integrated into the company's total effort.

One device for bringing a wide range of employees directly into the monitoring and analysis process is the employee task force, or employee focus group, or quality circle. Such a group typically consists of employees charged with spotting means for improving company productivity and quality of work life. Some companies currently charge their focus groups with spotting issues that need to be watched. In Chapter Four, Coates and Jarratt express concern that a task force charged with issues monitoring may be ineffective because it is temporary; they prefer a permanent position or department for issues identification. In this case, companies can have their cake and eat it too: A permanent unit for issues identification and analysis can ask employee task forces to be alert for emerging issues. Revolving membership on task forces is then an advantage because constantly having new persons looking for issues makes the company less likely to develop myopia. A permanent office that receives task force recommendations provides the best of both worlds.

The task force system is vital for another reason. Companies can be alert to issues that come to their attention through public complaints and local protests. The task force system fosters the technical analysis needed to estimate the explosiveness of the issue should it become known to the public. Task forces are critical to this process because, without the protection and mandate of the group, technical experts often refrain from revealing trouble spots. Experts may be insensitive to the explosiveness of an issue because they have hard evidence of how safe something is, such as processes involved in nuclear generation, whereas reporters and the general public respond more emotionally. The task force has still another advantage:

Employees are more likely to identify trouble spots when they can do so through channels created for that purpose. If the company is sensitive enough, these will never even emerge. The problem will be eliminated in its earliest stages.

## Keeping Track of Issues

Conversations with successful issues managers suggest that issues management programs break down if they fail to assign responsibility for handling each issue. As long as issues management is viewed narrowly as a staff function where one or two persons are responsible for forecasting, monitoring, analyzing, prioritizing, and handling the communication effort, the program will struggle and likely fail.

Issues tracking and formulating a public policy plan should be closely integrated. The public policy plan is the guiding force behind the internal and external tactics used to manage issues. It states the company philosophy, broad goals, and specific tactics that support the strategic plan. Developing the public policy plan helps a company decide what changes to look for and what must be changed as the company strategically manages its business plan. Those who prepare the public policy plan should look for stress points and opportunities in altering operations and communicating with key publics. The public policy plan should contain at least the following kinds of information: (1) the company mission, including public policy goals, (2) a statement of corporate responsibility, expressed in objetives, (3) a summary of the issues most likely to affect company operations, (4) an estimate of bottom-line effects on the business plan, including suggested business opportunities, (5) tactics to be used to reposition the company in its public policy environment, (6) short- and long-term communication objectives and tactics, (7) key personnel and their responsibilities for implementing and controlling the plan, and (8) measures of success.

An inattentive company risks letting an issue sneak up or slide through the cracks. Both outcomes are minimized by a tactical system that specifies who is watching for each issue. It makes explicit to the persons involved in the issues management network how they are responsible for assisting in this process. This system assumes that most issues do not change dramatically or quickly. Rarely do several issues make major changes at the same time. Consequently, one person can manage several issues while doing regular staff and operations activities.

Not every employee is qualified to decide whether an issue is worth putting into the system. But each employee, especially executives and managers, should know what person or group to contact about an issue that seems to warrant monitoring. Surveys and other methods can help the issues management team determine whether the issue deserves serious attention.

Someone must be accountable for seeing (1) that each issue is constantly monitored, (2) that its impact is calculated and discussed internally and externally, (3) that internal and external liaisons are established to handle the issue, (4) that its relationship to operations is clearly understood and alternative modes of operations considered and weighed according to cost-benefit analyses and value implications, (5) that goals are set for managing the issue (in the context of the total plan), and (6) that the progress of issues management is measured. This plan assumes that appropriate management persons sign off on the execution of the plan and periodically review its progress. The accountable person must make periodic reports on the success of the plan—and confer with those associated with the issue if major changes occur. This plan places one person at the hub in the process to handle each issue in conjunction with liaison people, inside and outside.

One of the most demanding aspects of issues management is the creation of internal procedures for handling issues so that they receive appropriate and balanced attention rather than getting tied up in the corporate bureaucracy or getting lost. Issues may fail to receive appropriate attention when people do not know who is responsible for their management or when several persons are trying to manage the same issue at the same time without proper coordination. The issues impact assessment and control form presented here is designed to help management and cognizant personnel keep track of each issue. The simplicity of this form allows each issue to be included in a

Issues Impact Assessment and Control Form.

1. Issue
2. Cognizant person
3. Internal liaisons
4. External liaisons
5. Relationship between this issue and other issues
6. Persons/special-interest groups/companies responsible for promoting the issue
7. Stage of development
   Priority 1: Legal/administrative litigation
   Priority 2: Legislative watch
   Priority 3: Prelegislative
   Priority 4: Potential legislative
   Priority 5: Emerging issue
8. Implications of this issue for the company mission (with cost estimate)
9. Implications of this issue for the company code of operating standards (with cost estimate)
10. Potential impact of this issue on operating procedures (with cost estimate)
11. Alternative operating procedures (with cost estimates)
12. Stress points associated with this issue (responses that seem required)
13. Opportunity points associated with this issue (profit options made possible by the issue)
14. Communication strategies
    a. Targeted audiences
    b. Message content—the company's perspective on the essential facts in the case
15. PAC strategies
16. Trade association strategies
17. Lobbying strategies
    a. Company/industry stance on the issue
    b. Liaison with others supporting the company stance
18. Measurable goals for assessing the management of this issue

company's data base and electronic (E) mail system (with appropriate security), so that the persons involved can access the files at any time to determine the status of an issue or to add comments. This kind of document serves an important monitoring and reporting function that allows management and other personnel to know what is being done on each issue. The document gives liaison personnel the mechanism to provide timely input to the appropriate person.

Before an issue is entered into the impact assessment

form, it must be discovered and given preliminary analysis. This operation demonstrates how issues management is not linear — it is a complex of interactive, ongoing activities. How does an issue come to be logged into the issues management system? One person, even if assisted by a committee, must finally determine that an issue warrants surveillance. This decision comes about whether the issue was discovered by an employee, identified by an extensive monitoring process using public opinion polls, or raised through employee task forces.

Use of employee groups, whether specially assigned issues task forces or ongoing focus groups, has several advantages. It opens a dialogue on public policy and operating standards that allows all levels of the company to scrutinize the fit between public standards, corporate philosophy, and operations. It acquaints management with a segment of opinion often known only to lower-level personnel who are intimately involved in operations or have customer contact. Participation in or access to focus groups can help personnel at all levels become more dedicated to creating a partnership with key publics. The persons involved can quickly recognize their responsibilities for advancing the public policy plan. This technique can make the company more aware of how public policy can create opportunities that lead to rewards as well as minimize losses by early detection and prevention.

Once issues have been identified for monitoring and someone has been assigned to shepherd each one, the issues analysis process is well underway. A next vital step is creation of issues position papers that can be used to disseminate the company public policy position to key players. To support the public policy plan, some companies create and circulate a public policy issues analysis statement to set the tone for the issues management process. (Chapter Six explains how one company uses a computer data-base system to make its policy statement available.) The policy statement can outline each major issue, discuss its potential or actual impact on operations, state the company's position, and supply issues messages for use in the company's internal and external communication effort. This document can be divided by short- and long-term issues.

Some companies publish this statement as often as every quarter. The frequency of its publication depends on many factors, chiefly how much scrutiny the company is receiving from outside and how quickly any position becomes outdated.

The public policy issues analysis statement serves at least three critical functions. It makes key readers aware of priority issues and the company stance on each; it analyzes the consequences of the issues and describes the internal and external tactics being used; and it shows that company executives are serious about identifying public policy problems and are doing something constructive to solve them. Companies that have adopted this device report that nothing else they have done makes mid-level operations managers aware of public policy so quickly. This document can be used strategically to channel information and policy positions to a wide range of key employees who, in turn, inform and influence other employees. Eventually, this information and influence make their way outside the company to persons who come into contact with employees.

## Integrating Issues Management into Operating Procedures

*It is wisest to identify and correct a problem in company operations before the problem is discovered by regulators or an activist group.* This internal policing, or control, process is vital. How each company integrates issues management into its operations differs according to its mission and the extent to which it will suffer careful and hostile public and regulatory scrutiny. The chemical industry is a good example of one where several leading companies have integrated issues management systems into their operations. Overt efforts to eliminate problems before they mushroom can lower employee uncertainty about company operating standards. Part of the value of such efforts is to constantly remind those involved in issues management that as the number or sophistication of critics increases, so does the uncertainty surrounding the management of public policy. Any scheme for estimating the power and vulnerability of a company vis-à-vis its critics must consider their numbers and their sophistication for applying pressure.

**Issues Sensitivity Matrix.**

|  | | (low) | Public Scrutiny | | (high) |
|---|---|---|---|---|---|
|  | | 1 | 2 | 3 | 4 | 5 |

| | | 1 | 2 | 3 | 4 | 5 |
|---|---|---|---|---|---|---|
| (low) | 1 | 1,1 | | | | 1,5 |
| | 2 | | | | | |
| Internal Controls | 3 | | | 3,3 | | |
| | 4 | | | | | |
| (high) | 5 | 5,1 | | | | 5,5 |

The issues sensitivity matrix reproduced here illustrates the correspondence between high external scrutiny and the need for high internal controls. External scrutiny is the degree to which a company is carefully watched by activist groups, regulators, legislators, and critics in the media. Internal controls are the measures (including rewards and punishments meted out through employee appraisal) used to minimize friction between company operations and acceptable operating standards. Internal control may include such efforts as industrial hygiene, pollution control, quality control of product and service, environmental impact, and personnel services. The matrix helps a company estimate whether its controls are appropriate for the degree of scrutiny. To use this matrix for diagnosis, find the row that represents the estimated degree of internal control your company is applying to the aspect of operations relevant to a particular public policy issue. Then find the column that represents the estimated degree of public scrutiny over that aspect of operations. The box where that row and column meet shows the approximate adequacy of internal controls to degree of scrutiny. For the best fit, the row and column numbers for that box should be the same. Some companies and issues will need to be 5,5 because of high scrutiny; others may be 1,1.

A classic example of a high-internal-control company is

Dow Chemical, which early in 1970 established its Ecology Council to develop and implement a program designed to make operations managers responsible for averting environmental problems. Over the years this body evolved into a Public Policy and Issues Committee that encompasses nonenvironmental matters as well. The committee has spawned Issue Management Committees on specific topics, such as waste minimization.

One of the first outcomes of the original Ecology Council was creation in 1972 of the Product Stewardship Program, whose objective was to make operations managers responsible for assessing the health and safety implications of each stage of product development both for employees and for the public. In support of its commitment, the council issued pamphlets under the company president's signature. One such pamphlet, entitled "Product Stewardship Is Good Business," took a positive stance on corporate responsibility, saying, for instance, that product stewardship "enables us to anticipate, find, and solve potential problems before they become real human or environmental hazards." This is one of several statements Dow lists in various documents circulated internally to guide employee behavior. This list carries the consistent theme that product stewardship *is* good business. These documents remind employees of this theme.

Whether such concerted effort is needed in a particular company is an individual matter. Those companies that have been subjected to the most scrutiny have the greatest incentive to avoid errors of operating philosophy and tactic. The strategic management system depends on clearly stated standards, including those specifying the quality of manufacturing or fabrication. It may be necessary to require that vital details, such as welds, exceed national specifications. Some companies, such as Dow, believe that national code specifications are sometimes too low and have created even more stringent standards. This kind of procedure makes managers not only aware of the corporate operating philosophy and standards but also responsible for looking for latent and emergent issues that will only come to the attention of people in close contact with the technical aspects of operations. Employees who handle technical requirements are in the best position to know the latitudes of criticality that surround operating standards. Matters such as the necessary thickness of pipes or the quality of welds are best assessed far from boardrooms or public affairs offices. For this reason, issues management must be diffused throughout a company. Standards must be openly debated by employees who have the incentive to critique procedures without fear for their positions.

What constitutes a high-scrutiny company? Those whose operations or products relate to the health, esthetics, and security of the public and employees are prime candidates. The escape of chemicals at a Union Carbide plant is more likely to bring widespread fear and hostile outburst than is check kiting by an investment house. Neither activity is acceptable by public standards, but problems that relate to public health and safety will need the closest scrutiny.

The following chapters explain how a company can look externally by searching for public policy issues and reassessing planning premises. Coates and Jarratt discuss the difficulties of spotting emerging issues and knowing which ones can affect a company. Markley discusses a technique that can help a company know whether it has identified the personnel most capable of knowing which issues are vital and how they will impinge on operating philosophies and tactics. His analysis is designed to locate the internal opinion leaders who are crucial to collecting and assessing relevant information, the individuals whose support is crucial to development and implementation of the public policy plan. Kasser and Truax explain how issues analysts can develop company position "papers" that are made available to key players through a shared data base.

# 4

# Mapping the Issues of an Industry: An Exercise in Issues Identification

*Joseph F. Coates*
*Jennifer Jarratt*

Can the trends and emerging issues shaping an entire industry be identified and mapped? If so, would it be worthwhile in terms of improving issues management across the industry? Would such a mapping put the options open to a particular company in dealing with an issue into a different perspective?

A likely candidate for exploring the feasibility of such mapping is the electric utility industry. Because of its structure, it is affected by issues arising from many causes in many places across the country. The electric utility industry is a nationwide, regulated industry operating under several different forms of ownership: investor-owned, government-owned, and cooperative. Each company operates within a limited geographical region, although there are holding companies. Grids create physical networks within the industry. The same basic technologies operate across the country but in varying mixes, reflecting the local situation.

Some issues are sharply localized or even company — or site — specific; others repeat over a substantial number of organizations or locations; and still others are industrywide. Some issues are so widespread as to cut across many industries and organizations. Consequently, attempts to map the problems of an industry may prove challenging, and the lessons may be generalized to many other sectors.

Among the specific questions to be looked at as a result of such a mapping are:

- Whether the issues for a company are the same as or different from the issues for an industry.
- How widespread an issue may be.
- To what extent the concept "emerging issue" is useful or misleading for an industry or a company.
- Whether mapping the industry's problem has specific implications for a company.
- Whether mapping has specific implications for industrial associations.
- Whether people inside and outside an industry see the same issues or perceive the same issues in the same way.

The centerpiece for this chapter is Figure 1. This diagram notes seventy-seven topics in fourteen clusters, or issue areas. Arrows show the most direct interaction among clusters. The rest of this chapter deals with the preparation of that diagram and its implications.

### Sources

The raw material for the diagram comes from several sources. One author (JFC) interviewed ninety persons inside and outside the electric utility industry, including specialists in issues management for the Electric Power Research Institute (EPRI). The primary purpose was to develop a research agenda in issues management (Coates and Jarratt, 1986). Incidental to those interviews, the interviewees were asked to suggest specific emerging issues in the electric utility industry. The purpose of that request was to determine whether concentration on the issues of one industry would suggest additional research topics in the issues management process.

Figure 1. Trends and Issues Shaping the Electric Utility Industry.

**Personnel**
- Technical recruitment
- Worker right to know
- Pay equity
- Cutbacks
- Need for new management

**Public & Social Pressures**
- Lifeline service
- Public confidence
- Public participation
- Access to mail
- Single-issue politics
- Business adopting public-interest-group strategies
- Direct action (terrorism)
- "No risk" ethic

**Planning/Management**
- Conservative foot-dragging
- Forecasting
- New federalism
- Customer orientation
- Factionalism in industry
- New designs for user/customer facilities

**Economy/Financial Forces**
- State of the economy
- Regional development
- Cash glut
- Bankruptcies
- Ratemaking/paying
- Capital availability
- Tax

**Nuclear**
- Safety
- Cost
- Decommissioning
- Waste disposal
- New design strategy (French model)
- Revival
- NRC

**Structure of the Industry**
- Regulation/deregulation
- Diversification
- New business
- Competition
- Opportunities
- Holding company model
- Municipalization

**Environmental**
- Short-term
  – NIMBY
  – Toxics
- Long-term
  – CO2
  – Nuclear
  – Acid rain
  – Groundwater
  – Water
- Emerging
  – Solid waste
  – Indoor air
  – EMF
  – Past practices
  – – Liability compensation

**Demography**
- Family size
- Income
- Aging
- Immigration
- Internal migration

**Personnel** / **Interfuel Competition**
- Cost of fuels
- Exhaustion of fossil fuel

**New Technologies**
- Central power
- Upgrade
- Cogeneration
- Distributed technology
  – Fuel cells
  – Solar
  – Photovoltaics
- Microelectronics
- Conservation
- A jackpot technology?

**Demand**
- Load growth
- Load stability
- New facilities
- Aging infrastructures in older communities
- Demand management
- How power is used

**Supply**
- Foreign dependency
  – Canada
  – Mexico
- Brownouts
- Wheeling
- Capacity
- Embargo
- Cost of power
- Extending plant life

**Transmission**
- Capability
- Reliability
- Rights-of-way
- Equal access

**Changes in Business & Industry**
- Decline of smokestack industries
- Rise of information society
- Migration of business & industry

A similar inventory of emerging issues was taken in two workshops held in conjunction with the same project. Having extensively discussed the research needs and opportunities in the issues management process, we thought that a review of issues specific to the electric utility industry would evoke further suggestions about researchable questions on issues management.

In neither the telephone interviews nor the workshops did identifying a family of issues in a specific area draw forth many additional candidates for the research agenda on the issues management process. They did produce a large body of material on the issues of the electric utility industry. In one workshop, for example, 130 specific issues were identified, some of which, however, either were redundant or were variations on another issue.

A second source of issues consisted of workshops with middle and senior managers in specific electric utilities, with labor unions, and with other groups not associated with the project noted above. A third source of information was a group of environmentally related projects for the Edison Electric Institute. Another source was the continuing monitoring of issues and problems by each author. All in all, some 200 people have been involved in providing raw material for Figure 1.

## The Raw Material

Because of the wide variety of sources, the broad variation in knowledge among the respondents, and the knowledge or shared belief imputed to the interviewers by the interviewees or to other workshop participants, statements of issues came in a variety of forms. Sometimes merely a phrase, sometimes a full sentence, sometimes a mini-lecture was used to express an issue. Justifiably or not, there was a tendency for the strong feeling of shared awareness to permit telegraphic communication. For example, the word *deregulation* would carry the message. However, the respondents sometimes felt that it was necessary to expand on concepts such as deregulation, in order to indicate that it was not the typical kind, as now associated with the breakup of AT&T; some felt that it was likely to be implemented at the state level; that it would be tied to the search for business opportunities within a continually existing regulatory frame-work, or that it was linked to a number of general and specific opportunities for diversification within individual utilities; or that it was to be driven by competition, and where that competi-tion might come from; or that it would be promoted by certain kinds of technical or economic shifts such as the move in trans-mission to a common carrier status. Some respondents devel-oped their themes extensively. Consequently, the raw material is variable in its depth of detail. One of the obligations assumed by the authors is making heads and tails out of it all. Putting it all into some form or pattern was the purpose of the diagram.

### Findings

Some findings are in order related to this material:

• Few respondents made any obvious or clear distinction between a current issue and an emerging issue. The temporal elements seem to be overridden by such considerations as im-portance, scope, and the individual's particular knowledge. For example, the cluster of items associated with nuclear power are already well and widely recognized, but they were put forward as spontaneously and vigorously as were emerging issues associ-ated with cogeneration or changing corporate liability.

• The few respondents who did emphasize the emerging nature of their candidate topics often did so with a sense of discovery and great enthusiasm for having come upon some-thing new. But their enthusiasm was often tempered by the sense that the issue might turn out to be insignificant, a "flash in the pan," or narrowly localized.

• Almost everyone's individual list was short. One work-shop came up with 130 separate items yet, typically, respondents in interviews would give us 2–5 items each. In the interviews, we pressed gently rather than forcefully with the question "Are there any additional issues?" The usual response was "No, none that occur to me," or other phrases that reinforced or legiti-mized a short list.

- Those who identified issues tended to concentrate on a group of related issues. We found people who were particularly prolific in identifying environmental issues tended not to move over into personnel issues, supply topics, new technologies, or interfuel competition. Similarly, those who focused on the structural issues in the industry tended not to be particularly attentive to demography or personnel questions. Thus, we have found among the respondents a narrowness rather than a catholicity in awareness. Put differently, responses tended to be neither tightly grouped nor broad-sweeping in their scope but, rather, lumpy and clustered.

- Generally, the respondents did not cast the problem or issue into a network of related items but instead presented it more or less free-standing. Notable exceptions were the discussions of the structure of the industry. Using "restructuring," "regulation," "deregulation," "new opportunities," or "competitiveness" as starting points quickly carried respondents into talking about other items and often led to "municipalization," that is, the takeover of utilities by local governments, "cogeneration," "wheeling," and "alternative suppliers."

- The issues were rarely expressed from a stakeholder point of view or as conflicts. They were most frequently expressed as either a phrase or a question. Phrases may represent a legitimate shorthand, just as the teenager says, ". . . like, you know," or they may represent a respondent's bias toward seeing many of these issues as technically manageable problems, rather than situations calling for strategies directed at conflict resolution.

- The three most frequently mentioned issues were restructuring, nuclear affairs, and acid rain. None of these issues is, by any reasonable standard, emerging. They are widely discussed, elaborately studied, and at the center of attention of great numbers of people in the industry, and in government and environmental groups. They all, however, affect companies in the industry differently. The opportunities, pressures, and pace for restructuring, the commitment to nuclear power, and the relative production and attributability of consequences from acid rain vary widely across the companies of the industry.

• Issues internal to the industry and internal to individual corporations were, in the authors' view, surprisingly prominent. They tended to fall into three categories. One category dealt with problems of accommodating change within the industry, driven by either internal or external forces—for example, the problem of recruitment of a new generation of engineers and technical specialists. A second category represented internal issues coming from the changing structure and competitiveness of the industry, such as dealing with work-force cutbacks, planning, or new technologies. A third category was hostile to the industry's management and used such characteristic phrases as "conservative foot-dragging," "inadequacy of planning," and "complacency." This last category contained items difficult to frame as issues, which might more properly be characterized as continuing management situations or corporate cultural characteristics widely shared or thought to be widely shared in the industry. This third group consists of managerial questions which do not lend themselves straightforwardly to a stakeholder or issues management analysis. There do not seem to be any clear policy options for the industry or company, and there do not seem to be any discernible consequences associated with the allegations against the management. One can conclude, therefore, that either some people tend to sweep all kinds of concerns under the rubric of issues, or the concept of issues may be more embracing than some of the earlier writings suggested.

• Many of the issues were interpreted in almost contradictory ways. In many cases, the interpreters were aware of the contradiction. For example, diversification was seen by a number of respondents as both inevitable and so desirable that it should acquire the status of a corporate goal. Others saw it as a great threat to their own company and to the industry. The reasons were sometimes curious: One person claimed the industry lacked an entrepreneurial management, so the pressure for diversification is a threat of disruption in the industry. There was even uncertainty as to what the dominant drivers in diversification were. Some saw it within the framework of regulation; some saw it coming out of reduced regulation; some saw it as primarily driven by more conventional economic factors, particularly the search for continuing return on investment.

- A catch phrase is often helpful in expressing a complex situation and facilitating discussion. For example, the widespread public resistance to selection of specific sites for energy facilities, such as transmission lines and power plants, comes into sharp conflict with an even more widely held desire to have safe, sound, reliable low-cost energy and the implicit need for new facilities. The catch phrase for this type of issue is "NIMBY"—"Not in my backyard."

- There was often an emotional quality accompanying the expression of the issue which bore no relationship to the overall significance of the issue, the frequency with which it was mentioned, or the emotion or lack thereof that other observers attached to the same issue. This suggests that, inside an organization, one should be wary of enthusiasm, animus, or emotion as a measure of significance to anyone but the individual.

- There were no striking differences between insiders and outsiders in issues identified, that is, between those in the industry and those outside the industry, in terms of the kinds of issues which they saw as important. There were occasional imputations by those outside the industry of bad guys, malefactors, or fault within the industry. Insiders, when critical, tended to be critical in terms of managerial competence, perspicacity, entrepreneurship, but not on the axis of "good guy," "bad guy." Insiders were generally more prolific in citing issues. The insiders tended to have a more extended knowledge of particular subjects or, at least, spoke of them in greater detail. They also seemed to have a wider awareness of some of the more emergent issues. This, of course, is a good sign that suggests that they are attending to business.

- People in the related industrial associations seemed on the average to have the broadest sweep of knowledge. However, there seemed to be forbidden zones or blind spots in their awareness. In contrast to staff in specific companies, association folks seemed to have greater difficulty in being critical of the industry or its management and practices. Similarly, they tended to see issues in more technical terms, not in conflict terms.

- There is no clear, straightforward, or universally useful categorization of the issues. A study of Figure 1 will show that many of the issues could be put in different categories or a new category could be created. This implies that any such diagram should be used only as a starting point. An organization- or company-specific diagram should tie to both the corporate culture and the structure of that organization.

- The uncertainty about the best categorization of the issues also highlights the value of attending to issues in other businesses and industries. For example, one has to be attentive to other businesses to understand such questions as energy demand and supply, workers' right to know, and the economic health of the community.

- The complexity and number of issues suggest that issues identification and analysis responsibilities should not be left to the novice or to someone who knows only one industry.

- A particular cluster of issues may be usefully and even readily fanned out into a more complex body of issues, each of which has its own network of connections. The block titled "Environmental" in Figure 1 consists of three main subcategories. To illustrate that issues interlock, nest, and can be defined in terms of more specific issues, Figure 2 fans these subcategories out in a longer but still significant list of issues. On close examination even these issues readily may be expanded into more specific issues. Issue 17, groundwater contamination, in Figure 2, may be expanded into two or three dozen subsidiary issues.

- Review of all our raw material makes it clear that frequency of mention is no clear guide to the emergence, the newness, or the freshness of an issue. Restructuring the industry and the associated issues of regulation, deregulation, diversification, and new opportunities to some extent represent new and emerging considerations. But the second most frequently mentioned issue, nuclear affairs, is really a cluster of well-recognized, stable, long-time concerns. Perhaps some new or newly significant questions, such as decommissioning aging facilities or

**Figure 2. Environmental Issues Affecting the Electric Utility Industry.**

1. Environmental issues as a catchall category.
2. Nuclear power.
3. Decommissioning of nuclear power plants.
4. Low-level radioactive waste.
5. Nuclear-waste reprocessing.
6. Acid rain.
7. Indoor air pollution.
8. Carbon dioxide and trace gases in the atmosphere.
9. Atmospheric loading.
10. Solid-waste incineration.
11. Synergistic effects of air pollution.
12. Cross-media contamination.
13. Clean coal plants.
14. Visibility protection.
15. Alternative power supplies.
16. Environmental effects of new technologies.
17. Groundwater contamination.
18. Water.
19. Water quality.
20. Underground leaking from storage tanks.
21. Aquifer recharge site limits.
22. Hazardous wastes underground.
23. Toxic-waste disposal.
24. Hazardous materials.
25. Trace metals.
26. Hazardous substances—the list is expanding.
27. Old sites.
28. Solid-waste disposal (toxic and nontoxic).
29. Cooling line PCBs.
30. Wood preservation.
31. Disposal of treated wood.
32. Disposal of old street lights (PCB in ballast).
33. PCBs.
34. Superfund.
35. Underground lines.
36. EMF (electromagnetic fields), fear of health and genetic effects.
37. Transmission line siting.
38. Migratory Bird Act/siting transmission lines.
39. Plant life extension.
40. Coal gasification.
41. NIMBY (Not in my backyard).
42. Environmental liability of the utility.
43. Retroactive environmental liability.
44. Emergence of an environmental agenda which is being linked to international issues such as disarmament, world peace, and nuclear affairs and to an emerging religious perspective.

design strategies for a revived nuclear industry, do represent new aspects of a chronic issue. In contrast, the third most frequently cited issue, acid rain, seems by no stretch of the imagination to be a new issue. It seems to be on the fast track to congressional resolution in the next few years. The fourth most frequently mentioned area is the cluster of issues on the environment already noted in Figure 2.

### Taking the Issue Seriously: Implications for Management

A safe assumption is that no utility is subject to all of the issues implicit in Figure 1. However, every utility must be subject to a substantial portion of them. How, within the present corporate structure, can these issues be handled? We pursued this question in several workshops, asking participants in each case some variation on the following questions: "Identify the portion of Figure 1 which you believe applicable to your utility or to a typical utility. Next, define the elements or key structural components of your, or of a typical, utility: board, CEO, executive committee, operating units, finance, planning, personnel, government liaison, consumer affairs, and so on. With that map of the organization in mind, how would you usefully relate the issues to your organization in terms of the structure of the organization and flow of knowledge and authority? How can the structure you identified cope with the complex of issues you acknowledge from Figure 1?"

In general, the respondents shied away from radical conclusions—for example, that the structure of the corporation is so basically at odds with this complex of issues that it must be revised. Instead, the responses tended to shoehorn solutions into the present structure. Two of the most popular solutions were:

- Create a task force.
- Create a new office.

The difficulty with each of these solutions is that the task force is, by definition, temporally finite. Consequently, it may do well at issues analysis, in establishing the state of the problem, or even in defining some company options. But, as a short-lived entity, it probably lacks the continuity, clout, and capability to follow through.

The new unit suffers from a similar problem but in a different dimension, that of corporate scope. Any new organizational entity, by virtue of being a unit, has limited authority and responsibility, and yet the arrows on the diagram implicitly show that any significant issue overlaps multiple interests in any corporation. No unit, new or old, can be given plenipotentiary power. The unit is likely to be given some analytical and persuasive function, but we know from a great body of corporate experience that persuasion is a thin reed on which to lean. The short-term, the pressing, the immediate, have the almost irresistible power to distract attention from the longer-term. As Henry Kissinger put it, "The urgent drives out the important." There seem to be no ready solutions in the direction of what needs to be done, namely to wheel the entire organization around to being attentive to emerging issues and to cooperative collegial joint actions. In other words, the addressing of a complex of issues of this sort may cut so deeply into the corporate culture as to require radical, not incremental, accommodation.

## Conclusions

- It is practical to map the issues of an industry.
- There is no general best way to state an issue. There may, however, be a best way to state a specific issue from a company or an industry point of view.
- No one, nor any small group, knows all the issues.
- Emerging and emerged may be less significant characteristics of an issue than are the relative awareness of the issue and its present or potential importance for a specific affected group.
- Some issues, when compared with others, may call for collective analysis, policy, and action, rather than for individual corporate response or accommodation.
- Some issues may sweep so broadly as to cover areas of the

society well outside the individual corporation or even the
industry—for example, workers' right to know or terrorism.

- "One man's meat is another man's poison" is well borne out
  by the strikingly different attitudes toward some developments and the associated issues. The clearest examples of
  that maxim are attitudes toward cogeneration and wheeling.
- A pall of negativism, defensiveness, and hostility characterizes much of the agenda. Even in those cases where it is
  clear that the situation can be interpreted as an opportunity—for example, new technologies, energy conservation, and changing worker attitudes—many saw only the
  short-term, disruptive, dark side. Whether this same pattern
  applies to other industries is an important open question.
- The staff functions associated with various models of issues
  management—scanning, monitoring, issues analysis—are
  fully compatible with the pattern of complexity of the map
  (Electric Power Research Institute, 1985). The map reinforces the value of these staff functions. What is unclear, and
  compounded in its confusion by the complexity of the map,
  is the potential implication of the overall collective or integrated effects of these issues on corporate structure, function, organization, and culture. The overall implications of
  the map may far exceed implications of each issue taken as
  an individual topic. Therefore, the likely problem for those
  involved with issues management is when and how to go past
  merely treating each issue in terms of its emergence, its
  implications, and the associated action plan.

### What to Do

There can be very little doubt that the emergence of issues
follows a strikingly regular pattern, often covering a period of
decades. From the earliest glimmers of an emerging issue to its
final embodiment in law, public policy, and accommodating
standard practices, at least a dozen stages in the evolution of an
issue can be identified. The pattern, of course, is most clearly
seen in retrospect. The skill and art of the issues manager lie in

his or her ability to identify the unfolding issue and the stages it is passing through at the moment.

Any organization, in coping with emerging issues, is well advised to be positive and forthcoming about the issues, rather than negative, secretive, adamant, isolated, or given to denial. Consequently, at the early, middle, and late stages of an emerging issue, one can support cogent actions leading to institutionally and socially more positive outcomes. For example, drawing on a recently completed analysis (Heinz and Coates, 1986), the following actions are appropriate:

| *Early/Middle/Late Stage of Emerging Issues* | *Suggested Actions* |
|---|---|
| E, M | Probe how your business operations, manufacturing process, services, or other activities tie to potential concerns on the issue. |
| E, M | Explore whether there may be an indicator jurisdiction or precedent in state and local government or overseas. |
| E, M | Creatively explore how definitions might change in the legislative, bureaucratic, or court discussions. Definitions determine the scope of legislation. |
| E, M | Consider raising an issue yourself in the spirit of being first and positive. |
| E, M, L | Note whether there have been any commissioned studies by the executive branch or the Congress. |
| E, M, L | Know the members and the key staff of the relevant committees. |
| M | Identify the other affected parties and anticipate their concerns, positions, and responses. You are not the only affected party. |

| M, L | Monitor bills for how the issue is being framed, the remedies posed, and their relationship to prior legislation. Anticipate to what extent old legislation might be used as a model for the new situation. |
| M, L | Know the legislative calendar for reauthorization. |
| M, L | Keep an eye on media events. |

# 5

# Conducting
# a Situation Audit:
# A Case Study

## O. W. Markley

It is said that, in the early days of the American space effort, Wernher von Braun had a standing offer of a champagne party for any project team that discovered a potentially catastrophic error and surfaced it before it could cause mischief for others. Von Braun's insightful policy was based on what is sometimes called the "cybernetic view of error," where gaps between "is" and "ought" are seen as indispensable signals for improved management (as in a midcourse correction), rather than as evidence of wrongdoing, to be hidden if possible (as is done when acting in accordance with the "political view of error").

That the spirit of this early tradition has been so strongly kept alive over the years is one of the main reasons that manned space flight was feasible to develop with so little loss of life. The case study described in the chapter is written in support of this tradition.

### Context and Purpose of This Chapter

Early in 1984 the top management at a large public-sector organization responsible for development and operation of high-technology manned space-flight systems realized that a number of transitions lay ahead and that new approaches for planning and managing complex change might need to be developed if these challenges were to be met. These expected transitions included the following shifts:

- From near dominance of free-world manned space activities by a single institution to a business environment driven by many institutions and factors.
- From a dominant organizational mission emphasizing innovative *development* of manned space-flight systems to one more concerned with ongoing *operations*, involving both an expected increase in flight rates and the necessity of continual retrofitting of old systems to incorporate new technological advances, rather than "building anew."
- From the serving of a single dominant programmatic mission within the organization to major responsibility for two programmatic missions, but with insufficient budget lines added to prevent intense competition for highly qualified personnel and other scarce resources associated with "turf territoriality."

To ensure that sufficient organizational capacity existed or could be developed for timely and effective management of those transitions, it was decided that one or more surveys should be conducted to document perceptions held by key constituencies (civil servants, contractors, and customers) regarding:

- What the future was likely to hold—both for the organization in general and for their own sphere of responsibilities in particular.
- The nature of significant transitions ahead, especially those necessitated by the growing flight rate of one major activity and the development phase of the other.
- The ways planning and operations should shift so as to anticipate and better respond to such changes.
- The capacity of various constituent organizations and units for making and managing the changes that might be necessary and for operating successfully in a significantly changed environment.

The purpose of this chapter is twofold: (1) to describe how a situation audit of perceptions at the public-sector organization was conducted and how this method of approach might prove useful elsewhere; (2) to introduce several state-of-the-art theories/tools/practices that are particularly suitable for organizations facing the challenges of managing high-technology development or utilization in a turbulent, competitive business environment.

## Methodology

*Initial Data Collection.* As is sometimes done in this type of audit, the research began with a formally defined sampling framework, a detailed interview protocol, and a quantitative questionnaire survey instrument—in short, the type of approach that is considered good practice by university-trained survey researchers. In pilot testing, however, it quickly became apparent that this type of methodology was inappropriate.

Overall, only a few respondents reported that they considered themselves particularly knowledgeable about strategic planning. Most had never given much thought to the wide range of factors that might affect the parent agency, the organization, or their particular organizational unit during the coming decade. Moreover, few meaningful incentives were felt to exist that would justify thinking about concerns lying beyond the day-to-day ones. Given that there was already overmuch to handle, why worry about these concerns as well?

Detailed interviews using a preestablished sampling framework and focusing on specific transitions that might lie ahead and on the capacity of existing planning and management processes to deal with them were therefore not feasible. Instead a method of approach was devised in which respondents were selected by means of a "snowball" sampling process (Wygant and Markley, 1988) and asked the more general sort of questions typically posed in a "situation audit" (Steiner, 1979).

The *snowball survey* is an interview sampling method in which the interviewer starts with a small number of respondents, perhaps five, known to be particularly knowledgeable about the topics of concern, asking two general types of questions to each and to subsequent respondents who are selected by virtue of their being most frequently nominated by their peers:

1.   What are your considerations about X?
2.   Whom would you recommend as a particularly knowledgeable person about X that I might also talk to?

A significant advantage of the snowball survey is that it quickly and efficiently identifies the more knowledgeable opinion leaders in an organization and the views they hold. Both are crucial resources in addressing complex questions of organizational transition — an advantage to which I return in the discussion section below.

   The snowball survey also encourages people to speak directly to the specific factors that they see as most significant, and in their own words — as opposed to having to answer within the preestablished framework of the researcher. This, of course, is of enormous value to the issues management researcher, who wants to identify emerging issues and ideas whose "time has not come" but may be "just around the corner."

   The *situation audit* is a type of inquiry most frequently associated with the practice of strategic planning, where an attempt is made to identify those *emerging issues and concerns, strengths and weaknesses, opportunities and threats* that most significantly bear on an organization's ability to survive and fulfill its mission, especially in competitive or turbulent business environments. Sometimes called "SWOT analysis," the use of these categories serves to focus the inquiry on longer-range considerations than would receive attention if no focus were given to the interviews at all.

   In the revised method of approach, the snowball survey and the situation audit were combined by formulating the following four questions:

1.   What are your views regarding future transitions facing the organization and your own unit in it?

2. How adequate do you judge the capacity of these organizations to be for dealing with such transitions?

3. What are the main strengths, weaknesses, opportunities, and threats embodied by the organization and your unit as regards strategic planning and management?

4. Whom would you recommend as particularly able to speak to these issues in a knowledgeable way?

It is important to note that these questions proved more useful as initial probes to stimulate discussion (after which the interview followed the lead of each individual respondent) than as formal questions to be asked in a standardized fashion, as in a structured interview.

*Content Analysis of Interview Data.* To assist in interpretation and the drawing of inferences and recommendations, the interview data were content-analyzed, using a set of six categories often found useful in an organizational audit. Based on the "Six-Box Model" (Weisbord, 1976; Burke, 1982) and the "MIT-Metanoic Organizations Model" (Kiefer and Senge, 1984), these categories are as follows: (1) *vision* (What business are we in?), (2) *motivation and influences* (What sets us in motion?), (3) *structure* (How do we divide up the work?), (4) *relationships* (How do we manage conflict?), (5) *supporting mechanisms* (How do we align and coordinate our efforts?), and (6) *leadership* (How do we keep the above factors in balance?).

*Final Data Collection and Feedback.* At the conclusion of the foregoing tasks, a one-page quantitative survey was sent to all who were interviewed, both to lend credibility to the otherwise qualitative results and to provide something of a temporal benchmark of perceptions following the STS Mission 51-L tragedy in which the orbiter *Challenger* was destroyed, the lives of its crew members lost, and many new transitions not foreseen at the beginning of this research project set in motion.

As the last step of this research, a process similar to "survey feedback" (Burke, 1982; Block, 1981) was initiated, which is still underway. At the beginning of this phase, selected opinion leaders in the organization were invited to review with the author the findings noted in the next section before they were presented to the CEO in a briefing format. This was followed by other "discussion briefings" to various audiences within the organization.

## Findings

To recapitulate, the central purpose of this research was to assess and increase the capacity of the client organization for effectively handling unavoidable transitions, emerging issues, and change. To best serve this end, a first survey, of civil service personnel only, was conducted to derive three types of findings:

1.  Documentation of *perceptions* held by key managers and staff professionals of future transitions and planning issues — particularly those having make-or-break significance to fulfillment of the organization's mission.
2.  Identification of *state-of-the-art theories, tools, and practices* that could significantly increase the organization's capacity to respond to such challenges in a proactive, rather than a reactive, fashion.
3.  Drafting of *recommendations* — with particular attention to specifying action items that were in good alignment with the traditional norms and customs that predominate at this organization and thus would be feasible to implement successfully.

Because the first and third classes of findings are largely proprietary in nature and are still being responded to by the organization's management team, the remainder of this chapter will focus on the second class of findings: state-of-the-art theories, tools, and practices identified as having particularly great potential for increasing the organization's capacity for "issues management and strategic planning." Owing to length constraints, however, only three such items will be mentioned: (1) a situational intelligence model, (2) the cybernetics of first- versus second-order planned change, and (3) four key methodologies for strategic development. Each will be discussed in turn.

*A Situational Intelligence Model for Strategic Assessment.*
Many readers may be familiar with the concept of situational leadership—the realization that there is no one "best" management style for all situations but, rather, that managers should be able to use different styles of management, depending on which one best fits the situation at hand (Hersey, Blanchard, and Natemeyer, 1979; Hersey, 1985). The same principle applies to the types of information needed for effective management, especially during times of environmental turbulence and change.

Though something of an oversimplification, a good answer to the question "What are the minimum requirements for good management?" might be (1) the ability either to *control* all variables having make-or-break significance for one's mission or to *forecast* the behavior of those that cannot be controlled accurately enough to anticipate and control their effects and (2) the ability to discern situations where neither control nor forecasting can be done satisfactorily and to substitute *intelligence-based strategic methods* in their stead.

The framework shown in Figure 1 is based on this insight. Arraying the two dimensions of controllability and forecastability against each other makes it easier to see the "situational relevance" of four important tools for management intelligence. The first three are frequently taught in business schools:

1. *Management information systems*—Collection, storage, summary reporting, and selective retrieval of historical, pragmatic data for short-range forecasting, planning, management, and assessment of activities and accomplishments. Frequently updated, the data provide *indicators of the status quo*.

2. *Predictive forecasting*—Anticipation of trends, trend discontinuities, and other projected occurrences expected to influence current plans and activities in significant ways. Revised periodically or when necessary, forecasts yield *indicators of the expected or "most likely" future*.

3. *Long-range planning*—Coordination and alignment of long-range plans and operational programs with corporate bud-

**Figure 1. Situational Intelligence: Matching the Type of Management Information Strategy to the Characteristics of the Situation.**

|                                                               |                  | Ability to *control* the issue being considered | |
|---------------------------------------------------------------|------------------|:----:|:----:|
|                                                               |                  | *HIGH* | *LOW* |
| Planning time horizon, relative to degree of environmental    | *NEAR* (high)    | I    | II   |
| turbulence (that is, *forecasting accuracy*)                  | *FAR* (low)      | III  | IV   |

SITUATION I:   *MANAGEMENT INFORMATION SYSTEMS*
                Indicators of the status quo
SITUATION II:  *PREDICTIVE FORECASTING*
                Expectations of the "most likely" future
SITUATION III: *LONG-RANGE PLANNING*
                Longer-term projections of influences, activities, and accomplishments
SITUATION IV:  *STRATEGIC METHODS*
                Alternative forecasts, contingency plans, scenarios, and situational management strategies

gets at all levels. Updated infrequently and requiring high commitment if implementation is to be more than rhetorical, long-range plans produce *longer-term projections of influences, activities, and accomplishments.*

The fourth "methodology" is the focus of this book. Traditionally it was something that good managers and executives had to learn gradually in the school of hard knocks; it has emerged only within the past decade or so as a flexible set of concepts, methods, and tools for dealing with environmental turbulence and uncertainty.

4.  *Strategic navigation* (perhaps more accurately termed *"experimental methods for turbulent times"*) — Identification and assessment of critical planning issues; advance formulation of

alternative strategies for proactively responding to anticipated challenges that otherwise would eventually have to be
dealt with on a "crisis reaction" basis; and development of
personal and organizational competencies that respond to
the challenges of emergent conditions. Done on a regular
basis or when needed because of "emerging issues," it provides management with a workable approach for *strategic
intelligence and shared foresight.*

The essence of "strategic assessment" is quite closely related to a second state-of-the-art concept, this one based on
recent advances in cybernetic theory.

*First- Versus Second-Order Cybernetics.* A recent line of
development having particular promise for high-technology,
systems-oriented organizations is based on cybernetic theory.
Among other ingredients, it involves a distinction between what
have come to be called "first-order" and "second-order" change.

For our purposes, a helpful way to view the notion of
second-order change is in terms of epistemology—how we learn
and know things. Morgan (1982) describes it this way: "Single-
loop learning, the mode embodied in a thermostat, involves the
detection and correction of error in a fixed context. Double-
loop learning involves the detection and correction of error in a
context that itself can be questioned and changed.... With
single-loop learning an organization can learn to achieve given
goals and objectives efficiently, but it does not question the
nature and appropriateness of those goals and objectives.
Double-loop learning... involves a questioning of such
grounds; *it requires organization members to question and change
contexts, including values, policies, goals, objectives, and theories in use,
in an ongoing fashion"* (p. 527; emphasis added).

First-order (change) theories, tools, and practices tend to
be more suitable for what are defined in Figure 1 as Situations I,
II, and III, whereas environments having Situation IV characteristics tend to require second-order approaches. The following four references provide both a theoretical and a practical
overview of second-order change and how to manage it: Levy
(1986), Hoffman (1985), Brown (1979), and O'Conner (1978).

The first two are more theoretical, describing second-order thinking and how it came to be applied to the management of human systems problems; the second two are more practical, providing guidelines for applying methods that, historically, have been most frequently attempted in business corporations.

As most practitioners know, it is frequently not feasible to implement either first- or second-order planned-change methods successfully in real-world organizations unless special methods for managing change are used. The apparent "resistances" to the successful implementation of issues management and strategic planning practices can often be avoided by "human/organization development" (HOD)—participative activities that are custom-designed to create an atmosphere of understanding and support among managers and other key stakeholders whose cooperation is needed (Hultman, 1979; Block, 1981; Burke, 1982; Freeman, 1984). For this reason, HOD methods are included in the "state-of-the-art synthesis" described in the next section.

*Integrated Methodologies for Strategic Development.* Figure 2 lists four key methodologies that have gradually emerged as preferred ways for meeting the challenges of management in turbulent times. Readers may find it useful to study Figure 2 long enough to work out for themselves how these approaches fit together as a whole before reading on. Using the terminology introduced above, these four approaches can be thought of as methods for (1) *assessing* the degree to which first-order and/or second-order change approaches are needed in any particular situation and (2) *implementing* either or both strategies for planned change, as the case may require.

Using common single-word descriptors, the four methodologies of Figure 2 can be thought of as essentially involving *intelligence, forecasting, planning,* and *development.* Though something of an oversimplification, this characterization is useful because these four methodologies are individually suitable for meeting type I, II, and III situations, especially when used with *first-order* change methods. But taken together as an integrated set of methods for *second-order* planned change, they provide the

**Figure 2. Methodologies for Strategic Development.**

1. Issues, Intelligence, and Assessment
   (Development of strategic outlooks on key planning issues needed for
   anticipatory management)
   - Environmental scanning
   - Issues identification
   - Environmental monitoring
   - Issues management
   - Other methodologies—for example, lobbying, public relations
2. Strategic Forecasting and Scenario Development
   (Analysis and visualization of current trends, emerging events, and
   other forces for change and how they may influence planning issues
   having make-or-break significance for the organizational mission)
   - Predictive forecasting
   - Contingency forecasting
   - Alternative future scenarios
   - Other methodologies—for example, technology/environmental
     impact assessment
3. Strategic Planning and Policy Development
   (Development and/or updating of mission, objectives, strategic policies,
   tactical programs, and operational resources needed to realize the
   organization's mission—even in the face of unexpected changes in its
   environment)
   - Operational planning
   - Long-range planning
   - Contingency planning
   - Planning of planning
   - Other methodologies—for example, "back of the envelope" think-
     ing, "networking," and "muddling through"
4. Human and Organization Development
   (Fostering of a valid sense of vision regarding new priorities and
   facilitation of human and organizational realignment, creative renewal,
   planned change, and other outcomes necessary to achieve them)
   - Situation audit
   - Survey feedback and organization development
   - Training and human resource development
   - Other methodologies—for example, quality circles

types of anticipatory intelligence necessary to manage successfully in spite of a turbulent (type IV) business environment.

In corporate applications where it is a definite liability to
use concepts that are perceived as excessively theoretical or
"academic," it is preferable to use the simpler terminology,

perhaps not even mentioning notions such as "second-order change" unless carefully introduced in management training workshops as part of a larger effort.

For reasons of simplicity, each will be briefly introduced as a first-order method of approach.

*Intelligence.* For present purposes, *intelligence* may be thought of as an ordinary-language term for issues management. Because this general methodology is treated in such depth by other chapters in this book, nothing further need be said about it here, except to note that in many organizational settings (including the one described in this case study) the term *issues management* is not a popular one.

*Forecasting.* Two comments are in order regarding forecasting. First, about accuracy. As Ascher (1978) has shown, one of the most important determinants of forecasting accuracy is the validity of the assumptions the forecaster makes about the cause-and-effect relationships at work in the field under consideration. The validity of these assumptions is a more powerful determinant of accuracy than is the sophistication of the forecasting methodology used.

Ascher's finding is a powerful reason to invest in environmental scanning and monitoring activities, for "assumption lag" (which he defines as what happens when an expert's views become inaccurate owing to unnoticed changes in his or her fields of expertise) is often a principal source of error in forecasting.

Second, it seems to be a human tendency to underestimate the degree of turbulence and uncertainty present in any given situation. The practice of regularly using alternative future projections, where an attempt is made to somehow "bracket" the range of plausible variation by having a high estimate (the "upside"), a low estimate (the "downside"), and one involving structural change among the principal variables involved (the "wild card"), is often a good way to compensate. The short Conference Board report *Planning Under Uncertainty: Multiple Scenarios and Contingency Planning* (O'Conner, 1978), though almost ten years old, is still one of the best guidebooks to practical alternative futures work in business corporations.

*Planning.* Again, two observations. The first is reminiscent of Lindblom's controversial article "The Science of 'Muddling Through'" (1959). It is simply this: *For most people, "back of the envelope" methods work best—it's just that you've got to know what to write on the back of the envelope!* Here also is a powerful argument for the systematic collection and dissemination of "issues intelligence" throughout a corporation, so that different people can use it in whatever ways make most sense.

The second observation comes from having watched a number of "issues" exercises collapse of their own weight because there was no effective way to separate the wheat from the chaff. A frequently recommended way to reduce the number of issues is to evaluate each candidate issue on two dimensions—its probability of occurrence and its relative impact were it to occur. Though useful, this is not by itself sufficient, for it does not get to the essence of what issues management is all about—corporate survival and fulfillment of mission.

A workable way through this difficulty is to define critical "planning issues" as those topics that have make-or-break significance for survival and mission realization and to cluster the issues that result from an environmental audit into a workable number. Obviously this is an exercise in which top management must be involved if normal resistances to information that threatens the status quo are to be transcended.

What this process can look like is schematically outlined in Figure 3. This approach is much less complex and detailed than parallel conceptions advanced in most of the leading texts on strategic planning (see King and Cleland, 1978; Steiner, 1979; Abell and Hammond, 1979) but is quite graspable by practical managers, who typically have their own intuitive methods of analysis through which the clustering described above can be done. Alternatively, formal clustering methods can be used, as in the SRI study *Assessment of Future National and International Problem Areas* (Schwartz, Teige, and Harmon, 1977).

*Development.* Unfortunately, formal evaluations are rarely made of the degree to which the results of environmental assessment, forecasting, and planning are meaningfully used by the audiences for which they were originally conducted. When such evaluations are done, they usually show that only a small portion

Figure 3. A Simple but Comprehensive Model of Strategic Planning.

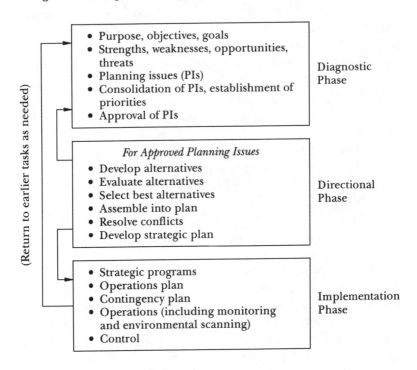

of the intended implementation ever takes place (O'Conner, 1978; Berg and others, 1978). The reasons for this unfortunate state of affairs are many. From a procedural standpoint, one of the main difficulties is the frequently erroneous "better mousetrap" assumption—the notion that if a good idea comes along, people will automatically adopt it.

Most people resist having to change the boundaries of their ideas and their organizations to fit emergent changes in the environments in which they and their organizations exist (Michael, 1973). It is not enough to simply collect, analyze, and communicate cognitive information about emerging environmental issues and their relevance for corporate planning and policy. Activities must be undertaken through which human and organizational capacities for change can be "developed" hand in hand with a collective understanding of the issues that make change necessary.

There are many human/organization development (HOD) principles that are important to consider regardless of what type of organization is involved (see, for example, Block, 1981; Burke, 1982). For present purposes, however, it is important that any *general* HOD methodology work equally well for first- and second-order planned-change strategies and that it also work equally well in high-technology, systems-oriented organizations and in more conventional, bureaucratic ones.

It is not yet known how many current training and development approaches can meet such demanding criteria. One approach that is reputed to do so involves the following elements:

- Establishing an updated and revitalized sense of purposefulness, vision, and mission for the organization.
- Alignment of all key leaders and organizational units in their pursuits.
- Development of personal ability and mastery, which inspire individuals and lead them to higher levels of achievement.
- "Resonant" understandings of organizational design and functioning, particularly in relation to how the organizational units together function as a system.
- Fostering of a balance between intuition and rationality; between technical and human relations outlooks and concerns; between formality and informality of the "official" planning and management processes; and so forth [adapted from Kiefer and Senge, 1984; Kiefer and Stroh, 1984].

## Discussion

*Situation Audit Methodology.* To recapitulate, this chapter described how a brief audit of strategic planning and issues management was conducted at a large, high-technology, public-sector organization. Because the audit focused to a large extent on "ideas whose time has not come," it is understandable that most managers at this organization had not thought enough about the topics of the study to make conventional survey methods feasible. This methodological finding is almost certainly generalizable to corporations that are just beginning to become involved with issues management and/or strategic planning.

Use of the combined snowball/SWOT survey methodology offers more than just a way to overcome this difficulty. A significant property of this innovative survey methodology is that it provides a quick and inexpensive way to identify key opinion leaders within a firm. These, of course, are precisely the people whom fledgling issues management and strategic planning activities need in order to overcome well-known resistances to implementation. Knowledgeable opinion leaders are particularly useful on formal advisory panels or participative task forces in support of corporate strategic planning and issues management activities, as well as in more informal "networking" activities.

*Recommended Approaches.* The audit also identified several state-of-the-art theories, tools, and practices having particular relevance for corporations trying to survive and grow in the intensely competitive and rapidly changing world of high-technology systems, processes, and products. Of these, the distinction between first- and second-order planned change is especially relevant for "leading edge" firms that frequently have to undergo transitions from development-oriented to operations-oriented planning and management activities in connection with new generations of technology.

Because implementing these approaches often requires a considerable investment and is not without risk, it is important to note the existence of research evidence that firms engaging in strategic methods such as these tend to be more profitable than those that do not (Thune and House, 1970; Ansoff and others, 1970; Karger and Malik, 1975). Figure 4 illustrates the "bottom line" gain in management effectiveness that such methods make possible.

If the potential inherent in all such methods is to be realized, however, it is vitally important to practice the time-honored principle of "Adapt, not adopt," as well as the "cybernetic view of error" introduced in the opening sentences of this chapter. In other words, strategic development methodologies such as those listed in Figure 2 must be "(re)invented here" if they

**Figure 4. Phases in the Evolution of Strategic Decision Making.**

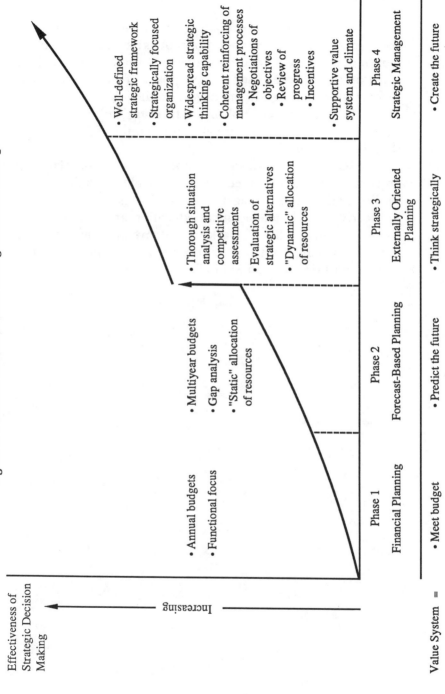

| | Phase 1 | Phase 2 | Phase 3 | Phase 4 |
|---|---|---|---|---|
| | Financial Planning | Forecast-Based Planning | Externally Oriented Planning | Strategic Management |
| Value System = | • Meet budget | • Predict the future | • Think strategically | • Create the future |

are to fit well with the prevailing management culture of a corporation and to enlist the support of its managers. Often this may mean the avoidance of academic-sounding terminology (such as this chapter used for purposes of introducing new theory) when talking with managers on the job.

How best to accomplish the training and development necessary to accomplish these ends is the topic of a new survey soon to be undertaken.

Finally, it is worthwhile to note that strategic planning and issues management methods are valuable, not only as a way to directly improve management effectiveness, but also as an indirect way to do management education and development. Given the universality of "back of the envelope" management methods in many, if not most, corporate settings, this may be the most important application of all.

# 6

# Integrating
# Issues Management
# and Corporate
# Communication

*Stephen J. Kasser*
*Greg Truax*

Because large companies are so much in the public eye, they are a likely target for public criticism. Some actions, such as plant closings, draw expected responses from the public and reaffirm the need to stress that the company is being the best corporate citizen it can but sometimes has to sacrifice a local operation to protect its operations (and jobs) elsewhere. Other issues, such as the safety of a product, can take a company by surprise. Issues like this one must be "listened for," and actions need to be taken before the issue gains widespread publicity. Unfortunately, issues like product safety often surface suddenly in the form of a lawsuit, with attendant media coverage.

With both kinds of issues—those where the need for a communication plan can be anticipated months in advance and those that surface unexpectedly—it helps if the corporate communications department has an action plan in place when the issue "hits." It is best if all the planning has been done. For

*Note:* The authors thank Thomas Ruddell, vice-president for corporate communications, for providing the motivation, environment, time, and resources that enabled them to design, install, and administer the Tampa Electric issues management system.

example, although a corporation manufacturing many products may believe all of them, in good faith, to be safe, its corporate communications department needs well-thought-out issues contingency plans just in case the safety of any product line is called into question.

On the proactive side of corporate communications, most corporate managers have a keen sense of responsibility to their customers. They want to know what their customers are thinking, what they want to know, and how best to communicate with them. They want to know what employees think about management decisions and what communications can best keep employee loyalty and morale high.

On a deeper level, a corporation can make changes in marketing strategy or corporate policies as the result of public or employee opinion. But to be sure of such decisions, the company's "listeners" should be well trained in what they do, and the mechanisms for listening should be reliable.

A systematic issues management function operated by trained professionals answers these needs.

In a utility environment, the "public opinion franchise" to operate is extremely important. Any substantive quarrel between the utility and its customers can end up in the state capital with a regulatory commission as referee. So it is doubly important to listen, to be ready to communicate, and to change or defend corporate policy when and where appropriate, as soon as the issue becomes clear and the correct decision becomes apparent.

It was to answer needs such as these that the authors were charged with the responsibility of designing and installing an issues management system for Tampa Electric Company, an investor-owned electric utility in west-central Florida. This chapter describes the system that worked for us. Although we are not certain of its uniqueness, we believe our emphasis is different from that of most "issues managers." We found this out during our preliminary research, which consisted of interviews with public relations professionals involved in "issues management," and an extended period of research during which we read most of the literature available on issues management. Most corporate communications practitioners involved in "issues management," we discovered, were not doing what we needed to do. It seemed that *issues management*, like *virtue*, was a term that had a variety of definitions. For some practitioners "issues management" meant an augmented governmental affairs function and the ability to anticipate legislative or regulatory events and to act early to prevent unwelcome legislation or regulation. For others it meant a long-term approach to corporate communications or public relations, anticipating the issues of the next decade and planning accordingly.

It became apparent at Tampa Electric that what we needed to develop was an issues management system to drive, or power, the entire corporate communications function. We could not, for example, just concentrate on lobbying, while putting out newsletters, videos, and brochures that were not in agreement with our issues effort. And although we recognized the need to look ahead to the currents of public opinion in the 1990s, what our utility needed was a process that would help us anticipate issues in the short term and be prepared to communicate when we needed to. We discovered that we needed to do what others did, and more.

More often than not, an "issue" for us arose as (1) a controversy either in or expected to be in the news media, (2) pending legislation or regulatory action, (3) a subject of recent customer inquiry, or (4) a subject brought to our attention by in-house experts, consultants, or industry experts—usually with a sense of urgency. The short-term nature of such issues is obvious.

## Codifying Usually Informal Processes

We were aware that our goal was something that corporate communications shops should already be doing, but we expected to codify what for most corporate communications departments seemed to be an ad hoc process. This process often included talking to the trusted contacts in the company, using the "beat" approach to issues (where one communications professional would cover a certain set of issues), and trying to be as fully prepared as possible.

Our effort was to differ from others' mostly in degree of organization. A greater degree of organization has two benefits. First, you are seldom surprised by a breaking issue, having made an effort to identify and research all possible issues. Chances are that your key people outside corporate communications have already been contacted for their expertise and that a company position or even a complete communication plan has been developed and entered into a computerized issues management data bank, where it can be referenced in a few seconds using a keyword search. Second, when an issue does break suddenly, the "skids have been greased." Staffers almost always have the facts at hand or know whom to contact in, say, Engineering or Accounting or Environmental Planning. And the contact person, having participated in the preparation to communicate on other issues, knows the issues management process and knows what is expected of him or her.

### The Day-to-Day Process

The day-to-day process followed at Tampa Electric approximates as closely as possible the process specified in the flow chart in Figure 1.

*Scanning and Forecasting.* First, as is emphasized in much of the literature on issues management, we devised a scanning function. Boxes 1 through 21 and I and II in the flow chart represent the scanning effort.

Staffers have daily contact with:

1. In-house subject experts. Depending on the importance of the issue and other factors, the contact may be a casual telephone conversation or a formal meeting. It may be initiated by Corporate Communications ("What's the latest on this issue?") or the expert ("We thought you people should know that the Public Service Commission is about to . . ."). Usually at Tampa Electric the contact person will be the manager- or director-level person who has the greatest technical knowledge of the issue. However, on issues of the greatest importance, the issues management staff might have to meet with the senior vice-

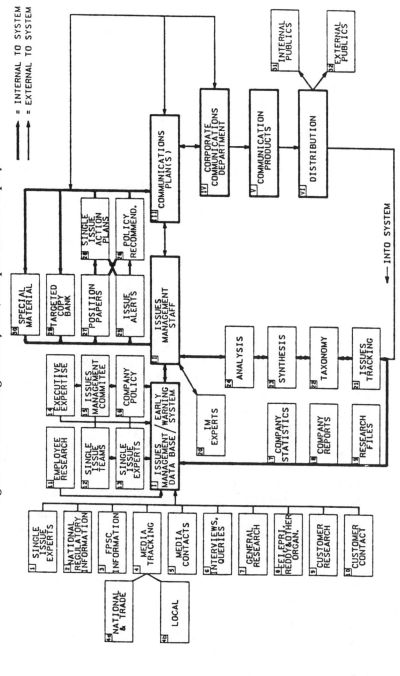

Figure 1. Issues Management System, Tampa Electric Company.

president over the department most concerned with the issue or even with the CEO.

2. A variety of local, regional, business, trade, and financial publications that are clipped daily or when published. Clips are filed by subject for quick future reference. Soon, keyword searches of the issues management data base will also reference the clips file.

3. An on-line wire service from the Edison Electric Institute (national trade association of electric utilities), which includes clip files for almost 200 news, trade, business, and financial publications.

4. Publications of the Florida Electric Power Coordinating Group, Florida's trade association of electric utilities.

5. Local, regional, trade, and business reporters, editors, and editorial boards, with whom we worked hard to establish solid relationships.

6. Customer Inquiry Department staffers who alert us whenever a customer brings up a potentially important issue.

7. Employees who are active in community groups and who have daily contact with customers through their jobs or through the Speakers Bureau. They have been asked to come to the issues management administrator with anything they think might be an issue.

8. Employees on company task forces dealing with particular issues. For example, the issues management administrator or another representative of Corporate Communications sits on most company committees or task forces considering major company decisions or policies, so that any issues arising can immediately be put into the issues management system and research begun.

9. The results of employee opinion surveys.

10. Company executives. In the future, Tampa Electric plans to have an executive-level issues management committee: a round-table discussion of major issues every three months.

11. Company policy documents. These are circulated to the vice-president for corporate communications, who routes them to the issues management administrator. This ensures that the company position papers in the data bank continue to

conform to company policy. Where there is a conflict, the issues management system is brought up to date; or Corporate Communications may make a recommendation that a particular company policy be changed.

12. Reports circulated by the Federal Energy Regulatory Commission, the Florida Public Service Commission, and other regulatory bodies, as well as reports generated in the U.S. Congress and the Florida legislature. These are circulated to the issues management staff by appropriate in-house experts who receive these reports.

*Relationships with Other Departments.* Instead of making issues management a companywide process immediately — as many had done, with high-level forums and task forces — we attempted to have a fully functional, systematic process embedded in the Corporate Communications Department before "going public." Therefore, although issues management "powers" the content of most company communications, we designed and sold the function as the research side of corporate communication.

The consultative function was there: The issues management system enabled corporate communication practitioners to give more informed advice to other departments. Eventually, companywide presentations on issues management and a formal, quarterly senior management round table on issues management are planned. But issues management already affects policy decisions in all departments, because it strengthens the consultative function of the Corporate Communications Department by providing the communication professionals with more information, better organized.

This approach contrasts with the way we discovered most companies initially approached issues management. The usual approach was to *begin* with director-level forums to "hash out" the issues companywide, then to deliver a document to Corporate Communications for that department to use as it saw fit. But this approach contained some flaws. First, there was no mechanism in place for the Corporate Communications Department to use the information, and it might even conflict with the existing orientation in Corporate Communications. Second, the senior-level people on the "issues management task force" would be operating in something of a vacuum without an ongoing issues management process already in place to support their efforts, give them more information, and immediately put their insights into practice.

The ongoing issues management process in Corporate Communications also makes the "early warning system" possible. Contacts throughout the company are coached to recognize significant developments in their areas and to bring them to the attention of the issues management administrator or another contact in Corporate Communications. Corporate Communications is admitted to the planning process in a number of departments; this way, representatives of Corporate Communications can detect issues surfacing and understand their significance for corporate communication. New information is continually "tested" against information in the data bank, to detect patterns. Finally, the excellent wire services provided by the Edison Electric Institute, their on-line bulletins and alerts, and newsletters and other publications of the National Association of Manufacturers and other such organizations give the issues management staff insight into developing issues in other parts of the country before they reach our service area. These sources of information are all part of the extensive scanning function in issues management—the early warning system.

*Processing the Issues.* Simultaneously with the scanning process detailed above, the issues are "processed" in the Corporate Communications Department. Issues-intensive materials are stored in the computerized data base. Also in the data base are calendars listing upcoming regulatory hearings and company statistical reports, updated monthly. All this information is accessible by keyword search. This process is represented by boxes 22 through 26 and I and II in Figure 1.

The data are analyzed with two purposes: to discover which issues may require communication or other action in the near future and act accordingly (our main emphasis) and to discover long-term patterns in time to make plans.

Top-priority issues are selected, in consultation with in-house experts and management in the Corporate Communications Department. Final decision concerning the treatment in the system of issues rests with the vice-president for corporate communications. Once an issue is judged significant enough, the issues management administrator or other designated staffer writes a position paper on the issue. This person interviews experts in the company and consults literature in the data base. If departments disagree on the company position, he or she offers counsel. Still unresolved aspects of the company position are taken up by the vice-president for corporate communications and other officers. The position paper is then used whenever the company communicates on the issue; for example, it can be used as content for employee communications or as notes for the media relations staff to use in answering inquiries from the media.

If the issue is important enough, the issues management administrator or other designated staffer generates a complete communication plan on the issue. This plan details both the messages to be communicated to various audiences and the media to be used, as well as the time frames, and which staffers are responsible for developing which materials. Again, the vice-president for corporate communications decides, with the advice of his staff, which issues are important enough for this treatment.

If the position paper results in insights about corporate policy that indicate changes are in order, the vice-president for corporate communications functions as a consultant to other officers and the CEO, bringing the new information to their attention and making policy recommendations.

If the issue does not warrant a position paper or if it is closely linked to an issue already in the system, the issues management staff will generate more-informal documents, such as "media responses" (notes to be used in answering inquiries), "issue alerts" (circulated within the department and to key personnel in other departments when an issue demands immediate communication), or "issue bulletins" (more-routine updates).

Whatever documents are prepared, they are first circulated inside the Corporate Communications Department for comment, back to the subject matter expert for sign-off, and then to Corporate Communications management for approval. If the issue involves more than one outside expert or department, the company position is arrived at by consensus, the issues management administrator or another Corporate Communications representative acting as consultant.

If differences of opinion cannot be resolved at the manager or director/expert level, a meeting of more-senior personnel in the pertinent areas is called.

When the company position is firm and sign-offs are complete, often a calendar is added. The calendar simply presents a schedule for the development of materials and the times for release of certain information. For example, a calendar might include the deadline by which all research should be finished, as well as the dates of a paid advertisement and a newsletter that will communicate on the issue. Such calendars facilitate coordinated action between Corporate Communications and other departments participating in the communication effort, such as Customer Services or Environmental Planning.

If it is an issue where the company prefers not to communicate until asked, the documents are put into the data base for quick reference when needed.

This system gives the company as much notice as possible about hot issues, where communication will soon be necessary. But even when issues arise without warning, the issues management system usually contains extensive related materials, making the research job easier. Since the issues management data bank is highly organized, it is easy to access related data quickly. Moreover, issues management at Tampa Electric has a well-structured set of procedures for crisis communications: We compare new issues with data already in the system, contact appropriate subject matter experts, write up media responses, get sign-offs, and so on. The relationships between ideas, and between people, have already been structured.

*Communicating.* At the appropriate time, the communication plan is implemented, using the media available to the company: a monthly newsletter to customers with a circulation of about 360,000 (research shows a readership of almost 90 percent), other bill stuffers on special topics, interviews with reporters, news releases, and paid mass media advertising where appropriate. This process is represented by boxes III through VI and 31 and 32 in Figure 1.

These communications often take place along with the company's ongoing public communications for conservation and marketing purposes, via the above-mentioned customer newsletter, bill stuffers, media interviews, and paid newspaper and television advertising. Sometimes, however, an issue warrants a *special* interview with the media, a letter to customers' homes, or even, rarely, a paid newspaper ad or television commercial devoted to a single issue.

The plan usually also identifies actions necessary from other departments, often divisions of Customer Services. Most often these other departments have received our recommendations before the plan is implemented, through the vice-president for corporate communications, so they too are ready when the time comes. An example is preparing telephone representatives to expect calls on a certain subject because of upcoming communication efforts. The "reps" are given sufficient background to prepare them for the expected questions from customers. Unexpected questions or persistent callers are routed to Corporate Communications.

The key to the entire effort is that virtually all communicating is done in the context of issues management. Stories in the customer newsletter, bill stuffers, even paid advertising—all are managed by people who participate in the system. Consequently, one of the most important functions of issues management is simply to coordinate the efforts of practitioners in preparing to communicate—both Corporate Communications professionals and people in other departments.

### The Long-Term Versus the Short-Term Process

Although many of the systems we reviewed and many of the materials we read put long-term forecasting first, we put it last. Our primary concern is to be as prepared as possible to handle breaking issues.

Long-term, our interest is in anticipating the less-than-obvious issues that may become important suddenly in the future. Often, by the time such an issue breaks, the months or years of preparing or communicating—or even changes in corporate policy—have partly or completely defused the issue. The longer in the future the probable maturing of the issue, the more issues management can become a consultative function, guiding the company's ongoing communications and advising policy makers. Examples of such issues in the utility industry are shared by most manufacturing industries: safety, product liability, environmental impact, diversification and other corporate financial issues, the effects of tax laws on a corporation, and so on. These major issues will be with us always. However, they generate immediate crises from time to time. The goal of the issues management function is to be prepared to handle the crises, while attempting to influence the long-term resolution of the issue.

That is why Tampa Electric communicates regularly with customers on many issues that have not yet generated crises. For example, the customer newsletter carries many stories justifying the price of electricity, even though public opinion on this issue generally intensifies only when rates are being changed for some reason. When such issues mature, our ongoing effort means that we have an educated public to deal with. "Maturing" can come in the form of a newspaper article, a lawsuit, an attempt by an environmental group to change the wording of a regulation, and so on. Since such events often occur without warning, the company's early preparation on the issue helps to generate a fast, competent reaction and, to some degree, an audience prepared to listen.

Many issues likely to mature soon appear regularly in an intradepartmental publication, a list of the twenty most important issues facing the company at a given time, with a supplementary list of all issues in the issues management system. The list of the top twenty issues contains brief summaries of the company positions on the issues and any background material that can be helpful to users of the list. This list functions as a quick guide to the entire issues management data bank. It can also be circulated, when appropriate, to individuals outside the department or used by department members when speaking to company groups.

## Conclusion

At Tampa Electric, we are doing what seems logical for any corporate communications department to do. We prepare to communicate in a systematic manner, and we anticipate the need to communicate as much as possible. Codifying this process into an "issues management system," we believe, enables us to communicate more effectively.

The "issues-driven communication process" has resulted in efficiencies in Corporate Communications (less reinventing and better use of materials already in the system), has helped to produce quicker and more complete preparation for media inquiries, and has helped to coordinate the vast array of messages communicated by the company.

For companies planning to set up an issues management process, we recommend that it be integrated as completely as possible into the normal corporate communications or public relations process.

# PART THREE

# Communication Campaigns for Influencing Key Audiences

## Introduction by Robert L. Heath

Issues management, once thought to be little more than governmental affairs and advocacy advertising, has matured to encompass a wide range of activities. Nevertheless, issues communication will continue to play a vital role in public policy battles by reaching opinion makers who are in a position to help the company solve its public policy problems. This section proposes that an effective communication campaign begins with a tactical plan based on estimates of which public policy/public opinion problems will yield to communication. Coupled with this decision, planners should consider how to make communication efforts cost-effective. The section discusses the design of the communication plan and offers criteria to measure its success.

Each of the chapters here discusses an aspect of the communication effort. Mary Ann Pires explains how to build coalitions with external constituencies. Herb Schmertz shows how to use op-ed ads as a form of issue advertising to affect opinion makers. Phil Cates draws on his experience as a state legislator and company lobbyist to explain the requirements of effective lobbying. And Herbert E. Alexander concludes that political action committees do not control politics; they increase the likelihood that their sponsors will have access to candidates and elected officials. Central to these articles is the theme that issues communication takes place in a political arena. There its job is not merely to achieve understanding and concurrence but to reach the persons who can exert the right influence at the right time.

### Issues Communication: A Long-Term Effort

A short barrage of self-serving issue ad messages will rarely win public opinion and stop legislation or regulation. Issues communication should be a long-term effort. *Communicate constantly and vigorously with key audiences to build lasting understanding and harmony.* Resolving to communicate with its various publics in good times as well as bad can keep a company from having to communicate only after it has been "caught." Starting to communicate late in the campaign puts the corporation at the mercy of its challengers; it finds itself responding to issues raised by outsiders, often adversarial ones. Substantial advantage goes to those voices that first define an issue and bring up the values and motives needed to create public clamor. Being on the defensive, having to refute a position others have laid out, strains a company's credibility and creates public skepticism about its veracity and its openness. Playing catch-up can lower a corporation's confidence in its communication experts. The executive who begins by asking communication to accomplish more than is reasonable may end by concluding that communication practitioners are useless because they fail to extinguish all the fires that occur.

Conversely, social concern and a commitment to perform in ways the public thinks ethical are worth announcing. This kind of message can foster corporate image and support marketing efforts by helping to differentiate the company and its products or services from its competitors. The public truly wants to know about company operations and learn that companies are working to satisfy public expectations (Ewing, 1982; Heath and Douglas, 1986). Reaching an audience to tell it good news about the company is often difficult because good news is not as attention-getting as bad news. But even if the attention of the general public is hard to capture in such matters, that of the media, legislators, and regulators is not. And all communication tactics must be viewed in light of where they fit in the total mix of activities. If the media, legislators, and regulators are aware of a company's long-term concerns and commitment, they are likely to investigate *before* jumping to conclusions when they hear bad-news claims about a company from activist groups. And if a company spokesperson has communicated continually with them, they are prone to call that person to see whether he or she has a reasonable explanation. In making this long-term commitment, a company communication plan requires several components.

*Planning.* A successful communication campaign begins by being part of effective strategic planning to consider which public policy issues will yield to communication efforts and which ones will not. Because of the hostility and rigidity of opinions surrounding some issues, some communication efforts will not succeed and therefore are not cost-effective. Taking a stand on some issues is not politically or tactically expedient. The planning process must consider when it is better to change company mission, philosophy, or operations than to wage a communication campaign. Public relations, public affairs, or any other corporate communication department cannot buffer an irresponsible company from its critics. Survival demands that companies recognize the reality that hostile stakeholders can discredit their statements and severely constrain their operations. Strategic planners should look at the short- and long-range public opinion, public policy picture to determine what must be said and what should be said, to whom, and with what potential effect. This stance is motivated by the conviction that communication must be judged, at least in part, by standards of cost effectiveness and good will.

*Goals.* The way the goals of the communication plan are framed and the tactics executed depends on how much external scrutiny the company receives and how effectively it has communicated in the past. In this regard, the communication plan should grow out of useful goals, some quite broad but most rather narrowly focused. (1) For instance, broadly framed, the plan might call for key publics to be involved in the creation and passage of legislation that maximizes public and corporate interests. More narrowly, the goal might be to inform a key audience of the perils of inadvisable legislation and motivate it to contact particular congressional representatives to oppose that legislation. (2) The plan can educate key stakeholders about corporate operating needs and philosophies. The objective is to have the audience believe that the company is acting correctly in doing business as it does. (3) It can blunt or defeat legislation or regulation by showing that it is ill advised. (4) It can dispute allegations about an industry or a company. (5) It can gain agreement with the company's view of contested norms and values of corporate behavior. (6) It can support favorable legislation and regulation. In each case, the goal becomes more narrowly focused when the planners decide what cognitive effects and behavioral responses they want to achieve with each targeted audience.

*Personnel.* A company needs trained communication specialists who have the skills and personality to wage a political struggle. Issues communication differs from other corporate communication efforts in that it always occurs in the context of politics. It is most credible when executives and operating personnel act as spokespersons. Executives, managers, and communication professionals must have communication skills and be part of a carefully coordinated communication plan that is well thought out, accurate, political, and candid. Effective issues communication assumes that employees are a targeted audience that needs to understand the company stance on key public policy issues. Employees, properly informed and incorporated into the issues effort, can be effective spokespersons for the company position.

*Budget.* Corporate communication requires a budget sufficient to accomplish its goals. The budget should allow use of the best available channels to reach targeted publics. New communication channels are becoming available—cable television, videoconferencing, and highly sophisticated, computer-

generated letters to be used in direct-mail campaigns to legislators. With vast data-base operations, grass-roots populations
can be segmented and supplied with different versions of letters
that need only be signed and sent to the legislators.

*Long-Term Commitment.* Corporate communication practitioners often complain that executives call on their services
only after an issue has advanced so far that the response options
are narrowed considerably. They hear executives grouse, "If PR
had been doing its job, these agitators would not be hounding us
with a bunch of unreasonable demands."

*Timeliness.* The success of a campaign is increased if its
messages are supplied at times when they can have the most
effect. In every communication campaign, the types of communication that should be used and the likelihood of their success
change as the issue progresses into the legislative and regulatory stages. As an issue becomes increasingly politicized, a
company can more accurately sense who the key audiences are
and what they need to know. In this way, the communication
effort can become easier. But at the same time, changing the
opinions of influential members of society becomes more difficult. Once an issue has become politicized, the scrutiny it receives and the amount of disbelief company statements encounter increase dramatically. When an issue has entered the
legislative stages, lobbying and grass-roots involvement become
viable options, but activist groups will also be working to have
their lobbyists and grass-roots followers fully involved. The
likely victor in this encounter is the one who can most satisfactorily reach the opinion makers. And who the opinion makers
are changes with every issue. In various combinations, they are
the media, activist groups, juries, courts, other companies in the
industry, companies in other industries, or key segments of the
general public.

*Honesty and Coherence.* All messages communicated externally must present an honest and coherent picture of the company. Drawing on the "product good will" to be achieved by
using high design specifications, Ford Motor Company proclaims, "Quality is job one." Such claims will be carefully scrutinized in the court of public opinion, where the single example

of a poorly manufactured car weighs much more heavily than routine production of cars of acceptable quality. Product and service ad claims have their counterparts in public policy debates. How much of a leader is Ford in the effort to achieve automobile safety, even if that means supporting additional legislation? How well does Ford do on automobile performance tests, such as the crash tests? Fast-food chains have come under scrutiny because, although they claim their products are nutritious, they have been criticized for including high levels of salt and animal fats in the products. The public demands that issues and product, image, or service advertising coincide. It is issues management's task to see that they do.

*Candor and Openness.* Candid and open communication has substantial marketing value. In contrast to the problems that resulted from the lack of customer responsiveness exhibited by A. H. Robins, Procter & Gamble opened itself to those concerned that the Rely tampon might have contributed to toxic shock syndrome (TSS). When the Food and Drug Administration presented data to P&G that suggested that Rely was producing a higher incidence of TSS than other tampons, P&G made two responses. The first was to carefully and objectively reassess the data and do its own research, realizing that it must eventually reveal the truth, not cloud it. P&G sought to determine the degree to which it was culpable. Second, partly because P&G believed that its product did not contribute to a statistically greater incidence of TSS, P&G went to the public to discuss the issue. P&G contacted those who complained about the product and sought permission to obtain medical data that could be used to better understand TSS in general and its relationship to Rely. Efforts to contact the public, a public information advertising campaign, and quick removal of the product from shelves won favorable public opinion for P&G. These examples demonstrate the balance among strategic planning, responsible operations, and communication tactics.

## Trends in Communication Styles

By the 1960s, two major kinds of corporate communication had become refined: (1) public relations designed to foster company image and product publicity and (2) product and service advertising. But the new public policy arena called for a tactic to use in response to the hostility voiced by various publics. The new tools included governmental affairs and issue advertising, or, as some called it, advocacy advertising. Issues communication was not new — its origins go back well before the turn of the century — but it was not a refined form of communication in the 1960s. Consequently, the initial reaction by many company communicators was to apply the philosophies and tactics of image and advertising campaigns, which are often little more than glib generalities. Some communicators went too far the other way and presented so much information in margin-to-margin text that only the most curious and diligent reader would have read it. Since then, the tactics have been further refined.

Slowly, a coherent corporate communication philosophy is forming. Three books help us understand what is going on. Sethi (1977) questioned how such campaigns should be conducted. One campaign he discussed, that by American Electric Power System, used xenophobic attacks on rich Middle East oil producers in hopes of causing public opinion to swerve toward the use of high-sulfur-content coal without proper flue gas desulfurization. The choice posed was a polluted environment or highway robbery by Middle East oil barons. Other charges by the campaign were so outlandish that they were easily discredited. The upshot of this analysis was a fairly resounding condemnation by Sethi. Because of this and other uninformative and misleading campaigns, Sethi called for ways to control issue advertising.

A bold stance in behalf of corporate interests is being advocated by Herb Schmertz (1986) of Mobil Oil. As demonstrated in his chapter here, his approach to issues communication combines political warfare with an effort to correct the platform of fact and intimidate irresponsible journalists. Mobil's stance was different from that of other oil companies during the embargo years. Mobil undertook an extensive informational campaign to show what it was doing to clean up the environment and to increase oil production. It avoided the simplistic terms other oil companies used to justify the gigantic profits that were being reported at the same time gasoline shortages were occurring. Schmertz and Mobil have worked to keep in mind the self-interest of the reader who always looks at corporate communication through the perceptual screen of "What's in this communication and the corporation's activities that will help or harm me?" Schmertz has helped communication practitioners and operations executives know what to do when "60 Minutes" or the *Wall Street Journal* calls.

The third contributor to the new communication style is Philip Lesly (1984), who tempers an exclusively communication orientation with the understanding that issues management is never totally divorced from a power battle with activist groups. The political aspect of issues management takes us beyond a mere communication battle; the contest can come to public policy votes that require attracting and using political resources. Rather than focusing on the media, as Schmertz does, Lesly looks more at activist groups. His book lists many practical communication strategies designed to counter these groups' activities. Lesly tries to prepare communication and operations executives to know what to do when they battle activist groups.

All three of these works have contributed to the understanding of issues communication. Three key conclusions are apparent.

• Issues communication differs from image public relations and product and service advertising because it deals with a different kind of message, one designed to help people understand complex policy issues in an atmosphere of controversy.

• Issues communication is not merely designed to correct the record by eliminating misunderstanding. It grows out of a conflict paradigm that acknowledges that the efforts involved may go beyond understanding into the realm of political victory.

• Issues communication requires the same kind of long-term commitment that is devoted to product and service advertising. Issues communication is not crisis communication, something trotted out when a disaster occurs. It is a response to the fact that if companies do not help the public understand what they are and how they function, they will have to suffer the consequences of what others say. As Lesly says, "Activists love vacuums" (p. 152). If companies do not help prevent information and power vacuums, then someone else will, and with ease.

The mistakes of issues communicators in the 1960s and 1970s led to several refinements. One is a willingness to adopt the high profile, typified by Mobil. Companies have begun to adjust to criticism by responding energetically when they are right and the critics are wrong. A second response is the low profile. Gone are the ill-designed blasts of the previous decades that too easily characterize the critics as irresponsible and un-American. Massive campaigns broadly scattered throughout newspapers and magazines have lessened. Communication efforts appear to be more narrowly targeted to key audiences. This gives companies more control over the impact and cost effectiveness of their issues communication. A third trend is an orientation toward the self-interest of the audience rather than the company. Gone, for the most part, are the obviously self-serving statements about the interests and needs of the sponsoring companies. Apparent in most issues communication is an awareness that a targeted public is most likely to respond favorably when appeals are couched in its self-interest.

## Forming the Communication Agenda

A vital part of issues management's contribution to strategic planning is the ability to forecast and plan for short- and long-range communication outcomes. In the same way companies commit to continually promoting their images, products, and services, they need to help their key publics understand what is required to operate a safe, environmentally responsible company that treats its customers and employees with fairness and equality. In the broadest sense, the communication agenda will grow from a company's commitment to comment on relevant facts, values, and policies.

*Establish a Platform of Fact.* Establishing a platform of fact has the short-term goal of correcting false statements opinion leaders make about the company and its operations; response to incorrect statements needs to be immediate. Comment on other statements of fact has the long-term goal of achieving a true and candid understanding of the company. This communication objective is met by the following strategies:

- Responding to misstatements by the media, activist groups, and other opinion leaders.
- Helping key groups understand the way the company does business and what it needs to operate effectively and profitably.
- Ensuring that claims about products and services are accurate, honest, and fair.
- Working with legislators, the media, and activists so that they understand the company and the industry.
- Communicating with special-interest groups as potential allies.
- Communicating continually with segments of the public that read newspapers and news-and-opinion magazines.
- Treating employees as vital audiences and as partners in issues management. Well-informed employees can be ambassadors of good will and information.
- Telling shareholders about operations, even when the news is bad. Shareholders are often fickle insofar as they may run from companies as soon as trouble arises. But for everyone selling stock, someone else is buying. Self-interested readers also make excellent communicators if they are well informed on policy issues.

*Establish a Platform of Value.* Values are one of the most problematic aspects of corporate communication. Public values used to evaluate company operations change, both in content and in priority. Consequently, the communication effort should include short- and long-range communication outcomes. In the 1960s, values did not change at less than three- to five-year intervals. But new values seemed to come up overnight, especially for companies that were not vigilant. The Reagan years have produced a slow change back toward the values of the 1950s, but this interval should not lull companies into believing that a new cycle is not beginning. The public opinions being formed today will be used to evaluate corporate practices three to five years from now. Every company and trade association should be considering what values are being formed and by whom.

Some changes will result because of predictable monetary evolution (such as the increase of the federal deficit) or demographics (the graying of America). Other changes come about because of incidents that cannot be totally predicted, such as the oil embargo or the crises at Three Mile Island and Chernobyl. A third major source of change is public debate that slowly shifts the beliefs, attitudes, and values of society. For instance, it took years for people to become convinced that various kinds of pollution posed health and esthetic problems.

If they learned nothing else from the 1960s, companies came to realize that their operations are subject to constant reinterpretation. That decade demonstrated that companies could no longer assume no one cared how business was being conducted. Americans left the 1950s believing that the business of America was business and entered the 1980s with the view that the business of America is achieving quality of life. This philosophy translated into a demand that companies be more people-oriented. The prevailing view of what constitutes a quality life is not always self-centered. Some groups genuinely believe their efforts will lead to a general increase in the quality of life for others; many other people and activist groups more narrowly seek only a quality life for themselves.

Corporate behavior is evaluated by four broad values: (1) esthetics (a world where each person can enjoy quality of life), (2) fairness (each person can trust the claims and commitments of others, especially companies; the public believes it should not have to read the fine print), (3) equality (each person can believe that his or her interests will be afforded the same importance and just treatment as everyone else's), and (4) security (each person can believe that his or her physical and mental well-being is not jeopardized by company activities). These values help a company to establish a long-term communication agenda by thoughtfully addressing how it strives to achieve harmony with each of its constituencies on these issues. Rather than telling the public how they must think on these

values, companies are advised to monitor these issues as eval-
uative criteria to know how they serve the public. Companies
must describe how they meet or are trying to meet each. They
can probably do little to change the content or priority of
society's values, but they can help vital publics know that they are
sensitive to these values and work to respond to them.

These values are typical of a smokestack society. What new
values will be added as our economy becomes more service- and
information-based has yet to be determined. But even today,
scholars are discussing such topics as invasion of privacy, employee dislocation, and information disparity. Whether and how
such issues will be influenced by public policy discussion are
uncertain at the moment, but companies are wise to look for the
trends and indicators that will influence the values environment
for their business.

*Establish a Platform of Policy.* Public policies are actions
being taken or considered, and companies' statements on their
consequences or advisability can explain the harm an ill-advised
policy will do to the audience. If a company's communication
efforts on platforms of fact and values succeed, those required
by policy debates will be lessened.

In the midst of public policy battles, a company should
never forget that its various publics are self-interested. Messages
must be designed to relate to the interests of the public. Sometimes this is extremely difficult to accomplish. But this task will
make companies aware of their publics' interests. If a company
cannot show that an action is in the public interest, communication is likely to fail. Even more important, the company may be
working on the false assumption that the public is there to
support it rather than positioning itself to satisfy various publics' interests. If a public cannot be brought to see that a policy is
not in its interest, then perhaps the company's analysis is false or
misdirected.

## Measuring the Effectiveness of Issues Management

Before discussing ways to assess the effectiveness of the
communication plan, it is helpful to examine the criteria by

which the total issues management effort is evaluated. How can the success of an issues management program be measured? The answer: Effective issues management brings harmony between a company and its many stakeholders. A company's issues management effort must be measured by its ability to do what the company wants done—as long as the outcomes are legal, responsible, and ethical. The criteria for measurement grow out of each company's or industry's game plan. The company must ask: Did we accomplish what we set out to do? And was what we accomplished vital to bringing harmony? Not that a company needs to have everyone in total agreement with it; indeed, the public policy game implies that sometimes only a majority of persons on a committee is sufficient for success. But the larger objective is to bring as much harmony as possible. The criteria for issues management grow out of its major functions: listening, analyzing, planning, controlling, and communicating.

*Listening.* Success at listening is gauged by the extent to which the issues management program accurately senses the emergence of issues and monitors their development. The key question: Do major issues and activist groups come about and grow to significance without the company's awareness?

*Analyzing.* A company's issues analysis program is effective if it produces understanding of the substance and implications of each issue as it develops. Joined to this analysis is the ability to understand the motivation behind the issue. How an issue develops depends on the accuracy and explosiveness of its substance and on the motivation people have to fight for it. Analysis is effective if issues managers can understand what stance is best to take on any issue to advance the company's interest in the context of establishing a partnership with the stakeholders relevant to the issue. Some issues can be safely ignored. Others require corporate adjustments in operation, philosophy, and mission. Some issues can be argued successfully to help others to accept the company's position. The key question: Did issues analysis locate the opportunities as well as the stress points created by the public policy contest?

*Planning.* Is planning adequate to maximize profits while minimizing friction among the key stakeholders?

*Controlling.* Is the company able to control its personnel and activities so that they comply with prevailing regulations, legislation, and standards of corporate responsibility? Issues management has developed to salve the pains companies suffered at the hands of their critics. If the relationship between a company and its publics produces no pain, then issues management is successful. *This is different from saying that in times of peace issues management is not needed.*

*Communicating.* How are we to assess the effectiveness of the communication plan? Issues communication is designed to help key audiences understand the company and realize that its operating needs are compatible with the public interest. Without measurable objectives expressed in the public policy and communication plans, a company cannot truly know whether it succeeds or fails. The pragmatic reality is that a campaign is only as good as an issues manager's ability to know where the leverage and stress points are.

*Audience penetration:* This criterion asks whether the company's issues messages are getting through to the targeted publics. Polls and similar methods can be used.

*Understanding:* Do key publics accurately understand the company, its mission, and its operating needs? Does the public believe some vital untruth about a company or industry? In this vein, the U.S. Committee for Energy Awareness ran print ads soon after the Chernobyl incident to inform key publics that the design of nuclear reactors in the United States is different from and superior to that of Soviet reactors. Polling, scanning, and use of external focus groups can identify negative attitudes toward a company or industry, based on inaccurate information, among key publics. Theoretically, correct information will change attitudes. A company can ask whether key publics understand the company and are satisfied by the kind and amount of information available.

*Willingness to support a company or industry position by acting in favor of it:* How willing is a stakeholder to act *with* or *against* the corporation or industry in support of grass-roots activist agitation, legislation, or regulation? We all know that opinions are different from actions. People may have opinions but be unwilling to act on them. In a grass-roots situation, the company must assess the likelihood that people will act on convictions against or for the company's interest. Companies often find that activist groups can be allies who can be mobilized in behalf of a company or industry position.

A company's campaign is successful if it has the grass-roots power resources to wage an effective battle with legislators and activist groups. As will be discussed by Fritz Elmendorf in Part Four, the public, including several activist groups, was willing to support the bankers' opposition to the 10 percent withholding provision for savings interest and stock dividends.

*Image of company, industry, product, or service:* This criterion asks: Is the image such that key publics easily believe the worst about the company, industry, product, or service? It is hard to tarnish some companies' reputations, whereas others are easily damaged. Reputation is a major component of image and is vital to issues management.

*Agreement and support:* Questions of value and policy may alienate the public from a company: The public may understand the company but not approve of its behavior. The measurement criterion is this: Do the values of key publics correspond to the company operating philosophy? Each key public has a set of criteria (a mixture of values and policy positions) that it uses to measure the quality of a company's performance. If these match the company's, harmony exists.

*Conflict with media or activist groups:* The criterion is this: Are the media and activists creating unfavorable opinions among key publics about the company's activities and philosophies? The media and activists need to keep issues alive to be effective and can do this by posturing themselves as acting in the public interest. The media can appear to be doing a public service (even if their real purpose is to sell media time and space). If the media have no stories and if activist groups cannot point to problems, the company's operations and its communication campaign are successful. Success is measured by the degree of harmony between the company and the media or activist groups.

An allied measure is the extent to which the parties share

values and views on policy issues. Values and policies are contestable, but a company must always be ready to admit that it is in error and be willing to compromise. However, the company must not acquiesce easily. Mobil Corporation mitigated some media criticism by pointing out where reporters were in error. It confronted the media as being hypocritical and unfair. In response to both tactics, the media became more sensitive to the need for fair and accurate reporting (Schmertz, 1986). Similar outcomes can be expected from the company's relationship to activist groups.

Another measure is the degree to which key publics support the stance taken by the media and activist groups. If the media and activist groups lose their credibility, they lose their power. The company can measure the extent to which it compares favorably with the media and activist groups as a credible source of information.

*Conflict with legislators/regulators:* This criterion brings us to power politics. Here the measurement question is: How likely is a legislative or regulatory body to pass guidelines that the company opposes? At times legislators or regulators take a harder line toward a company than is supported by public opinion. An example is the outdoor advertising industry. Generally, the public supports the presence of reasonably attractive billboards, but nevertheless legislators have passed ordinances to ban such signs. The communication campaign is successful when legislators and regulators cannot accurately claim to be acting as an expression of public sentiment.

These criteria are offered to help decide whether issues communication is successful. The key to a successful campaign is determining what must be said to what audience with what effect. That is the more difficult part. The easy part is finding out whether the campaign is having its desired effect.

Issues communication efforts vary in the kind of messages and strategies used. No easy prescriptions can be made. But the four chapters that follow offer an array of practical suggestions. These chapters represent the range of activities typical of issues communication: corporate communication, advocacy advertising, and political activities, especially lobbying and electoral participation through political action committees (PACs).

# 7

# Building Coalitions with External Constituencies

## Mary Ann Pires

In the beginning, there were friends — and enemies. Corporate America warily eyed the plethora of activist groups emerging in the 1960s and 1970s, and the activists glared back.

Little love was lost between the two. Stereotypes were the order of the day. To many corporate executives, the activists were wild-eyed radicals, bent on destroying the private enterprise system. To the activists, the corporate types were greedy, arrogant operators who preferred to function behind closed doors.

Interestingly enough, the genesis of the business and interest-group factions is identical: the unique American political system. Among its hallmarks are the rejection of a powerful central state and the concept of individuals and voluntary organizations seeking to affect the political process. Yet, likeness is in the eye of the beholder. When I began working in the public policy area in the late 1970s, few corporations perceived that they had much in common with public interest groups, and vice versa. Suspicion abounded.

What follows is one person's account of the evolution of the external (constituency) relations function from, if not "day one," at least "the early days" — for it must be acknowledged at the outset that public interest activism by no means *began* in the 1960s, nor did the responses to it. Both have been hallmarks of our democracy since its earliest days.

What did begin in the 1970s, largely in response to the

185

public-interest-group activism of the previous decade, was serious corporate attention to this phenomenon and a systematic approach to it. I was fortunate to be a part of that development, in my position as the first constituency relations manager for Texaco, Inc.

Like many other giant corporations, particularly those in the petroleum industry, Texaco had come head-to-head with the growing power of consumer activists in the 1960s and 1970s. It was an enlightening experience. One has only to look at the activists' list of notable achievements during this period to understand the alarm of some in the business community. The various public interest groups were able to increase the role of government regulation in such areas as the environment, occupational health, and product safety standards. In short, the activists were riding high. Add to this the public's disenchantment due to the gasoline shortages of 1973 and 1979, and the petroleum industry, in particular, faced a real challenge. How to deal with the increasing public hostility? How to maintain leverage in the public policy arena, in the face of a widening credibility gap?

Texaco, to its credit, sought answers to these questions in the late 1970s. It employed an audit of national consumer leaders, conducted under the auspices of a Washington, D.C., consulting firm. The findings amounted to a "good news/bad news" story. The bad news was the confirmation of public hostility toward the industry and its enormous credibility problem. The good news was evidence of a genuine opportunity for companies to help shape the sociopolitical environment in which they operated. The opportunity lay in opening lines of communication with nontraditional constituency groups: in essence, reaching out to one's adversaries. Beyond that, it lay in developing cooperative, energy-related programs with them that might cast new light on certain issues and alter stereotypes on both sides. Ultimately, it might even result in the activists' supporting business on selected issues, and vice versa.

With this as the goal, Texaco set up a formal constituency relations function in 1980. As its manager, I was charged with developing a program.

Researching the literature extant on activist group/corporate dialogue at that time was a simple task. There was little. Discussions with the Stop & Shop Companies in Boston to explore their work with consumer panels revealed it to be interesting and productive but totally product-oriented rather than issue-oriented. In fact, a number of companies were using product-related consumer dialogues and panels, as evidenced by the growth of such organizations as the Conference of Consumer Organizations (COCO) and the Society of Consumer Affairs Professionals (SOCAP). However, their agendas, too, were largely devoid of topics having to do with interaction between businesses and interest groups on *issues*.

Within the petroleum industry, Mobil, Shell, Chevron, ARCO, and the American Petroleum Institute itself had begun to reach out to major national constituency groups, and their experience proved helpful. Yet, given the dominant role of corporate culture in shaping such a program, it remained for Texaco to construct its own program largely from the ground up. This we did, drawing heavily on conversations with consumer leaders, what published articles did exist, and the consulting firm's advice. What we "constructed" initially was actually a philosophical framework within which such a program would operate:

- Strive for long-term relationships with public interest groups, not expedient encounters.
- Start by listening to what the groups have to say, to their needs, issue concerns, and so forth. Don't propagandize. Listening provides the clues that can lead to future cooperation.
- Don't overpromise. Since the function was new within the company, caution was needed, primarily to avoid creating false expectations on either side.
- Be prepared to give as well as get. To operate any other way borders on manipulation. Reciprocity is a legitimate expectation of all parties to such activities.
- Treat people decently, respecting confidences.

If all this sounds as though it had been lifted from a Scout handbook, the fact is, it works. Yet, the nature of many corporations is such that anything simple, anything predicated on common sense, tends to lack appeal. Thus, interestingly enough, for the handful of public affairs specialists doing corporate outreach in the early 1980s, the challenge was often not so much mastering how to work with adversaries as maintaining the support of their own managements to enable them to do what instinct and common sense dictated. For many of these "pioneers," building an *internal* constituency for the function demanded the lion's share of their time and energy.

We gave considerable initial thought in the Texaco program to objectives. What was it we really wanted to accomplish? Our overriding objective was to be able to influence public policy on issues affecting the company. (Delineating the objectives of a program like this is critical. Ideally, all the internal parties at interest need to participate in formulating those objectives, and everyone has to back them. This is important for two reasons: (1) so others understand what you are about when you explain it to them, *without* hidden agendas, and (2) so you can measure the effectiveness of the program. Many a good public affairs program has been red-lined out of existence because it could not show measurable results.) Secondary objectives of the Texaco program were to open lines of two-way communication with influential public interest groups; to share energy information with the groups; to provide a focus for interest-group/issue information within the company; and to develop cooperative, energy-related programs with the groups, wherever possible. All these objectives were met within three years.

As one surveys the landscape of activist groups in this country, with hundreds of them active, the question is often where to start. This is not the challenge today that it was in 1980, when reference books were scarce and many groups had a lower profile. But it is still an imposing task. Our approach was to use informal research—a combination of the sources mentioned earlier—to identify the principal organizations speaking for broad segments of the population: the elderly, those with disabilities, minorities, consumers, women, environmentalists, and so on. Admittedly, this was a crude segmentation, neither all-encompassing nor mutually exclusive. But it served its purpose, which was to help us select for personal contact a few groups from among hundreds.

To further refine the universe of what was at this stage fifty to sixty groups, we examined such factors about each as its membership, its issue interests (was energy one?), its internal communication vehicles, and whether it had dealt with corporations in the past. Through this process, certain groups emerged as likely prospects for dialogue. An example would be the American Association of Retired Persons (AARP). With 20 million members, an interest in energy as it affects the elderly, both a popular magazine and a newsletter, and a willingness to work with corporations, it was a paramount prospect.

Having identified about a dozen "top tier" target groups and another dozen second-tier ones, we picked up the phone. We spent a year making contact with the groups, candidly explaining our purpose in wanting to meet with them and asking whether they would give us the opportunity to get to know them and their issue interests. We assured them they would have an equal opportunity to get to know us.

If there was any hesitation on their part—which would have been understandable, under the circumstances—it did not show. No one said no. The dialogue began, one on one. Generally, I met with the staff person responsible for issues in the public interest group. We then went back and shared impressions, information, plans, and so on with our respective organizations. Soon the stereotypes—"big oil," "radicals"—began to fall away. Over the course of many meetings and conversations, information about both parties' needs, issue priorities, and the like was exchanged. We found that we did not disagree about everything. We actually found we had some objectives in common.

As these dialogues were going on, I worked to build a structure within the company of key individuals and departments with whom this new-found information could be shared: the strategic planning department; the government relations staff—both the D.C. office and our network of state public affairs staffers; often, the human resources department; and, of course, the public relations department, through which pertinent information was shared with senior management.

This task became easier as the benefits of interaction with the interest groups grew increasingly obvious. One of the foremost benefits accrued to our issues management program: Our conversations and cooperative activities with the public interest groups over several years provided the best early warning system for emerging issues, bar none. Given the usual "maturation" cycle for an issue—eight to ten years—we found that the opportunity to be present when issues are "seeded" in the discussions of these activists, possibly participating in these formative discussions and certainly getting a much longer lead time in which to address them, is invaluable. This aspect of working with external constituencies positions it squarely in the issues management arena. This "intelligence gathering" is part and parcel of the first stage of issues management—namely, issues identification—and, as such, has definite bottom-line impact.

Besides discussing things, we and the interest groups *did* things together. A number of activities took place with such organizations as the AARP, the Consumer Federation of America, the NAACP, the American Coalition of Citizens with Disabilities, the American Association of University Women, the National Council of La Raza, and the League of Women Voters. All were related in some way to energy issues—but from the standpoint of the *clients'* (interest groups') needs as well as our own. We took our cues from them. The activities included, for example, media training for leaders of several groups, issue briefings, energy workshops, weatherization clinics, assistance with mailing lists—for the most part, in-kind support.

All this served to build relationships. Credibility and trust grew with each honest dealing. By 1983, just three years after the function had been established, we felt comfortable in broaching certain industry issues with selected groups, by way of enlisting their active involvement. Selecting both the issues and the groups very carefully, to increase the likelihood of a match of issue to group priorities, we were successful in putting together our own coalitions around such big-ticket issues as natural gas deregulation, credit-card surcharges, and lead phase-down.

No coercion was involved. The coalitions resulted from a mutuality of interest in given issues. There is no other sound basis for coalition building.

Coalition building is a subject in its own right and one that is assuming increasing importance with the proliferation of single-issue groups. This latter phenomenon, incidentally, is singled out by the League of Women Voters' respected former legislative director (now membership and development director) Isabelle Weber as the most significant public affairs change of the past decade. "In my twelve years with the League," she notes, "I've been struck by the *explosion* of single-issue groups." There has been a concurrent "boomlet" in coalitions, as author and columnist Kevin Phillips recently pointed out in his newsletter, *Business and Public Affairs Fortnightly.* The 1986 edition of the *American Society of Association Executives Directory*, he notes, "profiles 120 different coalitions in 70 subject matter areas."

The fact that coalitions are enjoying such a bull market reflects a maturation in the art/science of business/interest-group relationships. During the past several years, business/consumer relations have undergone a dramatic shift from confrontation to cooperation. In fact, a recent nationwide survey of consumer leaders, conducted by the Society of Consumer Affairs Professionals, found 71 percent of them now supporting working relationships with business. It appears that we have entered a new era, one in which business, consumer, and government representatives are disposed to work together for mutually beneficial goals.

Considering the tentative nature of such alliances even six or seven years ago, the speed of this evolution is remarkable. It has several causes. For one, we have seen the emergence of a new breed of savvy, sophisticated consumer leader—an educated professional, knowledgeable about how business works, diplomatic at shaping a public image. Such leaders as Stephen Brobeck, executive director of the Consumer Federation of America, and Raul Yzaguirre, president of the National Council of La Raza, come to mind. In 1986, Yzaguirre said to me, "All of us have become more sophisticated—business, in realizing that it often has a commonality of interests with the advocacy groups, and the groups, in realizing that there are natural allies in the business community." He went on to say, "Interest groups now see business as more variegated, as opposed to the sterotyping of before." Ellen Haas, founder of the four-year-old Public Voice for Food and Health Policy and an activist for many years, puts it another way: "No, the movement hasn't died and it hasn't gone underground. It has lowered its voice, matured, become more diplomatic, and sought victories by linking up with unlikely allies" (quoted in Sinclair, 1986, p. D1).

By the same token, business representatives are more rational in *their* approach, less inclined toward reactive knee-jerk behavior, more disposed toward anticipating issues, than even two or three years ago. And that has a lot to do with the new breed of CEOs to whom many of them answer, CEOs who are spending more than half their time on external relations. That involvement has done a great deal to dissipate the insularity that formerly made the job of the public or governmental affairs person so precarious.

Of equal significance, we are dealing with a new kind of legislator in many states. Finally, the emergence of a true professional class of public relations/public affairs specialists has also given great impetus to coalition building. In my experience, it is they alone who have the necessary combination of training and interpersonal skills to function in the role of facilitator/mediator, which is at the heart of this activity.

Another possible reason for the shift toward coalitions is a greater disposition toward risktaking. As that stellar public affairs specialist Mae West once observed, "Given the choice of two evils, I'll take the one I haven't tried before."

My own theory, however, is that we have moved from confrontation to cooperation because the latter works better. It is more cost-effective and far more productive. Its real payout is that it enables business to anticipate and respond to emerging issues.

What lessons about coalition building can be learned from the efforts of pioneering companies like Texaco?

1. *Define your objectives.* That includes not just what your company or association hopes to accomplish but, equally important, what stake others have in your issue—and just who those others are. This may sound simple; but it is this initial, critical step that I find is most often overlooked in the "rush to results."

At the Texaco program, we had developed extensive background on every group we approached. We had profiled the group, met with its leaders, worked with them on some non-legislative project, and so forth. In short, we had got to know them and allowed them to get to know us—and test us. From that interaction came insight and a degree of trust. At a minimum, there came a sufficient credibility to allow us to broach legislative issues with those groups, within two or three years of contact, and get a hearing.

Any issue has natural allies. They are identified every day. What presents the real challenge, and the real reward, is throwing the net wide enough to bring *un*natural allies into one's coalition. Building such a broad-based coalition requires mutual trust and appreciation for one another's self-interest, and that means working with others in one's organization, too—the public relations people, the contributions staff, the strategic planners, the lawyers, the operations people. It is the business of building relationships, not putting together deals. It is slow, unglamorous, and sometimes hazardous—but it works.

2. *Know your issue.* Here, I do not refer to mastering all the technical aspects of a given issue, although a person certainly must. But once she has done that, she must analyze the issue further to communicate its most popular aspects, in English. The message must be simple and cogent.

There is a place for expert testimony, we all know that. But it must be orchestrated carefully. Its use must be controlled. Exercising such control will not make one popular with industry co-workers, perhaps, but the objective here is to get *others* to "buy into" the issue. To do that, they will need to understand it. The public affairs person is the all-important interpreter, who simplifies technical issues so they can be easily understood.

If others are assisting in issue discussions, it is important to make certain that they, too, are knowledgeable about the subject of their communications. Otherwise the effort may be counterproductive.

3. *Build the alliance.* This may involve individualized meetings with other groups; or it may be appropriate to call several groups together for a meeting on the issue. On occasion, telephone conversations may be sufficient to bring a particular ally on board.

Ideally, one can build an alliance without making it seem to be the creature of one's company. There is no question that this is delicate, but if one assesses the strengths and weaknesses of others in the coalition as they join it, furnishes them with adequate background information, identifies other available resources, assesses the contribution each party can make to the coalition, and assigns tasks accordingly, the effort can assume an identity of its own. Building a coalition that is truly a joint enterprise, of course, entails committing to a shared process of decision making. You will not be calling all the shots unilaterally.

Having built an alliance, one needs to develop that all-important consensus. The coalition has to reach decisions and perform. Useful aids toward this end are—

- A paper from which everyone can work.
- A list of decisions and assignments that need to be made.
- A strategic plan. This includes goals, tactics, and a timetable. Among the most useful tactics are a joint policy statement, media contacts, lobbying, direct mail, surveys, and grassroots efforts.

Someone will need to make assignments and follow them up. If one of the constituent organizations of the coalition is not holding up its end of the bargain, then someone must get on top of the situation immediately. That person must find a way to provide the help the constituent organization needs. Insist on accountability.

All these process considerations are essential to the smooth operation of the coalition. But they have an even greater significance. If those in the coalition can work well together on the mechanics, it may make developing a consensus on final objectives much easier.

4. *Maintain flexibility.* It is a fact of life that we seldom get our own way, completely. So, too, with coalitions. They involve negotiation and compromise. To negotiate effectively, one will need to have had a civil relationship with the other parties at interest—a point about which I will have more to say in a moment—as well as a clear mandate from senior management and a degree of flexibility. Coalitions begin with negotiation among the allies; they conclude with negotiation involving adversaries. Negotiation is a continuing part of the process.

One will need to test one's own ideas on others in the coalition. It may be necessary to give way on some points. And eventually, of course, one will need to develop that all-important compromise with those on the other side of the issue. Compromise is at the core of policy making. The consensus that various interests achieve is what motivates legislatures and administrators in government to act. That consensus comes through well-timed compromise.

5. *Treat people decently.* Sounds simple enough, doesn't it? Yet here is what it involves:

- Listening. Not just to be polite, but listening for clues to what is on the other group's agenda. In this way, one may be able to mesh some goals and objectives, rather than merely flatter them. Often I found that one point raised by a given group provided the start of a dialogue. Listening has other advantages. You learn things, and you become better able to sensitize your senior management. Listening will also reduce your chances of making a fool of yourself. As Calvin Coolidge so aptly put it, "If you don't say anything, you won't be called on to repeat it." Talking to excess is an occupational hazard for people in public relations/public affairs. Most are good at talking—but it is a temptation to be constantly resisted.

- Respecting other people's time. One should treat someone in a consumer or public interest group with the same courtesy as a hospital patient. Phone ahead for an appointment. Show up on time. Be succinct in what you have to say. Don't overstay your welcome. And don't forget to say thanks. (Come to think of it, those are the same guidelines a smart executive uses with his or her CEO!) Sending some follow-up material on the issue is also a good idea.

- Keeping confidences. Never, never, never knowingly do something that will undercut or harm your coalition contacts. That does not mean depriving your management of useful information. But safeguarding the position of a key contact will often make it necessary to protect a source, or embargo information for a period of time, or control the dissemination of information. Do it. It is essential to the long-term value of that relationship to *your* organization.

- Giving as well as getting. It is inevitable that others will ask you to help them, in any variety of ways—perhaps by providing in-kind services, by acting as a sounding board, by providing public support or testimony on one of their issues, or by funding a project or a function. Do not get involved in coalitions if you are not prepared for this kind of reciprocity. It comes with the territory. And the sooner you educate your senior management to that reality, the easier your life will become. Public interest and consumer groups in this country are not for sale. It is not a matter of "buying your way in"; it is a matter of understanding that most streets in this world are two-way.

The idea of treating people decently may seem trite, but repeatedly in my work with public interest groups, I heard horror stories of companies violating these civilities. They left a trail of burned bridges, in the press of trying to influence a given vote. Needless to say, when the next critical bill came around, it was difficult to revisit these contacts.

Remember that companies and organizations, just like individuals, have reputations. And, just like individuals, they have networks. Civility in your dealings with others, whether they are in your coalition or outside it, will serve you well in the future. Conversely, the word will get around if you double-deal, try to mislead, or simply run roughshod over others. I call this last technique the "bull-in-the-china-shop approach." Unfortunately, I have observed a good bit of it through the years.

6. The final lesson is *maintain your contacts*. Once you have achieved a particular objective, do not ignore those with whom you have worked. Keep in touch, even if only by an occasional phone call or an exchange of information, lunch perhaps. And stay available to those who have assisted you. If possible, expose your coalition contacts to others in your company, and vice versa. It breaks down the stereotypes. It is also wise to keep some line of communication open to those who were on the other side of the issue. Respect them. They will likely reciprocate. And remember, tomorrow's issue may prove to be even more important than yesterday's. It may well call for a new coalition, new allies. The adage that politics makes strange bedfellows has never been more true.

The foregoing guidelines to successful coalition building take on added significance when one considers that the maturation of the parties at interest, the proven viability of a cooperative (as opposed to confrontational) approach, and the limitations inherent in direct lobbying all point toward greater reliance on coalitions in the future. I believe that many of these coalitions will be business-related and will focus on modifying the present nature of corporations. They will, for the most part, continue to be ad hoc coalitions, dealing with single issues. Many of those issues will be state issues as this level of government assumes greater importance.

A public affairs focus exclusive to Washington, D.C., will become increasingly passé, as will a preoccupation with domestic issues. Business and the interest groups are realizing that they must have multilevel impact—in municipalities, in state capitals, in Washington, *and* abroad.

Further, the coalitions of the future will be "easier" ones, in many respects. They will be more relaxed, for, as Stephen Brobeck observes (personal communication, 1986), "Public interest groups are more willing to talk and work with business, to accept compromise"—and so are the more progressive corporations.

If I seem sanguine about the future of coalition building, it is because I believe there are some corporations in this country willing to take the long view, corporations that will opt to build trust, rather than simply "do deals." They will grasp what a handful of others already know from experience: that in building trust with external constituencies, one builds relationships. If those constituents trust you and your organization, chances are they will stand by you when you err, or are under attack, or even possibly deceive. It is these relationships of trust, in an age when the corporation is no longer viewed solely as an economic entity but a social one as well, that will spell the corporate success of the future.

8

# Reaching the Opinion Makers

*Herb Schmertz*

Over the years, we at Mobil Corporation have come to view public affairs differently from the way most companies traditionally have. Essentially, we believe that running a public affairs program is like running a political campaign.

Most political campaigns, of course, are geared to elections; so each one has a beginning, a middle, and an end. Our campaign goes on. From time to time, we may have victories or defeats. But the whole process is never-ending. We are always out there trying to win votes for our positions.

If Mobil is running a political campaign, it follows that our strategy must be a *political* strategy. Political strategy involves planning. It means assessing a company's present position, making projections, identifying campaign objectives, and laying out a program to achieve them. In short, a political public affairs strategy has much in common with corporate planning to achieve strictly economic objectives. Such a strategy, however, is far different from conventional public relations strategies, which are essentially defensive. Of course, a company should defend itself when attacked. But a political strategy involves leading, not following. It means taking the initiative in raising issues. It means abandoning the low-profile posture of many public relations operations. In a word, it means confrontation.

*Confrontation*, of course, is a word that makes people feel uncomfortable. People think confrontation has to be unpleasant, destructive, or rude; so they tend to avoid it, even when it is clearly needed. At Mobil, we think differently. We think confrontation can be good for you. We believe in getting issues out in the open. We say what we think, without waiting to be asked.

People in our society often talk about an idea whose time has come. But life is rarely that simple, and new ideas do not just suddenly appear on the scene as if by divine revelation. More often than not, the development and acceptance of an idea are a subtle, layered process—something like throwing a stone into a still pond and watching the ripples move out.

Most new ideas gain currency and acceptability because they are discussed by people who are regarded as important. I hesitate to use the term *opinion maker* here, because that term has been overworked and its currency cheapened by Madison Avenue. But the fact remains that certain people in our society are seen as creators or arbiters of public policy. Some have attained that rank because of the positions they hold in government, religion, business, or education. Another group consists of members of the news media. Others are listened to because of their intellectual or academic credentials, such as teachers, professors, and researchers. Still others are active in consumer or environmental groups or in show business. Finally, there are those who are listened to because they are prominent. "In every town in Texas," LBJ once remarked, "there's a guy who lives in a big white house on a hill. These are the guys I want with me."

No corporation, no matter what its resources, is likely to change public opinion. Your actual purpose here is far more modest: to inject yourself into the debate and to make sure your viewpoint is heard by the intellectual establishment. Whether anybody actually pays attention depends on the quality of the ideas—and the way they are presented.

There are several ways to achieve this. One is to make sure that you (or, if you are a public relations professional, your top management) are knowledgeable on the key issues and able to articulate your views in meetings, in interviews, and during social occasions. Another is to be sure that your voice (or, again, the voice of your leadership) is heard directly through bylined articles in newspapers and magazines and even letters to the editor. A third way is through public speeches and debates, especially if they are reported in the press.

We at Mobil have specialized in a fourth way—issue advertising—which I will be discussing here in some detail. But no
matter which route you take, the principle is the same: You have
to express yourself as clearly and as intelligently as possible. If
you are unable to present a convincing argument based on hard
data and sound philosophy, you will fail.

At the same time, what you say is only as effective as how
you say it. Don't be a complainer, because the public does not
respond to a company that whines or carps. But people admire a
fighter, and they respect an organization that sticks its neck out
when it considers itself to be in the right. Whether it is an op-ed
article, a letter to the editor, or an issue ad of the sort I will be
discussing here, make your prose feisty, without being disagree-
able, and you will find an audience who will pay attention to
your arguments.

I am going to dwell at some length on the Mobil op-ed ad
program because it has been unusually successful. In political
terms, the ads constitute the platform on which we run. Each
week, in effect, we add another plank or reinforce a previous
one. To continue the analogy, we are continually seeking new
supporters among the undecided, and one way we do this is by a
continuing series of position papers on the important issues of
the day.

We at Mobil are proud of our op-ed program, but we are
by no means its only admirers. We are continually hearing from
authors, publishers, and colleges who want to reprint our ads in
textbooks and from graduate students who want to write about
them in dissertations.

Several years ago, a study by the International Advertising
Association concluded that the Mobil program is "the single
most significant campaign of this nature ever undertaken, regardless of country." And Milton Moskowitz, a columnist who is
known for his criticisms of big business, has given us the ultimate compliment. "Most corporate advertising," he says, "is still
only flatulent rhetoric. Most companies are just talking to each
other to make their directors feel good. But I'm in favor of what
Mobil is doing. They are more aggressive than most of the others

and far more effective. They get under your skin, which is the way to start a real dialogue."

In 1970, when our op-ed program began in the *New York Times*, there were at least three major issues facing the oil industry. First, we at Mobil were concerned that, in the relatively near future, America and the rest of the free world would be vulnerable to politically motivated oil cutoffs from foreign governments. Owing to a rapidly depleting supply of domestic crude oil, the United States was becoming increasingly reliant on foreign sources of energy. As we saw it, this fundamental change in America's energy supply was bound to have significant and possibly even dangerous effects on the political, social, and economic fabric of our nation.

Back in 1970, however, the prospect of an energy shortage was just about the last thing on people's minds. The economy was prosperous in the land of plenty, and anyone who foresaw a different scenario was regarded as a latter-day Chicken Little. Still, we were concerned about the future. We argued strongly for action that would lead to a greater supply of domestic energy, including the deregulation of natural gas and oil prices, the opening up of offshore drilling opportunities, increased nuclear power, and a more balanced and realistic policy of environmental legislation.

This last issue — the environment — was our second major concern. The 1960s had seen the emergence of a powerful environmental lobby, partly because the environment served as the perfect "motherhood" issue for a good many politicians and journalists. Everybody was in favor of clean air and clean water, which made it conveniently easy to vilify those who expressed any reservations about the goals or methods of the new movement.

But those who served in the management positions of large industrial corporations knew full well that perfectly clean air and perfectly clean water could not be achieved without spending truly staggering sums of money. We were the ones who had to worry about the cost of these programs. Of course we favored a clean environment; who wouldn't? But it was clear to us that there would have to be some trade-offs between what was ideal and what was realistic. At the time, this was a message that few people wanted to hear.

The third issue that concerned us was that American business institutions were under fire as never before. As a number of polls had made all too clear, big business in general and the oil industry in particular had suffered a significant erosion in public confidence. In some circles, these antibusiness feelings were widened to include a deep skepticism about our entire free-market economic system.

In the face of these growing attacks on business, we knew we had to make a significant response. Although most other corporations were silent, this ostrichlike response was not our style. Starting with Rawleigh Warner, Jr., our new chairman, the management of Mobil was eager to participate in the national dialogue. We were ready to speak out on a host of economic and political issues. The only question was how.

At around the same time, editors at the *New York Times* had just decided on a major change in the paper's editorial page. In an effort to open up the paper and to feature diverse opinions and commentaries by both staff columnists and guest writers, the *Times* instituted what soon came to be called the op-ed page — that is, a second editorial page opposite the original one. The management of the *Times* decided to devote a quarter of this new page to advertising — at a small premium over the regular rates.

The kind of advertising that the *Times* had in mind for its second editorial page would not be designed to sell goods and services. Its purpose, rather, was to allow corporations to enhance and polish their identity. This is traditionally referred to as "image advertising," a technique that occasionally leads me to suspect that the company in question is spending more money to publicize its good deeds than it spends on the deeds themselves. Image advertising is always warm and never controversial. Its objective is to tell the reader how great your company is, and its motivation, in a phrase, is to get people to love you.

For us at Mobil, however, the advertising space on the op-ed page represented a very different kind of opportunity. Here was an ideal chance to speak our mind to opinion makers! In using that term, I do not mean that we had in mind a small elite. While from time to time our ads might be directed toward one person—the president of the United States, for example—or toward a small group—say, the members of a congressional committee—for the most part we wanted to reach anyone who would expend the time and effort to read our messages. In other words, if you cared enough to read our point of view, you were enough of an activist for our purposes, and we were delighted that ours was one of the viewpoints that you were being exposed to.

Although there was no line for this kind of advertising in our public affairs budget, we quickly signed up for a series of thirteen ads on the op-ed page.

Now that we had made a commitment, it was time to formulate some basic decisions regarding the nature of our ads. One thing that was clear from the start was that, unlike our product advertising, these issue ads—or advertorials, as they came to be known in the press—had to be written in-house. When you are dealing with important issues of public policy, it is unfair to expect that your ad agency can understand your business and your thinking well enough to express your views on the issues of the day. Moreover, the timeliness of the ads and the necessity of having them cleared by top management required that the turnaround process be as fast as possible.

We also decided to make the ads fairly substantial. Instead of seeing our messages in terms of conventional advertising, the model we had in mind was the thoughtful newspaper editorial. This might mean, on occasion, that our messages would be fairly long and complex. But we felt that the public had a right to know more than our conclusion. We decided to show the intellectual basis for our arguments, so that the reader would be aware of the various assumptions we hold and the philosophy that influences our views.

At the same time, we certainly did not want to be ponderous. And so we attempted to develop a crisp style that would convey a well-supported viewpoint to a sophisticated audience without boring the reader.

Another critical ingredient was accuracy. Because our

program was bound to be controversial, we realized that we could not afford to make any errors. Our credibility was on the line, which meant that even a minor mistake could destroy months of good work. So from the start, it was clear that our research would be as important as our writing.

When it came to matters of tone and style, we wanted to take the offensive without being offensive. Our messages would be urbane and, when possible, good-humored; they would not be pompous or bland. They would comment on issues, but they would also show other facets of our corporate personality by celebrating good works and excoriating ineptitude. Our ads would also, on occasion, serve to wheedle, cajole, josh, and admonish our readers.

Finally, there was the question of how the ads would look. I remember insisting that those messages that dealt directly with issues of substance should contain no illustrations. Although my view prevailed, the decision was far from unanimous.

The other esthetic considerations were arrived at more easily. It was clear that the ads would have to fit in with Mobil's distinctive graphic style. At the same time, they would also have to be suitably integrated into the two-page editorial spread in the *Times*. It sounded easy enough, but this turned out to be a fairly tricky proposition. If our ads were too similar to the other columns on the page, they would run the risk of getting lost in the crowd. If they were too different, they would end up fighting with the rest of the paper. Eventually we arrived at a suitable compromise.

Even before the first ad appeared, we understood that this project carried with it certain risks. We knew, for example, that our speaking out in the *Times* would inevitably serve to invigorate our opponents. And it did not take a genius to realize that our approach would quickly activate that well-entrenched coalition of politicians and self-appointed public guardians who opposed the oil industry on principle and who would not hesitate to single out Mobil for rebuttal and attack.

We were also aware that it might take many months before our ads yielded any real results. For this reason, we committed ourselves to the long run. We decided that if our project lacked continuity, it was probably not worth doing in the first place.

Despite all our worries and cautions, we were genuinely excited about this new opportunity. We saw ourselves as practicing the ancient and honorable art of pamphleteering—only instead of distributing our tracts from door to door, we found it more economical to pay the *Times* to serve as our delivery system.

Our first op-ed ad appeared on October 19, 1970. "America has the world's best highways and the world's worst mass transit," read the headline. "We hope this ad moves people." Although Mobil's economic health has always been tied closely to the continuing use of private automobiles, we were convinced, especially in view of the possibility of an oil shortage, that the United States urgently needed more and better mass transit.

To our delight, this first ad generated a great deal of attention. Many readers paid attention simply because the position we took seemed to be at odds with our basic economic interest. Certainly this was the first time that a major oil company had come out publicly for improved public transportation. By questioning the wisdom of continuing to build expensive highways, we infuriated several constituencies that had traditionally been our allies, including the heavy equipment industry, the construction industry, and, most of all, the other major oil companies. These groups saw our advocacy of mass transit as a betrayal, and they did not hesitate to let us know of their disappointment.

On the other side, many of our long-time critics were also caught off guard, because with this one ad we were undermining the convenient monolithic image of the industry that everybody loved to hate. Some of our liberal critics smelled a plot and waited for the other shoe to drop. They are still waiting.

By the time our thirteen ads ran, it was already clear that our messages had been noticed, read, discussed, and reprinted. During the following months, we continued to buy space in the *Times* on an ad hoc basis. Finally, after a year or two had gone by,

# America has the world's best highways And the world's worst mass transit.

# We hope this ad moves people...

In recent years the United States has developed a really superb highway system. It's been built with tax revenues earmarked specifically for road building.

But the highway construction boom has been accompanied by a mass transit bust. Train and bus travel in this country, with few exceptions, is decrepit. The air traveler suffers increasing indignities despite bigger, faster planes.

Greater New York is a typical example. You can depend on commuting to and from Manhattan—but only to be undependable and slow. On public transport, the 25 miles to Westfield, N.J. takes 75 minutes at an average speed of 20 miles per hour. The 33 miles to Stamford, Conn. takes 60 minutes at 33 mph. The 26 miles to Hicksville, L.I. takes 55 minutes at 28 mph. When you're on time.

You have to be a stoic with stamina to use public ground transportation for a trip beyond the commuting range. Fly to a nearby city? You can hardly get at our congested air terminals, either by land or air. The ride to or from the airport often takes longer than the flight.

Mass transit seems to work better abroad. Americans are agreeably impressed by the fast, comfortable, and attractive subways in foreign cities. Intercity trains in other countries make ours look pitiful. Japan's high-speed Tokaido line carries more than 200,000 passengers a day. Clean, comfortable French, German, Italian, and British trains regularly attain speeds over 100 mph. European railroads are already planning or building expresses that will do better than 150 mph.

Yet, in the United States, new mass transit systems are for the most part still in the wild blue yonder.

Providing for our future transportation needs will require very large expenditures. We believe there's an urgent need for legislators to reexamine the procedures used to generate and expend transportation revenues. Such a review may yield the conclusion that special earmarked funds are no longer the best approach.

In weighing priorities, no decision-maker can ignore the increasing congestion on those fine highways of ours, especially in and around the great urban centers. But more and better mass transit could stop traffic jams before they start. Just one rail line has triple the people-moving capacity of a three-lane superhighway.

It costs less—in energy consumption and in money—to move people via mass transit than on highways. Thus mass transit means less air pollution.

It also means conservation. Whether the energy comes from gasoline for cars, or fuel oil, natural gas, or coal for electric power plants, it's derived from a diminishing natural resource. So we think all forms of transportation should be brought into a national plan for safe, rapid, economical ways of moving people—consistent with the wisest use of our energy resources.

While Mobil sells fuels and lubricants, we don't believe the gasoline consumed by a car idling in a traffic jam (carrying a single passenger, probably) is the best possible use of America's limited petroleum resources. Our products ought to help more people get where they want to go.

To us, that means a green light for mass transit . . . soon.

# Mobil.

This ad appeared in *The New York Times* on October 19, 1970

Rawleigh Warner called me one day and asked, "Why don't we do this every week?"

"Maybe we should," I replied, "but I don't know whether we can sustain it. Let me see if we can get a dozen ads into the hopper." We did, so I went back to Warner and we agreed to continue the project on a weekly basis. We have been doing it ever since.

The *Times* has never interfered with our op-ed ads, even when we have directly taken issue with their editorials. There was only one case of censorship, and it was more amusing than disturbing. Early in 1971, Mayor John Lindsay and 11,000 sanitation workers found something they could agree on: plastic garbage bags. The mayor signed into law a bill allowing New Yorkers to use approved garbage bags instead of the old metal cans. This was a program that we at Mobil were eager to support—first, because it made urban living just a little more pleasant, and second, because we ourselves were in the plastic-garbage-bag business.

Now, it was clear to just about every New York resident that one of the biggest garbage problems in the city concerned Monday's disposal of the Sunday *New York Times*. To deal with this problem, and to encourage the use of plastic garbage bags, we developed an ad whose headline read "All the News That's Fit to Print Today Is Trash Tomorrow."

Apparently we went too far. Although the *Times* had no objection to the content of our ad, they asked us to change the headline because it spoofed their corporate slogan. It was a reasonable request, and we changed the headline to the rather more prosaic "Neat News for Waste Watchers." Fortunately, this one incident has constituted the extent of our problems with the *Times* over our program. In view of our repeated and unsuccessful attempts to present similar ads on television, we have always been very appreciative of that fact.

For the first couple of years, the ads were done catch-as-catch-can, with writers being assigned on an ad hoc basis. Jack Tolbert, a talented veteran writer who was manager of our public relations department, wrote most of the early ones. Over time, we started bringing in other writers. In the early years, the writer was responsible for his own research; more recently, those two functions have become separated.

It is not surprising that our greatest challenge over the years has been to maintain our original spirit of spontaneity. Although that task has grown increasingly difficult, even today our ads are rarely prepared more than two or three days before publication.

Over the years, Mobil's op-ed ads have dealt with a wide variety of issues. During the two oil crises of the 1970s, for example, we needed to dispel the widespread impression that the oil industry was to blame or that the oil companies were reaping unconscionable profits. In the wake of the oil crises, we have continually urged the government to adopt a workable energy policy and to let us step up the search for oil. And we have spoken out strongly against legislation that would tear apart the large oil companies.

Another of our major themes has been that everything in life is a trade-off. For example, it is certainly possible for our society to enjoy natural gas at artificially depressed prices. But if that is the choice we make, nobody can guarantee that there will be adequate and secure supplies.

Or to take another example, while it is possible to reduce automotive air emissions severely and abruptly in order to meet an arbitrary timetable, this program would make it impossible to also hold down costs and improve mileage. In short, we have tried to help people understand what options are open to them and what costs are involved in the various alternatives — matters that few politicians or journalists ever seem to talk about.

In 1974, we published a series of eleven ads in several dozen newspapers across the country, under the umbrella headline "Toward a National Energy Policy." This was the most comprehensive project of this kind that we had ever undertaken. The ads were long and fairly complex. But when we offered free reprints of all of the ads, assembled in an attractive little booklet, more than 11,000 people wrote in, requesting over 25,000 copies of the booklet.

Many of these people were college professors. Many others were in government. We also sent copies to every member of

Congress, every cabinet member, and to other members of the administration. In addition, we sent copies to 3,000 media people across the country, to about 10,000 educators, and to some 12,000 high-school libraries. This large-scale secondary distribution was our primary goal when we decided to prepare and publish the series.

When you are selling ideas, the results are especially hard to quantify. But it is clear that, through our op-ed ads, we have managed to bring some of our views into the public consciousness. We have won a certain degree of credibility with various key publics and have apparently convinced at least some of them that the oil industry is neither monolithic nor antediluvian.

In 1976, the Harris organization conducted a poll to learn how the American public viewed forty major corporations, including seven oil companies. Although the oil companies in general fared very poorly, the people surveyed thought more highly of Mobil than of the competition. In their view, Mobil was "committed to free enterprise," "seriously concerned about the energy problems," and "working for good government." In fact, the public perceived Mobil as the industry pacesetter on nineteen of the twenty-one public policy issues that were mentioned in the survey. Obviously, our op-ed program was a major factor in our favor.

Moreover, although we had not done any product advertising for nearly three years, the public rated the quality of our products and services higher than the other oil companies and equal to the average of the forty companies in the survey. I think that is evidence that even though we may be selling ideas, there are also some bottom-line benefits from our public affairs program.

While it would be presumptuous to suggest that our editorial messages have actually made the difference in the public's changing attitudes on certain controversial issues affecting energy and the economy, it does seem that some opinion leaders have been influenced by the arguments we have made. For example, we have spoken out frequently on excessive government regulation. By now, most Americans agree that the federal government has gone too far in its efforts to control American business and that all of this well-intentioned meddling carries a stiff price tag.

Similarly, we have had our say on the folly of price controls, a mistake that has become increasingly clear now that most controls on oil have been lifted. We have been equally outspoken on the need for a balance between jobs and growth, on the one hand, and a clean environment, on the other. By now, it seems, a majority of the public recognizes the need for sensible trade-offs. And it is interesting to note that jobs and economic growth were prominent issues in the 1984 presidential campaign.

In cases where our views have not prevailed or where they prevailed only in part, we have at least played a respected role in the debate and received a fair hearing. For a corporation, this is what makes advocacy advertising worth doing.

Over the years, we have also had a lot to say about the role of business in American life. On a number of occasions we have used our space to explain and defend America's economic system, which has been so little understood by our own citizens. We have supported efforts to reduce the federal deficit, and we have paid particular attention to private-sector reports on how the federal government can cut spending. Finally, we have been outspoken about the media's negative treatment of big business.

In addition to whatever intellectual effect our ads have had on the general public, our op-ed program has also produced several important fringe benefits among certain sub-publics. For one thing, our ads have had a salutary effect on our recruitment program. For another, there has been a parallel improvement in employee morale, especially among our executives, who have been delighted to see the company standing up for what we think is right. Many of them tell us that they are proud to be associated with an institution that does not cut and run when the bullets start to fly.

A third benefit of our op-ed program is its positive effect on shareholders. When we survey new shareholders, the second most prominent reason they give for buying our stock is their belief that Mobil will be active in protecting their investment from hostile government intervention and legislation. If we ever found ourselves in a proxy fight, I would like to think that this perception on the part of investors would be a significant asset on the side of management.

When it was clear that the ads in the *Times* were reaching their intended audience, we started to run them in other papers as well — the *Los Angeles Times*, the *Chicago Tribune*, the *Boston Globe*, the *Wall Street Journal*, and the *Washington Post*. At one point, during the 1973–1974 energy crisis, we were running our op-ed ads in a hundred different newspapers. But that was an unusual situation, and in normal times we've limited ourselves to half a dozen major dailies.

In 1974 we reviewed our op-ed program and concluded that we had put too strict a definition on who, exactly, constituted an opinion leader. While our messages were certainly reaching a good number of opinion makers, we were ignoring other important sectors of the population. Owing to the nature of our political system, people living in the heartland are often more influential in political terms than the eastern intellectuals. A fuel-oil distributor in Ohio, for example, or the woman who runs a feed mill in Missouri may have closer personal relationships with their respective members of Congress than the editor of a big-city newspaper has with his. Many congressional districts lie outside major population areas, and we were especially eager to reach these areas.

So in 1974 we embarked on a magazine campaign aimed at heartland-community readers. Our ads began appearing in places like *Time* and *Reader's Digest* and in such service-club magazines as *Rotarian, Kiwanian, Moose,* and *Elks.*

A few months after this campaign was started, I was invited to lunch by an ad agency that did corporate work for a large multinational client. The ad people were interested in stepping up their client's issue advertising, but they complained that Mobil's program of issue ads had preempted the field to the point that there was nothing left to do. I was flattered, but I strongly disagreed with their conclusion. Preempted the field? That couldn't be. I was convinced that there was plenty of room for a new concept in issue advertising, and I took it as a personal challenge to come up with one.

A few weeks earlier, I had been approached by an old college friend who was now the head of advertising for *Parade*, the Sunday newspaper supplement magazine. It was his view that we ought to be running our issue ads in his publication. I agreed that *Parade* was a good way to reach an entirely different group of readers, but I just could not see running our ads there. The ads were appropriate in the *Times*, but in *Parade* the environment was all wrong.

Then I hit upon an intriguing idea. What if we designed a different kind of ad, one that was more in keeping with *Parade*'s format? Over a couple of weeks we came up with the idea of a series of short takes that would look something like a gossip column. The new ads would deal with the same themes as our op-ed ads, but they would do so more breezily and informally.

We called the column "Observations," and for years we ran it in *Parade*, *Family Weekly*, and similar Sunday supplements. At its peak, "Observations" reached approximately half of the households in America through 500 different newspapers. Later, owing to budget considerations, "Observations" was put on a monthly schedule and moved to *Reader's Digest*. But I am convinced that *Parade* represents an unusually good media buy, and I have never regretted advertising there. If our budget allowed it, "Observations" would still appear in *Parade* every week. But for advertising that appears only once a month, *Reader's Digest* was more appropriate.

While it is always difficult to measure the impact of advertising, the effects of "Observations" were truly impressive. The readership scores in *Parade* for that column routinely exceeded by a large margin the average scores for other half-page black-and-white ads. Often, "Observations" did much better than big, four-color ads and occasionally even outran the editorial columns of the magazine.

We once commissioned a survey to determine whether "Observations" was really influencing people on public policy issues that we saw as important. We asked newspaper readers in three cities (Hartford, Connecticut; Davenport, Iowa; and Charlotte, North Carolina) for their views on seven provocative issues that we had treated frequently in "Observations." Then we compared their views with those of newspaper readers in three demographically similar cities (Providence, Rhode Island; Des Moines, Iowa; and Memphis, Tennessee) where "Observations" was not seen.

The poll results, based on fairly large samplings, showed significant differences between the two groups on a variety of issues, including nuclear power, limiting the government's role in business, and skepticism about solar energy.

We have always received a great deal of mail from "Observations" readers. Whether or not they agreed with us, most of our readers supported our right to express our views, and they took time to write to us. Many of them pointed out the vital role that "Observations" played in balancing the information they received from government and the media.

If your corporation is interested in a program of issue-oriented ads, you will have to face the problem of tax deductibility, so I will take a moment here to explain Mobil's position. By law, advertising is tax-deductible if it "presents views on economic, financial, social or other subjects of a general nature." But if the ads constitute lobbying, or if they take a position on the passage or defeat of legislation, they are not tax-deductible. To be safe, we take tax deductions for charity-related and public service ads but not for ads that deal with energy, the environment, or anything else even remotely connected with legislation. We submit all our ads to counsel for their opinion on tax-deductibility, and we have asked the lawyers to follow conservative standards.

At the same time, I have always been struck by what seems to me a blatant inequity. Why can a newspaper take a tax deduction for its editorials—including those that deal directly with legislation—while we at Mobil cannot? Why can a media corporation support a candidate while an industrial corporation cannot? To take an obvious example, most publications depend heavily on special third-class mailing privileges. And some of the larger publications are tied in to large conglomer-

ates. Why do we assume that these parties are necessarily disinterested observers or that they are never involved in a conflict of
interest? Eventually, when I retire and find myself in need of a
project, I would like to devote some time to looking into this
question.

In recent years, corporate issue advertising has become
increasingly popular. One reason for this development, I think,
is that the media have been unable to cover complex issues—
especially business issues—fully and accurately. As a result, both
print and electronic journalism are full of distortions and sim-
plifications that cry out to be corrected by advocacy advertising.

"Most advocacy campaigns," writes David Ogilvy (1983) in
*Ogilvy on Advertising*, "are too little and too late. They are addressed to the wrong audience, lack a defined purpose, don't go
on long enough, are weak in craftsmanship, and advocate a
hopeless cause. So they fail" (p. 126). Ogilvy's conclusion? Advocacy advertising is not a job for beginners.

Ogilvy is right to be cautious, but he overstates his case.
For corporations interested in advocacy advertising, I would give
the following advice: Stake out your objectives clearly. Be sure to
define the issues you want to address. Make sure that your top
management knows what is involved. They will have to do more
than approve the ads; they will also have to take the heat. And if
there is no heat, it is a sign that your ads are not very effective.

To the extent that it is possible, try to run the entire
program yourself. If you have your ads prepared by an outside
agency, they may be so slick as to turn off the people you want to
reach. Instead, hire the best talent you can find, and put your
energy into substance, style, and timeliness. Finally, be patient:
The results will not come overnight.

If you embark on an op-ed program, it is important to
develop a style that reflects your company's personality and to
stick to it. Whatever style you use, be sure to talk to readers in
terms they can personally identify with. Be consistent in what
you say and how you say it. Check all your facts carefully. And
above all, maintain your visibility. If you speak up only in times
of crisis, your credibility is sure to suffer.

But enough theory. At this point, I would like to present a few of my favorite "advertorials" — together with a brief commentary on each one — from among the hundreds that Mobil has published over the past decade and a half.

When our op-ed program began, we decided that we would occasionally take a broader view and that we would discuss such topics as the nature of our economic system. What makes it viable? Why does it work? What could lead it to stop working?

The ad "Capitalism: moving target" represents a group of a dozen or so philosophical messages about capitalism that we have been running over the years. Initially, these ads were designed for two purposes. First, we wanted to help combat the massive amount of ignorance about our economic system. A great many Americans — including some who are otherwise well educated — simply do not understand how the free-market economy works or why it has been so successful in our society.

Second, during the 1970s, we felt a pressing need to defend the free-market system at a time when its basic tenets were being called into question — especially among academics and intellectuals. In this ad and in others, we tried to speak directly to the concerns of the antibusiness reader.

Most of our ads are like conventional editorials in that we run them only once. But a few, like "Capitalism: moving target," are not time-bound, and every year or two we run them again.

# Capitalism: moving target

The list of things wrong with business in this country is almost endless. Nearly as long, in fact, as the list of what's right with it.

Perhaps the most frustrating thing about business, for those who keep trying to shoot it down, is this: Corporations are so tenacious that they will even do good in order to survive. This tenacity goes beyond the old maxim that man, in his greed for profit, often unavoidably serves the public interest. In times of crisis, business will even do good *consciously* and *deliberately*.

Nothing could be better calculated to confound business's critics than this underhanded tactic. The Marxist dialectic has it that capitalism must inevitably founder in its own inherent contradictions; that it contains the seeds of its own destruction. But business also contains the seeds of its own adaptation and survival.

Businessmen are pragmatists, and with their daily feedback from the marketplace, they readily abandon dogma whenever their survival instinct tells them to. It has become less and less a question of what they *want* to do or might *like* to do, but of what their common sense and survival instinct tell them they *have* to do.

Remember the Edsel? That was one of the fastest plebiscites in history. But it wasn't the American public that took the loss; it was the shareholders of Ford Motor Company. (Then, you'll recall, Ford changed course and bounced back with the Mustang, which quickly showed its tailpipe to the competition by breaking all sales records for a new make of car.)

Because it is keyed so closely to the marketplace and so responsive to it, private business is necessarily the most effective instrument of change. Some would call it revolutionary. Many of those who attack business fail to comprehend its constructive contributions to responsive change. And this sort of change is one of the basic reasons business manages to survive.

Not *all* businesses survive, of course. The record is replete with companies that expired because they didn't adapt rapidly enough to a new milieu.

While businessmen as a whole are not exactly social reformers, they do respond to criticism and to sustained social pressures. The alert businessman regards such pressures as a useful early warning system. The danger is that criticism can become a mindless reflex action that persists long after the basis for it has been dissipated.

Partly because of its ability to adapt—which is simply another word for responsive change—private business remains the most productive element in our society and on balance the best allocator of resources. If you decide to draw a bead on it, remember you're aiming at a moving target. Because, as we've said here before, business is bound to change.

Over the years, we have been deeply frustrated by the inability of the public or the press to distinguish between profits and profitability. It is true that, in terms of actual dollars, the oil companies have usually made large profits. But everyone in business knows that the absolute size of a profit tells you nothing until you also know the size of the company reporting it.

Unfortunately, this basic information is not necessarily understood among the general public. Most people are surprised to learn that, compared with the profitability of other industries, our rate of return has always been rather modest. Even in the so-called windfall years, our profit margins never got much above average.

Because profits are such an emotional issue, we have returned to this theme again and again. We have also stressed that to search for, refine, transport, and deliver new oil requires an enormous sum of money. And the only possible source for that money is our earnings.

Although there is room to reproduce only one ad on this theme — "If we tell you oil companies don't make enough profit. . ."— some of our other headlines have included:

We're one of the 10 biggest industrial corporations
   in the world.
You think that's big enough?
We're not so sure.

We're earning a lot.
We're spending more.
Sound familiar?

Are oil profits big?
Right.
Big enough?
Wrong.

# If we tell you oil companies don't make enough profit, you'll have a fit.
# Oil companies don't make enough profit.
# Sorry.

The international oil industry has to find a new Kuwait every year, almost.

Between 1970 and 1971, oil consumption in the Free World increased by 2.2 million barrels a day. That approximates the petroleum output from Kuwait—one of the world's largest producers.

Oil consumption today is more than double what it was 10 years ago. And the world will use more oil in the Seventies than it used in all previous history.

To achieve the equivalent of a new Kuwait every year from here on, oil companies must invest money on a scale that boggles the mind. Mobil alone will make capital and exploration outlays of more than $1 billion this year.

For the past several years, oil companies have been unable to generate enough capital from their operations. They have been forced to borrow more and more of their capital needs; and the interest on loans, as well as the loan payments, adds significantly to the cost of doing business and eventually to product costs.

Of all sources of capital, net income—profit—is most important. To help provide the capital needed for investment, profit must grow as demand rises.

But for years, profits have grown much more slowly than demand. Between 1969 and 1971, while demand rose by 20 percent, aggregate net earnings of 30 of the world's largest oil companies increased by just over nine percent. In the same two-year period, worldwide tax payments of these companies went up by more than 50 percent.

One of the main reasons for inadequate earnings is that prices for U.S. petroleum products are too low. Too low for the consumer's own long-term interest. In June, 1972, the wholesale price of regular-grade gasoline in this country was only about five percent higher than in 1967, the base year used by the government for such surveys. Since 1967, the U.S. cost of living has risen more than 24 percent.

If oil companies are to have enough money in the years ahead to make the investments they must make to meet people's growing needs, their earnings will have to rise faster. There is just no other true solution.

If you understand this basic economic reality, maybe the next time somebody suggests that oil companies are not making enough profit, you won't have a fit.

This ad appeared in *The New York Times* on June 29, 1972

"Musings of an oil person. . ." is one of my all-time favorites. The content was strong and the style was brilliant. But more than that—we took on a world-class media performer.

Early in 1974, Tom Wicker wrote an angry column in the *Times* that attacked the oil industry in general and our advocacy ads in particular. Reading the column, I could see that although Tom Wicker did not really like what we were doing, he had not put together much of an argument to make his point.

I immediately called my staff together and announced that we had to answer Wicker's column. The challenge here was not what to say, but to find the right format in which to say it. Charlie Pollak, one of the most creative writers we ever had, went out and wrote this one straight from the gut. Charlie insisted that it be typeset to look as if it had been done on a typewriter. He was right, of course, for here the medium is the message.

We have gone back to this format a number of times since, because it is an ideal way to express indignation, confusion, or anger. I would like to think that the reader can visualize a fellow sitting at the typewriter, banging away in righteous indignation.

# Musings of an oil person...

Wonder if oil company advertising isn't risking indecent overexposure these days. There's so much oil on the tube and in print. Gulf, Shell and Texaco all ran full-pagers on the same day last week in the Times. Mobil's on the Op-Ed page every Thursday. Why do we all do it? Some critics think the ads show the companies are conspiring to brainwash the public. Others think the advertising deluge proves we can't do anything right, not even conspire. But an oil company has to find some way of speaking its mind and letting the public know what's going on, especially now when oil companies are accused of being secretive. Have to take risk of moving Tom Wicker to nausea over the "...pious, self-serving, devious, mealy-mouthed, self-exculpating, holier-than-thou, positively sickening oil company advertisements in which these international behemoths depict themselves as poverty-stricken paragons of virtue embattled against a greedy and ignorant world." Tom turns a nice phrase, but doesn't he know we're frustrated in trying to get information to the public? Try to buy time on TV to say something substantive and the networks clobber you with the fairness doctrine. Same with radio. Several congressmen want the FTC to require a company to substantiate its idea advertising, just as if an idea were like a new toothpaste. Why don't they exhume Madison and make him substantiate the Bill of Rights? Sure, we can stick to print media to tell our story. But newspapers and magazines frequently don't understand the complexities of our industry. Only a few have oil specialists. And how many deadly news releases can we send them before they scream for mercy? Much better to use TV to try to reach the millions whose opinions about oil are swayed by what Cronkite, Chancellor and Reasoner say every evening. Briefly! In 30 seconds they can suggest enough wrongdoing that a year of full-page explanations by us won't set straight. Hate to be on the defensive all the time. Arm our top management people with facts and get them on TV panels and talk shows. They still look drab next to a politician making some wild allegation against us because he's running for something. Does he have to run on our backs? Sure he does--as long as there are gas lines. What do we tell the guy who's boiling mad at us--in our station or some other company's--after waiting two hours for the privilege of paying $1.10 for two gallons of gas? Are we going to tell him he's been wasting energy for years? No way. Tell him to lay off those jackrabbit starts? He'll find that out for himself. That Detroit's naughty for building big cars, that we shouldn't have built all those superhighways, that we're sorry we gave away all that glassware? Forget it. Should we remind him we've been warning for years that the energy crisis was coming? He'll mow down the pumps and who would blame him. No, have to focus on the positive things we can do. Tell him we're recycling the money he pays at the pump right back into oil-finding offshore, Alaska, anywhere. Into more refinery capacity. Into oil shale, synthetic fuels from coal, tar sands, far-out processes in the lab. Dammit, we're a can-do company in a can-do country. Give us a few years and we'll make gas lines just a quaint recollection of the mid-70s. In the meantime, try to reason with Washington against counter-productive laws and regulations. Fight the two-times-two-equals-five logicians who think the same outfit that brings you the U.S. Mail can find oil three miles under the ocean bottom. Give people the facts. Give them genuine information. Speak out. Persuade them to listen. Never bore them. If at first we don't succeed, bust a gut trying again. No other way. Or we all end up working for the government.

This ad appeared in *The New York Times* on February 28, 1974

One day Rawleigh Warner asked me, out of the blue, "Do you think you could do some fables?"

"I don't know," I replied. "It sounds like an interesting idea, so we'll give it a try." Over time, we turned out seven or eight little stories. Our fables attracted a lot of attention—not all of it favorable. Some people thought they were brilliant; our opponents insisted they were manipulative.

In my view, the real problem for our opponents is that we dared to present a moral to our story—a concept they thought they owned. Moreover, the probusiness forces did not normally use such "creative" techniques to get their point across, which was another reason that some people hated the fables. It was after this fable appeared that I formulated Schmertz's Seventh Law: The opposition will always defend your right to free speech so long as you have no hope of convincing anyone.

When "How the squirrel found himself up a tree" appeared, we were involved in a debate over price controls on energy. In our view, price controls would have provided no economic incentive to develop new sources of energy. But had we framed our argument in those terms, who would have listened? With the fables, we were able to make the problem understandable and even interesting to people who had no inherent interest in business. It was a communications breakthrough, as we were no longer preaching to the choir.

*A Fable For Now:*

# How the squirrel found himself up a tree.

There once was a squirrel who collected nuts and stored them. In this way, he was able to see himself safely through the long, hard, cold winters.

Other squirrels soon noticed how good he was at finding nuts, collecting them, and bringing them home. So they asked if he would do the same for them. They, in turn, agreed to pay him for his services.

Soon, he was finding and delivering nuts to squirrels near and far. As might be expected, nuts became harder and harder for the squirrel to find. Because the search became more difficult, it cost him more. (He had by now devised an ingenious transportation system to move nuts from one squirrel community to another.) So he raised the price he charged the other squirrels.

This, of course, caused some concern, particularly among those squirrels who weren't familiar with the nut gatherer's problems. Because they never had to look for nuts, they thought nuts must be awfully easy to find, harvest, and deliver. And so they appealed to the Supreme Squirrel.

He, in his wisdom, determined that a Furry Persons' Committee should determine what price the squirrel should charge for his nuts. The Committee set a low price, and all the other squirrels thought that decision was, in their words, "a real gasser."

"Now we won't have to shell out so much," they said.

On the other hand, the nut-gathering squirrel wasn't too crazy about the price that was set.

"Why should I knock myself out?" he said. "This is tough work, and if I can't squirrel away a little something for myself, I'd be crazy to look for nuts in hard-to-find places."

And so, his incentive gone, he stopped searching in those hard-to-find places. Pretty soon, he began to run out of nuts. Naturally, he started cutting back on deliveries to far-away squirrels. And, naturally, his customers were upset. They couldn't understand why there were not enough nuts to go around.

So, the first squirrel patiently explained: "You wanted nuts on your terms, and as long as I could supply them to you on that basis, I did. Because nuts were so cheap you used more and more. Now, they're just too expensive to find. Unless you get the Furry Persons' Committee to stop telling me what price I can charge, you're going to have to get along with fewer nuts."

Moral: When the Supreme Squirrel interferes with the pricing of nuts, it's enough to drive you up a tree. Which reminds us: The U.S. is still suffering from the Supreme Court's 1954 decision to let the Federal Power Commission regulate the price of natural gas shipped across state lines. In the government's eagerness to keep prices low, it hurt the industry's incentive to find more gas. Only decontrol of new natural gas can restore that incentive. And that's no fable.

## Mobil

This ad appeared in *The New York Times* on January 29, 1976

© 1976 Mobil Oil Corporation

During the national debate over divestiture, we wanted to point out that opposition to the breakup of the major oil companies was not limited to those of us with an obvious interest in preserving the status quo. We knew that we had to argue the case in terms of the public's interest, rather than the vested interest of the major oil companies.

In the spring of 1978, a number of newspapers, radio outlets, and television stations had gone on record saying that divestiture was a bad idea. We decided to reprint selections from their statements in an ad whose overall effect would suggest a unity of opinion from widely different sources—"Voices of reason."

In retrospect, our decision to reproduce the logos of the publications and stations that supported our position probably doubled the effectiveness of this ad.

# Voices of reason

A growing number of voices are being raised against proposals in the Congress to break up the large oil companies into smaller, less efficient units.

People without axes to grind. People outside the oil industry. Radio and television commentators and editorials. Newspaper editorials.

Of the editorials we've come across so far, more than 60 oppose divestiture, and only one urged passage of the legislation.

Here are samples:

**THE ARIZONA REPUBLIC** "Breaking up the oil companies would be a national disaster."

**KNBC** Los Angeles: "The over-riding fact is that bigness in oil companies isn't necessarily bad, when it takes billions of dollars in risk capital to go get the oil we all seem to want to keep using. If the politicians who're trying to climb into higher office over the bodies of America's oil companies really want to cut your fuel prices, we think they should stop monkeying around with more regulations and break-up threats, and let the forces of competition decide how big and how integrated an oil company should be." **The Los Angeles Times** also came out against divestiture.

## THE KANSAS CITY STAR

"The people pushing divestiture are not doing anything to ease the energy shortage or bring down prices; they are just playing to the political galleries by trying to sock it to Big, Bad Oil."

**The Hartford Times** "The effort by some liberal congressmen to force divestiture is so laughable that the initial inclination is to ignore the rantings as petty demagoguery. Unfortunately, history has proven that petty demagoguery, when ignored, all too often can succeed in achieving incredibly destructive ends."

**WLOS·TV·FM** of Greenville, S.C. "The philosophy behind these proposals is that 'big is bad,' which ignores the fact that big is almost always more efficient and productive. . . . More often than not, bigness benefits the consumer . . ." In neighboring North Carolina, Charlotte's WBT and WBTV added: "Sure, there are about 20 oil companies that are mighty big.

But it's because they're big that they've been able to afford the exploration, the drilling and the sophisticated distribution system that provided America for so long with cheap, dependable fuel—and that, even now, has kept us from being utterly swamped by the 500% increase in OPEC oil prices."

**THE SPOKESMAN-REVIEW** of Spokane: "A Federal Energy Administration study indicates that requiring oil companies to split up would result in less production and higher prices to consumers. If this is true, it would be a clearcut case of cutting off one's nose to spite one's face."

**THE INDIANAPOLIS STAR** "The industry as presently structured has served the nation very well. It could continue to do so if government would let it alone."

**TULSA WORLD** "At a time when the country faces a growing and dangerous shortage of domestic fuel supplies, it would seem incredible that Congress would attempt to punish people who are investing their money and talent in the search for new sources."

**DESERET NEWS** of Salt Lake City. ". . . instead of trying to break up oil companies, the government should get on with the job of formulating a rational and comprehensive national energy policy."

**San Francisco Chronicle** "Once big oil is broken up, who's next? It is logical to expect that the line will form on the left, of course, to bust up the automobile industry, steel, aluminum, the computer industry, and anything else big and inviting."

If you'd like a full file of editorials on this issue, write to:
Mobil Oil Corporation, Box E, 150 E. 42nd Street, New York, NY 10017.

# Mobil

Late in 1971, the New York Public Library announced that its Science and Technology Division was in imminent danger of closing down owing to a shortage of funds. This particular section of the library has always been of enormous importance to the business community, and we felt strongly that it deserved corporate support. In addition to making our own contribution, we used this ad to encourage other corporations to add their support. The response was terrific, and the Science and Technology Division was able to remain open. I only wish all our ads fell upon such willing ears!

# Help wanted. Urgent.

This isn't an employment ad. It is an urgent call for help.

The New York Public Library needs $86,000 in a hurry.

If the library cannot raise that amount by the end of this week, it will be forced to close its Science and Technology Division to students, researchers, and the general public.

This priceless asset that has made such a great contribution to intellectual and commercial life must not be lost for want of $86,000.

We urge the city, the state, banks, foundations, other corporations, and you to join with us and others who are aiding the library.

Send your tax-deductible contribution to Richard W. Couper, President, New York Public Library, Fifth Avenue at 42nd Street, New York City 10018.

Checks should be made out to: NYPL-Science & Technology.

Do it today.

Please.

The need is urgent.

## Mobil

This ad appeared in *The New York Times* on December 27, 1971

© Mobil Oil Corporation

"The U.S. stake in Middle East peace" turned out to be one of the most controversial messages we've ever run. Owing to the nature of the oil business, our information from the Middle East tends to be fairly reliable. In 1973, we had the strong impression that tensions between Israel and the Arab world were close to the boiling point. But we were concerned that our own government did not perceive this risk as being real. When we approached the State Department with our concerns, they told us not to be alarmists.

We thought it important to point out that America, too, had a stake in Middle East peace, if for no other reason than the prospect of a major disruption in our oil supplies in the event of war — a possibility that in our view was growing more likely every week. The ad did not mention Israel because we didn't want to focus here on the rights and wrongs of the Arab-Israeli conflict. The issue at hand was simply the future of America's oil supply, which boiled down to the need for recognizing the strategic importance of Saudi Arabia. Our critics accused us of running this ad at the behest of the Saudis, but there was no truth to this charge.

Three and a half months after this ad appeared, war erupted in the Middle East. It was followed by the Arab oil embargo.

# The U.S. stake in Middle East peace: I

Oil and natural gas supply over three-quarters of the energy used in the United States.

Our society literally cannot live without adequate oil supplies. We could not even grow our own food without oil to power farm machines, much less continue as an industrial society.

U.S. oil consumption is rising rapidly and will continue to, even though we must become much more efficient in our use of energy. Yet domestic production of crude oil is actually declining now. We already have to depend on other countries for over a third of the oil we use. In another seven years, or less, we will be relying on foreign sources for more than half our oil.

This is the prospect even if a pipeline is built to bring oil from Alaska's North Slope to market in this country, and even if large additional oil reserves are found and produced off the U.S. East and West Coasts.

Canada, Venezuela, and Nigeria, among others, are substantial exporters of oil to the U.S., and increasing volumes of their oil will probably come here. The North Sea is a promising area, but this oil will be consumed in Northwest Europe. Additional new oil provinces in various parts of the world will probably be brought into production over the coming years.

However, based on everything we now know, the Middle East is the only region in the world with large enough reserves of oil to meet the inevitable increase in U.S. consumption. Like it or not, the United States is dependent on the Middle East even just to maintain our present living standards in the years immediately ahead.

Of all the countries in the Middle East, the U.S. must look primarily to Saudi Arabia and Iran for oil. Each of these countries has its own unique needs and problems and opportunities; later in this series, we will have more to say about this.

Of these two countries, Saudi Arabia has the most oil—more, in fact, than any other nation in the world. Its reserves can support an increase from the present production level of about 8 million barrels a day to 20 million barrels daily. Iran's reserves can support an increase in production from about 6 million barrels a day now to around 9 million barrels daily. Mobil has substantial interests in the oil reserves of both countries—and substantial supply obligations to millions of customers around the world.

We in the United States must learn to live with the peoples of these two countries and to understand that they look to us for policies that recognize their legitimate interests and aspirations. If we want to continue to enjoy our present life style, or anything approaching it, then—no matter how much more efficient we may become in the use of energy—we will have to understand the changed and still-changing conditions in the Middle East and in the rest of the world.

If our country's relations with the Arab world (Iran is not an Arab state) continue to deteriorate, Saudi Arabia may conclude it is not in its interest to look favorably on U.S. requests for increased petroleum supplies. The government of that country has the power to decide how much oil is to be produced within its borders. And to what countries that oil can be shipped.

In the last analysis, political considerations may become the critical element in Saudi Arabia's decisions, because we will need the oil more than Saudi Arabia will need the money. That country could reduce oil exports 3 million barrels a day below *present* levels and, with its small population, still finance its domestic development programs with a comfortable margin for reserves. Its present reserves of foreign exchange—dollars, pounds sterling, and gold—exceed $3 billion and will reach about $5 billion by the end of this year.

Thus Saudi Arabia has no urgent financial incentive to increase oil production to 20 million barrels a day, or even to increase it at all.

It is therefore time for the American people to begin adapting to a new energy age, to a vastly changed world situation, to the realities with which we will have to learn to live. Nothing less than clear thinking, a sense of urgency, and a grasp of what is at risk can lay the base for achieving a durable peace in the Middle East.

So we say: It is time now for the world to insist on a settlement in the Middle East, backed by ironclad and credible guarantees from the United States and the Soviet Union, among others. A settlement that will bring justice and security to all the peoples and all the states of that region. Nobody can afford another war in the Middle East. Nobody. *Nobody.*

None of us can any longer go on just hoping the situation in that part of the world will somehow resolve itself peacefully. Because the alternatives to a just, peaceful, and lasting resolution have become intolerable.

**Mobil®**

In the spring of 1980, the Public Broadcasting Service decided to show a British docudrama called "Death of a Princess." The show told the story of a princess in an unnamed country—it was clearly Saudi Arabia—who had an illicit love affair and was subsequently beheaded by the authorities.

I was familiar with the show, which had previously been aired in England. In the guise of a documentary, "Death of a Princess" had perpetuated a libel about the people and religion of Saudi Arabia. Moreover, the showing of the film on British television had led to strong diplomatic protests from the Saudis and adversely affected British commercial interests in that country.

We ran the ad "A new fairy tale" only after the most serious and careful consideration, and only after we concluded that some statement had to be made about the nature of the show. We were fully aware that by running the ad we would be giving "Death of a Princess" a great deal of publicity, which would probably serve to increase its audience.

But we also felt that it was important to be clear about the consequences of the show. Among other problems, the fact that "Death of a Princess" was being aired on public television might lead other nations to believe that it enjoyed the support of our government. In fact, the State Department deplored the program. But we were doubtful whether America's unique separation of powers would necessarily be appreciated abroad.

Naturally, our opponents claimed that we were trying to intimidate the Public Broadcasting Service and that we had tried to prevent the show from airing. At no point did we make any attempt to stop the show, either through the ad or through other channels. Our goal was not to censor "Death of a Princess" but, rather, to let the viewing public know that this particular story was also libelous and offensive to one of our strategic allies.

# A new fairy tale

On May 12, a number of Public Broadcasting Service stations are scheduled to show a television film which purports to depict certain events and practices in Saudi Arabia When this film was aired several weeks ago in Britain, it caused Saudi Arabia to express its objections to the British Government In Saudi Arabia's view, the film misrepresented its social, religious, and judicial systems and, in effect, was insulting to an entire people and the heritage of Islam.

As a consequence, the following transpired:

● According to *The New York Times*, the British Foreign Secretary sent a letter to Prince Saud Al-Faisal, the Saudi Foreign Minister, expressing his "profound regret"

● *The Times* also reported that the British Foreign Office issued the following statement "It is most unfortunate that Anglo-Saudi relations should have been damaged by a film for which the British Government was in no way responsible and which it could not prevent from being shown on British television or elsewhere We hope it will be possible to restore relations on their normal level as soon as possible"

In our opinion, the proposed showing of this film on public television in the United States raises some very serious issues

1 If we are going to have a free press, what responsibilities and obligations to the well-being of the nation does that freedom impose upon television stations and other media?

2 What are the implications of the fact that congressional appropriations to public television supported, at least indirectly, the production of the film and, if shown, the facilities for dissemination?

3 Does the public regard fictionalized "docu-drama" accounts loosely based on some historical event as accurate portrayals of those events, even though fiction is mixed with so-called fact? Many serious commentators have raised questions about the "docu-drama" format

We believe that if a free society is to survive, we must openly and candidly discuss these issues so that an informed public may make rational judgments

## 1 Obligations of a Free Press

We all know that in the U S, our Constitution guarantees a free and unfettered press However, implicit in that guarantee is the obligation on the part of the press to be responsible Clearly, the people of the U S have the right to expect that the media will not abuse its privilege The public will have to decide whether a "free press" is acting responsibly if it presents a fictionalized story of "events" and thereby demeans another nation's religion and possibly jeopardizes U.S relations with that nation

## 2 The Role of Government Support

Here we have a curious contradiction. Congressional appropriations have indirectly made possible the television structure which helped produce and will disseminate the show We are not suggesting that congressional grants to public television should contain substantive restrictions nor are we suggesting our government in any way is responsible for the film We know, however, that other nations may not understand how one branch of the government may deplore or regret a film offensive to a friendly country while another unwittingly supports it financially

## 3 The "Reality" of Docu-drama

It should be understood that this film is not a news documentary. Rather, it is a drama using actors whose roles and dialogue have been scripted by a writer and, both in terms of visual portrayal and dialogue, must be classified as fiction. Yet, the claim will be that it is a factual presentation of a series of events. In this case, we are not dealing with the rights of a free press to express its views. Rather, we are dealing with a controversial film which most of the viewing audience will take as fact and thereby reach incorrect conclusions. Many television reviewers have raised serious doubts about this type of television which so blurs the distinction between fact and fiction that the viewer doesn't know one from the other.

This issue was discussed in a letter to *The New Statesman* by Penelope Mortimer who worked with Antony Thomas, the show's producer "I was involved with the project for almost a year and present at most of the interviews I accompanied Thomas on his ten-day trip to Saudi Arabia and was with him in Beirut in September 1978 With the exception of Barry Milner, who had already sold his story to the *Daily Express*, Rosemary Buschow, and the Palestinian family in Beirut every interview and every character in the film is fabricated. The 'revelation' of the domestic lives of the Saudi princesses—man-hunting in the desert, rendezvous in boutiques—was taken entirely on the evidence of an expatriate divorcee, as was the story of the princess first seeing her lover on Saudi television No real effort was made to check up on such information Rumour and opinion somehow came to be presented as fact the audience foolishly believing it to be authentic, is conned

That is why we say the show is a new fairy tale

## 4 Conclusion

We hope that the management of the Public Broadcasting Service will review its decision to run this film and exercise responsible judgment in the light of what is in the best interest of the United States

## Mobil

This ad appeared in *The New York Times* on May 8, 1980

The ad "Why do we buy this space?" is one of my favorites, and I cannot understand why we did not think of running it years earlier. By 1981, our program of advocacy ads had become a popular topic of discussion in the press, the business world, and even the universities. There was a considerable amount of speculation about why, exactly, we had embarked on the program and what we stood to gain from it. In view of this, I thought it would be a good idea to address the issue straight on. In the process, of course, we revealed another level of our corporate personality.

# Why do we buy this space?

For more than 12 years now, we've been addressing Americans with weekly messages in principal print media. We've argued, cajoled, thundered, pleaded, reasoned and poked fun. In return, we've been reviled, revered, held up as a model and put down as a sorry example.

Why does Mobil choose to expose itself to these weekly judgments in the court of public opinion? Why do we keep it up now that the energy crisis and the urgent need to address energy issues have eased, at least for the present?

Our answer is that business needs voices in the media, the same way labor unions, consumers, and other groups in our society do. Our nation functions best when economic and other concerns of the people are subjected to rigorous debate. When our messages add to the spectrum of facts and opinion available to the public, even if the decisions are contrary to our preferences, then the effort and cost are worthwhile.

Think back to some of the issues in which we have contributed to the debate.

• Excessive government regulation—it's now widely recognized that Washington meddling, however well intentioned, carries a price tag that the consumer pays.

• The folly of price controls—so clear now that prices of gasoline and other fuels are coming down, now that the marketplace has been relieved of most of its artificial restraints.

• The need for balance between maintaining jobs and production and maintaining a pristine environment—a non-issue, we argued, if there's common sense and compromise on both sides, a view that's now increasingly recognized in Washington.

Over the years, we've won some and lost some, and battled to a draw on other issues we've championed, such as building more nuclear power plants and improving public transportation. We've supported presidents we thought were right in their policies and questioned Democrats and Republicans alike when we thought their policies were counterproductive.

In the process we've had excitement, been congratulated and castigated, made mistakes, and won and lost some battles. But we've enjoyed it. While a large company may seem terribly impersonal to the average person, it's made up of people with feelings, people who care like everybody else. So even when we plug a quality TV program we sponsor on public television, we feel right about spending the company's money to build audience for the show, just as we feel good as citizens to throw the support of our messages to causes we believe in, like the Mobil Grand Prix, in which young athletes prepare for this year's Olympics. Or recognition for the positive role retired people continue to play in our society.

We still continue to speak on a wide array of topics, even though there's no immediate energy crisis to kick around anymore. Because we don't want to be like the mother-in-law who comes to visit only when she has problems and matters to complain about. We think a continuous presence in this space makes sense for us. And we hope, on your part, you find us informative occasionally, or entertaining, or at least infuriating. But never boring. After all, you did read this far, didn't you?

## Mobil

This ad appeared in *The New York Times* on February 9, 1984

The "Observations" ad reproduced here is a good example of how we used that series to discuss some of our negative experiences with the press. The tone is more informal than in our op-ed ads, and the whole texture of the ad is very different. And yet the content is similar to what we are saying each week in the *Times*.

# ⊙bservations

**Good news blues.** *"All I know is just what I read in the papers,"* cracked humorist Will Rogers back in the 1920s. Today, some things that you <u>don't</u> read in newspapers, or see on network TV news, are what you <u>ought</u> to know—especially about **energy**, a field where reporters too often go **tilting at windmills.** Well, as a top journalist put it, *"bad news sells better."*

**Silent knights.** For much of the media, *"covering"* the oil industry means putting a wet blanket on good cheer. A recent example–the heavy silence that greeted government economist Richard Greene's report in the Labor Department's May *Monthly Labor Review.* **Rising energy costs mean more additional sources of energy,** he said…more gas and oil wells completed in six months last year than in all of 1973…more jobs created in the U.S. oil and natural gas industry–almost 50 percent more <u>after</u> rigid price controls began to soften. Quite a contrast to the crusading critics' charges that the oil industry squanders money on *"department stores and circuses."*

*"And that's the opinion of the management of this station…"*

**Surprise!** Sometimes good news is so astounding that the media may be too dazed to report it. Take the recent revelation from Harvard's Energy and Environmental Policy Center. Seems U.S. oil companies <u>undercharged</u> customers by **$5 billion** during the supply crisis following the Iranian revolution. *"We were surprised ourselves,"* said one of the report's authors. But *"the data is clear…major [oil company] prices fell behind the rest."* The reason for the big companies' lagging prices? <u>Pressure from the media and threats from politicians going *"after the most visible and thus the largest"* targets.</u> So who's ripping off whom?

**A little learning….** If the media had properly covered either of these studies (and admitted that some past stories about oil industry "wrongdoings" were inaccurate), <u>you and the rest of the public would have benefited.</u> Some media-watchers have suggested that the fairy tales concocted by *"energy experts"* could be eliminated if reporters **go to school to bone up on energy.** Not a bad idea, especially now, when kids are hitting the books again. After all, as the poet Alexander Pope said: *"A little learning is a dangerous thing."*

---

**It's a fact:** Oil industry profits are big news in the media…but both publishing and broadcasting have been <u>more</u> profitable than oil over the past five years, based on return on stockholders' equity.

---

# Mobil®

In the last few years, of course, the situation has changed. World oil prices have dropped way down, and oil products are plentiful and less expensive than they were. But major issues remain, even though the political climate is more favorable than it used to be. So we will continue to stay in the public eye, for at least two good reasons.

One, we cannot afford to go "in" and "out" with our kind of program. A company loses credibility if it goes public only when it needs support. It must *be there*, and it must vary the mix. It must be pleasant, amusing, or public-spirited some of the time, if it wants an audience when it has something to complain about. That means visibility — week after week, in the same space — a continuing, dependable presence.

Two, we at Mobil think there is a continuing need for business voices in the national dialogue on public issues. If more such voices had spoken up during the past fifty years, perhaps more people would have questioned our economic direction, and business would be in a better position. Because the media still give a hearing to antibusiness critics, qualified or not, and because businesspeople are portrayed as venal and corrupt on many television programs, business needs a voice of its own *in* the media — a voice that cannot be silenced or blue-penciled to make its message innocuous.

So, if I were asked to advise other organizations on the conduct of public affairs, I would say: *Speak out, continually and consistently, and do not be afraid of confrontation.*

Because Mobil is one voice among many, it is impossible to pinpoint precisely what we have achieved. However, I think we *can* claim that such a policy has worked well for us:

- We have greatly improved our own image — and maybe that of the oil industry — since the 1960s. Key target groups, including the news media and members of government, *do* understand us better than they did. They do not love us — we do not expect that — but they respect us more.
- We are recognized as an outspoken, responsible company with high visibility and high credibility.

- We have sparked public debate on many issues important to us.
- We have provided the public with an alternative source of information on major national issues.

And I think I should add: We have had a lot of fun running our political campaign. We still do.

# 9

# Realities of Lobbying and Governmental Affairs

*Phil Cates*

Lobbying is vital to effective issues management. It provides two-way communication between a company and a select group of listeners. The information a company gains by listening to legislators and regulators can help it understand the currents and shoals of public policy. This information may find its way into strategic planning—but the major value of lobbying is to help the company have an effective voice among regulators and legislators. This model of lobbying flies in the face of the stereotype of lobbyists as deep-pocket spenders trying to unfairly manipulate the political process. The primary role of lobbying is to bring about or prevent legislation in a company's interest, which also is in the interest of those who count on the company to deliver goods and services, pay wages and taxes, and provide profit and dividends. The ideal of effective lobbying is to help achieve reasonable, sound, and fair public policy.

There are many kinds of lobbyists. From schoolteachers to cab drivers, everyone in this country has an opinion on how our government should be run. When I tell people I am a lobbyist, their first reaction is often one of not knowing how to relate to a lobbyist or even what lobbying is. I sense that the common perception of a lobbyist is of some sort of "fat cat," doing easy work, throwing plenty of money at issues he or she may favor. Not so!

Why include the subject of lobbying in a book on issues management? Not only to describe the do's and don't's of lobbying but also to describe the role lobbying plays in the American political and governmental process and the importance of lobbying in protecting profit margins for business and industry. This latter goal is of particular value to issues management.

A lobbyist is defined as anyone who represents a particular position on an issue before a public decision maker. A public decision maker may be an elected official or an appointed regulatory officer. As my fellow lobbyist Jack Dillard stated in a 1983 speech, when "you add up all the so-called 'special interests' represented by lobbyists—schoolteachers, cab drivers, small businessmen, insurance salesmen, laborers, farmers, ranchers, oilmen, doctors, public employees, bankers, automobile dealers, wholesalers, retailers, pro-abortionists, anti-abortionists, environmentalists, real estate agents, manufacturers, pro-ERAers, anti-ERAers, and so on, ad infinitum, you will, in the aggregate, have far more than the sum total of all the people in the United States. In other words, it is 'We the People' whom lobbyists represent."

Lobbying involves representing an interest, that of the company or organization for whom the lobbyist works. But larger interests are also at stake. To balance the interests involved, a lobbyist must be realistic without losing his or her identity or integrity. In the legislative arena, maintaining one's realism can be a challenge. In the world of politics, many forces appear unrealistic when judged against the lives most of us live. Many facts of political life may seem unreal to the majority of people.

As well as being realistic, a lobbyist must keep a sense of integrity. Peck (1978), speaking about life in the business world, says, "The road that a great executive must travel between the preservation and the loss of his or her identity and integrity is extraordinarily narrow, and very, very few really make the trip successfully." Peck makes this statement when discussing the "selective withholding of one's opinions from time to time in the world of business or politics if one is to be welcomed into the councils of power" (p. 62). Simply put, in lobbying, one's personal opinions or feelings will often differ from the political reality. Keeping one's opinions or feelings separate from the realities of the political and legislative worlds is a tough but essential task for good lobbying. Those who can be political realists have a chance to be effective lobbyists. Those who do not accept political realities do not have a chance to be even mediocre lobbyists.

The three sections of this chapter will address the reality of working in the legislative arena. As you will see, there is no one right way to integrate issues management, public policy, and the legislative process, but there are many wrong ways to approach the task of lobbying. The first section cites examples of non-professional approaches and offers definite guidelines for one professional approach. The second section is a case study that illustrates one successful effort. The last section tells of the responsibility of business and industry, and to some degree other groups, for participation in the political process through responsible and professional lobbying.

## Making It Work in the Legislature

Good lobbying is far more than following procedures and applying skills. It is more art than science. Professional lobbying is the result of strategic planning and of integrating issues management, public policy, and the legislative process. Passing, killing, or amending a bill for your client or employer is justification enough for the funding and implementation of sound issues management programs—even though many corporate executives view lobbying as a necessary evil and support it uncomfortably.

Lobbying is a discipline different from public relations, public affairs, media relations, environmental affairs, corporate law, community affairs, and a number of other staff service functions, although it interfaces with all these functions. Lobbying demands the same relationships, skills, and working knowledge of operating divisions as the other staff service departments under the umbrella of "public affairs."

Lobbying is as important as other corporate disciplines. Productivity measured in profit margins is protected by good lobbying. If governmental affairs is mixed with marketing or any other function, the conflicting results expose profit margins to the legislative wilds that any smart executive seeks to avoid. Political carnage of business profit is a virtual certainty when business fails to maintain the proper legislative relationship. Corporations will in one way or another pay homage to the political system and especially to the legislative process.

Several basic procedures must be followed and adequate attention given to details. For instance, the force of both civil and criminal penalties exists in all fifty states and on the national level to ensure that those who practice the art of influencing politicians will do so within clearly defined limits. Legal restrictions set the boundaries of what a lobbyist can and cannot do. Important for successful lobbying is knowing and implementing what a lobbyist should know and do and knowing but not doing what should not be done. It is important to know when not to be seen or heard and to have the self-control to do so. This calls for a well-tuned sense of timing in applying the interpersonal skills of lobbying, and it is what makes lobbying an art rather than a science.

This point was made resoundingly during the 1983 regular session of the Mississippi legislature, when the house and senate members were asked to complete an official ballot to select the recipient of the "Worst Lobbyist" award. The guidelines, as recorded in a Jackson newspaper account, clearly identified what legislators considered necessary attributes for a successful lobbyist. The lobbyist must "tell the truth whenever possible; provide free food and drink at every opportunity; not become a pest." The Jackson newspaper article also mentioned two views of lobbyists widely shared by legislators as well as business executives: (1) "scumbag, palm-greasing, slick-operating sleazes" and (2) "protectors of the democratic process."

The first is a jerk and the second is a saint. Neither of these describes today's professional lobbyist. Some, though, have not faced this political reality. Having served eight years in the Texas house of representatives before becoming a lobbyist, I know what I appreciated and what I found abrasive from the lobbyists

working the legislature, as we dealt with well over 20,000 bills
and resolutions during this period.

Mike Hazle, a colleague in my department at Tenneco, has
corporate state governmental affairs responsibilities for twelve
western states. He made the point best about what a lobbyist
should not be when he was describing our lobbying operation to
a high school teacher in Houston. The teacher had asked what
advice to give his students about preparing themselves to enter
the lobbying profession. Hazle told the teacher that the last
person a corporation would want representing its interests before a legislative body would be a "jerk." Here the word *jerk*
means someone who is stupid, foolish, and unconventional to
the point that people seek to avoid that person. In the political
arena, a business has enough problems without having a "jerk"
representing its interests. However, one need not be a beauty
queen, a superjock, or an Einstein to best represent business in
the legislative arena. Extreme personality types should be
avoided. I have known good lobbyists who were good athletes,
smart, and so forth. But I have known none who was a "jerk."

Like any other component of our system of government,
lobbying, if not kept within bounds, can be dangerous. The
reporting of abuse is the most public part of the lobbying
profession. When abuse occurs, the public often learns from
media reports the details that strike terror in the hearts of
executives and managers responsible for lobbying programs.

The rest of the world may view the oil and gas companies
as united in their lobbying efforts. It would make sense for an
industry that has such bad public relations and so few friends in
the press or in the legislative assemblies, as well as in the public
as a whole, to be united so as to best face all this opposition.
However, it is not united. The truth is that oil and gas company
lobbyists sometimes seem to dislike one another more even than
they dislike their enemies outside the industry. This makes lobbying tough. The intraindustry hatred is the most intense between marketing personnel. It seems to me that some company
marketing people would rather damage the entire industry than
lose a marketing advantage to another company.

Several times I have heard oil companies' governmental

relations people remark about the lack of agreement among companies concerning a bill before a state legislature. These comments extend to the lack of strategic unity to work members of a legislative body for or against a bill on which the industry agrees in principle. After listening to these frustrations, with which I often agree, I point out that if we agreed and worked in unison on every issue, we might do great harm to our government by exercising so great an influence. Other lobbyists, knowing how much I love to win legislative battles, smile and admit that winning on every legislative issue might not be in the best interest of good public policy or maybe even our business interest.

An effective business approach to governmental affairs was best described by Gordon Bonfield in a speech on the external environment made to Texas A&M M.B.A. graduates in September 1983. Mr. Bonfield is a senior vice-president and group executive responsible for Tenneco's external affairs functions. When speaking about the lobbying structure of Tenneco, he described the real-world approach that Tenneco takes toward lobbying activities: "They lay out options and deal in the art of the possible. It's rare that we obtain what seems the ideal solution to us."

No lobbying program can be effective without support and understanding from the highest levels of the organization. This is especially true for corporate lobbying. The support must be consistent. The understanding must be realistic. In this regard, management must understand how lobbying can serve the company's interest. For instance, taxation and regulation are threats to achieving and maintaining necessary profit margins. Good lobbying may not produce profit, but it can reduce or eliminate the loss of profit. When a business is overly taxed or unduly regulated so that its profit margin is diminished or destroyed, the company will suffer. The lobbying program should be well balanced between the flexibility to deal with political realities and corporate accountability. Then resources are neither wasted nor used to abuse the system.

In addition to receiving top-management support, lobbying must be expected to perform a vital range of functions. The major function of lobbying is to communicate with persons who can influence the future of the company. Monitoring is another vital function. To be most effective, however, lobbying should not be limited to monitoring and report writing or to entertaining or spending money on elected and regulatory officials.

Lobbying is often limited to monitoring and reporting legislative and political activities when governmental affairs responsibilities are included in corporate departments with other responsibilities, such as corporate law, public affairs, public relations, media relations, or marketing. A natural desire for the corporate executive or manager who lacks experience in the political arena is to require continual reporting by the governmental affairs operatives on their activities. The danger is that the monitoring and report writing will become the dominant function of the program. Passing legislation, killing legislation, or amending legislation will be secondary to reporting, and influencing legislation on the company's behalf may not even be at the forefront. Some people charged with so-called lobbying duties are lost in frustration because of an incorrect or blurred understanding of what those duties entail. They do not have a realistic understanding of politics or lobbying.

Sometimes when management finds its company is taking a beating in the legislative arena, it decides to spend vast sums on officials or on hiring more legislative operatives. A few lobbyists follow the old philosophy of relying exclusively on wining and dining legislators or spending money on gifts for officials. Certain of these practices may be within the limits of the law, but they can nevertheless be counterproductive if they are not in good taste. There are a right way and many wrong ways to spend money directly on officials. The law must always guide this activity, and good taste must always limit this practice to a greater extent than the law does. A successful program does not consist totally of spending money on entertaining, feeding, or buying gifts for elected officials. Successful lobbying is not that simple.

Any effective lobbying effort will consider the advisability of involving key company personnel in the effort. Some corporate executives, managers, and other employees are gifted at putting the company's best foot forward in the governmental affairs arena. However, some people who are good in their business responsibilities do not realize the dangers involved in dealing with legislative and political matters. Insensitive and untalented businesspeople can hurt their cause by getting involved in governmental affairs.

One such story is about an oil company marketing manager in Florida who testified at a legislative hearing on his company's position about tax considerations for gasohol. The meeting took place several years ago, during the energy crisis. Oil companies were being credited with a great deal of responsibility for the crisis by many legislators. Legislation was blossoming in virtually every state and on the national level to divest the oil companies from portions of the oil and gas business. This particular legislative committee was considering a proposal to set a lower sales tax on gasohol than on other fuels as an incentive for production and use of synthetic fuels. A member of the legislative committee asked the marketing manager why his company wanted the proposal to pass. The manager, who was very good in the marketing area, responded by saying, in effect, that if the bill being considered were to become law, then his company, along with the other oil companies, would control the whole gasohol market, just as they did the oil and gas market. This hurt his position on the bill as well as the industry's interest on several legislative measures.

Another story is about a company's vice-president, a respected businessman, who testified before a committee in the Alabama house of representatives. Oil company lobbyists had the votes in the committee to pass the bill, and they had carefully explained their reasons for supporting the legislation to the house leadership and the committee members individually. None of the more than twenty committee members disagreed with the industry's position. This was a winning situation for the oil companies, which is rare in the legislative process. The committee testimony was little more than window dressing. Then the vice-president testified. He was doing well until one man on the legislative committee began flirting with a pretty clerk at the back of the room. The vice-president, at this point, made a statement that he did not appreciate this legislator's not giving full attention to the committee proceedings—especially the vice-president's testimony. Then he went on to say that if he did his job the way some legislators did theirs, he would have been fired from his company thirty-five years ago. Because of this testimony, the bill was defeated.

One last illustration of a kind of naiveté on the part of business when dealing with the legislative process: A group of company lawyers were called into a state capitol the day before a legislative committee hearing on an important bill. They were asked to draft a very technical amendment. After spending a full day and much of the night drafting the amendment, the lawyers were shocked and dismayed when the committee adopted the amendment without questions. Having worked out the reasons for including each word in the technical amendment, they were dismayed that the committee would accept their work without what they viewed as any concern for or understanding of the legal and technical issues involved. What they failed to understand is that a member of the legislature who is considering thousands of pieces of legislation is not interested in the legal or technical details as long as those who are experts in the area agree that the language will solve the problems.

"A good lobbyist is an honest and accurate broker of needed information," says Sam Genovese of the Tenneco state governmental affairs department. However, a good lobbyist, like a good legislator, cannot be an expert on technical details and legal ramifications for every issue. A person representing business interests in the legislative arena who wants to show how smart he is by discussing these technical details at great length with elected officials soon finds that legislators are avoiding him. Businesspeople are active in politics on an individual level. They have as much at stake as other people, if not more, in who is elected to public office. They have as much insight as anyone else, if not more, into what laws should be enacted. They have as much concern with the administration of these laws as anyone. But they do not necessarily know how to best represent a company's interests in lobbying a bill.

One of the best resources an organization has in the

political arena is its people, who make the company's position into a flesh-and-blood matter for legislators rather than just one of the many business positions on a given issue. Lobbying requires familiarity with certain skills and techniques. There are three essential characteristics of a successful lobbyist: (1) one's ability to pass, kill, or amend legislation for the advantage of a client, (2) one's personal credibility, and (3) one's ability to facilitate the flow of information or to educate company personnel as well as officials. If a lobbyist cannot pass, kill, or amend legislation, there is no other criterion to justify his or her salary or office space. This so-called lobbyist may have great integrity, know all the technical details on a given issue, and be a great debater. But these are window dressing unless the lobbyist can pass, kill, or amend bills.

The credibility of a lobbyist can be tried and found lacking by an elected official only once. A lobbyist can lie or mislead an elected official only one time. A lobbyist's personal credibility must be consistently maintained to have legislative clout.

The third essential is the ability to facilitate the flow of information or to educate. A good lobbyist can never know enough about an issue and should work to grasp the technical and general knowledge on a subject. But the lobbyist must use the information wisely to inform legislators, not to dazzle or bore them.

## A Case Study: Florida Divorcement Repeal

The issue in this case study was a state statute that prohibited refiners of oil into gasoline from owning and operating their own gasoline outlets. The statute, Section 526.151, enacted by the Florida legislature in 1974 during the height of the energy crisis, was known as the Florida gasoline retail marketing divorcement bill. A Florida court ruled the bill unconstitutional shortly after it was passed.

Ten years later, in the summer of 1984, a distributor of gasoline appealed this ruling to the Florida Court of Appeals, which overturned the lower court's decision, thus making the bill constitutional. The latest decision placed the commissioner of agriculture in the position of implementing rules and regula-tions to enforce the divorcement law. Despite a split within the industry and against the odds, key members of the industry lobbied the legislature to repeal the statute, which had been on the books since 1974. This effort was successful: On June 5, 1985, Governor Bob Graham signed into law Committee Substitute for House Bill 690, repealing Section 526.151.

Had the statute not been repealed during the 1985 legisla-tive session, Tenneco would have had to close, sell, or drastically alter the way it operated all its convenience-store gasoline out-lets in Florida—almost half of its over 400 such outlets nation-wide in 1985. Tenneco has a small share of the gasoline market, and that corner of the market is based on a directly operated convenience-store concept. Unlike major gasoline marketers, Tenneco does not have in place the middle distribution level known as oil jobbers. Tenneco could not afford to establish such a system. Tenneco, a relative newcomer as a gasoline retailer, had to build on a consumer-attractive gasoline marketing network to compete with companies that were already well established. The convenience-store concept allowed Tenneco to build a directly operated gasoline market business without the cost of a jobber distribution system. Under the statute, Tenneco would have been forced out of the gasoline marketing business.

Before the campaign to repeal the statute, Tenneco en-joyed a good image in Florida. An example of Tenneco's ac-tivities that helped in creating this positive image is the dona-tion of a retired offshore platform as a fishing reef in Florida waters in September 1982.

An extensive grass-roots and third-party campaign was essential to victory. A total of more than 5,161 written contacts with elected officials was achieved by—

- Non-oil-company Tenneco employees living in Florida (around 400 generated from Philadelphia Life, J I Case, and Car X Muffler employees).
- Tenneco Oil Company employees (around 545 generated).
- Tenneco Oil Company credit-card holders and retirees (over 3,475 generated).

- Documented third-party contacts instigated by Tenneco employees (at least 741 generated).

These were quality contacts, implemented directly by Tenneco. The all-out effort produced, conservatively, more than double this many legislative contacts. Mobil generated around 50,000 contacts through a postcard mailing effort that paralleled Tenneco's program. Never before, during my six years with Tenneco, have I seen so much effort by as many people on any other single issue.

The best form of communication with an elected official is the face-to-face approach; next is telephoning. Writing to elected officials is the third-best way to communicate with them if coordinated properly. Those who write to elected officials are often under the impression that they should use canned form letters, a certain "suggested wording" for a postcard or telegram, or, better yet, a word-processed letter. Quite the contrary! Rather than a telegram, a personalized word-processed letter, a printed postcard, or any number of other forms of written communication, there is no substitute for a handwritten letter from a voter to his or her elected official. Someone recently said that most members of the U.S. Congress can be swayed on any given issue by fifteen to twenty letters. The handwritten letter is rare in legislative mail.

During my eight years in the Texas legislature, I received fewer than twenty handwritten letters from voters in my rural legislative district. When someone cares enough to use her own words to voice her opinion on an issue, an elected official will personally read the letter. Form letters, telegrams, postcards, word-processed letters, and even individually typed letters are for the most part handled by the staff. Some legislators say they are a dime a dozen. Petitions are the least influential form of communication with elected officials.

Short of personal visits face to face or by phone, our first-, second-, and third-party constituencies were asked to send handwritten letters to their state representatives and state senators asking for repeal of the retail market divorcement statute.

The opposition included a major oil company and various others who joined it from time to time during the period of the repeal effort. In the end, only the major oil company publicly opposed the measure repealing divorcement. The jobbers, dealers, and other companies supported repeal. Even the sponsor of the 1974 bill to be repealed, Senator Curtis Peterson, did not vote against the repeal when it passed the senate. Not only did the senator not vote against the repeal, he did not use a valid point of order that would have delayed, if not defeated, repeal in 1985.

Senator Peterson's statesmanlike behavior in allowing repeal of a law he had placed on Florida's books ten years earlier raises an important point concerning the place of revenge in the legislative process. A friend, Stan Hudson, who once lobbied the Florida legislature, shared this thought with me in 1986: "Revenge is unforgivable for professional legislative consultants. Proponents should be appreciated and opponents should be forgiven. One cannot expect every legislator to agree on all bills, amendments, and procedures. For in the future there will be other issues, bills, and causes, and lobbyists will then need all the friends they can get. Those who burn their bridges behind them will soon lose their effectiveness." One basic part of human nature must be overcome to lobby effectively: the natural inclination to dislike someone who has done you in. The legislator or the lobbyist who is fighting you tooth and nail on a given issue may in the next moment be down in the ditch with you, working on your side for or against the next piece of legislation being considered.

For Tenneco, repeal of the gasoline market divorcement law was an effort that demanded our best lobbying. Every tactic that is legal and professional was used to achieve the repeal of the ten-year-old law. There is a political phrase that describes this effort best. When you want a politician in Texas to know he has your full support in his campaign, you tell him you are behind him with your "money, marbles, and chalk." This represents commitment of the necessary resources in the political process. For Tenneco, all the necessary resources were committed to winning this issue. Money was dedicated to campaigns;

time of our people was committed; and planning and strategy were developed. These were our money, marbles, and chalk.

There was plenty of lead time to work the issue. This is rare. Since many state legislatures meet for short periods, the response time to lobby on an issue is often very short. In Florida, the court of appeals rendered its decision in the summer of 1984. Establishing a procedure for the agriculture commissioner to promulgate the rules and regulations to enforce the law lasted through the legislative session, which did not begin until April 1985.

The effort to repeal the Florida divorcement law demanded the efforts of several full-time lobbyists. In comparing the merits of full-time and part-time lobbyists, Stan Hudson told me: "There are occasions when part-time lobbyists can accomplish their goals; however, their responsibilities are usually limited to minor issues and writing general reports. Part-time lobbyists normally work only while the legislature is in session and . . . may or may not represent several clients simultaneously. Many years ago a lobbyist's reputation was judged by the number of clients he represented. The more clients—the better his reputation. After a few sessions of wasteful spending, conflicts of interest, and ineffective results, it was concluded this method was penny-wise and pound-foolish."

The best time to visit an elected official is when there is no pending legislative matter in which you have a vested interest. For a part-time lobbyist this is more difficult than for a full-time lobbyist. The campaign season, when elected officials are seeking your help, is a very good time to make legislative contacts. The contacts on which a sound working relationship between a lobbyist and an elected official are built, however, must go beyond the election season. The best time would most likely be between legislative sessions. When you can stop by the legislator's home or office, tell her you are not there to ask for her vote or help on anything, and wish her well—then you have done the best in establishing a personal relationship that in the future may give you the opportunity to explain your position on an issue.

In Florida, the strategy was to maximize our political

leverage through campaign contributions, direct contacts with company employees and their local legislators, telling our story through the media, brokering the information to the legislators, the legislative staffs, the governor, and other statewide elected officials, getting our third-party constituencies involved on our behalf, and working to keep the industry as close to our position as possible. Whenever possible, a local company employee, a colleague with our oil company—Phil Brooks—and I would meet with candidates to deliver contributions across the state. This was carried out before the elections in the fall of 1984.

Contrary to what may be popular opinion, you cannot pass, kill, or amend a bill solely because of campaign contributions. The most you can expect from making a campaign contribution to an elected official is the entree to explain your position on a legislative matter and the willingness of the particular official to help you if he or she can. We expect only to be able to communicate with a candidate to whom we have contributed. There are those both making contributions and receiving them who attach a different meaning to contributions.

Being questioned about a legal violation in dealing with campaign funds has caused many candidates to lose their elections. Some lobbyists have been rendered ineffective and even imprisoned for such offenses.

From time to time the staff of our department at Tenneco is called on to get out the votes of our employees, especially in national elections. As a part of this effort, the October 1984 issue of *Tenneco Topics*, our in-house employee newspaper, carried two articles emphasizing the importance of the elections on November 6. One of these appeared under the heading "VOTE AMERICA—YOUR VOTE COUNTS":

### EMPLOYEE KNOWS EVERY VOTE COUNTS

"Every vote counts in an election."

Phil Cates, regional coordinator for Tenneco, Inc., governmental affairs and a former State Representative in Texas, can attest to that. Cates won his first nomination to the House of Represen-

tatives by just two votes. He jokes that if his parents
had not voted, he would not have won the race.

"I was twenty-four, still green in politics, and
had graduated from West Texas State University
just the year before," explained Cates. "Friends
from my church, school, and community organizations urged me to run. Little did we know what a
close and memorable race it would be. We all
learned how much every single vote counts.

"Unfortunately, only a minority of people
vote, which means that a minority of citizens run
this country," said Cates. "We all should be more
responsible and accountable in the election of our
public officials."

Voting is essential to being a good citizen. Being a good citizen is
basic to being a good lobbyist. To be a good lobbyist, one must
assist in giving campaign contributions and getting out the vote.

In addition to putting money were it counted in Florida,
Tenneco mapped the strategy and directed the personnel to
mobilize the first-, second-, and third-party constituencies. The
industry also sought public support through the media and
legislative hearings process. The first-party constituents were
employees who could lose their jobs unless the law was repealed.
These were the most effective people for repeal in communicating with legislators. Next came the second-party constituents—
other non-oil-company Tenneco employees within the state who
could effectively support repeal with their elected officials. Tenneco Oil Company credit-card holders and retirees could do
likewise. Finally, third-party constituencies consisted of vendors
who would be adversely affected if gasoline outlets in Florida
closed, as well as banks and organizations such as the state and
local chambers. All these were activated. This could be seen in
the letter files and telephone logs in each senator and representative's office.

These letters had substantial impact on the media. Editorials and legislative reports in both the print and the electronic media identified Tenneco as the company on which re-

peal would have the most impact. It was as though some reporter had been reading the legislators' mail on the issue. The capitol reporters do have a close working relationship with most legislators in Tallahassee. Since Tenneco was most affected by divorcement in legislators' minds and in public opinion, the risk of having our repeal effort labeled as a profit grab by big oil companies was avoided.

One big oil company placed itself on the other side by talking about how small, directly operated companies were the strongest competition for big oil companies. Opposition of our effort to repeal the bill, coming from a big oil company, helped our effort by dispelling the potential argument that divorcement would in some way control or hurt big oil, an argument that had been effectively used for divorcement in Alabama and Georgia.

The big company's opposition was good for another reason: It made a strong argument that involving government in business operations most often is poor public policy. Governmental involvement in pricing and marketing of a product often hurts the consumer. Part of the package included in the repeal bill was language that would regulate pricing of certain fuel below "cost." This would, in theory, prohibit on a state level what is described as pricing below cost in order to drive competition out of business. In this case, the claim by the big oil company failed to garner support because allowing divorcement to be the law in Florida permitted more governmental regulation of free enterprise than did the bill we passed.

The prohibition of below-cost sales that would injure competition was the compromise with jobbers to be included in the bill to get their support for repeal of divorcement. For Tenneco, faced with going out of the gasoline marketing business, prohibiting below-cost sales was a price well worth paying. For the big oil company opposing repeal, which has an extensive jobber network as well as some directly operated company-owned outlets, the principle of keeping government out of the marketing of gasoline was more important than repealing divorcement.

Part of a letter from a lobbyist for one of the big oil

companies about the Tenneco effort will cap the story and show why we were successful in spite of the odds against getting the bill repealed. Mike Kumpf, lobbyist with Standard Oil of Ohio, wrote to Art Rutrough of Tenneco: "Our industry really had an uphill fight in reaching a compromise in Florida to repeal the retail divorcement law there. Those companies, like yours and mine, which saw the political necessity for the compromise were often criticized by fellow companies. We were also subject to a great deal of personal stress, due to the intensity of the negotiations with the jobbers and our own individual corporate positions and needs."

The letter continues by praising Tenneco's team efforts and the skill of our lobbyists who worked effectively with the Florida legislature. By working together and achieving reasonable compromise, we were successful. The Florida house and senate voted unanimously to repeal divorcement.

## Responsibility for Good Public Policy

How do the activities illustrated in the Florida divorcement case, such as writing to elected officials or giving campaign contributions, come together to pass, kill, or amend legislation for the benefit of the organization while also contributing to good public policy?

A lobbyist's style is important, but not to the degree it was a few years ago. More important today in lobbying is the "selling" of one's position on an issue by showing how that position contributes to the establishment or maintenance of good public policy. This is important to elected officials. This, for them, is good politics. They want to be seen promoting what is in favor of good public policy. A position can be sold to politicians on this basis even when it is an uphill fight.

The work necessary to build the case for a position on a legislative matter can no longer be replaced by charm or personality, although one's style must be appropriate in selling the argument for or against a bill. There is seldom, if ever, time to check back with corporate headquarters, since a bill can be considered and passed in a matter of days, if not hours.

The private sector should be concerned about the development and maintenance of good public policy. This must be an ongoing process.

In his book *America's Third Revolution,* Irving Shapiro (1984), former chair of the board of Du Pont, says, "All sorts of institutions in society have been unwilling, for one reason or another, to restrain immediate wants in favor of longer-term benefits, their own included. Leaders in government, labor, and business have worn blinders and seen issues too narrowly. Each group has maneuvered for its own gains without asking where such a chain of events would probably, even inevitably, lead" (p. x).

A number of excellent lobbyists share a commitment to maintenance of good government while they work to benefit their clients' interests. They press hard for the client's position; they use style and present the best arguments for that position; they accept reality and therefore deal in compromise rather than harbor unrealistic expectations. Those who would revert to the old days when style and personal friendship were all that was necessary to pass, kill, or amend a bill are out of touch. Today, style and personal friendship are very important, but less so than the larger issue of one's position on a legislative measure as that position makes a contribution to good public policy. The business lobbyist must follow a path of preparation, presentation, and acceptance of the reality that one rarely obtains what seems the ideal solution.

Although the emphasis in government has moved away from style and personality, shifting toward substance in the form of a business position's contribution to good public policy, some things remain the same. One notable constant is that a business must maintain a professional lobbying program.

The Texas Association of Business has a motto that has not lost meaning as the emphasis in legislative arenas has shifted from style to substance. As long as we have the governmental and economic system in place that we have had in this country for more than 200 years, the significance of this motto will not change. This motto is "Get into Politics or Get out of Business."

Lobbying is an essential component of our system. It must stay within due bounds. But in a representative democracy, lobbying is an integral balancing mechanism through education of elected officials and equally through emphasizing the necessity of good public policy for the client's economic and political well-being.

### ❖❖❖ 10

# Soliciting Support Through Political Action Committees

## *Herbert E. Alexander*

The essence of political action committees (PACs) is that they are delivery systems. They developed in the private sector and then were legitimized by the courts and the Congress, in each case to deliver money to politicians. This PACs have done so successfully that they have generated a great deal of controversy.

PACs also deliver information to their members and to elected representatives whose campaigns they help support. Obviously, issues affect the internal and external environments of both PACs and their sponsors. The PACs' role in the political process is to spend their money on political issues, communication strategies, and lobbying—tasks requiring skills in persuasion and in interpersonal relations.

### PACs Defined

The notable growth of political interests in organizations, including activist groups, environmental action committees, antinuclear coalitions, women's caucuses, gay-rights advocacy groups, senior citizens' alliances, and a host of others, indicates that many citizens recognize the value of organized political action. Enactment of the Federal Election Campaign Act of 1971 (FECA), with its 1974, 1976, and 1979 amendments, encouraged the growth of political action committees, many representing these very issue groups but many, of course, representing business, labor, and other interest groups as well (Alexander and Haggerty, 1981).

A PAC is a political arm organized by a corporation, labor union, trade association, or professional, agrarian, ideological, or issue group to support candidates for elective office and, by inference, to defeat others. PACs raise funds for their activities by seeking voluntary contributions, which are aggregated into larger, more meaningful amounts and then contributed to favored candidates or political-party committees.

This traditional definition of PACs, however, fails to convey fully their function in the political arena. More descriptively, PACs can be defined as effective solicitation systems with outreach potential to attract greater participation. They are the most visible evidence of the exchange of big givers for big solicitors; by this is meant that the FECA's imposition of contribution limitations not only diminished the potential for big givers but also put emphasis on seeking out larger numbers of smaller contributors, a process effectively achieved through group efforts.

Thus PACs are tools or mediating structures legitimized by law. They act as an institutionalized outreach by providing a process to gather contributions systematically through groups of like-minded persons for whom issues are a cohering element in their political activity.

To solicit funds, groups have employee or membership lists and hence great outreach potential. For example, corporations have three characteristics essential to effective fund raising — large aggregates of executive and administrative personnel (and shareholders for publicly held companies), internal means of communication, and goals that are affected by politics. Labor unions and environmental groups, among membership organizations, have similar characteristics. The PACs of such groups are only too willing to spend money — and corporations, labor unions, and trade associations can use treasury or dues money to establish and administer their PACs and raise funds for them — in order to aggregate small donations into more meaningfully sized contributions to candidates they want to support. Candidates could not afford to reach out to all eligible corporate employees or union members, but PACs of such organizations can. This functional analysis of PACs as solicitation systems spurring participation leads neatly to a conceptualization of PACs as organizations whose growth was inevitable given the needs for political money compounded by low contribution limits requiring that big money be raised in smaller sums, thus facilitating delivery of both money and information about issues.

### Genesis of PACs

Before the enabling provisions of the Federal Election Campaign Act, there were very few corporate PACs. Extant PACs were mainly labor PACs. Among the earliest corporate PACs, although they were not called PACs then, were Aerojet-General's Good Citizenship Campaign, established in 1958, and Hughes Aircraft's Active Citizenship Fund, organized in 1964. But not until the 1974 amendments permitting government contractors to establish PACs, and the Federal Election Commission's 1975 SUNPAC decision (AO 1975-23), did corporate PAC growth take off.

Robert E. Mutch, a political scientist, has written about the uneven historical development of PACs: "PACs are formed to pool small contributions from large numbers of people; this explains why labor unions, whose primary political resource is their membership, created such funds as early as 1943, while corporations, whose primary political resource is their treasury, saw no reason to do the same. But when Congress limited the amount of money an individual could contribute, it also closed, or at least narrowed, a loophole through which much corporate money had flowed. This unpleasant fact put corporations, for the first time, in the position of having to solicit contributions; precisely what PACs were invented to do" (Mutch, forthcoming).

That political action committees should come under fire from individuals and groups espousing the cause of political reform is fraught with irony, for the PAC phenomenon is in many ways a consequence of early efforts to reform politics.

In the 1950s political reformers in New York, in California, and elsewhere launched movements to replace the patronage-hungry, nonideological political-party machines still dominant in many large cities and state capitals with an issue-oriented politics that would attract an emerging segment of the electorate: the growing numbers of college-educated, suburban-dwelling voters who prized ideas and dialogue and espoused such far-reaching causes as civil rights, equality of opportunity, protection of the environment, and preservation of world peace. In significant measure this reform movement succeeded, but over the years the issues many voters cared about narrowed, or at least changed, as single-issue groups evolved in unexpected ways. Yet all the emergent PACs, whether corporate, labor, or ideological, are supremely issue-oriented—a goal the reformers long sought.

Another reason for the growth of PACs is the shift from geographical, or neighborhood, politics to socioeconomic, or interest group, politics. Corporations and labor unions, for example, are socioeconomic units replacing geographical precincts. Because the workplace and the vocational specialty have come to attract the allegiance of the politically active citizen, loyalties to PACs are replacing loyalties once enjoyed by the political parties. PACs can focus on single issues or give priority to emerging issues and still survive with small but devoted constituencies, whereas parties must be more broadly based in order to thrive.

The number of PACs registered with the Federal Election Commission (FEC) has risen dramatically, though no longer at the rapid rates of the 1970s. Their numbers increased 123 percent from 1976 to 1980, only 57 percent from 1980 to 1984. Rates of increase differ by category, some types growing much faster than the overall rate. From 1974 to 1984, the number of corporate PACs more than doubled, from 809 to 1,682. Since 1980 the numbers of corporate PAC registrations at the FEC have begun to level off. Through the years, the number of labor union PACs grew slowly, since few new unions were formed and some mergers occurred. In addition, there are many more corporations than there are unions. Today, almost half of all registered PACs are corporate, and they outnumber labor PACs more than 4 to 1 (Federal Election Commission, 1986).

The 1979–80 election cycle was the first in which contributions to congressional candidates by corporate PACs surpassed contributions by labor PACs. In the 1985–86 election cycle, labor PACs contributed $31.0 million to Senate and House candidates, while their corporate counterparts gave $49.4 million.

Since 1980, the fastest-growing group of PACs has been the nonsponsored ones, mostly ideological or single-issue, without ties to either corporations or unions. Some of these PACs make independent expenditures to support or oppose candidates, but most other PACs—corporate, labor, and trade association—do not.

### Business-Related PACs

The focus of this chapter is on "business-related" PACs, a more meaningful classification than corporate PACs alone. This category includes the corporate sector but also the trade association PACs whose orientation serves the business community; these include general groups, such as the Business Industry Political Action Committee (BIPAC), and specific groups, such as the American Bankers Association's BANKPAC. BANKPAC's activities supplement the work of the banking corporate PACs, enhancing the overall effect. But this too can be misleading, because corporate and trade association PACs are not monolithic. Some serve "high tech" industries, others' interests are of the "smokestack" variety; some favor high tariffs, others do not; the steel PACs and the aluminum PACs compete, as do the banks and the thrifts. Because of competition or divergent interests, the business community does not all march in the same direction.

In the mid 1980s, the corporate PAC movement has matured while its growth has leveled off. Current developments include near-saturation in solicitation of defined executive and administrative employees, a leveling off of response rates, and a modest growth in the amounts of average contributions. Particularly during 1985–1986, mergers and takeover attempts, as well as the oil glut, led to many corporate staff cutbacks, reducing the eligible universe of employees to be solicited by such PACs and leading to new strategies for giving.

Yet PAC contributions to candidates have grown apace. In 1974 PACs contributed $12.5 million to candidates for the U.S. Senate and House; in 1984 the figure was $139.5 million—a more than 1,000 percent increase.

However, PAC contributions play a far more limited role in campaign funding than many critics suggest. They are a negligible element in the direct financing of presidential prenomination campaigns—in 1984 they made up only 1.2 percent of the prenomination campaign funds of the major candidates. Their role in congressional campaign financing is greater but far from dominant. What most often gets media attention is the continued increase of PAC contributions to federal candidates, both in absolute terms and as a percentage of total receipts. For example, some 28 percent of the funds raised by all Senate and House candidates in 1983–84, including primary losers, came from PACs, compared with 26 percent in 1981–82. PACs provided 34 percent of the funds donated to House candidates and 21 percent of those donated to Senate candidates (Federal Election Commission, 1987, p. 1). Private individuals—including the candidates themselves—continue to be by far the most important source of campaign funds for congressional candidates. In the 1983–84 election cycle, private individuals accounted for 47 percent of all funds contributed to major-party House general election candidates and 61 percent of funds given to Senate general election candidates (Democratic Study Group, 1985). Other sources are political parties.

### Role of PACs in Influencing Legislation

Much of the criticism of PACs centers on common themes: that contributions give PACs undue influence over election results; that PACs favor incumbents and thereby decrease the competitiveness of election campaigns; that PAC sponsors enjoy extraordinary access to officeholders and exert decisive influence on legislative decisions, often making it impossible to achieve consensus on important matters of public policy. The list of harmful effects goes on, each claim buttressed by an appropriate horror story. Many of these claims are based on loose talk and weak analysis, unable to withstand close scrutiny.

Members of Congress continually confront choices, face conflicting goals, make trade-offs. Members, however, are most attentive to the preferences of their constituents, at least the majority of those voting for them. After all, people, not dollars, vote, and the priority is to get elected. Members also have their own personal values and have concepts of the national or public interest; for the most part, they are not easily moved from their basic beliefs.

The problem of PACs is not that they create pressures on issues; such pressures exist for all politicians, who must take stands and make daily decisions on public policy and are expected to prioritize the issues, to focus on the essential ones, and to mobilize majorities within legislatures. The basic need is for congressional leadership to overcome the conflict that results from the diversity and fragmentation generated by the proliferation of issues that the Congress addresses.

Critics' claims about PAC influences on legislative voting patterns are often based on hearsay or on facile correlations between PAC contributions and legislative results. But simply to posit a cause/effect relationship between interest-group contributions and legislative decisions reveals a simplistic understanding of what influences legislation.

Author Elizabeth Drew (1983), for example, suggests that provisions in the 1981 tax-cut bill that benefited independent oil producers resulted from efforts of the Reagan administration and House Democrats to outbid each other for securing independent oil money from individuals and PACs. Columnist Robert J. Samuelson (1983), however, builds as convincing a case that the issue at stake was not whether Republicans or Democrats would attract the greater sums of campaign money from independent oil producers but who would wield decisive influence in the House of Representatives: the majority Democrats or the Reagan White House. Thus no simple explanation is conclusive.

That campaign money may at times influence the voting behavior of lawmakers is undeniable. But to assign a near-monopoly of influence in the formulation of most legislation to PAC contributions ignores the rich complexity of variables that affect the process. For example, psychological pressures affecting voting by members of Congress include many other factors: job or reelection security, going along with the party, friendships with other legislators or lobbyists, personal idiosyncrasies, prejudices, and fear of ostracism.

Contributions of campaign money clearly do not assure contributing groups the legislative outcomes they seek. Business or labor groups may not always or even often get what they want. They more often have enough votes to block legislation they do not want: They are what are called veto groups, and they exercise their vetoes when needed.

The complexities of the elective and legislative processes make the drawing of a causal relationship between contributions and legislative votes suspect. This is not to suggest that contributing money is entirely ineffective. Campaign money may help an incumbent sympathetic to an interest group's political goals retain office or help a sympathetic challenger win a seat. On specific issues with no clear partisan or ideological content or no clear relevance for a lawmaker's constituents, PAC contributions surely may tip the lawmaker's vote in the PAC's favor. University of Virginia political scientist Larry Sabato explains their limited impact this way: "Do PACs buy votes? Yes, they do sometimes on low-visibility issues, issues where there's very little press focus, where groups like Common Cause don't aim their fire, and where there are no competing interests to counterbalance one particular PAC's desires. But, obviously, these sort of issues are rare" (quoted in Alexander and Haggerty, 1984, p. 58).

To quote another political scientist, Frank J. Sorauf (1986, p. 111): "Scholars have not found it easy to cope with the problem of trying to establish relationships between money and votes in large. . . numbers of role calls in a congressional session. The most successful attempts have found only a small positive relationship." What is most often found is stronger correlations of legislative voting to ideology, party, or constituency interests than to contributions.

In reality, the narrower an interest is, the easier it is to organize people emotionally involved in the issue; since narrow issues tend to have low visibility, it is easier for members of Congress to vote for the measure. Even though a group may have a single-issue PAC or have a small following, numerous similar PACs may be organized, as banks have done, thus enabling large aggregate amounts, well above the $5,000 maximum for a single PAC, to be given to favored candidates. And, of course, groups form coalitions with others to achieve their political goals.

In one study, John R. Wright (1985) concluded that money is given more to influence election outcomes than specific roll calls. Accordingly, he suggests that members of Congress need to cultivate relationships with local PAC officials, not Washington lobbyists. In many groups, of course, such as BIPAC, networking is important, with word of an endorsement and contribution by the "lead" PAC followed by locals or even unrelated PACs that do not have the capacity to research the voting records.

When election outcomes are the motivation, the purpose is to change the complexion of a chamber, to tip the balance of thinking or of parties, or to elect more business-oriented or labor-oriented members. Take, for example, the election of a probusiness or prolabor member of Congress. PACs know that they do not have to lobby the member on how to vote; they know by his or her orientation how the candidate likely will vote on relevant issues. They give because they sense the candidate is favorably inclined on their issues. Many PAC contributors are ideologically motivated, and the desire is to help elect like-minded candidates. Money does not create a philosophy so much as money follows a philosophy. Issues are often less important than basic posture.

This viewpoint was well expressed by Andrew Mollison, a journalist: "If PACs don't have influence, then the people who run them are not fulfilling their fiduciary duty to the people who have the money." But he made clear that he did not mean the kind of influence exercised over legislators "who wouldn't go along with you unless they get the money." Rather, the idea is to get candidates into office "who you know [are] going to be predictable. You search them out, you find them out, you back them. That's a much better way to do it" (quoted in Alexander and Haggerty, 1984, p. 64). Many PAC and issues managers have found this basic posture relevant even when a single issue is at stake.

But the choice is not always between a labor-oriented or a business-oriented candidate, or between a "good" or a "bad" candidate from the PAC's viewpoint; often there are gradations of views on a spectrum.

### Techniques of PAC Managers

Many years ago Alexander Heard (1960) wrote that what contributors sought was access, the opportunity to present one's case, perhaps to get a sympathetic hearing on an issue or a series of issues. Access helps to explain the many PAC contributions to members of a committee dealing with legislation affecting the company or industry the PAC represents; often contributions are made indiscriminately to members of a committee, Democratic as well as Republican, liberal as well as conservative, so that lobbyists can feel free to discuss legislation. Access also helps to explain why corporate PACs, for example, at times give to labor-oriented members, perhaps because the member sits on a committee important to the company.

PACs tend to favor incumbents over challengers. But so do individual contributors. Historically a far larger percentage of incumbents than challengers are successful in each general election. Each incumbent enjoys the advantages of name recognition and the benefit of allowances for salary, staff, travel, office, and communications, whose worth over a two-year term has been put at more than $1 million ("Advantages of an Incumbent Seeking Re-election," 1980, pp. 1–4). These factors contribute significantly to the high reelection rate of incumbents in the

House—but not the Senate, where higher levels of visibility lead to greater vulnerability. Since relatively few contributors, whether individuals or organized groups, are interested in giving money to candidates who seem to have little chance of winning, incumbents garner a disproportionate share of campaign funds from all sources—some 72 percent in 1984, whereas challengers received 16 percent and open-seat candidates 11 percent (Federal Election Commission, 1985, p. 3). In the latter two categories, money is often concentrated on a few contests. In open-seat contests, individuals and PACs tend to give more generously because the contest may be competitive.

Even among those PACs that generally have favored incumbents over challengers, the mere fact of incumbency is not enough to guarantee a contribution. Other factors may also affect a PAC's decision whether and how much to contribute: the candidate's party affiliation; the candidate's business or labor bias; his or her need for campaign funds; and the competitiveness of the race. Finally, PACs keep box scores and need many winners to "prove" their effectiveness with their donors.

PACs, however, may be in proactive or reactive modes. If the former, they seek to influence policy makers early, looking for candidates to support who are or may soon be in a postition to carry the banner over the long term. Reactive posture is responding to immediate electoral situations and to requests for funds. Although the latter is inevitable to some extent, it is important to seek out future issues and future key players, perhaps to start early to build coalitions that may be essential later.

Occasionally there are tensions between the Washington representative of a corporate PAC and the management at the company headquarters; the lobbyist needs to talk with members day after day and so recommends at least token contributions, whereas the company management may be more ideological, more business-oriented, in its recommendations for contributions. The lobbyist must rely on the PAC to provide funds for the many receptions and dinners that are obligatory in legislative advocacy. If the lobbyist has reason to call on an elected official or the offical's staff, he may consider attendance at fund-raising events critical regardless of views that headquarters executives may hold of the official. However, corporate PAC managers usually work at company headquarters and may be more sensitive to the wishes of top management; sometimes the chief executive officer will make a commitment that the PAC is expected to fulfill.

The issues manager of a corporation tends to view the PAC as a means of transmitting information about issues to employees — for example, helping set up "key contact" members among PAC participants and arranging rallies or events in the orchestration of crucial issues. PACs serve as a focus of politically interested persons who should be a good audience to hear about issues. The issues that PAC members hear about, in turn, help to generate larger contributions and new contributors. PAC members also help convey corporate views to the political world, often through "key contact" programs. Once a problem is identified and a position on possible solutions is determined, the PAC is a useful vehicle for disseminating information to influentials.

While candidates, particularly challengers, often approach the PAC for funds directly, the wise PAC manager keeps an ongoing dialogue with the lobbyist and the issues manager to keep abreast of votes and the major issues involved. Votes on issues affecting the company are the usual measurement standard, but astute PAC managers will, at times, ignore the conventional wisdom by eliminating or reducing the contribution to the incumbent and backing the challenger. In any case, close communication and coordination among the PAC manager, lobbyist, and issues manager are crucial, and each needs to understand what top management expects.

Turning to strategies, the combined efforts of the PAC manager, issues manager, and lobbyist are needed to identify issues important to the company, to select the public officials it is necessary to communicate with, and to make decisions on the apportioning of money. But anyone in management may raise issues to be considered for action.

Timing can be critical. Obviously it is better to get at an issue early, to seek to contain it and head off any larger controversy later. Too often, PACs are called in at the end to fix a problem, if possible, by contributing, when earlier attention might have forestalled much of the fallout. The principle is to get in earlier, when an issue is smaller, rather than later, when the only option may be to try to "buy it off" in order to resolve it favorably.

Because different PACs have different goals and because they are sponsored by different organizations representing diverse cultures, they go about their business in different ways. The manager, whether of a corporate, trade association, or union PAC, has two basic problems: how to raise the needed money and how to dispose of it wisely from the perspectives—ideally harmonious—of its sponsors and its members.

Normally a political action program is used by organizations to acquaint their PAC eligibles with the imperative issues facing the industry/company/union. Over the years PAC managers have found that the more people know about the legislative process, what is being proposed, and how it will affect their jobs and paychecks, the more apt they are to contribute and to become involved in other ways.

One effort used by corporate PACs to relate giving to issues is the reception to honor a member of Congress or, on rare occasions, the challenger to the incumbent. The format of the meeting usually includes questions, and there is a preannounced adjournment time. This arrangement has a great deal of appeal to the candidate. The candidate may receive an honorarium from the sponsoring organization, has the opportunity to request individual or PAC contributions, and can present himself or herself in the best possible light. The event appeals to members of the organization in attendance; it is a sponsored social. It is usually held in an elegant location, and without such an event few members would have the opportunity to meet a member of Congress or a candidate in person.

Lately these modest gatherings are being augmented by more sumptuous gatherings including slates of candidates and diverse groups of PAC managers, sometimes sponsored by a trade association. As most of the PAC managers know one another well, and the candidates know many of the PAC managers, such gatherings are often good-humored and relaxed. These relatively intimate events not only provide the candidate with opportunities for as many multiples of $5,000 as the number of PAC managers in attendance; they also provide the PAC managers quality time to push their "detached overview" of issues or legislation.

The information delivery system of a PAC can take many forms. One enterprising oil company PAC manager used his presentations not only to provide issue information but also to find out what the legislative concerns of the employees were and then convey them to the candidate of choice. He also parlayed the information gleaned into a presentation for the leaders of national party committees, making him an invaluable source of information and at the same time permitting him to express the opinions of corporate and industry officers to highly placed political leaders. This rapport with leaders on the national political scene provided the PAC manager with a great deal of credit within his industry and PAC communities, permitting him to leverage his PAC's contribution potential considerably beyond the $5,000 legal limit. "Inside dopesterism" can play a postive role in conveying issues to politicians.

As another example, a major western bank chairman realized that in order to battle the eastern financial institutions bent on "invading" his territory, he would have to enlist the aid of his employees. (A bank has a disproportionately large number of employees in the eligible PAC class because of the number of "officers" who fit that category established by the FECA.) The PAC proved to be the ideal vehicle for managing this issue. After each quarterly meeting of the board of directors, a high-level group, consisting of the chairman of the board, the executive vice-president for public affairs, the chief lobbyist, and the PAC manager, would hold meetings in major bank locations. A slide presentation, shown earlier to the board of directors and including income/profit/loss charts, was made by the chairman; the public affairs officer discussed the global problems affecting the bank; the lobbyist talked about proposed legislation; and the PAC manager made the solicitation for more members or for increased contributions. Members of the PAC were provided with newsletters and receptions and were invited to volunteer for a three-day political training program in the state capital and later in Washington, D.C. That bank PAC became one of the fastest-growing financial institution PACs in the country.

Although some basic manufacturing, production, and financial industries have been making issue-related presentations for some time, it was not until recently that many in the retail trade began to develop PAC skills. They felt the need in order to respond to the Textile and Apparel Trade Enforcement Act of 1985, which would have restricted imports of fiber and cloth. The bill was vetoed by President Reagan, and many in the industry claim that the efforts of the retail PACs were effective in preventing an override by Congress.

Association PACs operate under different constraints that can be both an advantage and a disadvantage. They can solicit the employees of their member organizations for financial support, but legally only one association per year is allowed to do this. Once an association PAC receives permission to solicit, it must compete with the organization's PAC for the individuals' funds. This awkward problem is often resolved by placing a senior corporate officer on the association solicitation team, providing an analytical service that the corporation can justify for support as "educational" or an unusual service difficult for a corporation to perform alone.

One western-state PAC has a paid director who spends considerable time interviewing candidates, staff, and political consultants to gather periodic updated analyses of each key race. Members of the association receive copies and an oral briefing. Contributions by the association PAC are made based on a vote of the members, who are usually corporate PAC managers. The analyses and established contribution levels the association PAC provides form a solid base on which the member PAC committees, chaired by the PAC manager, make their decisions for their corporate PACs.

## Indirect Lobbying

Money is not the only tool used by organized groups to press their interests. When the Reagan administration proposed major cuts in Social Security in 1981, Capitol Hill was deluged with letters from worried senior citizens who had been mobilized by a coalition of so-called gray-lobby groups. The proposal was withdrawn. Such indirect lobbying, utilizing volunteers engaging in grass-roots activities, can be very effective. Many corporations have voluntary programs through which employees and stockholders are urged to contact their congressmen and senators regarding issues affecting the company; one energy corporation has a "hotline" communication for employees and stockholders who sign up to participate, and which is activated only for crucial votes on relevant legislation, so as not to reduce effectiveness by overuse.

One interesting case of indirect lobbying involved allegations that passage of the All-Saver Certificates for savings and loan associations as part of the 1981 tax law resulted from a Democratic effort to raise campaign money from savings and loans. Probably more influential in Congress's decision to approve the All-Savers plan was the ability of the savings and loan industry to mobilize depositors to write and call their representatives advocating support for the plan. Similarly bankers were able to defeat a bill requiring that they withhold for tax purposes a portion of interest on depositors' savings. They achieved this not so much by contributing PAC funds to key congressmen, though they did that, but more tellingly by encouraging depositors, particularly senior citizens, to write and telephone members of Congress, voicing opposition to the measure. (For a contrasting view, see Drew, 1983, p. 46.)

"I don't care if the National Rifle Association didn't give one penny through PACs," observes tax lobbyist Charls Walker. "They would still have a very big influence in the Congress of the United States. The same is true of automobile dealers. The same is true of any group that is so widespread and relatively cohesive as those groups are" (quoted in Alexander and Haggerty, 1984, p. 62).

There are many inequalities in group resources — whether in money, skill, or numbers of people. For example, there are far more used-car buyers than dealers, but they are not and cannot be organized. Sen. Robert Dole (R.–Kans.) pointed out, "There aren't any Poor PACs or Food Stamp PACs or Medicare PACs" (quoted in Drew, 1983, p. 96), suggesting that unorganized population segments without campaign funds to contribute are disadvantaged in their efforts to make their voices heard. Yet there are food stamp programs and child nutrition programs and Medicare programs because legislators and government policy makers identified with the needs of the unorganized poor and because the public approves of programs to benefit them. When budget reductions occur, these sorts of programs suffer but most often by a decrease in the rate of increase.

The focus thus far has been at the federal level. To partici-pate in the processes affecting campaigns for federal office, PACs must register with the Federal Election Commission and submit periodic disclosure reports. But corporations also have interests at the state and local levels, and so PACs similarly may be established at the state level and thus regulated by state law. In some states there are no prohibitions of corporate contribu-tions, and accordingly corporate treasury money, as dis-tinguished from PAC money, can be contributed directly to candidates or party committees. At the state level, ballot issues may also attract corporate attention, sometimes from out-of-state companies. Direct corporate contributions can be made to ballot issue campaigns, and corporate PACs may not need to be involved. Where direct corporate contributions are permitted by state law, their amounts may be much greater in the aggregate than PAC contributions.

### Conclusions

Competing interests, of course, may cause what James Madison (1787/1948) called "the mischiefs of faction," but they also bring to society ideas and values of great worth. Moreover, the ability of individuals to band together in interest groups to articulate their viewpoints and press their demands is the only reliable guarantee against dominance by government or the media, which could lead to the emergence of a single "accept-able" viewpoint. In short, Madison's answer is not to deny the right to associate and to organize — or, by extension, to lobby or to contribute. Rather, it is to seek to ensure that no group (or collection of groups) will dominate and that all kinds of groups will be able to participate through their dollars or skills or voting members.

The reference to articulation of views as a counterweight against dominance by government or the media is amplified by a statement made by Sen. Phil Gramm (R.–Tex.): "PACs did not create political power. Political power exists because the government sets the price of commodities, because the government grants contracts, and because the government is a megaplayer in the economy of the U.S. . . . The power which PACs have, they have taken away from other special-interest groups. They have taken some power away from the media. It, therefore, comes a little shock to me that the media almost uniformly support limiting PACs. They have taken power away from the political parties and, as a result, there are those who would like to see the political parties strengthened by limiting PACs. Not surprisingly, virtually all such organizations want to limit PACs" (quoted in Zuckerman, 1985, p. 6). Gramm's statement points up that government and the media, in fact, are themselves forms of interest groups that may advance views on election reform and other subjects to further their own influence.

More than 150 years ago, Alexis de Tocqueville (1835/ 1945, pp. 198–199) recognized that in America "the liberty of association [had] become a necessary guarantee against the tyranny of the majority." The freedom to join in common cause with other citizens remains indispensable to our democratic system. The pursuit of self-interest is, as Irving Kristol has pointed out, a condition, not a problem. Most groups behave in such a way as to maintain and further their positions and status as they see them. What is essential is to elect to public office people who are enlightened enough to ensure that special interests are kept subservient to the public good.

*PART FOUR*

# Working Through Trade Associations and Public Information Organizations

## Introduction by Robert L. Heath

Parts One through Three have described issues planning, analysis, and communication primarily from the company's point of view. Part Four examines the vital analysis, planning, and communication roles performed by trade associations and public information organizations. Trade associations differ from public information organizations; typically, the latter is a coalition of firms and interest groups that join to share the costs of national advertising campaigns. Trade associations are often thought of narrowly as only lobbying in behalf of an industry. They lobby, but they also perform issues monitoring and analysis, seek voluntary industrywide adoption of standards of operations, conduct technical and public policy research, and communicate issue positions to the members and to targeted audiences through various means of issues communication, including issues advertising. To think narrowly about the activities of associations and organizations is to miss many vital roles they play in the management of public policy issues. These groups contribute to issues management by seeking a united stance.

To explore these themes, Part Four features four case

studies: the data-base system (NAMNET) recently created by the National Association of Manufacturers, the issues advertising campaign of the U.S. Committee for Energy Awareness, the grass-roots campaign of the American Bankers Association against the 10 percent withholding provision, and the issues analysis efforts of legal counsel for the American Beverage Alcohol Association.

Robert Wiebe's excellent history, *The Search for Order: 1877–1920* (1967), demonstrates how trade associations worked in the early years of this century to achieve industrywide standards to lessen the chance that an ethical company would be penalized for the irresponsibility of others in the industry. At the turn of the century, when the federal and state governments began to regulate some industries, several trade associations were created. Some, especially the National Association of Manufacturers (NAM), worked to gain adoption of standards, through government and voluntary agreement by companies, in order to regularize commercial (particularly interstate) practices.

Through association, members of an industry can agree on uniform operating standards that can bring orderliness, whereas otherwise they could be torn apart by ruthless competition not in their best interest or that of their consumers. A few corporate leaders and scholars such as Milton Friedman (1962, 1970) favor a totally free marketplace. In the best of all worlds, this philosophy can win, but the marketplace alone does not protect people from product and service misrepresentation or from hazardous operations. Industries are often too vast to function effectively in a totally free marketplace. Too many consumers and responsible businesspeople suffer under such circumstances. The "free-market system" spirit can lead to business practices that are contrary to the public interest or harmful to the industry. High product standards and honest advertising claims can be driven out of the marketplace by shoddy products and misleading claims. Trade associations can help businesses self-regulate through voluntary codes of practice.

No industry operates effectively for very long without voluntary or mandated codes. The industries with the most self-regulation typically suffer less from rules promulgated by government agencies. Some legislation and regulation is actively sought by leading members of an industry, particularly through the vertical trade associations. The trade association offers mechanisms for discussing and adopting voluntary codes of operation that give an industry more control over its own operations and minimize the kinds of regulation that become more of a nuisance than an aid. Rather than categorically opposing regulation, most businesspeople favor those standards which keep irresponsible members of their industry from doing business in ways that can lose public trust or which enable the whole industry to profit.

As well as serving many other ends, trade associations can position themselves to prevent legislation and regulation that is not in the interest of their sponsors. They also argue for favorable legislative and regulatory measures. By taking this stance, associations at times receive a bad image, tarnished further when their lobbying efforts are perceived as too narrow or selfish. Nevertheless, any trade association worth its cost must provide legislative monitoring and act as a clearinghouse for the flow of important information between companies and government officials. It can develop an agenda for legislative or regulatory action that combines the collective weight of the members of the association.

In this age of growing regulatory and legislative sophistication and increasingly complex operating environments, trade associations find themselves pressed with many problems. Performance is the key issue. They often have to struggle to hold members together under difficult circumstances where some feel that their interests have not been adequately served. Anyone who believes that companies speak with one mind should visit, even briefly, with a leader of a trade association. Such conversation soon reveals how splinter groups pop up, sometimes even to oppose the original association, if policies are not developed quickly and in a fashion that maximizes business opportunities for all members and minimizes unfavorable forces of the marketplace. Not all the members of an association play by the same rules and standards. Large interests often conflict with small ones. Time is money, and no interest wants to wait for a cumbersome association that takes too long to formulate and advocate policy positions.

Individual efforts by companies often attract less attention from legislators and regulators than is possible through the collective efforts of an association. This advantage is particularly important when companies are small and scattered around the United States. Associations offer means for creating coalitions. Collectively, companies can receive a favorable hearing, draft legislation, and contest legal cases that often cost more than they could afford individually. Sharing the costs of massive national communication campaigns can make such a campaign affordable. And when communication does not succeed in changing public opinion or mitigating regulation, the association is an excellent means by which the member businesses can reestimate their practices in light of new public standards. In this case, trade associations play a constructive role by introducing public policy considerations into industries' business plans. Trade associations help companies share issues-tracking costs and provide communication networks and political contacts that small companies otherwise could not sustain.

To achieve this last goal, some associations realize that they must adopt the most advanced and streamlined communication techniques and technologies to keep pace with the demands of the information age. Gone are the days when associations could achieve their goals by depending on conventional mail and telephone systems. The National Association of Manufacturers (NAM), headquartered in Washington, D.C., offers an interesting example of how an association can use advanced communication technology to assist its members.

NAM's size and scope require an extensive data retrieval and communication network that can operate at state-of-the-art speed and efficiency. NAM, a voluntary association organized in 1895, is made up of more than 13,500 manufacturing companies, 80 percent of them with fewer than 500 employees. In addition, the National Industrial Council (NIC) of NAM includes 47 state manufacturers'/business associations and 85 industrial relations associations. There are also 125 vertical manufacturing trade associations affiliated with the Associations Council of NAM. Together, these groups represent 85 percent of American industry. With this diversity of constituents, NAM is challenged to provide relevant and timely information to its members on which to base policy positions and communicate those positions to employees, shareholders, and the public.

The National Association of Manufacturers operates primarily on the national level. It operates fourteen policy committees organized within five policy departments. Over 3,000 corporate executives of member firms serve on these committees, which cover five major issues areas: government regulation, competition, and small manufacturing; industrial relations; international economic affairs; resources and technology; and taxation and fiscal policy. The policy committees recommend to the NAM board of directors new or amended policies in areas of present and future national concern to manufacturers. A two-thirds vote of the board is required for approval. These official policy positions are implemented through NAM staff lobbying, communication, and public affairs activities, plus NAM members' contacts with their congressional representatives.

This brief description of NAM sets the context for appreciating the advantages to be gained by computerizing its communication system. NAM realized that today's businesses rely heavily on computer-based resources. To increase industry's effectiveness, information must be arranged in a useful format and disseminated rapidly and efficiently.

These goals are being realized at NAM through an NAM-sponsored public policy network accessed through local telephone dial-up facilities. (NAM uses the private network capabilities of The Source Telecomputing Corporations.) NAMNET: The Public Policy Electronic Network permits NAM members and affiliates to access NAM information electronically. It provides for electronic communications among NAM, state manufacturers'/business associations, manufacturing trade associations, industrial relations associations, and manufacturing companies and their corporate representatives in Washington.

NAMNET, which went on-line February 2, 1987, serves a variety of interests. It enables its subscribers to—

- Monitor the progress of federal legislation.
- Obtain information on particular issues for congressional contacts, speeches, and communication with employees, stockholders, members, and press—including issue analyses developed by participating public policy institutes.
- Monitor NAM's policy goals and objectives on particular issues and participate in actions in support of these goals and objectives.
- Create profiles on members of Congress (using the CON-GRESS DIRECTORY and VOTING RECORD data bases) for use in developing lobbying strategies, focusing communication with Congress, and developing background for use by political action committees.
- Facilitate coalition building.

An electronic communication package permits users to—

- Communicate electronically with NAM and with other system subscribers to receive information on legislative alerts, approve NAM testimony, and exchange issues data.
- Communicate with individuals and subgroups such as NAM policy committees, manufacturers'/business associations, and manufacturing trade associations.
- Receive notices of NAM meetings and publications.
- "Post" requests for information and share experiences on particular issues.
- Create bulletin boards for particular subgroups or issues.
- Participate in on-line conferences.

Access to certain commercial data bases allows users to—

- Monitor, and scan electronically, national and state press coverage of issues of concern to their organizations.

This is an impressive array of services available on-line to NAMNET subscribers.

Many of these services are standard in commercial and private-club computer networks. With NAMNET, the association serves its members by combining a variety of computer-assisted communication options.

A good example of this, and one of the most important features of the system, is NAMTRAK, a federal legislative tracking system initiated by NAM in-house in 1984. It provides up-to-date information on NAM's priority legislative issues. Fifty-seven issues were on-line at the close of the 99th Congress. Two kinds of reports are available on each issue. A one-page *NAMTRAK Status Report* provides —

- Current status of legislation
- Outlook
- Bill summary
- NAM position and policy goals
- Recent NAM activities in support of its position

Longer NAMTRAK background reports include —

- Political analysis, House and Senate
- Point-by-point bill summary
- Coalitions
- Communication theme, including pro and con arguments
- Origin and history of the issue
- Additional information such as statistics and related bills

As the network grows, tracking key state issues is expected.

The CONGRESS DIRECTORY data base furnishes information on current members of Congress, congressional committees, and governors. Members of Congress can be "sorted" according to various characteristics. The VOTING RECORD data base shows how each senator or representative voted on issues of key importance to industry. Votes are selected because of overall significance to business and relationship to NAM policy positions.

NAMNET also includes a daily legislative update — *Capitol News* — and a weekly legislative summary. Media Communications consists of NAM news releases, editorial comments, and similar messages. From the news menu, users can access

United Press International, Associated Press, and financial news and market reports.

The Associations Council of NAM has created a data base, restricted to its members, to help identify potential allies for a wide range of legislative coalitions or general association activities. Nearly seventy associations, with interests and concerns in over 145 different issues, participate. Data include, and can be sorted by,

- Issues of concern to each association
- "Resident" association expert on the issue
- Capacity for grass-roots mobilization
- Political action committees
- Federal agency contacts
- Other association programs and activities that may relate to lobbying capabilities or interests

By developing NAMNET: The Public Policy Electronic Network, the National Association of Manufacturers has made major strides in keeping pace with its members' information needs and has increased the likelihood that it will remain a cohesive and vital force to its members. (NAMNET is directed by Jane Work, assistant vice-president, legislative analysis.)

The chapters in Part Four present three case studies. The first describes the issues advertising efforts of the U.S. Committee for Energy Awareness. The second shows how the American Bankers Association waged its grass-roots campaign against President Reagan's 10 percent withholding tax provision. The final study demonstrates the analysis effort performed by legal counsel in the alcoholic beverage industry.

In the first case study below, Edward L. Aduss and Matthew C. Ross provide an insider's view of how a public information organization, the U.S. Committee for Energy Awareness, and a major advertising agency, Ogilvy & Mather, work together to inform and influence public judgment on a controversial issue. They show how the need for concerted communication effort often spawns public information organizations, which, in contrast to trade associations, have a narrower, more focused task of conveying information to key publics in behalf of spon-sors. Rather than taking stances on individual pieces of legisla-tion or regulation, these organizations seek mainly to educate key publics to create an environment of favorable public opin-ion. Groups that attempt to communicate publicly in behalf of industries encounter many problems in the development of an issues stance and agenda and the creation and dissemination of issues advertising. These efforts can be substantially improved by an agency that is able to commit the needed personnel resources to understand the unique problems of an industry and to solve the difficult task of conducting issue advertising.

Next, Fritz M. Elmendorf explains how an industry di-vided stood no hope of opposing a pet tax proposal by the extremely popular Ronald Reagan. At stake was an Internal Revenue Service rule that would have required banks and sav-ings institutions to send 10 percent of each customer's interest to the IRS. The campaign against this proposal cost too much for any single bank or savings association to afford. Not every bank or savings association had access to the kind of public relations/marketing counsel that was available through collective effort. As the point of the spear, the American Bankers Association helped its sponsors defeat a major piece of legislation.

Finally, Abraham M. Buchman, general counsel to the American Beverage Alcohol Association, discusses how legal counsel can help perform the issues analysis an industry needs for cooperation. This analysis is vital to the interests of indus-tries that must do business in an arena of conflicting regula-tions, among the states and between state and federal govern-ments. Perhaps no industry needs a collective effort of this kind more than wholesalers of spirits, beer, and wine. Having a cen-tral clearinghouse for scrutiny of legal rulings is particularly valuable. In any complex industry, efforts to achieve uniformity and share expenses through collective actions are quite fruitful. As well as performing issues analysis, counsel provides its opin-ion to the members of the association by memorandum and newsletter. It addresses national and international bodies to establish dialogue with those who will regulate and those who will be regulated. This dialogue sparks discussion that can isolate key problems and develop solutions. Without the dialogue, the regulators would not have easy access to carefully formed opinions on the operating needs of the industry. Often, as bills and regulations are formulated, they are circulated among trade associations' legal counsel for review. This does not result in wolves regulating wolves. It is evidence of a healthy partnership between the regulators and the regulated in an effort to make operating practices meet prevailing standards acceptable to the public while also acknowledging the needs and integrity of the members of an industry. Counsel for a trade association can assist its members in changing rulings, regulations, and operations in a uniform and orderly fashion.

# 11

# Integrating Efforts of Advertising Agencies and Public Information Organizations

*Edward L. Aduss*
*Matthew C. Ross*

As issues of public concern have become more complex, so have the methods used to address them. The availability of information, coupled with the public's desire and, in many cases, need to know, has created an American society of information seekers. It has become an accepted responsibility of government, business, and industry, as well as professional groups, to provide the public with more and more information.

As Americans have become more informed, there is a great deal more for them to be informed about. Since 1970, the amount of information available to the public has increased beyond even Alvin Toffler's expectations. The ability of the mass media to disseminate information quickly and broadly is outstanding. Television, radio, magazines, and newspapers provide us with a continuous flow of facts and figures.

Simultaneous with the increase in available information has been the increase in the complexity of issues facing society. Some issues are now so complex that individual companies cannot by themselves mount an effective campaign to address the major issues facing them. One solution is for the companies

affected to leverage their resources and to form a public information organization (PIO).

Once formed, the PIO must develop programs to communicate the industry's positions on the agenda of issues to the
targeted audiences. To do so typically requires the involvement
of an advertising agency. But an agency accustomed only to
standard product or service advertising approaches may be
largely ineffective at dealing with the intangibles of issues and
public opinion. The agency must understand the mission of a
PIO, as well as the unique aspects of issues-oriented advertising
and how it can affect public opinion.

The development of issues-oriented advertising is both
challenging and frustrating. The challenge is obvious: how to
present an issue in terms both provocative and persuasive so as
to affect the attitudes of millions of people. Although presenting
issues is a relatively new use for advertising, issues-oriented
advertising is based on classical advertising theory, involving
such concepts as the value of different forms of information
exposure, learning/forgetting theory, and the process of information assimilation.

Issue advertising is similar to package goods advertising
in that both seek to communicate distinctive benefits that will
lead to a particular behavior. In package goods that behavior is a
purchase. In issues management it is less well defined. It might
be political action (or inaction); it might be social action (or
inaction); or it might be coalition building for future actions.

The frustration comes from the difficulty of accurately
measuring results. The effects of any issue advertising campaign
must be judged in the context of the prevailing environment.
Media coverage, legislative actions, and industry news are only
three of several sources of information that color the public's
perception of the issue campaign's message. Issue advertising,
because it is sponsored, may be among the least credible of the
voices trying to get the attention of the public.

If the environment is overwhelmingly negative, the goal of
the campaign might be to halt or stabilize declining public
attitudes. In a neutral environment, the goal might be publicly
sponsored initiatives on public policy. Unfortunately, most is-

sue advertising campaigns are initiated because the climate of public opinion has deteriorated significantly. They must proceed like a tugboat working to reverse the course of a large ocean liner — first, motion in the present direction must be slowed and stopped; only then can movement in the opposite direction be initiated.

By some estimates nearly $2 billion was invested by corporations and their trade associations in 1986 to affect public opinion on issues. And, with significant evidence of effectiveness, it seems likely that the use of issue advertising to influence public attitudes will continue to grow, in terms of both issues addressed and budgets applied. The public will also, no doubt, become more sophisticated in its acceptance of and reaction to issue advertising. Consequently, the demands made on both the agency and the PIO to develop effective and efficient campaigns will increase. Coordinating and integrating the various activities and responsibilities of the client PIO and the agency will become more difficult, yet more imperative.

The purpose of this chapter is to identify and discuss the various activities performed by the PIO and its advertising agency. The U.S. Committee for Energy Awareness and Ogilvy & Mather are used as examples to show how one PIO selected an agency and developed a successful issues-oriented advertising campaign on an issue of significant complexity and concern.

### The Public Information Organization

Public information organizations (PIOs) have served business, industry, and the public since before the First World War. Over time, the functions of these organizations have grown considerably, and their operations have become quite sophisticated.

The PIO, as its name implies, provides the public with information it can use to better understand a particular product, industry, or issue. This serves the needs of the public and the organization, as the information provided may favorably influence public opinion on issues of importance to those supporting the PIO.

Unlike lobbying groups, the PIO does not directly communicate with public policy makers. Its efforts are directed at clearly and accurately providing information to the public so that public policy can be influenced by the weight of an informed public opinion. This indirect effort relies on the availability of the mass media and attempts to balance reporting in those media that may focus on only the most extreme aspects of an issue. As this effort is an indirect one, change must be understood to be slow. Virtually every program instituted by a PIO must be looked at as a long-term investment involving a considerable expenditure of resources, human and financial.

The first commercial American nuclear power reactor began producing electricity in 1960. For the next eighteen years, the utilities focused their efforts on building a nuclear power industry. They largely ignored critics and let the Atomic Energy Commission (AEC) carry the burden of informing the public of the benefits of nuclear energy. In 1974, public opinion polls showed that some 55 percent of the American public answered the question "How would you feel about a nuclear power plant being built in your community?" favorably. That same year, the AEC was broken up and the government eliminated the nuclear-energy public information program. Almost immediately public support began to drop. The Three Mile Island (TMI) incident was certainly an event of significance for the industry, but in the context of public support, it only promoted an already established and significant decline. By the time of TMI, only 34 percent of the people surveyed responded favorably to the question of building a plant in their community.

Recognizing that the lack of public support could seriously threaten its viability, the electricity industry set out to take over the role of the old AEC and to talk directly to the public about nuclear energy and its benefits. To do this, the industry rechartered an existing organization as the U.S. Committee for Energy Awareness (USCEA). The USCEA's mission was to promote a public debate using facts to encourage the development of a balanced U.S. energy program for the future. To do this, the USCEA had to become proactive. Rather than responding to critics of the industry, it had to set the agenda for public debate.

The organization had to have a clear understanding not only of the technical issues involved but also of the social and economic issues as viewed from the public's perspective.

The U.S. Department of Energy (1986) estimates that, by the mid 1990s, America's need for electricity will have increased 45 percent since 1980. Just as America has become more informed and information has become more accessible, our nation has also become more electrified. A reliable and reasonably priced supply of electricity is essential to America's economic growth and national security. There is no doubt that coal and nuclear energy have helped supply, and will continue to help supply, that electricity well into the next century. The public should understand this, and if it does, USCEA believes the needs of America's electricity industry will be served, as well as the public's need to know.

The U.S. Committee for Energy Awareness is a public information organization that provides information on a variety of energy issues, with a particular focus on electricity and its sources. The organization is committed to the idea that an informed electorate can exert a positive influence on the nation's energy policy makers. The energy crisis of the 1970s clearly showed how important energy is to America. The USCEA seeks to keep energy and energy-related policies and issues on the national public agenda for debate and discussion.

The USCEA has as its members electric utilities, architect/ engineers, equipment suppliers, labor unions, financial institutions, major energy users, mining companies, and others who are concerned about America's energy needs. It uses a committee/subcommittee structure to actively involve members in the development and evaluation of various programs and activities. The major committees are chaired by members and report to a board made up of CEOs of member organizations. The subcommittees are chaired by USCEA staff members. In every case, direct member involvement is solicited and encouraged.

The formation of the U.S. Committee for Energy Awareness stemmed from the electrical utility industry's belief that, to supply this country's growing demand for electricity, it was vital to maintain nuclear-generated electricity as an element in the energy supply mix. Further, its founders understood that nuclear power used to generate electricity could not continue to play a major role in the U.S. energy supply without public approval. Explaining the mission of the USCEA, its president, Harold B. Finger (1986, p. 7), said, "We set out to influence the national agenda of energy issues — indeed, to *define* the nuclear energy public information — to assure that the positive accomplishments get the attention they deserve." As he continues, "We set out to reach the tens of millions of the educated, politically active Americans who influence national policy. We realize that the support of this target audience is essential if we are to overcome the obstacles to utility investment in future electrical capacity. Their support is also important to complete the plants now under construction or even to continue operating our existing fleet of plants."

Specifically, USCEA selected a primary target audience of college-educated, upper- to middle-income people, aged twenty-five to sixty-four, who are community leaders and influentials. Although the organization's goal is to educate and inform all Americans, budget limitations and media realities will not permit that. The hope in targeting the primary group described above is that this segment of the public will receive the message, assimilate it, and then carry it forward to others in their communities.

The major theme of the advertising program, developed through extensive research, is America's need to rely on its own resources, not to be dependent on any foreign power. This message is both factually supportable and emotionally involving. The challenge is to communicate it effectively and engagingly to the targeted audience. To do this, USCEA uses the three major media for its advertising: television, magazines, and newspapers.

Television reaches many millions of viewers with straightforward points about nuclear energy and coal. *Awareness* of USCEA's TV commercials also draws attention to USCEA's more comprehensive print ads. USCEA's research shows that people who frequently view USCEA television commercials are more aware of USCEA print ads on the same subject matter than people who see the same television commercials less often.

In light of this information, USCEA designed its advertising campaign with synergism in mind, so both TV and print would contribute. The television commercials are literally thirty-second animated versions of the print, but with a simpler, more emotional presentation of the message.

USCEA's magazine ads are designed to reach the target audience described earlier. They appear in magazines that attract thoughtful readers and information seekers. Each detailed ad focuses on a specific part of the USCEA message. Research shows that people read these ads more than other corporate ads. They find the copy believable and authoritative, with interesting facts.

The "Energy Update" series of newspaper ads run by USCEA appears in the *Wall Street Journal*. These ads are designed to present a single key message point through a bold headline and graphic, with short, to-the-point copy that supports the headline and gives important information that is of interest to the reader. The ads give the "good news" side of the nuclear energy story that usually does not get media coverage.

## The Advertising Agency

Ogilvy & Mather, one of the world's largest agencies, employs thousands of people across a global network of over 200 offices. In addition to creating and placing media advertising, the agency offers a panoply of related services, including market research, direct marketing, public relations, lobbying, and specialized advertising (such as corporate, financial, recruitment, and Yellow Pages). The company has or has access to increasingly extensive and complex data bases covering such areas as purchasing patterns, demographic trends, attitudes and values, life-styles, and media viewing/reading habits. In contrast to the 1950s and 1960s, today the business of advertising is at least equal parts inspiration and science.

To provide the necessary services to its clients, Ogilvy &

Mather is organized around the concept of account teams. The number of persons in an account team will depend on the size of the client's budget and the scope of services required. A "typical" account team will have representatives of the creative department (an art director and a copywriter), a planner and a buyer from media, a researcher, a traffic (work flow) coordinator, a broadcast production manager, a print production manager, a billing coordinator from financial, and an account executive. The account executive works most directly with the client and coordinates the activities of everyone else on the team. Most team members will work on other account teams as well. The USCEA account team has nineteen persons directly involved and working on the account.

When USCEA began looking for an advertising agency in 1983, it recognized that it needed an agency that could function as a full marketing partner. From an initial field of over forty agencies, USCEA eventually selected Ogilvy & Mather. The criteria for selection went beyond services, resources, and relevant experience. The selection team recognized that the quality of the client/agency relationship would depend on personal chemistries and a clear understanding of the role of advertising in the mission of a PIO.

For the agency to have and maintain the thorough understanding so necessary to the creation of accurate and persuasive advertising on so complex a subject would require the agency and client teams to spend a considerable amount of time together, often under pressure to meet timetables and deadlines. So the selection team paid particular attention to the individuals who would be working on the account. From the agency's perspective, it was also important that everyone working on the USCEA account be ethically comfortable with the issues involved. So, as staffing assignments were developed in each department, people were asked about their attitudes on nuclear power. Those with concerns about working on the account were given the opportunity to decline the assignment. (Most agencies have similar staffing policies to allow people to decline working on products such as cigarettes, liquor, or pharmaceuticals.) The ensuing four years have seen numerous personnel changes at the agency as people have been rotated to other assignments, but matching personalities and personal attitudes are still primary considerations.

## Strategy Development

Although the most obvious expression of the agency's work is the advertising it creates and places in the media, the most important aspect of its efforts is in the area of strategy development. The strategy behind the advertising is the key determinant of the advertising's success or failure. Strategy development is perhaps the single most difficult aspect of the USCEA advertising, for it demands information and creativity, plus an understanding of how to present information so as to most beneficially affect attitudes. A basic, yet critical, premise of strategy development is that the sequence in changing an attitude is attention, then awareness, then comprehension, then assimilation, then change.

For most issues, the number of people firmly committed pro or con is small in proportion to those who may have opinions but are uncommitted. The committed pros and cons are typically those people who are more interested in, and consequently better informed on, the subject. The uncommitted are less involved in the issue and are therefore less inclined to seek out information on it. The challenge is to present information to them in such a way that it not only is interesting and educational but also gives them a reason to care about the issue. This is what the strategy does. It focuses and orients the presentation of the information so that people can care about the issue and pay attention to the message.

If funding were unlimited, virtually every uncommitted person would be a target for the advertising message. But funding is always limited, and national advertising, though still highly efficient at reaching large numbers of people, involves significant expenditures. So decisions must be made early in the strategy development process to identify that segment of the total audience in which a change of attitude will produce the most significant results toward the PIO's goals. This segment may be selected according to demographic, geographic, or psychographic considerations or some combination of the three.

Whereas the responsibilities for the rest of the advertising process are discrete and well defined, in the area of strategy development the responsibility is fully shared between client and agency. The agency's research team works with the client's research staff to review existing research and draw out conclusions and implications. The account executive then works with both research groups to develop strategy alternatives, which are reviewed throughout the agency. Then USCEA's research staff conducts any additional research with the targeted audience that is deemed necessary. This may include qualitative research (such as focus groups) or quantitative research (such as opinion polls). The qualitative research is particularly useful for developing a perspective on the dimensions and emotionality of various issues. The quantitative research helps rank-order messages and combinations of messages. This research is analyzed jointly by both research staffs. From these analyses come the recommended strategy. Since the development of the strategy determines to whom the advertising message is most efficiently and effectively addressed, what the message (or messages) should be, and how this message will be delivered to the audience, it requires input and involvement from virtually every department of the agency as well as from USCEA's senior staff. Only after the strategy has been developed and approved can work begin on the actual advertisements and the media plan detailing their exposure to the audience.

The USCEA/Ogilvy & Mather relationship is one organized for productivity, recognizing the agency's capabilities and responsibilities as well as the client's capabilities, responsibilities, and final authority. Within this structure the agency has the right and the responsibility to present its opinions and recommendations factually and forcefully. If the client disagrees, this may put the relationship on a somewhat adversarial plane, but the final decision is always the client's, and after it is made, there is no further dissent.

## Advertising: Development and Implementation

The USCEA advertising program is built on three types of research: strategic, diagnostic, and attitudinal. Strategic research is used to identify issues and the persuasiveness of various messages in addressing those issues. As stated earlier, a key element in successful issues advertising is the development of a message strategy that gets people involved in the issue. If the message strategy is ineffective at doing so, advertising developed from it, no matter how clever, will fail. Although strategic research is typically conducted annually, the message strategy is continually reviewed as a part of the ongoing program of diagnostic research.

Diagnostic research is done on both print and broadcast advertisements. The ads are tested in rough form to determine their ability to communicate information credibly and persuasively. From the results of this research, the ads are revised and produced in finished form.

Attitudinal research is done regularly to measure attitudes and opinions across a range of issues relevant to the advertising. Since issues advertising has no product or service to sell, results are often difficult to measure. As a further complication, public opinion is often swayed by the environment of current events. Although single events do tend to exert an influence, public opinion is highly elastic and often returns quickly to the level just prior to the event. Each wave of attitudinal research is a "snapshot" of the opinions of the audience. Although a single "snapshot" may distort public opinion, a series can show reference points and trends.

In each of these types of research, the research design and subsequent analysis are done jointly, but the actual research is contracted by and done under the direction of USCEA's research staff. In this way, control of the research is clearly and demonstrably with the client. It is essential for all concerned that the results of the research be above reproach.

From the approved strategy, the agency's teams go to work. The creative team begins developing ad topics and concepts for individual advertisements and commercials. These are developed in rough layout and storyboard form.

Since USCEA is an organization whose primary purpose is to communicate, and since the topic issues are highly complex, USCEA's senior staff takes a particularly active role in the development of the advertising program. This is not only for technical accuracy but also for tone, emotional content, and consistency within the overall strategy.

In a sense, the advertising program can be considered one of USCEA's products. Great care is taken to ensure that this product is of superior quality and highly marketable. All elements of the advertisements are reviewed in various stages of initial development, when the research is analyzed, and again in final form before release to the media. It is a time-consuming process, but it is essential. The advertisements not only must be accurate but also, to be truly effective, must be consistent with the messages the audience is receiving from other information sources.

While the creative team has been working to develop advertising, the media team has been developing and evaluating alternative media plans. Depending on the targeted audience and the budget, as many as twenty options may be reviewed. Each of these is put through a computer analysis to determine its performance against previously defined media criteria. After these analyses have been completed, the account management and media teams meet and review the results with USCEA's vice-president of advertising. From this meeting comes a recommendation that is presented to USCEA's senior staff. The final approved plan is then purchased by the agency's media buyer.

After the media schedule has run, the media team will run a "post-buy analysis." That is, the actual viewership reports for the radio or TV shows within which the commercials were placed and the actual magazine or newspaper circulation/sales figures for the issues in which the print advertisements appeared are now compared against the planned exposure levels for the advertising. This analysis tells the media planner how good the estimates and his assumptions were in developing the plan.

From the diagnostic research, the agency and client research teams recommend revisions to the ads. The account and creative teams meet with USCEA's senior staff and determine which, if any, changes should be made. From this meeting, the advertisements and commercials go into final production. The agency's creative, traffic, and production groups perform or contract for the required services to turn layouts into finished full-color magazine ads, storyboards into finished television commercials with full sound and motion. Throughout this final phase the account team is responsible for coordinating and keeping all timetables and budgets on track. The next thing the client sees for final approval is the finished product. Shown here is a print advertisement as it actually appeared in national magazines.

### Clearance

Every advertisement is accepted by the medium—newspaper, magazine, or broadcast—subject to final approval. Generally speaking, this final approval deals with whether claims made in the ad are truthful and whether the advertisement is in good taste. Before any USCEA ad is submitted to any station or publisher, it must be approved by the agency's legal department. All claims must be factual and supported before the ad can be cleared internally.

In print advertising this process is, for the most part, routine. It is also totally subjective in that each editor or publisher can decide independently on each ad as he or she sees fit.

These decisions may reflect the editor's views of the editorial environment of the magazine. They may also be a direct result of personal attitudes and opinions held by the editorial staff. For instance, a few years ago the publisher of a leading national women's service magazine rejected an advertisement for men's underwear on the grounds that it was lascivious. The advertisement showed a full frontal view of a male model wearing underwear briefs. This advertisement had been approved by a wide variety of other national magazines. The issue in which it had been scheduled to appear contained an editorial on the best kinds of bar soaps. This story was illustrated with a photo-

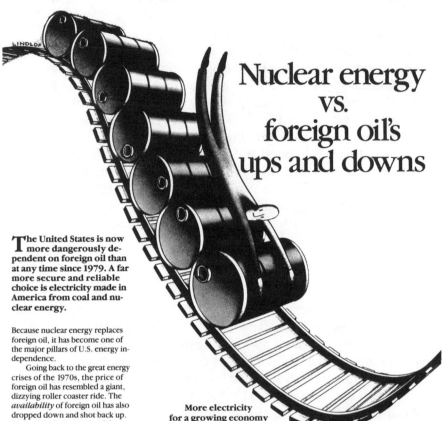

# Nuclear energy vs. foreign oil's ups and downs

**T**he United States is now more dangerously dependent on foreign oil than at any time since 1979. A far more secure and reliable choice is electricity made in America from coal and nuclear energy.

Because nuclear energy replaces foreign oil, it has become one of the major pillars of U.S. energy independence.

Going back to the great energy crises of the 1970s, the price of foreign oil has resembled a giant, dizzying roller coaster ride. The *availability* of foreign oil has also dropped down and shot back up. And we don't even control the roller coaster—others do.

Consider this ominous statistic: in the first half of 1986, even at today's low prices, America had to pay over $20 billion for foreign oil. That's a lot of dollars leaving this country, adding to an already huge trade deficit.

### Nuclear energy cuts oil imports

Clearly, the more energy we use in the form of electricity from coal and nuclear energy, the less oil we have to import.

Nuclear-generated electricity has already saved America over two billion barrels of oil, with billions more to be saved before the turn of the century. That's why it's so important for our energy self-reliance.

### More electricity for a growing economy

Our economy needs plenty of *new* electrical energy to keep on growing. Almost all of that new energy is coming from coal and nuclear electric plants.

The truth is that nuclear energy is an everyday fact of life in the U.S. It's been generating electricity here for nearly 30 years. Throughout the country are more than 100 nuclear plants, and they are our second largest source of electric power. As our economy grows, we'll need more of those plants to avoid even more dependence on foreign oil.

### Safe energy for a secure future

Most important, nuclear energy is a safe, clean way to generate electric-

ity. U.S. nuclear plants have a whole series of multiple backup safety systems to prevent accidents. Plus superthick containment buildings designed to protect the public even if something goes wrong. (It's a "Safety in Depth" system.)

The simple fact is this: America's energy independence depends in part on America's nuclear energy.

For more information, write the U.S. Committee for Energy Awareness, P.O. Box 1537 (RC1), Ridgely, MD 21681. Please allow 4-6 weeks for delivery.

Information about energy
America can count on
U.S. COMMITTEE FOR ENERGY AWARENESS

As seen in the October 27, November 3 and November 10 issues of TIME and Newsweek and the October 27 and November 10 issues of U.S. News & World Report.

graph of the rear view of three naked women in a shower, of the type found in a spa or sports facility. The editor felt that female nudity was acceptable while male near-nudity was not.

Broadcast is, however, different. In 1978 Congress amended the Communications Act of 1934 to "encourage" the use of television (thought to be less accessible than print to issues-oriented groups eager to express their opinions) to present fair, accurate, and balanced coverage on issues of public importance and controversy. However, since the fairness doctrine requires a television station or network to provide free air time to legitimate groups whose views on an issue deemed controversial differ from those expressed on that station or network by an advertiser who paid for commercial time, the net effect has been a disinclination by the networks and individual stations to accept issues-oriented advertising. The question of what issues are controversial is subjective and is open to challenge by interested groups. Sometimes the results of the fairness doctrine are in direct opposition to its original, announced intentions, as illustrated by the refusal of all three networks to air the W. R. Grace *Deficit Trials* commercial.

Over the past four years, USCEA's animated television commercials have appeared on all three television networks. To accomplish this, both client and agency met repeatedly with representatives of each network's clearance department (called "Standards and Practices") at various stages of each commercial's development and production. In each case, these meetings were set up and orchestrated by the agency's legal counsel and held individually with each network's staff in their offices. At these meetings, questions on language, imagery, and verification of statistical data were discussed. These discussions clarified each party's concerns and resulted in agreements on the appropriateness of each television commercial for airing on each network.

In this process, the agency coordinated and directed the contact and discussions with the networks. The client was responsible for researching and presenting statistical data supportive of claims or conclusions put forth in the commercials. In each case, network approval given at the initial storyboard/

concept stage is conditional and subject to final approval of the finished commercial. So it is possible to have a concept approved, take it all the way to finished production, and have it rejected in final form. Although this is the exception, it can happen.

### Advertising Coordination

An important aspect of any smoothly operating public information organization is coordination.

First and foremost, coordination at the internal level is key. At USCEA, for example, the senior staff, which consists of the president and CEO with the vice-presidents of advertising, public and media relations, research, and program operations, meets as needed to carefully review advertising in development and as planned for the future. At these meetings staff members can offer creative input and, more important, can see what USCEA's advertising is and will be. In addition, the advertising can be reviewed and checked from a technical standpoint. One of the worst things a PIO can do is to put out information that is incorrect or inaccurate.

When appropriate, USCEA's vice-president of finance and its director of membership development are asked to attend advertising review sessions. Their attendance provides an opportunity for review of budget and advertising costs and gives the director of membership development a chance to examine ways to use USCEA's advertising to help design a fund-raising program.

USCEA's staff meets with members of the advertising agency at coordination meetings. Exposure to agency staff gives USCEA's staff members the chance to discuss what is necessary to properly develop the advertising and also serves to build a good working relationship and team spirit.

Just as coordination with staff people is important to the success of any advertising program, that program must be in concert with the other functions that make up the PIO's total program. The vice-president of advertising meets regularly with the vice-president of public relations and the director of membership development. These meetings include regular reviews of strategy, goals, and objectives.

USCEA has a rather extensive review procedure used by its membership to examine program elements at various stages of development. Although this system can be lengthy, and at times frustrating, it is not unusual for a PIO, and it does work.

USCEA's board of directors receives regular status reports from the Programs Committee, which reviews advertising, public relations, and research in progress. The Programs Committee is divided into several subcommittees that review, evaluate, and contribute to advertising, public and media relations, research, and membership development. In short, the Programs Committee oversees USCEA's entire program.

This committee system not only helps members stay involved but permits them to contribute to the development of the program. It also provides first-hand industry insight into the program and lends support to projects that will later be presented to the organization's other committees and then to the board of directors.

Presence of the agency at these meetings is important, since it provides the agency with immediate information and direction and provides the membership with the knowledge that the agency is involved, informed, and concerned.

### Lessons Learned

The USCEA/Ogilvy & Mather relationship is unique in the way that every such partnership is unique. The mission, the particular tasks, and the operating environment all vary from situation to situation. But, in reviewing the history of this particular relationship, several things stand out as possible reference points for others.

First, the client and agency must both clearly understand and commit to specific objectives for the advertising. Without this commitment, the advertising will lose its focus and, as a result, its effectiveness.

Second, there must be a full measure of trust between

client and agency. All relevant information must be shared and all opinions fairly considered.

Third, understand that no matter how much research is done, the final decisions come down to judgment. The research can reduce risks, but it cannot eliminate them. Advertising is not a science and therefore requires personal judgment.

Fourth, the advertising must work as an integrated part of the whole program. To maximize the efficiency of the program, the messages and audiences must be consistent and coordinated.

Fifth, accept that the program is hostage to the news environment: Negative media coverage can undo the best efforts. In a hostile environment, holding the line on public opinion may be the only possible goal.

And last, the right strategy can greatly simplify a complex problem and lead to dramatic and highly effective advertising.

## Summary

Groups with vested interests have always sought to influence public policies. In the past these efforts have been aimed directly at policy makers. Now, more and more of these groups are recognizing the opportunity to effect changes in public policy by utilizing the leverage offered through issues-oriented advertising in the mass media.

But, successful issues-oriented advertising campaigns are the result of an understanding of the processes involved and a dedicated collaborative effort between client and agency.

As much as it is a cliché, it is also a fact that the client/ agency relationship is a marriage. The ones that survive and prosper are the ones that are flexible, mutually supportive partnerships. The review presented here of the USCEA/Ogilvy & Mather relationship is a snapshot. In truth the relationship is as complex and as provocative as both the issues and the people involved.

12

# Generating Grass-Roots Campaigns and Public Involvement

*Fritz M. Elmendorf*

Application of modern market research tools to a grass-roots lobbying effort was the key to the monumental success of the campaign to repeal a provision of the 1982 Tax Equity and Fiscal Responsibility Act (TEFRA) requiring the withholding at source of 10 percent of individual interest and dividend income. The American Bankers Association (ABA) did not pioneer the use of product market research tools to formulate a strategy for a grass-roots lobbying campaign. However, the massive success of the effort is credited as the hallmark of a new style of public affairs: the grass-roots campaign.

Withholding of taxes on interest and dividend income is an old idea whose advocates point to the success of wage withholding in ensuring compliance with the nation's income tax laws. The notion that income taxes should be withheld as interest and dividends are accrued had been considered as far back as during the implementation of wage withholding for federal income tax and had been seriously proposed during the Truman, Kennedy, Johnson, Nixon, Ford, and Carter administrations. The idea had always been dropped, usually following strong protests from the banking and thrift industries. Previous to the 10 percent withholding campaign, the banking industry had opposed these measures through traditional lobbying. During incarnations as recent as the Carter administration, grass-roots opposition had been voiced through senior citizens' organizations, in particular the American Association of Retired Persons.

The Reagan administration, like its predecessors, was in search of ways to raise additional revenues without the appearance of a tax increase. This need was exacerbated by the prospect of $200 billion annual deficits following the administration's initial round of tax cutting in 1981. Because of the enormous pressure to find revenues, withholding was first proposed in the spring of 1982 as a means of increasing compliance and accelerating tax payment flow. Following traditional lobbying by bank and thrift industry groups, Senator Robert Dole, then chairman of the Senate Finance Committee, publicly announced that withholding was being dropped from the "revenue enhancement" package.

The administration and the Senate had set a target of raising $100 billion over three years in TEFRA. Producing such a package without a direct increase in income taxes was a monumental task, requiring feats of sleight-of-hand and enormous political coercion. As Senator Dole, working with Secretary of the Treasury Donald Regan, struggled toward this goal during the summer, 10 percent withholding was reborn at a late hour. Because of revenue projections that the withholding provisions would raise $8 billion over three years, the largest single item in a bill containing dozens of "cats and dogs," Senator Dole declared it to be the centerpiece of "revenue enhancement."

Aware of the political sensitivities of withholding, Congress added provisions to exempt most senior citizens and others with low account balances. While providing for political expediency, these provisions vastly complicated the mechanical aspects of withholding faced by paying institutions.

A conservative Republican junior senator from Wisconsin, Robert Kasten, bucked his party leadership and offered an amendment to remove withholding from the bill. His amendment, voted on in the early hours of the morning as the Senate struggled toward final passage of TEFRA, was defeated 50 to 47. The only concession made to banks, thrifts, and other paying institutions was a delay in the effective date to July 1, 1983, to allow time to prepare for an exceedingly complicated and expensive task. Congress and the Treasury had shown little understanding of the difficulties and expense of the withholding process, particularly as magnified by the complicated set of exemptions designed to mollify key constituencies, primarily the elderly. Bankers, in the business of handling other people's money and aware of the associated sensitivities, intuitively knew that withholding posed customer relations problems of nightmare proportions. Yet, withholding was now the law of the land, the linchpin of a historic effort to improve the nation's compliance with tax laws and reduce budget deficits that threatened dire economic consequences.

Bankers are civic leaders, and no group was more concerned about the consequences of budget deficits at that time. Further, the nation's largest banks were better equipped operationally to implement the withholding procedures. The process would be more difficult for banks that were smaller and less automated. The large banks wisely saw the political advantages of protecting the interests of smaller banks as well. Moreover, bankers were concerned about a possible backlash of ill will in Congress that might be generated against them if they mounted an effort to repeal withholding. After all, during the TEFRA debate, banks had been repeatedly criticized for having a low effective tax rate. Many bankers felt the industry was vulnerable to tax legislation targeted specifically at banks.

With these different concerns, the ABA board of directors debated a resolution to seek repeal during its October meeting at the annual bankers' convention in Atlanta. After extensive debate, the board members broke to seek additional views from other bankers and reconvened to pass the following resolution:

> Move that ABA continue to articulate banking's opposition to withholding and that support be given to any politically valid opportunities to repeal the law.
>
> Further move that the initial emphasis of the Association be on a campaign to inform its members and through their efforts and others to inform

the public of the withholding issue and the impact
it will have on them.

The bankers had hedged their bets: They did not wish to
incur the wrath of Congress if there was no real prospect of
repeal.

As Barber Conable, then a highly respected member of
the House Ways and Means Committee, had earlier told a banking legislative policy conference, no amount of lobbying by
bankers would persuade Congress to repeal withholding; only a
large outpouring of public sentiment would do that.

This long narrative is necessary to properly set the stage
for the repeal effort, which eventually resulted in an estimated
22 million pieces of mail—more than the Vietnam War, Water-
gate, and the Panama Canal combined. The following chro-
nology summarizes the significant events in that effort.

*1982*

| March | ABA testifies against withholding. |
| --- | --- |
| May | ABA is informed withholding is a dead issue for now. |
| August | Congress passes 10 percent withholding law; no opportunity for ABA to object. |
| September | The Banking Leadership Conference (BLC) urges ABA to undertake a communications effort to inform its members and their custom-ers of the withholding portion of the law. If research shows significant interest, consider fighting for repeal. |
| October | ABA board meets three times during annual convention to hear pros and cons of repeal effort. All problems, corporate taxes, minimum taxes, political retribution, and so forth are out-lined. Board agrees to proceed with caution, making no moves until public sentiment re- |

search is completed and executive board is advised.

November
Four focus-group studies are completed; results could prove devastating to banking. Members of the public sampled—

- Blame the bankers for doing nothing to protect the customer.
- Do not want any outside source to touch their savings other than to report the interest paid.
- Resent the implication from Congress that they are "tax cheaters."
- Blame Congress for passing a "new tax law" without advising the public.
- Believe that the IRS is capable of collecting the taxes.

November (late)
ABA moves ahead cautiously, with plans for an education/information effort from individual bankers to their customers, the bottom line being *repeal*.

December
Executive leadership agrees to release the materials to the members and instruct staff to maintain a low profile. To be successful, the repeal must come from the customers at the grass-roots level to Congress, not from the bankers. Also agrees to rethink position at February BLC with an eye to change if customer response is low or lacking.

Congressional effort for repeal legislation at end of lame-duck session fails with 155 cosponsors.

*1983*

December–January
"Repeal kit" requested by approximately 9,000 member banks. Distribution of information to customers begins.

ABA joins with other financial associations to share progress of repeal effort and legislative data.

Congress returns and promptly introduces 20-plus pieces of repeal legislation.

ABA decides not to single out one piece of legislation.

February      BLC agrees to rethink repeal effort, to hear pros and cons, and as a result invites Sen. Robert Dole to address the conference.

Sen. Dole threatens the bankers in front of national media, thus angering the attendees at the BLC.

BLC hears; there is no turning back, it is now a people's issue, with millions of cards, flyers, and letters arriving on Capitol Hill.

Sen. Dole conducts tax hearing on banks. Sen. Long and other Democrats refuse to support him.

President Reagan blasts the bankers.

*Washington Post* and *New York Times* support Dole and the president.

March      Senator Kasten runs with repeal effort and attaches it to important Jobs Bill; he then wins an agreement to have it attached to the Trade Bill on April 15, setting the stage for a showdown.

Kansas State Bankers ask for and receive a meeting with top Dole aides; also see Sen. Dole and urge him to change positions.

April      ABA leadership tests customers' support for repeal through six focus groups and a national telephone survey. Results: 71 percent supported repeal and thought the IRS should do the job it is paid to do, collect taxes.

ABA top leadership visits White House and urges the president and administration leadership to hear the people.

Representatives of several large banks visit White House and tell the president they are not with the ABA.

Estimates on Capitol Hill place the mail against withholding and for repeal somewhere between 8 and 11 million pieces.

Survey data released to Congress and the press; Sen. Kasten's support mounts to April 21, where a final compromise results in a 91 to 5 vote in the Senate.

Attention turns to the House of Representatives; Chairman Dan Rostenkowski says the move for repeal will go nowhere but calls for hearings on June 2.

ABA sends letter to all House members, urging them to support the American public.

Rep. D'Amours moves closer to his 218 signatures for discharge of H.R. 500 — outright repeal.

| | |
|---|---|
| May 4 | Number 218 signs the discharge petition; House leadership agrees to vote on issue by May 23. |
| May 5 | Chairman of the Ways and Means Committee agrees to a vote next week. |

The first — and most important — step taken by ABA staff was to convene two focus groups in Chicago and take a sampling of public attitudes on the new law. We picked Chicago because it was mid-America and because we had a facility there that had been used in conjunction with ABA's Full Service Bank© advertising program. Each of these groups included equal numbers of men and women between the ages of thirty and forty-five who currently had incomes above $20,000 a year. In addition, attitudinal statements from the recent ABA Usage and Attitude study were used to classify respondents as either Solid Savers (Group I) or Involved Investors (Group II). On October 5, 1982, the ABA, working with Leo Burnett Company, Inc., our advertising agency at the time, conducted two group discussions with eight persons each. The discussions drew together a diverse group of people who had some interest earnings. ABA had prepared a simple, brief narrative describing the withholding law, since it was expected that knowledge of the new law, not scheduled to take effect for more than eight months, would be low. Additionally, a copywriter with Leo Burnett had written copy for possible advocacy advertising.

This focus-group research was limited compared with the amount of research that typically precedes product marketing. However, it was sufficient to assure us that we had found a genuine "hot button"—that the public was strongly opposed to the witholding of taxes on its interest and dividend income. Key findings, reflected in both group discussions, were:

- The general public had virtually no knowledge that the withholding law had been passed.
- The public was very distrustful of Congress and strongly resented the idea that such a law had been slipped through "in the dark of night" with no publicity.
- Members of the public were resentful that Congress did not trust them to pay the taxes they owed on interest income.
- They were suspicious of the banking industry and did not understand why the bankers had allowed such a law to be passed. Some felt that "there must be something in it for the bankers."

Opposition to the new law was intense and emotional and at a level not witnessed before by the ABA director of advertising, Allan Paro, a veteran of market research.

When presented with several versions of copy for a proposed advocacy ad, focus-group participants preferred straightforward language, relatively free of hyperbole, that informed them of the facts of withholding and gave information on how to seek its repeal. Several participants spontaneously offered suggestions on how to alert the public to the new law.

Focus-group reaction was so intense and the themes so consistent that we concluded that repeal was possible, if we were successful in alerting the public to the existence of the law before its July 1, 1983, implementation. The reaction also suggested that the public would take out its wrath against the banks, rather than Congress, if no public relations effort was launched earlier than July 1.

There are about 14,500 commercial banks in the United States, along with 17,000 credit unions and 3,000 savings and loans, all with a direct stake in the withholding issue. We knew that it was the customers of these institutions, not the managers, who would have to communicate to Congress their support for repeal. We knew that bank presidents across the country, working with their counterparts in savings and loans and credit unions, would have to take active leadership roles in mobilizing their customers to make their feelings known to Congress.

We knew that bankers, particularly community bankers who were civic leaders in their cities and towns across the country, were bitterly opposed to the law. We knew that, without their active leadership by the thousands, any efforts on the national level by the ABA would be unsuccessful. We did not know at that time to what extent those bankers would take the leadership reins.

The ABA, like any trade association, is most effective when it has the active support of its members. The trade association can develop the materials, but if its members do not use them, the effort is wasted. Conversely, the efforts (and budget) of a trade association can be multiplied a thousand times if it has correctly anticipated the interests of its members.

Following the focus-group sessions, the public relations staff developed a strategy for repeal and, working with its public relations counsel, Carl Byoir, Inc., produced a "repeal kit" for distribution to bankers. The strategy depended upon bankers at the local level using the materials provided by ABA to alert their customers to the new law and give them materials and information with which they could contact their legislators. ABA would provide national advertising and public relations support through its communications department.

It is noteworthy that all this activity was taking place in ABA's communications department, under the direction of public relations and marketing professionals. At this time, Congress was out of session, and the only role being played by the government relations group was to review materials for factual accuracy. These materials were developed in November 1982 and were designed for maximum impact when the new Congress convened in early 1983. We hoped that constituent mail would peak in February, convincing Congress of the need for repeal as one of its first acts of business.

The "repeal kit" consisted of—

- Three full-page, camera-ready advocacy advertisements, produced by Leo Burnett, Inc., based on the input from the two focus-group sessions.
- A speech designed for delivery to civic groups, with a segment that could be added to appeal to senior citizens.
- An op-ed-style editorial column, to be submitted (perhaps with modifications) under the banker's byline to the local newspaper.
- Sample letters to stockholders, to customers, and to Congress.
- An order form for postcards to Congress, which were designed to be included in monthly statements. These "statement stuffers" could be ordered preaddressed to the local representative and senators.
- An order form for posters and lobby displays.
- A sheet of instructions on how to use the materials to organize a local repeal campaign.

ABA initially ordered a press run of 5,000 repeal kits and announced their availability, free of charge, in ABA's weekly tabloid for members, *Bankers News Weekly*, with some attendant notice in the trade press. Not only was demand high, but we went to a second and then a third press run for a total of 15,000 kits distributed through February.

We computerized the address list of those receiving the kits for possible follow-up action, but as it turned out, none was needed. Nevertheless, the list told us that more than 7,000 banks had requested the materials (some banks received more than one copy), about half of all banks. Nothing approached this in precedence. When orders for statement stuffers surpassed the 10 million mark in January, we felt confident we had a good fight on our hands. The bankers had responded beyond our expectations. We awaited the public's reaction.

ABA helped to prime that reaction, initially through its Banking Advisory Program, which put a well-briefed group of bankers in local markets to do media interviews on various banking topics. The program, administered by the Byoir agency and its regional offices, was a very succesful grass-roots public relations program. In November, one of the Banking Advisors delivered the canned withholding speech to a civic luncheon group in Idaho, as one of a planned series of addresses. The ABA decided to use this speech to see how it played to the heartland. The crowd was very responsive to the call for repeal, and a local Associated Press reporter attending the lunch put the story on the state wire. This began what became a regular series of local stories on the new law. Pockets of public opposition were beginning to form, and the universal reaction reflected the attitudes discovered in our focus groups.

We developed a press kit containing information on the law itself and the repeal effort and mailed it to a national press list in January.

The ABA never seriously considered using television advertising, because it seemed incompatible with grass-roots advertising. ABA officials appeared on many talk shows. There was a great deal of media interest. Every time Dole, Reagan, or Regan blasted the ABA or discussed the measure, the ABA was asked to comment. These events actually kept the issue alive and further fired the grass-roots movement. If these officials had not attracted so much attention, the ABA campaign might have failed. The ABA case was likewise sustained on the front pages of newspapers.

Also in January, we purchased a single full-page ad in *Time* and *U.S. News and World Report*, running one of the ads originally developed by Burnett. We also bought the then-new "issues forum" page in *Newsweek* and wrote a narrative, under the byline of our association president, explaining our reasons for seeking repeal. The tab for the three newsweeklies, approximately $150,000, was our only advertising expense.

In January we started to get swamped with calls from local and regional reporters wanting more details about the new law.

As soon as Congress came into session, several members rushed to introduce bills repealing the withholding law, and dozens of others signed on as cosponsors. Meanwhile, a coalition of groups favoring repeal began to meet periodically, mostly consisting of the trade groups for banks, savings and loans, mutual savings banks, and credit unions. The major savings and loan trade group, the U.S. League of Savings Institutions, had developed its own repeal kit for its members, and the biggest credit union group, the Credit Union National Association, was busy providing its members with several million postcards.

With Congress back in session, lobbyists began discussing strategies for pushing repeal legislation. However, while lobbyists discussed repeal strategies among themselves, Senator Kasten seized the initiative in the Senate, and Representative Norman D'Amours, a junior Democrat from New Hampshire, led the charge for repeal in the House.

Opposition to repeal from the White House, the Treasury, and the Republican and Democratic party leadership in the Senate and House hardened as the repeal effort grew. The "insiders'" consensus was that repeal had no chance given that solid opposition.

At this time, in early 1983, the Treasury Department and Senate Finance Chairman Dole went on the offensive in support of the withholding concept. They argued that withholding would only penalize the cheaters who were not paying the taxes they owed on interest and dividends. They questioned the

motives of the ABA and denied that withholding would be
burdensome to either the public or the banks. They convinced
many editorial writers that the bankers were wrong, resulting in
many editorials critical of the ABA and the banking industry in
general.

While both the congressional and administration leadership were digging in their heels against repeal, a majority of
senators and representatives were cosponsors of repeal legislation. The issue exploded from the business pages to the front
page when Senator Kasten offered an amendment to repeal
withholding to major Social Security reform legislation, which
was the first major item of Senate business.

Senator Dole succeeded in doing what the ABA could not
do on its own: He put the withholding issue on the front page of
every newspaper in the United States and on the evening network news.

The banking industry, and the ABA in particular, was
roundly condemned, first by Senator Dole, then by Treasury
Secretary Regan, and then by President Reagan himself, who
pronounced himself fed up "to my keister" with the bankers.
They charged that the bankers had misled the public, but with
every new burst of criticism, a new round of mail flooded
Capitol Hill.

Pressure at high levels was brought to bear against the
ABA to stop its efforts, but what those in the White House,
Treasury, and Congress failed to realize was that there was nothing the ABA could have done at that point to stop the grass-roots
repeal effort. The grass-roots movement was genuine. It was not
based on false or distorted information; the information had
been presented to the public in a straightforward manner from
a credible source, their banker. Certainly, the information was
designed to reinforce the inclinations and prejudices of the
public. The public was suspicious of Washington. The public
resented the implication that they could not be trusted to pay
the taxes they owed. The public firmly opposed a direct reach by
the IRS into their bank accounts. The public felt cheated by the
lost opportunity for additional compounding of their interest.
These are all deeply ingrained public attitudes that were there

before the ABA formulated its repeal plan and will be there again in the future should Washington, in its folly, decide to resurface the withholding proposal.

The ABA repeal effort was relatively simple in design, and it was that simplicity that contributed directly to its overwhelming success. The message to the public was simple: Help us repeal a bad law. You are not a tax cheater, and you should not be penalized when there are better ways to target the tax cheaters.

Public opinion polls taken at various points during the campaign consistently showed that only 10 percent of the public supported the withholding law, while the overwhelming majority opposed it.

Some critics charged that the repeal effort was merely a postcard campaign and that preprinted postcards do not truly represent the wishes of the American public. While this is true to different degrees of many postcard and preprinted-letter campaigns, it again shows the degree to which repeal opponents misjudged public attitudes. Certainly, the campaign was "primed" with the use of preaddressed postcards and newspaper advertisements that included clip-out coupons. Institutions initially made it as easy as possible for their customers to register their opposition. It is true that a preprinted postcard carries much less weight than a handwritten letter. Signatures on a petition may carry even less weight, especially when collected in a bank lobby. But the initial flood of postcards was followed by handwritten letters, and deluge followed deluge with each front-page event. It was the millions of dollars worth of free publicity generated by Senator Dole and associates that demonstrated the sincerity and spontaneity of the public's reaction. Members of Congress could not visit their home districts without being besieged by constituents demanding repeal.

The ABA was not alone in this battle. It was joined by many other groups and trade associations. There was no coalition of effort—each group worked in its own way, but toward a common objective. The list of groups involved is impressive: Chamber of Commerce of the United States, Credit Union National Association, General Federation of Women's Clubs, Independent Bankers Association of America, Mortgage Bankers

Association of America, National Association of Federal Credit Unions, National Association of Mutual Savings Banks, National Association of Retired Credit Union People, National Savings and Loan League, National Taxpayers Union, Stockholders of America, Inc., and United States League of Savings Institutions.

It was the intensity of this clamor that led to a historic successful discharge petition which took the repeal bill out of the House Ways and Means Committee, where it had been bottled up by Chairman Dan Rostenkowski, directly to the House floor, where it passed overwhelmingly.

The Senate was completely stymied in its attempt to pass any important legislation, because of the prospect of a repeal amendment, until Senator Dole finally gave up. A face-saving compromise (if there was any face left to save) was fashioned, supported by ABA, that repealed withholding but instituted a complicated system for "backup withholding" that was targeted strictly at noncompliance.

Some groups have attempted to copy the ABA model and have failed. Typically what has been lacking is a genuine "hot button," or a clearly defined message. The ABA itself tried to determine whether a similar grass-roots campaign could be mounted to generate public support for a balanced federal budget. Extensive focus-group research failed to determine a clear or simple hot button. Although there is general support for a balanced budget, there is no consensus on a plan to get there. The issue of budget deficits is too little understood by the public. It is not seen as an immediate threat or as something that directly affects the household budget. Without strong feelings to arouse, the ABA made no further efforts to mount a grass-roots campaign for balanced budgets.

In "rolling over" the leadership of the House and Senate, as well as the White House, the ABA did create enormous ill will. Of course, the sheer volume of answering more than 20 million pieces of mail created animosity at the staff level, even among supporters of repeal. Many observers have said that the banking industry paid a heavy price for its withholding victory that eventually resulted in its poor treatment in the Tax Reform Act of 1986. However, some believe that the sheer power of the campaign gained the banking industry new respect. There is no hard evidence of a causal link between that effort and Congress's treatment of the industry on other issues, such as tax reform.

## Conclusions

The withholding repeal effort was historic in scope and will not likely ever be duplicated. The issue of withholding interest as it accrues on savings accounts is unique and is poorly understood in Washington. The extent of public arousal is attributed to the special attitudes Americans have toward their savings. Bankers played the role of Paul Revere, alerting the public to the impending law, and led the initial charge for repeal. Once started, however, the grass-roots movement had a life of its own, and repeated denunciations of bankers, which were the lead news items of the day, only served to sustain the momentum of those rallying for repeal.

The issue of reprisals is a genuine one, but if you really have the public on your side, as measured by standard marketing and polling techniques, then your cause is destined to prevail.

# 13

# Role of Legal Counsel
# for a Trade Association

*Abraham M. Buchman*

Uniformity is vital to many industries. Legal counsel to a trade association serves the important role of bridge between the varied efforts of the members of the association. Centralized counsel shared by members of the association spreads the cost of services and minimizes the likelihood that companies will unnecessarily pay for duplicate legal services or, even worse, conflicting legal opinions. Moreover, efforts to deal constructively with a highly regulated industry can be more productive when they are concentrated.

To appreciate the important role of legal counsel to a trade organization, one may consider the assistance that legal counsel offers to wholesalers of alcoholic beverages. To aid in this understanding, this chapter will examine the effort by the alcoholic beverage industry to achieve uniform regulation. This examination will be brought up to date with a brief case study of the current efforts to regulate the gray and parallel markets—an issue that divides an industry seeking to foster the orderly handling of business activities.

In an effort to bring uniformity to the alcoholic beverage industry, legal counsel assists a trade association in at least two vital ways: (1) communicating to members the ramifications of the legal issues so that supporters of the association can collectively voice their opinions on public policy and (2) attempting to bring about uniformity of practices to be in harmony with court guidelines on restraint of trade and price fixing.

## The Need for Uniformity: A Profile

Business cannot operate effectively in a regulatory environment that lacks uniformity and is constantly changing in unpredictable ways. Lack of regulatory stability often characterizes the operating environment of the beer, wine, and spirits industry.

Before it became national policy, prohibition was sometimes imposed at the local level and in some cases was statewide. For example, Kansas became a "bone-dry" state after passing a constitutional amendment in 1880, which was not repealed until 1949. During this sixty-nine-year period the Kansas state constitution decreed it a penal offense for any person to give another individual a drink of alcoholic liquor, be found in a place where liquor was sold, sell liquor, or merely possess any liquor.

The federal Volstead Act followed the passage of the Eighteenth Amendment and made the United States a country wherein any beverage in excess of 0.5 percent alcohol by volume was illegal except for religious or medicinal purposes. To facilitate the limited uses of alcoholic beverages, wineries and distilleries were operated during Prohibition under federal control until the passage of the Twenty-First Amendment.

Rather than being orderly, Prohibition created chaos in the alcoholic beverage industry. I witnessed the later years of Prohibition in New York City. There was little enforcement of Prohibition by either the state or local police. The little enforcement that did exist was provided by the local alcohol tax unit, and that was severely limited by too small a budget for the tremendous task it faced. As a result, a large portion of the population continued to drink alcoholic beverages, primarily distilled spirits, mostly obtained illegally.

During the Prohibition era, people would normally bring personal flasks of spirits or wine to their table at social functions. There were always some individuals who set up bars in hotel rooms. However, it was not uncommon for notices to be sent to guests invited to a public dinner party asking them to refrain from bringing any alcoholic beverages to the table because of the presence of a national figure who was known to be a rabid prohibitionist.

In the wake of the Twenty-First Amendment, the various states adopted their own alcoholic beverage control and enforcement statutes. There was little contact between state and federal authorities reporting applications and the issuance of state licenses or federal permits. Nor was there much communication about enforcement of the various state and federal laws and regulations. One must bear in mind that the federal Alcohol Tax Unit was part of the Internal Revenue Service and was operated primarily to control alcoholic beverage permits granted for the protection and collection of federal alcoholic beverage taxes. Federal and state offices were often divided between enforcement and permissive statutory philosophies, the enforcement section being interested mainly in penal enforcement (fines, jail sentences) for violations of the Internal Revenue Service laws. Many states were permissive and dealt primarily with the federally approved permittees that operated distilleries, wineries, and breweries, for the purpose of collecting taxes.

The major changes in post-Prohibition regulation of the alcoholic beverage industry occurred through the development of the National Recovery Act, the Federal Alcohol Control Administration Act, and the U.S. Supreme Court ruling in the *Schechter* case (1935). As a measure to help recovery from the Great Depression, the statutes of the NRA established pricing and other trade practices for many of the major industries. However, in the *Schechter* case, the Supreme Court ruled that all such statutes exceeded strict constitutional limitations and were therefore null and void.

Following the *Schechter* decision, Congress conducted many careful committee studies and enacted the Federal Alcohol Administration Act of 1935 (FAA Act). Since its passage the FAA Act has never been amended. The FAA Act was promulgated to control the issuance of permits, the issuance of certificates of label approval, advertising, and trade practices. Initially, the FAA Act was administered by a separate agency. Administration and enforcement of the FAA Act were placed under the control of the Alcohol Tax Unit following the urgings of the Hoover Commission to consolidate government agencies. Consequently, for the more than fifty years since, the director of the Alcohol Tax Unit (later changed to the present Bureau of Alcohol, Tobacco, and Firearms, commonly called BATF) has had the full responsibility and authority to enforce the FAA Act and regulations.

As a result of low budgets, administration of the FAA Act was initially limited to issuing basic permits and approving labels, thereby permitting the legal production, sale, and distribution of alcoholic beverages. Under the FAA Act, brewers and retailers were exempt from the requirement to obtain basic permits, because of administrative problems and because retailers were small, local businesses that operated primarily in intrastate commerce (Congress had determined that federal basic permits should not be required for such businesses). The penultimate clause further provided that the regulations of the FAA Act only applied to brewers and distillers in those states whose laws and regulations were similar or equivalent to the federal ones. Only after many complaints from members of Congress was there any significant enforcement of the advertising laws and regulations. More than thirty years passed before there was any real attempt at enforcement of the Federal Trade Practices regulations adopted in 1935.

The only substantial cooperation between the federal and state alcohol tax units during the first twenty years after Prohibition was a program conducted by the Alcohol Tax Unit to prevent refilling. This occurred when the Alcohol Tax Unit inspectors and laboratories found that some on-premise licensees were using illegal and sometimes poisonous methyl alcohol, without tax paid, to refill bottles and to make cocktails. As a result, for many years the BATF laboratories not only were used by the Tax Unit officials but also served the various states that wanted to have alcoholic beverages analyzed.

Cooperation with enforcement has been a continuing problem. There have been a number of isolated instances wherein a state official did send to the federal authorities facts concerning certain practices of a wholesaler that were beyond the jurisdiction of the state, and in some cases the federal authorities did bring action based on the information received. The states have also experienced little cooperation among themselves, except in the area of collection of state excise taxes. The states require monthly tax reports that show when alcoholic beverages cross their borders, and they therefore profit from checking with each other to verify reported shipments. Verification between state tax collection agencies guarantees that information reporting removal of alcoholic beverages from one state will be picked up by the receiving state, which can then collect the appropriate state taxes. It must be borne in mind that in some states the tax agency is separate and apart from the liquor administration. Yet in a number of states the arrangement resembles the present federal administration of both taxes and liquor laws in that the alcohol beverage control agency is administered as a division or bureau under the revenue department.

The lack of uniformity among the liquor laws adopted by the various states has led to many problems. For instance, during the time when Mississippi remained dry, Louisiana had become wet. A delegation of Mississippi officials went to the BATF in Washington and requested that the director not automatically issue wholesale or retail occupational tax stamps to anyone who made an application and paid the fee. The director explained that he had no discretion but was required by the Internal Revenue Service to have such stamps issued. A subsequent investigation revealed the following standard method of selling liquor in Mississippi. First, a possessor of a wholesale liquor stamp who did not have a federal basic permit would send a truck to New Orleans and purchase liquors. The licensed Louisiana wholesaler would report the sales in its monthly Louisiana tax report, showing removal of the spirits from Louisiana to Mississippi. This phase of the scheme complied with Louisiana regulations and exempted any payment of Louisiana state liquor taxes. The purchaser would then pay a "fee" to the county sheriff in Mississippi and was permitted to sell to retailers possessing retail stamps in the county. This procedure continued until Mississippi voted wet and adopted its own regulatory statutes.

During Prohibition and for a few years after repeal, the federal Alcohol Tax Unit actively enforced laws concerning occupational tax stamps. As a result, a number of criminal cases were brought by United States attorneys when there was proof of willful intent not to secure occupational tax stamps, usually to hide the fact of operating illegally without any state license. Later, the BATF operated in a similar manner during the time when federal laws placed the responsibility of enforcing the collection of gambler's stamps with that agency. And there was similar cooperative enforcement between the BATF and the U.S. attorneys. In recent years, however, with the exception of special types of cases such as task force cases, U.S. attorneys refused to prosecute FAA Act criminal violations and thereby required the BATF to resort solely to civil actions to collect monies due, including interest and penalties. The main exception has been the prosecution of breweries by U.S. attorneys, since the BATF has no authority to bring a permit action against a brewer who does not have a federal basic permit. Action against a basic permit has been the customary procedure used by the BATF for FAA Act violations by distillers, wineries, and wholesalers, all of whom have federal basic permits. The actions by the United States attorneys that resulted from BATF investigations have been settled by an agreed penalty ranging from amounts less than $100,000 to a single agreed penalty of $2 million. All these cases were based on investigation by the BATF of a brewer's violation of the Federal Trade Practices laws and regulations under the FAA Act.

Only in recent years has there been any cooperation between state and federal agencies. Recently the BATF was given lists of state licensees, all of whom must possess federal retail and/or wholesale stamps. A simple matching of the federal and state records revealed hundreds of licensees who had not obtained proper federal occupational tax stamps.

The most obvious demonstration of cooperation has been joint educational programs conducted under the BATF's leadership with the participation of state alcoholic beverage authorities in the particular state where such programs were conducted. The BATF has had a history of conducting educational programs when a major change took place in federal laws or regulations dealing with plant operations, sales, marketing, or taxes. In 1979 modernized trade practice regulations were promulgated, and a program was instituted providing for joint trade practice seminars in those states where the liquor authorities would agree to participate in such seminars. These joint seminars were first instituted in the western region and, because of their success, were extended throughout the rest of the country. Following the success of the joint seminars, permission was obtained to hold special seminars for individual large firms, conducted jointly by state and federal authorities at company offices. These special seminars have had an enormous positive impact on company compliance because the sales and marketing personnel were directly involved. The seminars have produced a more definite and positive understanding of the federal and individual states' interpretation of laws and regulations. The company seminars are further enhanced when state officials attend and explain their state's regulations and identify the regulations as either the same as, similar to, or contrary to the federal laws and regulations.

Despite efforts to increase cooperation and uniformity, problems still exist. Mainly because of severe budget limitations, the necessary follow-through by state and federal officials leaves much to be desired. Unless there is immediate enforcement by either the state or federal agency, the extreme competition in the alcoholic beverage industry pressures one firm to meet the types of illegal activities of a competitor. Unfortunately, the BATF procedures require too much time to prepare a case against a permittee, since the BATF must prove more than the commission of illegal acts — it must also prove that the illegal act resulted in exclusion of a competitor's product. Because of limited finances, federal and state agencies must rely on complaints from the industry. Complaints are rarely made because of fear of retaliation or because the complainant may be fearful that it too may be in violation. In view of the complexity of the regulations and the policy of the federal and state authorities to hold a corporate licensee or permittee strictly responsible for any and all acts of its employees, there are only a few licensees who have little fear that they could be found in violation of some laws or regulations after an intensive investigation by the state or federal authorities.

Under local option, there have been many diverse and surprising results. For instance, Florida, Kentucky, and Mississippi have permitted distillers and vintners to operate in dry counties. Even though Kentucky is known as the bourbon state, more than 50 percent of the state remains dry. Throughout the South there are large areas that have decided to remain dry or have changed from wet to dry counties. In some states where local option is permitted below the county level, there are places within a city where one side of the street is dry and the other side is wet. Needless to say, a proliferation of local dry areas exacerbates the problems of administration and enforcement of liquor laws and makes cooperation between federal and state liquor agencies even more difficult.

Enforcement has to be prepared to deal with complex issues. Florida is a classic case. In addition to the parallel- and gray-market activities, alcoholic beverages were being sold in packages that could not legally be sold anywhere in the United States because they did not conform with the FAA Act and were not capable of being legally imported into the country. At my request as legal counsel for some of the licensed wholesalers, a joint effort was undertaken by the BATF, U.S. Customs, and the state of Florida to correct these inconsistencies. This effort greatly reduced the amount of illegal activity.

The chief virtue of the Twenty-First Amendment was to allow individual states the opportunity to balance their communities' needs for temperance with individuals' preferences for consumption, in conformance with local and regional acceptance and norms. But this could not have been done without national action or involvement by the federal government as it related to functions that were and still are beyond the legal and practical capabilities of state and local governments in regard to interstate problems. Those within the industry as well as within the government are aware of the need to continue sound regulatory programs that require a strong federal presence. The BATF cooperation with the several state liquor administrations has fostered a partnership between federal and state authorities that has resulted in efficient regulation of the alcohol industry nationally and locally within each state.

The present joint regulatory effort between state and federal authorities provides the most effective means of ensuring adequate protection to the consumer against fraudulent products, of preventing unfair trade practices and unlawful competition that could lead to domination of the industry by its largest and most powerful members, and of ensuring that the considerable federal and state tax revenues generated by the industry are paid in full.

It is in the interest of all of the industry, as well as the liquor administrators, to have clear understanding and teamwork. Just as in any sport, if the rules are to be effective, immediate and uniform penalties must be imposed for violations so that the licensees and permittees who comply with the rules do not suffer when their noncomplying competitors continue their illegal activities because of delay or lack of enforcement by the liquor administrators. The following example demonstrates the kinds of efforts being made through trade association counsel to bring uniformity to a highly competitive industry.

### Gray and Parallel Markets

One of the most serious problems concerning distilled spirits, premium wines, and sparkling wines is the parallel and gray markets. Parallel marketing is a method of importation and sale of genuine goods (not counterfeit) in a manner different from the standard authorized computation and distribution system set up by the manufacturer. On May 14, 1986, John G. Hensen, senior assistant attorney general, Washington State Liquor Control Board, drew the following distinctions. *Authorized* in this context means *authorized by the manufacturer of the product.* "It does *not* mean that the 'authorized' importer or distributor has any additional license or other legal sanction from any governmental authority which is not also held by a parallel importer of the same product."

One of the underpinning assumptions of an import business is exclusivity of contract. When a company contracts to import a foreign product, it undertakes certain responsibilities and, in turn, should be able to assume that its efforts will benefit itself and not others who bring the same product into the country but without the same responsibilities and expenses. For this reason, the industry has attempted to combat the problems of gray and parallel markets by encouraging the BATF to intensify its efforts to see that imports meet stringent regulations aimed at protection in the public interest and by seeking primary-source laws in each state. Primary-source laws prohibit a wholesaler from receiving any product except that purchased from the primary source (brand owner) or its authorized agent.

Parallel marketing in alcoholic beverages has been seen throughout the world for more than ten years. However, it is only in the last few years that the alcoholic beverage industry has experienced such problems. Parallel marketing in the alcoholic beverage industry made its presence known in the trade through the "Oklahoma Connection." The state of Oklahoma required every supplier to sell to any wholesaler who wished to purchase its brands. Certain Oklahoma wholesalers would purchase wines and spirits and resell them to wholesalers in other states where there was no primary-source law. An early resolution of this issue may occur as a result of the decision in the Court of Appeals for the Federal Circuit in Washington in *American Lamb Company* v. *United States* (decided February 28, 1986). The court held that the International Trade Commission must consider and weigh all evidence gathered in its preliminary investigation in order to determine whether there is a "reasonable indication" of "material injury to a domestic industry."

The kind of difficulty parallel marketing can cause is exemplified by the stance taken by the Washington State Liquor Control Board. On December 9, 1985, the board proclaimed after extensive study that it had "decided to take advantage of the parallel marketing practices found in Europe and act as its own importer for certain distilled spirits and wine." The reason for this action, the board explained, was the refusal by U.S. importers "to lower the costs of the imports purchased by the Liquor

Control Board despite the fact that importers' costs in doing business with the board are lower than those locations where they must deal with private wholesalers and retailers."

The state of California has a primary-source law for spirits but not for wines. A large quantity of French and Italian sparkling wines, as well as expensive still wines, is being brought directly into the state by the Liquor Barn, the largest retail chain in the state. Liquor Barn sales represent approximately 12 percent of the total retail sales in the state. This is significant because California is the largest retail market for alcoholic beverages in the United States.

One major objective of beer and wine wholesale trade associations is to establish primary-source laws in their state that protect the investments of the wholesalers that bear the responsibility of spending money to promote their product. Parallel marketing is a serious threat to the national distributor, since parallel sales do not pay a proportionate part of advertising and they reduce gross sales and gross profits. There is no way to determine whether these products are of good quality, whether they have been properly stored, or whether the type of storage and distribution that they have been subjected to has affected their shelf life. Obviously, any bad product entering the United States through parallel markets would damage the good will of the brand. Paralleled products carry no liability insurance, and there is no record of distribution channels that is used to determine who is responsible for the product.

What does the Bureau of Alcohol, Tobacco, and Firearms (BATF) perceive as its role in this controversy? Stephen Higgins, director of the BATF, at a speech before the Distilled Spirits Council of the United States (DISCUS) on January 21, 1986, set forth the following position. He emphasized that the Federal Alcohol Administration Act (FAA) "makes no distinction between the activities of a 'gray market' importer and an 'authorized' importer, as long as both have the necessary importer permits." He repeated the labeling requirements that, according to some industry members, are not being followed by gray-market importers. Labels must meet three requirements: "(1) that the labels be in such form as to avoid consumer deception;

(2) that they provide the consumer with adequate information as to the identity and quality of the product; and (3) prior to and as a condition of release of such products from customs custody, the importer must furnish certificates, where issued by a country, with respect to origin, age, and identity of such imported products." The industry was successful in getting the BATF to intensify its efforts in the label approval area to ensure that such products contain all mandatory label information and not contain prohibited information that might deceive the consumer. Higgins emphasized, "In essence we are attempting to hold all importers of alcoholic beverages to the same standard of compliance with all U.S. laws and regulations." Industry pressures brought the bureau to agree to intensify its efforts "to ensure product integrity for all imported products."

Thus, through its legal counsel, the industry trade association has spearheaded two primary efforts that combat the parallel and gray-market importation problem: (1) seeking state-by-state primary source statutes and (2) liaison with the BATF to intensify government efforts to ensure compliance with all import regulations, especially those relating to labeling.

Throughout the many battles that confront an industry, association legal counsel, in support of the association, strives to keep the members apprised of the subtle changes brought about by court decisions and subsequent legislative responses. By framing the issues in litigated cases, association legal counsel will help the association's members identify and explore options responsive to the extraordinarily complex legal entanglements that follow the association's pursuit of clarity and uniformity.

# The Future of Issues Management

## Introduction by Robert L. Heath

Issues management is slowly maturing into a discipline and, in the process, is integrating a vast and diverse array of studies. As Coates and others (1986) observe, "The concept, insofar as it is a new future-oriented policy and planning tool, and insofar as it involves practice across many kinds of organizations, businesses, industries, and trade associations, is still evolving in terminology, technique, scope, and organizational setting" (p. 17). Seeing issues management as a vital activity rather than a fad, Wartick and Rude (1986) contend that its future depends on increased professionalism and, most important, on the ability of issues managers to help their companies take the right kinds of actions at the proper times. They observe that "regardless of what individual issues managers may be doing, their worth lies in how their work improves the overall IM process in the firm and how the overall process improves corporate performance" (p. 138). Issues management began as a means for filling a void discovered in company response systems during the 1960s. Now its challenge is to achieve permanence in all companies, as it has in some (Littlejohn, 1986).

Part Five describes the trends and discussions that are helping issues management emerge as a distinct and vital discipline, both by academic standards and in corporate practice. In Chapter Fourteen, James E. Post and Patricia C. Kelley share the results of interviews of public affairs practitioners to formulate eleven lessons that can be used to strengthen the discipline. In

Chapter Fifteen, Richard Alan Nelson forecasts the public policy implications that can be expected as we move into the "information," or "post-smokestack," economy.

A brief review of the major discussants can explain the themes and trends shaping issues management. This discussion has been prompted by the past two decades' revolution in thinking about corporate public policy options. This reorientation began because companies found themselves unprepared for the massive reevaluation of business activities spawned during the 1960s. The business environment of the 1950s was peaceful. It seemed that business was the business of America. A leading public relations practitioner, Edward Bernays (1955), seemed correct in advocating that the role of corporate communicators was to engineer consent for their companies' operations and philosophy. This paradigm seemed workable and guided the corporate communication profession for many years. Only the most astute observer could have spotted the seams in the fabric of consent that prevailed until the 1960s. But the new era of activist outburst made it apparent that if consent had existed, it had dissolved. Companies had not for a long time been made so aware that their public policy environment demanded skillful political combat.

One of the first major writers to note this failure was S. Prakash Sethi, who raised many corporate eyebrows when he challenged the prevailing approach to advocacy communication and corporate social responsibility. One book, *The Unstable Ground: Corporate Social Policy in a Dynamic Society* (1974), showed how companies were failing to recognize the changing operating conditions of public opinion and policy. In *Advocacy Advertising and Large Corporations* (1977), he deplored some companies' use of millions of dollars to engage in advocacy advertising that did nothing to narrow the gap between their performance and public expectation. He used glaring examples to propose careful self-regulation by companies and supported government regulation of company communication practices.

One early study aimed at helping companies monitor and manage issues was conducted by James K. Brown, *This Business of Issues: Coping with the Company's Environments* (1979). It laid many stepping stones for others to follow. Though short, this book is amazingly comprehensive. Brown was systematic in his effort to isolate the key factors to consider in identifying and managing issues. He saw the need to make corporate planning sensitive to public policy issues, claiming the results of this effort go beyond survival to offer market advantage. Issues management is responsible, he argued, for helping executives chart the future of their company. Sponsored by the Conference Board, Brown's book heralded a new era in corporate response.

Building on a decade of discussion of corporate social responsibility, Rogene A. Buchholz has meticulously examined the public influences that have played havoc with traditional business decision making. His analysis has been drawn together in three major works: *Business Environment and Public Policy: Implications for Management* (1982), *The Essentials of Public Policy for Management* (1985), and *Management Response to Public Issues: Concepts and Cases in Strategy Formulation* (Buchholz, Evans, and Wagley, 1985). These books have increased awareness of how managements are responding to their public policy environments. Buchholz's theme was summarized in this last book: "The manager in today's world must consider many additional factors in decision making beyond strictly commercial factors to run a successful business. A broad range of potential consequences must be considered before a decision can be made in almost all business situations." He observed, "To survive, the modern business organization must serve other constituencies besides those interested in profit. Managers at all operational levels must be aware of these important nonfinancial or nontraditional objectives, which can affect profits as much as more traditional concerns. They must develop the instincts and habits of mind to be aware of external influences that can affect the corporation" (p. 36). Charles Arrington, Jr., and Richard Sawaya (1984a, 1984b), while working in the Public Affairs Department of Atlantic Richfield, approached strategic planning from an issues management point of view, placing emphasis on forecasting and planned adaptation. They argued that issues management is more than simply institutionalizing standards of corporate social responsibility.

These works added to others that addressed issues management from a business management point of view. Lee E. Preston and James E. Post undertook a pioneering discussion in 1975 in *Private Management and Public Policy: The Principle of Public Responsibility*. They voiced the changing efforts by business managers to acknowledge public policy implications in their corporate planning. Post wrote *Corporate Behavior and Social Change* (1978) to make the adaptation to public policy constraints more systematic and less traumatic.

One spur to the new direction in corporate planning and communication was a more insightful understanding of the turmoil of the 1960s and 1970s. Many scholars examined the dynamics of social movements, particularly William A. Gamson (1968, 1975) and Anthony Oberschall (1973). But along with scholars, activists wrote how-to manuals, the most famous being *Rules for Radicals* (1971), by Saul Alinsky, who had waged many successful wars against such giant companies as Eastman Kodak and Marshall Field and such municipalities as Chicago. Alinsky laid out tactics and a governing code of ethics for those battling the power establishment. Here was a practical manual full of savvy advice for the special-interest tactician. His work was a robust call for people to work skillfully and thoughtfully to find the soft parts of the establishment's anatomy and "bite" until something good happened.

In the mid 1980s, several books presented detailed and varied approaches to the topic of issues management. Guy D. D. Stanley, in *Managing External Issues: Theory and Practice* (1985), applied a game-theory approach to analyze how companies can assess the pressures being applied and calculate the relative strength of the public policy combatants. His discussion is a comprehensive assessment of the tactics typical of the public policy battle. As Stanley argued, the consent that seemed to exist in the 1950s regarding corporate behavior met its death during the 1960s and 1970s. At this time, activist agitation got its foothold in the regulatory environment and became a potent force leading to a flood of regulatory measures of unprecedented number and breadth. In place of a consent model guiding company public policy efforts, Stanley advised issues managers to adopt a power resource management model, which sees the regulatory battleground as a tug of war where companies compete with special-interest activists and governmental regulators to maximize gains and minimize losses. Whereas public relations and public affairs work from a persuasion paradigm, Stanley contended, the most viable issues management model must be founded on a game-theory model that treats participants in a public policy struggle as rational decision makers, each seeking to maximize its wins. Stanley urged companies to acknowledge that the public seeks to maximize its self-interest, even by applying governmental regulation. For this reason, companies must respond to public policy contests from the same orientation. Public policy contests are not philosophical debates but contests of self-interest.

Other political scientists have contributed to the understanding of the public policy arena. The work of Herbert E. Alexander has been particularly useful in understanding the roles and influences of PACs—for instance, *The Case for PACs* (1983).

Two other recent books took a decidedly procorporation stance while achieving the kind of feistiness characteristic of Alinsky. Herb Schmertz, in *Good-bye to the Low Profile* (1986), offered sage and salty advice for dealing with the media. Unapologetic for corporate efforts to make a profit, Schmertz was convinced that the media need to be forced into accurate and responsible reporting. He encouraged companies to tell their story lest someone else tell it for them. Another strident and political view of public affairs was presented by the long-time public relations practitioner and textbook author Philip Lesly, whose *Overcoming Opposition: A Survival Manual for Executives* (1984) demonstrated a solid understanding of the needs and tactics of special-interest activists and advised managers to arm against them in the same manner and tone Schmertz employs against the media. This nuts-and-bolts manual, undergirded with an awareness of relevant social scientific research, was designed to help blunt the efforts of special-interest groups. Lesly grudgingly acknowledged the social value of agitators but took the side of corporations in the battle for public policy advantage, believing that companies are usually quite responsible and have a vital role to play. Lesly's advice is valuable because it comes from the trenches. Some companies may not like the rough-and-tumble spirit that runs through his book and Schmertz's, but one point seems clear: To survive and prosper, companies must be responsible and responsive while possessing extremely good political instincts and skills.

In a less contentious vein, W. Howard Chase, a pioneer in issues management, wrote *Issue Management: Origins of the Future* (1984) to flesh out his issues management process model. His volume offered a comprehensive treatment of what the discipline should include. Evidencing a strong commitment to corporate social responsibility, he advocated setting up early warning systems to spot and intercept special-interest activists at their earliest stages of development. Strong in its conceptual explanation of how companies should respond with issues communication, the book does not discuss, as Buchholz's and Preston and Post's do, what companies need to do internally to change operations to obviate public policy efforts.

Three other excellent books concentrate on the communication aspects of issues management. *The Public Affairs Handbook* (Nagelschmidt, 1982) contains an excellent assortment of essays and studies by leading public affairs practitioners who address public affairs efforts in general and issues communication in particular. This book presents the now-standard definition of public affairs as "a management function concerned with the relationship between the organization and its external environment, and involving the key tasks of intelligence gathering and analysis, internal communication, and external action programs directed at government, communities, and the general public" (p. 290). Unlike issues management, public affairs as defined this way does not address strategic planning, issue-oriented controls over operations, or the positioning of a company in its political/economic environment. S. E. Nolan and D. R. Shayon have drawn together several years of public affairs consulting experience in *Leveraging the Impact of Public Affairs: A Guidebook Based on Practical Experience for Corporate Affairs Executives* (1984). Their book takes an exclusively communication orientation but offers comprehensive models for laying out and executing the vital corporate communication function. August B. Stridsberg drew together research by the International Advertising Association in *Controversy Advertising: How Advertisers Present Points of View in Public Affairs* (1977). The primary value of this work is its presentation of survey results that help practitioners know what trends exist in tactics. One of the earliest books, and a solid study, this work helped pioneer the scope and nomenclature of issues communication. This study concluded that issue advertising falls into three categories: (1) defense of the company's views on a social or economic question, (2) aggressive promotion of a point of view, and (3) establishment of "a platform of fact." What this study misses is the awareness that the battle is not only one of fact and understanding. But the work is not so naive that it did not instruct its readers to remember that the adversaries are not likely to be the targeted audience. It treats advocacy communication as a battle of public opinion.

Because of the need to forecast issues trends, futurists have played a vital role in the development of issues management. Joseph F. Coates and associates, in *Issues Management: How You Can Plan, Organize, and Manage for the Future* (1986), concentrated on issues monitoring and analysis. Coates's specialty is developing early warning systems to help companies forecast public opinion shifts as an aid to their strategic planning and communication efforts. His research draws on that by Jane Work, of the National Association of Manufacturers. Her writing continues to play important roles in helping others to understand the dynamics of the public policy process. Serving in Washington, D.C., for many years has sharpened her awareness of what goes into public policy and helped her define the milestones that are used to measure the evolution of public policy issues.

Throughout the development of issues management, Raymond P. Ewing has combined corporate experience with a sound sense of theory development. His recent book, *Managing the New Bottom Line: Issues Management for Senior Executives* (1987) continues to exert his influence, which is felt in many ways. Though a skilled practitioner who earned acclaim as a leader for

Allstate Insurance's support for air bags and other automobile safety measures, Ewing has provided some of the most provocative conceptual ideas of what issues management is. He has shown the uniqueness and interconnectedness of public relations, public affairs, and issues management. At the same time, he has demonstrated how issues management has paralleled the development of strategic planning from budgeting through long-range planning to the complex process employed today (Heath and Nelson, 1986, p. 15).

Three writers have taken a decidedly anticorporation tack in criticizing corporate behavior in general and issues communication in particular. Robert G. Meadow (1981) made an articulate case that even product and service advertising is "political communication." He has argued that companies run the country by maintaining a stranglehold on the perspectives people use to view themselves, their needs, and the standards of happiness. He challenged the materialism inherent in these perspectives. Oscar H. Gandy, Jr. (1982), warned that corporate deep-pocket spending leads to distorted, one-sided analyses of public policy issues. He opposed tax deductions for corporate expeditures on issues communication because individuals cannot likewise take such deductions; thus, the Internal Revenue Service essentially subsidizes corporate public policy discussion. Making a similar case, Michael Parenti (1986) complained that companies have an undue advantage over unions and special-interest groups in public policy debate.

One irony of issues management is that public policy contests are good and bad. They are bad because they channel funds into activities that do not directly contribute to increased production. But they have a good side. Through the presence of critics, companies are forced to be responsive to those persons and groups whose lives and well-being they affect. Each contest poses strategic opportunities for a company's efforts to bring harmony between its interests and those of its stakeholders. Part of the adjustment problem facing each corporation is developing a strategic public policy plan that accommodates and balances the interests and desires of its stakeholders: shareholders, employees, competitors, colleagues, neighbors, regulators, legislators, consumers, and special-interest advocates, to mention a few.

Issues management employs company image, public consent, and political victories as means (not ends) to create a harmonious partnership with a variety of stakeholders. An issues management approach that narrowly concentrates on gaining all that its power can deliver, too narrowly applied, can bring out critics in full force. To maximize wins and minimize losses in support of a company's mission, issues management is best conceived of as a staff activity as well as a companywide attitude integrated into executive and line functions that aims to harmonize *and* maximize corporate and stakeholder interests. This view assumes that issues management can help bring the company's performance and prevailing standards into equilibrium and that companies are obligated, as citizens, to assist proactively in an enlightened effort to achieve the full potential of the free enterprise system.

The central theme in the emerging literature on issues management is that it is vital to a wide range of company activities and attitudes. Planning, supervision, and evaluation are made more effective if issues management comes into play at each phase of the planning and management process. First, the strategic plan can be designed and reassessed using data generated by forecasting the public policy environment and after careful consideration of the success or failure of the issues communication effort. Second, new tactical plans can be laid out for changing operations and communication strategies based on the success or failure of the public policy efforts. Third, a new strategic management philosophy can be created, especially in cases when the public policy efforts ease or constrain operations. Finally, one of the most valuable aspects of issues management is its ability to make planning and operating personnel cognizant of and responsible for public policy victories. All this goes on in an environment fraught with activist groups demonstrating various amounts of power and tactical sophistication as well as a context wherein various government bodies seek to regulate issue advertising.

Pondering the difficulties related to issues management's

becoming a well-defined discipline, Goodman (1983) looked at it as practiced inside companies and as a scholarly activity. He worried that companies spend more time trying to label issues than managing them. Companies are bombarded with too many issues and often lack ways to handle them. The problem of defining the discipline is exacerbated when divisions within corporations and scholarly writing lead persons to focus on a segment rather than on the total picture. As Goodman concluded, "The articles, writers, and editorial boards live in the same interrelated world but do not seem to recognize that this is the case. And business schools and corporations have failed to recognize that ambiguity and uncertainty exist."

Because of the information/public opinion foundation of issues management, some have argued that it is nothing more than the typical practice of public affairs and public relations (Ehling and Hesse, 1983). In part, this usage resulted because the term was coined by leading public relations practitioners such as Raymond P. Ewing and W. Howard Chase, who earned his reputation as an industry spokesman while at American Can Company. Chase (1984) in particular articulated a rationale for issues management that makes it an adjunct of communication, encouraging corporations to work to influence public policy and redirect interest-group pressure. He was also among the first to outline coherently why corporate leaders should aggressively counter widespread public suspicion of the private sector by engaging in proactive rather than purely defensive issues communication programs.

This brief review of the various approaches and contributions that are defining the roles and responsibilities of issues management leads to several conclusions. First, a turf battle among issues management, public affairs, and public relations can divert attention from deploying the full potential of corporate efforts to adjust to the political environment. Public relations and public affairs enter the scene to bring harmony between the company and key groups in the sociopolitical environment by solving communication problems. However, a communication remedy can assume that a communication breakdown is the only problem. Nothing could miss the essence of issues management further. A politically sensitive *management* theme of issues management is mandated because it is a broad executive function that consists in formulating and executing corporate policy in an environment influenced by public policy and public opinion. Failure to distinguish between managerial and communication aspects of issues management confuses the total function with its strategic tools.

Second, issues management, as a vital part of corporate planning, sometimes makes its contribution by showing that the best corporate strategy is to adapt to the current external public policy environment rather than change it. In this way, issues management supports strategic planning efforts to be sensitive to the vagaries of markets, economic conditions, competition, and other variables crucial to corporate success. Instead of employing standard external public relations tools (including advocacy advertising), issues management can in some situations proceed most effectively by infusing public standards of corporate responsibility into internal operating procedures. Issues management can even help reshape policies on product development, marketing, and product or service advertising. Moreover, many companies are finding that understanding and applying good ethics is good business — they attract and hold top-notch employees more easily, their customers are more satisfied and loyal, and they face fewer regulatory challenges.

No corporate function is better prepared to understand the limits of operating in a hostile environment than issues management. Ever sensitive to public responses, issues managers can work with management and operations personnel to be alert to the pitfalls of certain corporate activities and policies. Issues management cannot be effective unless holistic planning and execution are conducted with the objective of creating a harmonious relationship between companies and their many stakeholders. To balance public interest and selfish commercial needs, corporate social partnership demands a carefully coordinated effort at all levels of the company — executive, staff, and operations. Corporations can act in ways the public believes responsible while constantly seeking to avoid regulation that harms the public interest by making products and services bear unnecessary costs of unwise regulation. This new stewardship requires that corporate communication include informed discussion of the public significance of corporate activities — the advantages and benefits as well as the perils, costs, and limits. This approach to issues management makes it interdisciplinary, drawing together forecasting, planning, management, control, political maneuvering, communication, and ethics. It is all of this and perhaps more.

In the first chapter that follows, Post and Kelley look to the future by applying what they have learned about making public relations/public affairs vital to issues management. They isolate skills, philosophies, and responsibilities that should help companies increase the likelihood of surviving and prospering in the public policy arena. In the last chapter, Nelson forecasts the public policy implications of the post-smokestack economy. In the conclusion to this book, I look to the challenges that will face issues managers in the coming decade.

# 14

# Lessons from the Learning Curve: The Past, Present, and Future of Issues Management

*James E. Post*
*Patricia C. Kelley*

The modern corporation has become part of the bedrock on which American society rests. As Kenneth Mason has written (1986), the corporation is the central institution of our age. Not surprisingly, it has been buffeted by the many crosscurrents of American social and political life. For example, it is subject at the same time to the strains of egalitarianism and entrepreneurship, innovation and bureaucracy, economic expectations and sociopolitical pressures. The modern corporation is, above all else, a diverse, highly complex institution existing amid an even more diverse, complex social universe.

These pressures and discontinuities are not new. Many can be traced to the 1960s, and some as far back as the 1930s. But the past twenty years have been characterized by an extraordinary growth in the social and political complexity of the business environment. Companies have not been passive witnesses to this transformation. As Votaw and Sethi wrote in their well-known book, *The Corporate Dilemma* (1974), too often the corporation has been seen as part of the problem, not part of the solution to social problems. One reason is that the traditional values that govern organizational development and activity are frequently at odds with those that drive emerging issues, concerns, and social needs. This conflict is not surprising, but it has given rise to the need for an organizational mechanism that can discern the important elements of social change, translate and communicate information within the organizational hierarchy, and stimulate responses to legitimate needs.

It is within the context of the continuing quest for a responsive business corporation that the public affairs function has evolved in many American companies, and within that function, a special capacity for issues identification and issues management has been created. Arguably, were the environment not uncertain, unstable, and turbulent, there would be little or no need for issues management or corporate public affairs. It is continued uncertainty, instability, and environmental volatility that prompt the refinement and development of these important corporate functions.

This chapter deals with the general question of what has been learned about issues management, corporate public affairs, and the development of the responsive corporation. At one level, the answer is "A great deal." Our purpose is to be as specific as possible in discerning and articulating the learning curve that managers and organizations have traveled during these past two decades. To accomplish this, we have done three things. First, we have reviewed recent publications, speeches, and papers that discuss public affairs and issues management. Second, we have used the unique resources of the Boston University Public Affairs Research Program to focus on the lessons that public affairs practitioners have learned. And third, the junior author has conducted a set of interviews with public affairs managers in a variety of industry groups to gather lessons learned. Together, these three streams of information provide a broad assessment of what public affairs managers have learned in the past two decades and offer a perspective on how to meet the challenges of doing business in the modern political and social environment.

### The Responsive Corporation

*Lesson 1.* Companies have the capacity to consciously pursue strategies from among four basic approaches to a changing environment. They may choose to be inactive, reactive, proactive, or interactive toward the environment. Each of these response strategies carries costs and benefits.

Government's increasing impact on business activities, and society's willingness to voice its concern over questionable activities (note the impact that opposition to apartheid has had on businesses operating in South Africa), suggest a changing relationship with business that is historically significant. Business has become increasingly interdependent with government and society, a condition that means the organization's environmental uncertainty has increased. This change has affected managerial decision making within corporations, as social and political concerns are incorporated into basic strategic and operational decisions.

To truly manage interdependence of social actors with business, some mechanism is needed that can bring the concerns of social actors into the corporation. As Pfeffer and Salancik (1978, p. 43) note, "The typical solution to problems of interdependence and uncertainty involves increasing coordination, which means increasing the mutual control over each other's activities, or, in other words, increasing the behavioral interdependence of the social actors."

It has become a managerial axiom that successful response to environmental change requires efforts to anticipate change, get ahead of issues, and avoid situations where other actors or forces dictate corporate behavior. Further, the desire to be proactive has been tempered by the realization that "interaction" is more appropriate to the type of interdependence that exists in many settings. Collaborations such as those seen in public/private partnerships (Waddock, 1986) epitomize the spirit of an interactive approach.

*Lesson 2.* A responsive organization will tend, over time, toward an interactive approach toward the stakeholders in its environment. That is, dialogue becomes the key to an interactive approach.

Rather than just reaching outward to external groups, the organization needs to acknowledge and cultivate its interdependence with significant constituents. Issues management by public affairs departments is one response by the corporation to the increasing complexity in the environment. As organizations become more sophisticated, they internalize their external environments through organizational structures. This change is manifested not only in the changed name of the department—from *public relations* to *public affairs*—but in the responsibilities of the function.

For those companies that have successfully operationalized the public affairs function and made issues management part of corporate policy, dialogue and communication with external groups are a vital component. For example, in companies where a formal commitment has been made to issues management, public affairs managers have been highly involved in working with internal groups to establish policy positions and working with external groups by providing access to the corporation. Public affairs officers who had strong internal support often allowed external constituents access to organizational policy making. As one said, "We deal with groups that represent every interest in this community, from well-defined establishments like the elderly, minority groups, the disabled, to those involved in less-defined interests. What's interesting in communicating with them is that the access we provide to groups allows for interaction on a much calmer basis."

Allowing external constituents access to internal policy making was cited as one way to neutralize conflict. Because the organizations studied are visible and interactive, their comments suggest that a clear trend is emerging—to obtain input, prior to social pressure, from groups that company action might affect. "We've come a long way in terms of working with these organizations. We're really incorporating them into pretty much an ongoing dialogue. . . . This is in contrast to a few years ago, when we were kind of a company going our own way and having very little contact with community programs except for conflict. [This change] has been a very positive move for the company. It's lessened the hostility and created a more cooperative environment in dealing with all of our constituencies."

For an organization to make intelligent decisions, it must have accurate, reliable information. The greater the uncertainty of an issue, the greater the amount of information that must be gathered and disseminated to decision makers during its development. Information gathering is therefore a key function of the public affairs officer. He or she gathers information so that the corporation can make decisions that (1) minimize conflict with external constituents and (2) further organizational goals. This role is analogous to Galbraith's (1973) description of an organizational integrator, who "needs to be knowledgeable about the areas in question, capable of crossing attitudinal barriers and seeing things from different points of view, and able to speak the languages of the different [parties] to the decision" (p. 98). Thus, the substantive background and interpersonal skills of an individual performing this function for an organization are keys to his or her effectiveness. These skills are particularly critical to the public affairs officer's ability to manage conflict with external groups and assist in the decision-making processes of the organization.

> *Lesson 3.* An interactive approach does not mean the stakeholder is always right. It does mean the corporation is prepared to think in a flexible manner about actions that will narrow the gap between legitimate stakeholder expectations and organizational behavior.

Public affairs officers indicated that incorporating the public into decision making helps to prevent conflict and hostility. Many of those interviewed believed that including public responses to organizational activities strengthens the public affairs function by creating a "more than the bottom line" approach to decision making.

Arranging meetings for interest groups that may be affected by corporate policy makes the public affairs officer's job easier. Allowing external constituents to voice their concerns directly to the company has increased the speed with which potential conflicts get resolved. If external constituents are given access to decision makers, negotiation time on issues is decreased because the external group can have immediate input into decisions that affect it. Rather than creating undue delay through legal channels, issues can be framed and resolved up front. Access serves the function of formalizing the relationship between the company and its publics. One officer noted these changes in his company's relationship with stakeholders: "We're trying to formalize a lot of our current activities. For instance, we spend a lot of time with community groups, and we have written a community newsletter which we hope to publish three times a year. The first issue will go out in the spring. That's formalizing a relationship—acknowledging that this constituency is important to us."

> *Lesson 4.* Organizational memory depends on a cadre of managers who have lived though and thought about the experience of dealing with the public environment. This leads, in turn, to the development of an organizational structure such as a public affairs office to interact consistently with the political and social environment.

When relationships are formalized, public affairs becomes integrated into operational managers' decision making. The need for the public affairs officer to be "bilingual"—that is, able to communicate on two different levels—is lessened as line managers begin to incorporate political and social concerns into their decision making. Thus, the value of the information that public affairs officers collect and disseminate increases as the function becomes better operationalized in the company.

Public affairs officers held very strong feelings on the value of information and the role they played in disseminating it. They mentioned several reasons for valuing their role: company visibility; captive consumers; sense of responsibility; complicated, intersecting relationships with community groups; and past negative effects of withholding information.

The company's visibility in the community was cited as a

primary consideration in keeping interested publics informed of company activities. This consideration has to do with "winning people's respect," "involving others before there's a problem," and "being a responsible corporate citizen." Captive consumers, it was noted, "aren't afraid to take on utilitylike businesses," and they have the ear of regulatory and legislative bodies. Thus, their captivity resulted in a higher, rather than lower, level of communication. Managing consumers' expectations up front lowered the amount of conflict with which the company had to contend. Complicated, intersecting relationships with diverse groups were cited as a rationale for maintaining high levels of communication in order to fend off potential conflict. Finally, and perhaps most significant, were past negative experiences that had resulted from withholding information. One officer noted: "I don't think we were very forthcoming in telling our side of the story, so we were sort of improperly bludgeoned in the press." Withholding information on one issue resulted in not being asked for information on other issues of importance to the organization. "Every time the press ran an article on South Africa, they would not call us and ask us [about our involvement] but just repeat that we were the bad guys again. We were forever trying to explain those involvements to some of the activist groups in the community who felt very strongly about not doing any kind of business with South Africa."

Withholding information results in a cyclical process: The company's reputation is damaged, the company is viewed with mistrust by outside groups, and it is denied the opportunity to respond on other issues of importance. One senior officer noted: "Increasingly, large businesses are becoming indistinguishable from other visible presences in the community — like a sports figure or the mayor or anything else. When you are visible, you're the target and it certainly makes a point."

These experiences have heightened companies' awareness of the impact they have in the community, as well as their sense that the public is holding them accountable for their actions through the media. Thus, the need to inform the public and involve it in the company is reinforced.

### The Public Affairs Function

> *Lesson 5.* The public affairs function serves as a window: Looking out, the organization can observe the changing environment. Looking in, the stakeholders in that environment can observe, try to understand, and interact with the organization.

The "product" of the public affairs department is the smoothing of relationships with external constituents and the management of company-specific issues. The primary raw material of this product is information. Using information well was considered the process by which public affairs officers could deal effectively with both internal and external constituents. This included "telling it straight," "telling them what they need to know," and "speaking their language." Information, both internal and external, was considered the key to soliciting others' support.

Gathering and disseminating information had both practical and philosophical implications. One theme that recurred in many conversations, particularly those with younger officers who had recently entered the field from the public sector, was the philosophical convictions they brought to their job: "To be not just socially responsible but fiscally responsible in this day and age is so important. The change in the regulatory environment is such that if you're not part of the debate, you might get lost in the shuffle." Although these philosophical considerations were more strongly emphasized by public affairs officers who had entered the field through the public sector, they were also articulated by professionals who had entered the field from the line and had more public affairs experience: "I come from the perspective that people have a right to know everything that impacts on their lives. If you are a company that has a pipe running down the street, then [they] have a right to ask questions and you have a responsibility to answer them."

According to officers interviewed, the nature of heavily regulated industries is such that individuals in the organization feel they have "more obligations to the public than a manufacturing company." This feeling of obligation has developed since "just about everything [we] do has some kind of element. . . which requires dealing either with government agencies or local groups or municipal governments." The constant exposure to outside constituents may well have sensitized these companies to the need to deal with issues before the only option becomes one of reacting.

> *Lesson 6.* The legitimacy of the public affairs function is tied to its effectiveness as a means of organizational interaction with the political and social environment. The success of public affairs managers, however, is tied to their ability to span the boundary between the organization and the environment—that is, they must have internal credibility with senior and operating managers and external credibility with stakeholder groups.

Public affairs departments are boundary-spanning units. The crucial problem for a boundary-spanning unit is to help an organization adjust to constraints and contingencies that the organization does not control (Thompson, 1967). The individuals who work in such units serve as representatives/interventionists for an organization. They are, simultaneously, both on the periphery of the organization and integrally connected to the organization.

This inner/outer dynamic is emphasized by managers as a major constraint in performing the job. Effectiveness requires the use of two languages, and there is always a question of what to communicate. How well integrated the public affairs function is with other departments of the company often determines how effectively the officers can communicate internally. If the function has not become operationalized (that is, line managers are not sensitized to public affairs responsibilities), the ability of public affairs officers to use information internally is severely hampered.

Information is the key resource of public affairs officers. Through their ability to control and channel information about vital matters, they can become active participants in organizational decision making. This responsibility to gather and evaluate company-specific social and political information is unique, normally unduplicated by others in the organization, and can result in public affairs officers' having distinctly different relationships with other managers in the company. Specifically, a public affairs officer may be more distant—psychologically, organizationally, and often physically—from other members of the organization than from other boundary spanners because he or she represents the organization to the external environment and serves as the organization's agent of influence over the external environment.

Public affairs officers often note that if their position is not operationalized in the corporation, effectiveness is impaired. As one said, "It becomes very hard to communicate what we're doing. That's important to line managers who are used to evaluating things in terms of bottom line; it's easy for them to do that. It's easy for them to think of functions like public affairs and community relations as overhead—as expense centers rather than profit centers." Where the public affairs function is operationalized, however, communication is much easier: "If, as we are here, you're heavily oriented to the customer and community even on the line, then you have more internal responsiveness to what you're trying to do. We're service-oriented. The public counts for everybody [in this organization]."

Lack of operationalization of the function produces a constant "internal struggle." In companies that had not formalized issues management as a legitimate corporate function, officers found that a major part of the job was gaining support for performing their jobs. Methods included selected use of the CEO as leverage in obtaining other departments' support, sending out informational newsletters to keep employees informed on community/company issues, and "infiltrating" line management. One manager stated: "I believe in bringing pressure internally. One of my first goals when I came here was to educate the people in the company about the outside world—and to infiltrate all the departments so that I had some influence. It's a technical company—it's an operational company—and if I'm not involved and I don't understand what they're doing, then how the hell can I represent them?"

Public affairs officers need support, internally, from which they can proceed to reach compromises with external groups. Without internal support, one has no leverage in effecting negotiations. In other words, public affairs activities must be considered of importance to the organization and must be supported by management to maximize effectiveness. Internal support is particularly important because the public affairs officer often has no formal authority over others in the organization. Without formal authority, alternative methods of exercising influence must be found. Developing trust, contacts, and networks may be dependent on the personal characteristics of the public affairs officer. Among the more important personal characteristics are demonstrated competence in substantive areas; open discussion of interests and agendas; genuine interest in others as people and as resources; and active efforts to understand the situation facing others in the organization.

> *Lesson 7.* Communication is the key to effectively pursuing an interactive strategy of response toward the environment. Public affairs management rests on a foundation of dialogue and related skills in the political and social (public) arena.

One important task is to keep communication channels between groups open. This requires building a relationship of trust with others. All officers interviewed agreed that being honest and forthright with people, both internally and externally, was essential to success in the job. Simply identifying and analyzing issues of importance to various constituents are not enough. The officer must be able to find how these issues link with the company's long-term needs and strategic policy in order to get it involved before the issue becomes politicized. As one public affairs officer noted, "We not only have the task of communicating our position to the government on key issues, but we have to try to show people inside the [company] why issues are legitimate—trying to sensitize our internal businesspeople to issues in the community and to agendas of the community."

In other words, a primary task for public affairs is narrowing the gap between public expectations and corporate performance. Looking at this same task from another perspective, the officers need to open the corporation to the outside world. "When I first came here, the company looked at the community from an opposite perspective—strictly from a company perspective. When I came in, they realized they needed to have more direct contact with the people who were controlling their lives. But they had no idea how to make a policy or unify a message that would cross departments and have everybody on the same wavelength."

The skill of persuading each side to understand the issue from the other's perspective is the key to encouraging the dialogue and communication process.

## Issues Management

> *Lesson 8.* Issues management is an integrative approach for unifying three of the central responsibilities of the public affairs function: social and political intelligence, internal and external communication, and action programs targeted at key stakeholders.

Public affairs officers often define their role as that of an "issue framer." "We need to make sure we have as much information as possible and notice where other people stand on it." "In this job you need to get involved in a potential problem before an issue becomes defined. You don't want to have to react after the fact." In order to behave proactively, the public affairs officer needs to be able to communicate with diverse publics. "You need to network on the job to find issues of relative importance." For example: "If the company has a commitment to education in the city of _____, which it does, it pays to be involved in the education process. . . . Our involvement . . . helps to attract a better-educated work force. The process is cyclical."

Thus, by developing relations with external and internal constituents, the public affairs officer is better able to isolate issues of importance to the organization. By incorporating those issues into the organization and acting positively on them (if possible), the public affairs officer can solidify relationships and keep the lines of communication open. The process is self-perpetuating—obtain information, use it thoughtfully in developing a corporate response, and develop trust, which creates access to information. Throughout this cycle, reliance on relevant external sources is critical. Therefore, establishing and maintaining relationships with others is crucial to acquiring corporate-specific information and minimizing potential conflict.

> *Lesson 9.* Effective issues management requires that the practitioner transform the daily job of reacting to an agenda beyond his or her control into an anticipatory system for responding to environmental change, whether in crisis form or not.

The presence of a public affairs office is an important structural response to environmental dependence. However, the methods that officers in these departments use require considerable imagination, even "entrepreneurship." As one officer, who originally worked in the public sector, stated, "You're almost totally a victim of what's in the daily newspaper or what someone else sets for you as an agenda. You do have some control over determining what's important—what you're going to work on—but that menu does shift radically. That's one of the fascinating things about this job. Many people would find it very frustrating, also."

A major attraction of the job is its "unstructured" nature and the "broader perspective" it both requires and facilitates. These features make the area appealing for line managers who want less "restriction" in their job as well as individuals from the public sector accustomed to such uncertainty. The challenge, it appears, is to create structure out of what would otherwise be chaos. One method of creating such structure is to "define areas of concern yourself. Then you have more control over what's happening, and you can get more input in the policy planning process." The ability to scan the environment for emerging critical issues and allocate resources in advance of crises is another key to managing environmental dependence. Since the routine varies from issue to issue, the job calls for numerous intuitive and creative responses. "I think it's really hard to generalize about this job. Things really differ from day to day and issue to issue.... You asked what kinds of things are done routinely. There frankly aren't that many. My in-box, my calendar, my list of things to do—not much consistency."

However, a high level of frustration is inherent in ambiguous situations. Often this frustration results from the need to mobilize resources—both human and monetary—without recourse to formal authority. For example, one officer said: "It's hard to get the public to understand that the company can act only in a way which is technically feasible within the time constraints you're dealing with. On the other hand, it's hard to convince the company that the public has a right to know what will affect them." Because of the need to deal with two groups simultaneously and in different ways, officers feel that they spend a great deal of energy structuring their time and that of their staff to accomplish important tasks.

> *Lesson 10.* Personal skills are crucial to effective career development in this field, but greater levels of professional skill are now required as well. Professionalization of the corporate function is leading to professionalization of the field and a concomitant interest in professional standards. Although "hired guns" still thrive, their use will decline for all but narrow skill-specific problems.

Conflicts originate from a number of sources, including differences in information, beliefs, values, and interests or desires and resource scarcity. A public affairs officer has a number of options for managing conflict with external constituents. Most seem to favor bargaining and compromise rather than confrontation techniques. However, the ability to manage conflict requires an ability to clarify goals, illuminate alternatives, promote rigorous analysis, and encourage creative solutions to complex problems. As Galbraith (1973, p. 99) suggests, "The conflict resolution process causes individuals to be confronted, to place their egos on the line, to accept criticism, and to deal with role conflict due to multiple group memberships. In order to deal with these feelings, interpersonal competence is essential." Therefore, both strong information-gathering skills and interpersonal competence are preconditions to successfully managing conflict.

Effective negotiations with diverse groups require an appreciation that no one will support you consistently. One needs to be able to maintain relationships though disagreeing on various issues. One public affairs officer noted: "If there is someone opposed to you, either you avoid them or you try to sit down with them and see if you really do disagree. Often you find that you do, but maybe your areas of disagreement are smaller than you thought they were. And maybe there are areas where you can agree with them. And that's what you try to find. You try to find areas where you can work together."

Public affairs officers often show an ability to depersonalize potential conflict. "It was part of his job"; one does not "write off a relationship" because a peer or friend could not or would not support one's position. "You still have to work with that person on another occasion." Some see the ability to depersonalize conflict as one sign of the increasing professionalization of the field. The "old-boy, cigar-chomping network" in which favors were traded has given way to an era of professionals who have more substantive experience in business and government and who are increasingly able to make a real career out of public affairs. Thus, trade-offs, negotiations, and compromises are easier to develop. Public affairs officers consider themselves professionals. One officer used this analogy in describing his job: "It's like being a lawyer, in a way. You sometimes fight like crazy for your client, but when the dust settles, you go out for a drink. Really, it's a job and next time you may be on the same side. So you never take it to heart."

The conviction that the public affairs area has become increasingly professional is at odds with the image public affairs officers held of many others holding similar corporate positions. All but one of a dozen officers recently interviewed clearly stated that they were not "traditional public affairs" types. "Businesses that traditionally staff their public affairs functions with either senior officers readying for retirement or former state legislators are going to have to rethink some of these strategies. Public affairs traditionally has been male-dominated — it's been a lot of backslapping and drinks and sort of the old-style notion of what lobbying was all about." Most clearly indicated their disdain for the "old-style public affairs type": "I guess, on a personal level, some people might use personal relationships, but that's not something I'm terribly comfortable with." Another officer, who had entered the field from the public sector, stated: "I didn't want to be a public relations type. I thought there was a better way to do the job."

Most public affairs officers are aware of stereotypes the general public holds toward them, and they resist being labeled according to those stereotypes. All indicated that they saw the field moving toward an "increasing specialization and professionalization that isn't there now." Many believe that their companies are on the cutting edge of this change, primarily because of corporate visibility in the community and company experience in public affairs matters. A large number seem to share the perspective advanced five years ago in the initial Boston University study: "The public affairs function in American companies appears to be converging around a basic set of responsibilities and activities. At the risk of some oversimplification, the essential role of public affairs units appears to be that of a window out of the corporation through which management can perceive, monitor, and understand external change, and simultaneously, a window through which society can influence corporate policy and practice" (Boston University Public Affairs Research Group, 1981, p. v; see also Mahon, 1982).

To perform this role effectively, a company's senior management must define the nature of the job it expects to have done. When public affairs officers are considered merely lobbyists, they suffer from a too narrow definition and a negative stereotype associated with the image. "Most lobbyists bridle at the title. . . . They resent the name not only because of its unflattering connotations, but because it doesn't adequately describe what they do" (Berry, 1984, p. 114). Our conversations with public affairs officers make clear that this lack of understanding creates constraints on job performance internally and externally.

As corporate attitudes toward external relations change, becoming more positive, the caliber of personel hired to fill that role evolves as well. The job now demands that individuals come to their job with proven "policy expertise,... the ability to network (form coalitions), to utilize the media, and to develop lasting professional relationships with staffers and policy makers" (Berry, 1984, p. 43). Thus, the type of person hired for this position and his or her qualifications have changed. The person is becoming an integrator, one who "behaves in ways that remove possible impediments to information sharing and problem solving. Such individuals are difficult to find, and training technologies are not yet developed to create them" (Galbraith, 1973, p. 99). Such a role may best be staffed when the candidate has demonstrated competence in the areas of greatest uncertainty facing the organization. Thus, political expertise, plus an orientation toward organizational goals, maximizes potential effectiveness.

> *Lesson 11.* You cannot evaluate what you do not understand, but you can evaluate what you cannot count. There is no free lunch, which means that managers can count on the need to continue evaluating the effectiveness of public affairs and issues management.

There appear to be a number of concerns about how professionalization can best be accomplished. Suggestions included training public affairs officers in the substantive areas of the company, hiring individuals with demonstrated effectiveness in policy planning, and formalizing role responsibilities.

These changes may affect the evaluation of public affairs officers (Andrews, 1987). In the past there has been little systematic analysis of what constitutes effectiveness in public affairs or what criteria apply in evaluating these activities. A more concerted effort is being made, however, to conduct such analysis.

Yet, the ambiguous, qualitative, and informal nature of the job creates difficulty in determining what criteria to use for evaluating the job and how to apply them. "It's so different from a line manager's responsibility, where you have certain profit targets, maybe manufacturing quotas. You look at their job performance evaluation, which is one way to think about jobs. There are measurable goals line managers are supposed to achieve, and they show up on the bottom line. . . . We have very few ways to evaluate our performance, to plan our performance, to really guide ourselves."

Some officers believe that their company neither understands nor appreciates the value of the work being done by the public affairs staff. "And how do you evaluate that?" was a phrase commonly interjected in the interviews. This phrase followed descriptions of the work being done — for example, establishing a public/private partnership in education, gaining support from an unfriendly legislator on a bill, developing good media relations, or developing a good relationship with the city. All these accomplishments were clearly considered important by the officers being interviewed. But the concern persists that there remains in senior management a view that "you cannot evaluate what you cannot count."

Thus, a major portion of a public affairs officer's performance may be directed toward neutralizing conflict in the external environment, and this role is often not easily evaluated. In fact, one public affairs officer commented: "One of the primary things in being evaluated is the typical corporate thing of getting along in the company. It's always a matter of being able to cajole people into doing what you'd like them to or cooperating with them . . . we don't have line authority over anybody, so your supervisors can only see how you get along with other units in the company."

If measurement is difficult, evaluation is possible by improved objective setting. This means that the work being done undergoes constant redefinition. "There's a pretty constant effort in trying to define and establish, first of all, what you are trying to do and, second of all, how to determine what the standards are."

The sense of uncertainty about the worth the company places on these activities declines as the function is integrated into the policy-planning process. It was apparent, under these circumstances, that bottom-line orientation could be harmonized with a more sophisticated appreciation of the job: "So what if we review 5,000 bills a year? That says nothing about our effectiveness or performance. We can review one bill, and if it's the one that saves the company a couple of million dollars, or makes a couple of million dollars for the company, that's all you need."

Thus, the areas to be emphasized in evaluating performance may well not be the areas that are most measurable. Where managers place their time and energy is critical to long-term corporate effectiveness but may be difficult to incorporate into short-term performance evaluations. "If legislation that is detrimental to the company doesn't get passed, that's one way of knowing how well you've done your job. But really it's the relationships, having to build relationships and keep them stable, that counts. And how do you evaluate that?"

Lack of certainty is a part of the public affairs officer's job. One needs to be able to create order out of chaos, certainty out of ambiguity, and calm in a storm, which are clearly elements of the job. According to many public affairs officers, "The only way to do it is to do it." And, one hopes, the company will recognize that it has been done well. "In the end, the only way to show [the corporation] I know how to do my job is through example. I rely on my experience and instincts, which means a lot of times I'm nervous. Because you don't know. You never know."

## Conclusion

Issues management has moved along a learning curve. It has evolved through the awareness stage, when organizations acknowledge the need for such a function, through the trial-and-error phase of "what works" and "what doesn't work." What doesn't work is paying lip service to the function, filling the role with near-term retirees, and attempting to manage stakeholders on critical issues by avoiding them. What does work is—

1. Sensitizing the company's line management to the importance of its activities for organizational stakeholders.
2. Identifying issues early in their life cycle and beginning immediate dialogue with stakeholders on those issues.
3. Staffing public affairs/issues management positions with individuals who are substantively grounded both in the organization's goals and in public policy planning.
4. Creating an ongoing dialogue with interest groups who hold multiple stakes on a variety of issues of importance to the organization.
5. Creating strong information channels between those involved in issues management and identification and organizational decision makers.
6. Managing ongoing interaction between personnel responsible for issues management and line functions.

The constraints on public affairs officers in performing their job appear to follow from how well integrated the department is in the corporation, and that integration depends on the department's experience, the individuals who staff it, and the predictability of issues to be faced. The experience level of the public affairs function and its operationalization in the organization determine how effectively the public affairs officer manages external isues.

Operationalization of issues management in the corporate consciousness also appears to affect the evaluation of public affairs activities. Departments that are well integrated into a corporation's continuing operations reflect sensible criteria for evaluation. Less well integrated departments are more interested in trying to find bottom-line measurements of performance; that is, they are more internally oriented. This suggests that as the function becomes increasingly formalized, the organization becomes more comfortable with qualitative measures of job performance. Additionally, the more experienced a public affairs department is, the more capable it is of isolating its contribution to profits. Demonstrations of how certain activities resulted in cost avoidance for a firm and the move from coping to planning activities were measures used to determine the long-term effectiveness of public affairs activities. The consensus appeared to be one of "working smarter" — that is, seizing opportunities to perform and showing, through example, why certain approaches are appropriate. It is a reflection of the learning curve that successful managers and organizations travel.

Top-level corporate support for public affairs continues to be cited as critical to a department's success. This support was often, however, pointed out as a "thin reed to grasp." CEOs and boards of directors can and do change. Often, when these positions turn over, staff areas such as public affairs are hit first by corporate cost cutting. One interviewee, a recent survivor of a corporate merger, said that the first place the merged organization made personnel cuts was staff areas such as public affairs. He felt that if cuts had been proposed in overlapping line functions, there would have been support to prevent such cuts. The ambiguity of the public affairs function and the loss of CEO support, however, resulted in a net loss of jobs in public affairs.

In spite of the pitfalls that plague some dimensions of the public affairs officer's job, there is considerable optimism about the future. The increasing "professionalism" of the field and the requirement that applicants be substantively grounded are often cited as evidence that this function would continue to play an important role in business. The continuing struggle to define criteria to judge its effectiveness was considered critical in integrating public affairs into the corporate culture. Moves toward including qualitative performance measures in evaluations supported the officers' contention that highly developed interpersonal skills can and should be an integral part of the job.

The public affairs management field has undergone tremendous change over the past five years. Change will continue as the field moves toward professionalization and legitimization within the corporate world. This trend should help organizations move from coping with external demands to anticipating how demands can best be met within the technical and economic context of the organization. This is the essence of being a responsive corporation in the modern world. For the central institution of our age, that is neither too much nor too little to ask.

# 15

## Public Policy Implications of the New Communication Technologies

*Richard Alan Nelson*

From ancient prophets to modern psychics, the wish to understand the future has been a constant of human nature. If serious social scientists and crystal-gazing futurists are correct, the next decade of telecommunications changes will be of the same magnitude as Gutenberg's introduction of movable type or the mass production techniques that ushered in the industrial revolution. We are entering an exciting, yet vaguely terrifying, "postindustrial" period — a transition foreshadowed by past events but of a magnitude unprecedented in world history. Curiosity is a valid reason for seeking to know upcoming events, but for business leaders, coming to grips with trends is more important. After all, this analytical ability is a key management component in serving their companies. Given that change is inevitable, awareness of the interaction between issues management and social regulation is particularly useful to managers who want to guide their firms and industries proactively into what is being called the information age.

This chapter forecasts some of the more significant public policy challenges that will likely occur for business as such countries as the United States further evolve because of new communication technologies. We will be looking at several broad themes, including the changing nature of employer/employee relations, the building of new consensuses in public policy making, and the emerging need for an international perspective. Later these will be applied to nine information-based issues of continuing importance.

The future will bring new international uncertainties that result from trends begun over forty years ago. The economic and political structures erected shortly after World War II are becoming more dated and subject to realignments—with profound implications for American business. Acting as a catalyst to the possible end of "Pax Americana" is technology, long associated with American leadership. Ironically, the post-1945 rebuilding of Japan and Western Europe as markets also led to their reemergence as competitors. Balance-of-payments deficits and other forms of economic hemorrhaging are causing policy reevaluations in Washington and other capitals. Unreciprocated free-trade policies by the United States government and cutbacks in research and development funding by American industry have clearly aided in this transfer of innovation to countries in the Pacific Rim and Europe.

Broad public policy criteria typical of the heavy industrial era that define quality of life, such as security, esthetics, fairness, and equality, will continue to serve as forecasting guidelines as we move toward a twenty-first-century economy. But the specific content of future policy issues and corporate action alternatives is still hazy and uncertain. While industrial production will remain an important part of the economic mix, long-term growth will depend on the service sector becoming increasingly linked via telecommunications. Such linkages are becoming evident; for instance, business outlets are linked to central computers that monitor performance (such as sales per outlet), control inventory as can be seen at checkout counters in major supermarkets, contain financial data and funding in the form of centralized bank authorization, and offer news/public policy tracking services such as Lexis, Nexis, or Dialog. As we shall see later, social considerations and public policy implications in a nationalistic non-export-oriented "smokestack" economy such as the United States has been may well differ markedly from those of the predicted *inter*nationalist postindustrial one to come.

The new information age we have all been hearing so much about results from the merger of computer, communication satellite, microprocessor, and allied technologies. They are — for good or evil — reshaping some of the basic structures of society, the distribution and exchange of information coming to dominate our lives to an unparalleled extent (Porat, 1977; Boorstein, 1978; Dizard, 1982; Nelson, 1983; Beniger, 1986). Unfortunately, *information age* and *information society* continue to be imprecise terms because they are used differently by various writers. One of the better attempts at definition establishes as its information-society criterion an economy where more than 50 percent of the adult population is tied into a "vast electronic telecommunications network" at home as well as at work. This differs from more simplistic "information worker" models in that such individuals are able to "transmit and receive news, data, and entertainment through home telecommunications centers" and "telebanking, telecourses, televoting, telemetering, telecommuting, telegames, and teleshopping are common" (Salvaggio, 1983, pp. 2–3). Using this definition, one can see that the United States, where less than 5 percent of the population is truly telematically interactive, is now only at the entry stage of such an informational, service-oriented economy. Nevertheless, the work component (make and handle information) and the domestic component (consume information) are being developed and promoted by important forces in business and government as the key to future prosperity.

Telecommunications and other informational technologies promise increased American efficiency and a shortcut to a new, more productive service-oriented economy but also entail social dislocation and privacy dangers if misused. We are already witnessing the strains as well as benefits that the geometric growth in information creates. The marketplace for new technologies is now a battleground of supply push and demand pull. Suppliers of new equipment have pushed their products, in some cases leading to thousands of home personal computers going unused. In other instances, buyers' needs for products and software services have gone unheeded. Certainly, the widespread implementation of new technologies is bound to affect the competitive position of various enterprises.

Futurists studying how social systems will respond to such evolutionary pressures tend to concentrate on two broad categories of issues: (1) what the economic and cultural impacts of growing "informationalization" in the workplace will be and (2) how the increasing value of information will influence decision making about access to such information (democratization/equity versus authoritarian/inequity concerns). Each has broad importance to executive decision makers, but despite the voluminous "information society" literature, little thought seems to have been given beyond concerns over worker displacement/unemployment or the wonders of a networked office linked to satellite electronic cottages to the more fundamental *sociopolitical role* to be played by business in the twenty-first century. For example, what public policy initiatives or voluntary restraints will corporations need to implement in the near term if they are to marshal these changing information resources to set the agenda for, and control debate over, the redefinition of social responsibility standards that is sure to come? Corporations have always turned to self-regulation and voluntary policing to stave off intrusive government intervention, and it is likely that increasing attention will be paid to international issues. Change is a reality, and the business community is beginning to apply new technologies to advance its political as well as market interests. Rather than simply responding to political pressures, business interests are taking the opportunity to proactively adopt voluntary measures that enhance image while increasing profits.

One implication of seeing social responsibility as a profit center is that tomorrow's business executives will be challenged to expand their understanding of the role of culture, both within and without the organization. This need to be sensitive to culture is due (at least in part) to greater sophistication in our understanding of communication, to the internationalization of finance and banking, which gives greater importance to exports, and to population changes due to immigration that are resulting in the reemergence of multilingualism in the United

States. If they are to develop the human resources of their employees, managers will need to see beyond surface similarities and attributes based on demographic and psychological profiles. To accomplish this end implies a greater educational role for business and, more significantly, increased sensitivity to group differences. Examples:

- Expanded private/public partnerships for job training will have to take into account language and culture backgrounds as minority groups become majority groups.
- Marketing considerations will force greater linguistic and life-style sophistication internally as well as externally.
- Flexibility in work hours and physical location of employment, linked to increases in the number of part-time workers, will alter the traditional labor/management relationship.
- As informational inequities lead to social dislocation, business will be expected to bail out various levels of government.

The bottom-line result: Well-managed businesses will establish corporate cultures conducive to innovation and competitiveness before government forces such involvement. For example, if the United States is to compete effectively against countries with higher academic performance standards, how a new public/private educational partnership is going to be structured and funded could prove one of the major policy issues of the 1990s. The White House Office of Private Sector Initiatives has served as a catalyst for creating the momentum for the school/business partnership movement. But as Don Adams, editor of *Pro-Education*, points out, "Only a small number of school systems are enjoying the benefits of these cooperative efforts" (Adams, 1985, p. 25). Given the failures of U.S. education, greater future involvement by business in staff training and team development will be *required* to maximize employee organizational value and performance. This involves enlightened and responsible self-interest but also demonstrates the need for expanded corporate social intervention because of the changing economy, especially true for those whose business is information-based (such as computer manufacturers). Firms like Apple have a vested interest in preparing young people for a computerized world and already devote considerable equipment and expertise to education. It would be a mistake to underestimate the long- as well as short-term benefits such involvement can have in public perceptions of corporate social utility (Lerond, 1986).

The restructuring of the office information environment and robotization of manufacturing also mean a fundamental redefinition of corporate organizational structures — particularly at the line worker and middle management levels. Businesses must choose between trying to make the technology fit their existing model and adapting themselves to the technology. The latter seems to be more efficient but runs into opposition from those unwilling to change. Successful leaders such as Lee Iacocca at Chrysler, Carlo de Benedetti at Olivetti, and Wisse Decker at Phillips in the Netherlands have ensured the adaptation of their firms to changing political and market forces by implementing widespread use of new information technologies, speeding product development, increasing performance, reducing unit costs, improving quality, emphasizing more effective marketing, stressing customer service, and incorporating issues management as an essential component of their strategic systems. This approach requires an integrated method of doing business, with an articulated company philosophy, well-defined goals, productivity improvement programs geared to informing and motivating employees at all levels, establishment of specific project teams and task forces accountable directly to top management, and a system for performance review geared to making practical improvements at a departmental level by diagnosing problems and rewarding achievement.

These educational and human resource changes may seem common sense. Though not necessarily unique to an information society, they are not as typical today as one would imagine. In the future such employee development involvement should become more common where service is really required for business success if managements are to flexibly navigate the jolts and dislocations of a postindustrial information society

(Faulhaber and others, 1986). Not only are these innovations vital at the corporate level, but they may be required at the level of national policy as well. Commitment among business, labor, and government is important, not only because it enhances productivity, but also because applying information technologies to the production process tends to demand the wholesale introduction of new methods throughout the entire corporation and industry. The new international marketplace requires that government, business, and labor work together to support technological innovation and worker training. As Kazuo Ogura (1987, p. 23), the Japanese minister to the Organization for Economic Cooperation and Development, recently observed, "Such a revolutionary introduction of a new process demands an overall consensus among workers and management. What is necessary is not so much new skills or knowledge with which to understand or master new methods but rather a sense of mission or consensus about an inevitable process for survival in this competitive world." In other words, a social contract is needed among workers, company management, industry leaders, and government that has these forces working together to solve common problems rather than at cross-purposes.

Business organizations again have the opportunity to position themselves at the forefront of providing progressive solutions to such social needs. Ironically, the very speed of technological advance and the rapid implementation of communication networks by business enterprises point up the slow nature of governmental processes and regulatory response. Those in the private sector who lack a commitment to applying strategic planning to involve themselves in shaping issues may find themselves in unmarked and dangerous public policy territory, groping blindly into the future, whereas firms under progressive leadership have a window to tomorrow. Of course, issues management alone cannot change the fact that media coverage feeds public opinion and public opinion, in turn, influences public policy, but such activities do provide organizations with a realistic road map to their future problems and opportunities.

Issues managers may be able to apply new "wired" and

satellite technologies to help decision makers in government, business, and activist groups understand the often volatile forces underlying change. New communication technologies allow people to communicate faster, as is the case with videoconferencing, and provide greater quantity and quality of data, supplied through vast data bases. A second benefit of the new technologies is that getting accurate predictive trend information will become easier. Nevertheless, four basic problems remain: (1) As information becomes a more marketable commodity, access restrictions for at least some of this information will follow. (2) As information technology penetration increases, an information overload will be likely, making it harder to separate the important from the trivial. (3) This information glut will also increase the importance of analysis because faulty assumptions in using the data can lead to flawed conclusions. (4) As we move toward a more telecommunications-based social environment, it is important to recognize that the United States is handicapped. Unlike our allies and trading partners, we have traditions that rebel against the idea of a national industrial or information policy. In Japan and most European countries, for example, information technology is viewed as analogous to a public utility such as transportation and electricity, but there is no such consensus in the United States (Varan, 1987). Reasons for this difference include greater belief by the advanced foreign nations in an ongoing partnership between the state and business, stronger commitment to national planning initiatives enhanced by their parliamentary political systems, and lesser cultural clash because of their more homogeneous populations.

There are also historical reasons for this difference. Although American industrialism dates from the late 1860s, it took nearly 100 years (despite previous Progressive and New Deal–era legislation) to develop our current corporate social responsibility standards, which seek to balance corporate and public interests. Many believe (myself included) that federal policy should more openly support—rather than restrict—corporate communication, particularly that designed to take advantage of new technologies and provide key audiences with information on social, economic, and political problems. But even today there are continuing disagreements about what is socially responsible, differences that will be exacerbated by the lack of a clear-cut and consistently enforced national information policy. Decision making in the United States is more diffuse than in Japan or Europe, and domestic market forces (now incorporating interest groups) at present are the key determinant of the introduction, adoption, and use of various new technologies.

Continued imbalances in the international marketplace and demands to erect protectionist barriers will increase the pressures to intervene through public policy decision making. But while the old rules break down (partly because of new technologies), changing from a "government as barrier" to "government as partner" view will not be easy—particularly if this means legislation to restrict domestic and foreign access to information or enhance big-business oligopolies at the expense of small to medium-size enterprises. The paralysis that attends debate would delay implementation of measures to deal with the new realities—a disastrous result for American business if it finds itself effectively shut out of foreign markets while domestically undercut by imports. In other words, by miring ourselves in resistance to change rather than seeking ways to use new technologies for a broader public interest, we could bring on destabilizing stagnation and unemployment.

American business executives face a number of other key issues that, described in full, would outrun the pages of this chapter. This in itself is a problem, for it is not enough to track general news about a topic. Besides following the ups and downs of large and crucial issues such as energy development and health-care cost containment, the business analyst today needs to spot key subissues at the hub of controversy. In evaluating environmental protection, for example, also important are related subissues like waste disposal, air-quality regulation, acid rain, and managerial commitment to informing target audiences. Given this caveat, however, by selecting the issues that affect profits, we can cut down the list to more manageable proportions. What are some of these key concerns, particularly as we prepare for an era when new sensibilities are going to be required if the potential conflict between corporate policy and public concerns is to be lessened?

1. The new information society will call for further *re-definition of the public interest* and the role business plays in terms of social good. The change in the nature of the economy is creating opportunities for influencing the development of issues as new public policy concerns emerge, ranging from the responsibilities of multinational enterprises in international trade to domestic questions about whether antitrust legislation is still appropriate. The fact is that we do not yet know the ground rules of this evolving information, service-based economy, bringing with it sets of issues and questions not yet imagined which will take the traditional public policy variables of security, esthetics, fairness, and equality and clothe them with new meaning. Once reality fails to live up to its potential, as it invariably does, public interest concerns will be compounded by the falling to the wayside of many of the "information society's" most glittering promises when company, industry, and governmental actions fail to meet public expectations. For example, continued widespread uneasiness about the questionable impact of information technologies on traditional values may spark an unintended antitechnology backlash. As Ettema and Griswold (1988) note, "Enthusiasts of communication technology regularly pay homage to the idea that information and therefore informational media are *necessary* for public participation in a democracy. They less often consider what is *sufficient* to sustain such participation." Or as Ogura (1987, pp. 23–24) puts it, "Despite the growing interdependence among nations, the political mechanism, or assumption, underlying the democratic system in major countries of the world has not undergone substantial change. Politics is still heavily . . . anchored to the interests and concerns of domestic electorates and is rarely in tune with international considerations. . . . Popular concepts of economic reality in the contemporary world appear to be becoming more and more divorced from the true reality, and partly because of the instantaneous and far-reaching effects of the mass media. Under these circumstances, it is becoming increasingly important to build an international understanding

or general consensus on what should be done in each country. . . . The problem should be coped with by fostering a new dimension of human contacts commensurate with the development of information technologies."

2. Growing ambivalence toward authority, deepening mistrust, and increasing cynicism are raising *new questions about future stability.* Information, rather than acting to liberate the disadvantaged by breaking the cycle of deprivation, is taking on the status of a property right as an essential accoutrement of power. Computers make possible the cross-indexing and correlation of data on individuals, organizations, issues, and nations with unprecedented depth and speed. Government is seen as the typical watchdog for abuse, but what happens when the state is itself a potential abuser? No clear legal definition of privacy exists, for example, and many specialists argue that an information age inevitably requires a blurring of the distinctions between public and private. A touted new technique known as "computer profiling" is a case in point. It uses sophisticated software to scan data bases to create depth profiles of individuals having certain characteristics. For some of those targeted it can prove a boon, but for others linked to specific behavior (such as those with a bankruptcy or landlord dispute on their record) it can be more of a bane. Although computer profiling is most typically used in marketing and in credit checks, its uses extend to the political. The U.S. Secret Service is reportedly setting up a profile system to help identify potential assassins, a practice with much broader civil liberty implications as other agencies expand their efforts (Field and Neff, 1987).

3. As business becomes more data-oriented, that is, as more of what a business does involves manipulation of information rather than creation of a manufactured product, *the cost of gathering the information essential to one's business will probably increase.* Price jumps are likely despite competition and productivity gains among information suppliers, for not only will there be new equipment needs (cable TV, data scanners, computer applications, and so on) and more sources of information to consider and purchase, but the value of really useful informa-

tion will inflate. There is no reason not to believe that information will be priced differentially like other commodities. (For a
useful overview of the "corporate network" business telematics
considerations, see Belitsos and Misra, 1986). It is also likely
that, as has happened in previously developed communication
industries (print and broadcasting), the number of competitors
will eventually shake out into an information oligopoly.

4. Privacy, proprietary needs, international trade, and a
variety of other information access concerns will likely lead to
*increased policing of unauthorized data use*. In 1987 SRI International and a consortium of leading companies, including IBM,
3M, Aetna, Sears, and Wells Fargo Bank, formed the International Information Integrity Institute ("I-4") to protect members'
information assets from unauthorized use. I-4 coordinates with
federal agencies charged with computer security functions. Government regulation of information policy is a two-edged sword,
however, since many of the ways government gathers and uses
information are questionable on grounds of public sensitivities
about social responsibility. From a public policy perspective,
recent experiments in "computer matching" of records from
different governmental departments—using Social Security
numbers to track down military draft nonregistrants, student
loan delinquents, and unqualified welfare recipients—raise
warning flags for social libertarians concerned about "Big
Brotherism."

As another information issue, some federal executive
agencies are asking firms to restrict customer access to reports
and data bases prepared by other federal agencies worried
about technological and information espionage. For instance,
the Reagan administration recently asked that private data-base
companies not make available studies that the National Security
Agency and the Department of Defense consider of value to the
Soviet Union and other potential adversaries, even though the
information is unclassified. The resulting brouhaha led to the
official withdrawal of a 1984 policy memorandum written by
Vice-Admiral John M. Poindexter, then White House National
Security Adviser, to codify policy for keeping "sensitive" information from foreign agents. Poindexter's list of "national se-

curity or other federal government interests" included "economic, human, financial, industrial, agricultural, technological,
and law enforcement information" irrespective of whether the
federal government collected and stored it. Still on the books is
National Security Decision Directive 145, signed by President
Reagan, which outlines a new category of "information, even if
unclassified in isolation [that] often can reveal highly classified
and other sensitive information when taken in aggregate." The
chilling prospect of litigation arising from this directive remains, and of course, restricting access also imposes added costs
on legitimate domestic research.

5. Census data now are used to divide the country into
250,000 neighborhoods of about 250 households each, further
recombined by researchers using more than forty identifiable
socioeconomic categories and various demographic and psychological groupings. Marketing firms translate the concerns of
individuals into perceived group needs, whether they make up
an expanded and highly educated professional caste, a politically savvy "graying" post-forty-five-year-old generation, a growing linguistic minority, or one of an increasing spectrum of
other interests stimulating new public policy contests. Although
the number of representative activist groups created each year
peaked in the 1970s, the 1980s are witnessing healthy, ongoing
*growth in new activist organizations*—most geared to a narrow
single-interest or niche issue rather than broad public policy
spectrum concerns (Bergner, 1986a). The information age will
offer activists greater opportunities, as long as the information
they provide and the issues they raise have perceived utility, for
such concentration brings with it increased budgets and staffing, allowing activists to move from the agenda periphery to a
more central continuing news and consultancy role to form an
integral component of an information economy.

6. As part of their maturation, public interest groups are
extending their influence by increasing grass-roots networking
and *diversifying into multiple levels of policy making*, rather than
limiting themselves to either state/local, federal, or international
lobbying as they have in the past. Over 80 percent of the 250
groups analyzed in the latest edition of *Public Interest Profiles* by

the Foundation for Public Affairs are now active in two or all three of these levels (Bergner, 1986b). Although many groups have monitored the activities of various government bodies, the extent and level of sophistication practiced today would not be possible without computerization.

7. This diversification of interests is also true of business itself. One of the assumptions of contemporary economic planning is that we are moving inexorably toward an interdependent global future where the majority of employees will work for service organizations whose primary product is information. Even if American corporations were to agree in promoting a neoisolationist agenda, it would be difficult to decouple from the *global marketplace* we now find ourselves uncomfortably—but inextricably—in. With competition for U.S. markets intensifying rather than stabilizing, business leaders may end up finding themselves blamed for the failure of government leaders to establish coherent (let alone consistent) policies for such basic issues as trade and jobs.

Because of new technologies, this marketplace extends beyond products. Part of the problem stems from our uncompetitiveness in industrial wares ranging from shoes to steel; but whether we have what it takes to maintain economic leadership in a future telecommunications-dominated service economy is open to question. Indeed, it is one thing to talk about an information age, another to survive it commercially.

8. Growing economic and political interdependence is pushing governments, corporations, activist groups, and others to communicate to an unprecedented extent. Indeed, *instantaneous worldwide communication* via satellite is a reality, both for consumer news and for new far-reaching business-to-business applications. The invisible hand of the market is linked to the visible hand of public policy forces. In an information economy, the largest producers and consumers of information are the engines of government and business. Much of what is converted to news is packaged as a result of government and corporate spending and appears as "fuel" in the form of public relations, advertising, and other political/commercial communication. As has always been true, with ubiquity and indispen-

sability comes power, and with it the potential for abuse. Information clutter is only one concern; there are also imbalances in influence and credibility. As the value of such communication increases, business must increase the quantity and quality of its intervention in the public policy process if corporate interests are to be expressed without undue filtering by government. News media, as scholars have shown (Dominick, 1981; Theberge and Hazlett, 1982; Hess, 1984; Linsky, 1986), are more likely to act as a handmaiden of government and critic of business activities.

But what about "narrowcast" and other alternatives? Do they not make such fears obsolete by increasing distribution options and opening up a worldwide market for ideas as well as products? Satellite, cable, and other new telecommunications channels today present an almost bewildering ideational environment, raising new challenges and creating new opportunities (Heath and Nelson, 1986). This plethora of information creates a powerful clutter, in effect forcing key social institutions such as corporations to speak out vigorously if they are to be heard in debate over public policy and consumer issues. Internationally, as well as nationally, silence is too often interpreted as guilt. Technology makes possible a new dialogue at a time when social responsibility concerns are becoming an entrenched part of organizational personality, requiring business leaders to articulate their positions to a broad variety of critical audiences as corporations seek to respond to the host of intercultural social demands made of them. But effective communication requires that a corporation have a consistent voice. As Robert L. Dilenschneider, president of Hill & Knowlton, recently told a Houston audience, "The wired age we live in forces political and economic institutions to match their words and actions if they are to survive. The time has long passed where they can live behind words or say one thing and do another." Managers who fail to fully integrate communication planning as an essential, rather than add-on, element of their organization unnecessarily handicap useful interaction with their constituencies.

9. Then why do some business executives continue avoid-

ing openness? When the debate regarding how open businesses should be is over, the benefits from the expanding communication web have to be balanced against the problems stemming from an *opening up of the organization to negative scrutiny, particularly during a crisis.* New-technology companies have an advantage here over firms from more established "smokestack" industries. Since for the most part they have not been under press siege and their "products" lack such obvious environmental consequences, management can and usually does start off without being particularly defensive about its practices. We have no parallel such as "datatoxic waste" or "informational strip mining." That is the good news, but foretelling what horrors will be found in the information society must be part of a constant monitoring agenda for issues managers. For example, concerns about office computer "screen squint" and possible infertility associated with the manufacture of microchips are already being voiced. This potential for harm also raises new questions about the nature of the business social contract and whether efforts to create a single standard of "social responsibility" and "public accountability" are realistic given the many inconsistencies between alternative private and local/state/federal/international regulatory approaches and the types of new businesses we find emerging.

Even in an information/service-dominated economy, key traditional industries will continue to remain important. And we will likely see the two sectors working together cooperatively in many ways. Unfortunately, however, experienced business executives are often frankly uncomfortable with the power-sharing limitations on autocratic leadership implied by democratizing decision making through two-way communication. So we are talking not so much about how new technologies can be adapted for manufacturing needs as, at a more elementary level, about what making the commitment to more progressive public policy issue communication can mean to businesess today as well as tomorrow.

Enhanced telecommunication technologies make possible effective responsiveness to changing community needs, even for traditional industries. A commitment to openness and cooperation necessitated by an industry's vulnerability to public criticism and government intervention may well prove a benefit rather than a hindrance. A leader in this respect has been the chemical industry, through the National Chemical Response and Information Center and the Community Awareness and Emergency Response (CAER) Program, two initiatives launched by the Chemical Manufacturers Association (CMA) in the wake of the Bhopal tragedy. The center coordinates responses to requests for emergency and nonemergency information on chemicals and training for emergency-service personnel at the local level. CAER seeks to integrate industry emergency-response plans with those of communities where plants are located. These programs complement the efforts of the Chemical Transportation Emergency Center (CHEMTREC), set up in the early 1970s to serve as a twenty-four-hour clearinghouse for authoritative information on safely containing hazardous materials involved in transportation accidents.

CAER was born of two concepts: that the public should have access to information about hazardous materials and that communities should be prepared for emergencies. The CAER effort is an unprecedented industry initiative to establish a partnership with citizens, public officials, and emergency responders who live in communities with chemical facilities, according to Christopher Cathcart, CMA's manager of the CAER program. CAER further coordinates and cooperates with many groups within and outside the chemical industry. For example, CMA, the General Federation of Women's Clubs, the Association of American Railroads, and American Trucking Associations Inc. jointly developed a communication package to help citizens and community leaders begin emergency-response planning in cooperation with federal authorities ("Emergency Planning and the Right to Know," 1987).

## Conclusions

"What Is to Be Done?" Lenin once asked in a seminal outline of his thought (1902/1943). It is still a good question for contemporary executives to contemplate. Quoting the archetypical anticapitalist to a business audience may seem in-congruous, but on a more global scale we can draw a parallel to the era of uncertainty and opportunity he foresaw in the social upheaval of post-Czarist Russia. For today we are in much the same situation, with a curious mix of technological progress and social instability a seeming constant. The upsurge in jargon we have all had to add to our vocabularies, ranging from *microchip* to *modem*, simply reflects the tremendous technical advances ongoing in the information field. Our political lexicon has similarly advanced, including the term *issues management* itself, as we have become more sophisticated about the grass-roots interrelationship of business and politics.

In essence, two sets of problems remain. One requires foretelling the unique developments that a new information-based society will produce. The second may be the more diffi-cult—the problems we have inherited from the past, many of which will continue. This is to warn that, among other things, difficulties involving communication on public policy topics will persist. The business cadre has not been particularly effec-tive in communicating an ideology of capitalism or how indus-try is helping to solve social problems. Such failures have al-ready contributed to an erosion of confidence but could prove disastrous should the business community as a whole continue making this same mistake.

Beyond earning a profit, a basic task for today's executive leadership is to use the new information technologies to advo-cate the legitimacy and social worth of business, so that in the process of public policy making the role of competitive and efficient business as the generator of material well-being is ac-cepted and encouraged. Problems, of course, can be addressed by other means, but communication is essential to reach both mass and specialized audiences.

Standards of behavior for new high-technology and ser-vice-oriented businesses are not as well established as those for manufacturing, which have been developing over the past half century or more. Issues of esthetics (quality of work life), security (health and privacy concerns), fairness (the protectionism bat-tle), and equality (maximizing human resources) will carry over into whatever economy emerges in the next century. Drawing on the experience of their counterparts in the manufacturing sector, information-society-oriented issues managers have a unique window of opportunity to shape the agenda and to focus debate by calling for voluntary policy making before new protagonists arise.

In what may appear a rather polemical view (and probably is) and at the risk of being charged with retelling "old hat" observations, I think that, at the same time, the business community as a whole must join together to show that restrictions on communication and marketing limit the individual's right to be informed and to exercise free choice. Business communicators need to point out how the suppression of business rights is, more importantly, an infringement on individual civil liberties. Inaction could prove dangerous. The failures of the political system to control, let alone solve, continuing problems of drugs, poverty, security, and employment are acting to undermine constitutional freedoms and to invite backlash against corporations. Even today, commercially sponsored public policy messages continue to be a second-class form of speech in most countries (including the United States). It is not surprising that in the past ten years we have seen a concerted effort to apply global controls on business speech from such entities as the UN Centre on Transnational Corporations, the World Intellectual Property Organization, the World Health Organization, and UNESCO and the propagation of such concepts as the New International Economic Order and the New International Information Order. Similar critics exist in the United States, who may successfully implement their own proposed standards if business neglects to articulate its long-term worth, perhaps pointing toward a future not of deregulation but of greater regulation. Given all we know and all that remains to be done, should business men and women step aside for the new Lenins— unsympathetic ideologues and political manipulators who would further limit communication to ways they deem appropriate?

Though not necessarily a problem unique to an information age, the continuing battle over corporate communication gains significance as new technologies themselves become increasingly integral to business and society. Ironically, without the counterbalance of corporate speech, the real message of the information society could be the loss of freedom.

# Conclusion:
# Balancing the Interests
# of Competing Stakeholders:
# The New Role
# for Issues Management

*Robert L. Heath*

The end of a book offers an opportune moment to look
to the future, in this case the prospects for issues management.
This future is best understood in brief historical perspective.
The first modern decade of issues management, the 1960s, was
characterized by rage and an increasing awareness that companies could no longer conduct business as usual. The rage was
expressed by both sides. Activist groups were angry with what
they saw as rampant corporate irresponsibility; corporate leaders were disgusted by the criticism, which, to them, seemed
unwarranted and carping. The 1970s witnessed the emergence
of issues management primarily in the form of issue advertising,
which at times lied, distorted, and maligned while often overwhelming readers' willingness to wade through complex, self-
serving text. In the 1980s, issues management has matured into
a complex, integrated, and multifaceted discipline.

The next decade will offer many tests for issues management. One obvious challenge will be the continuing effort to
establish its legitimate and vital role in corporations — including planning and operations. A second challenge involves the
shift from a predominantly smokestack, industrial economy to

one where more and more employees will be involved in creating, storing, transferring, and marketing information, with its attendant hardware and software. This new commodity can be a blessing for our economy and will undoubtedly reshape our culture. But are there unforeseen public policy pitfalls? As increasing numbers of consumers and workers enjoy the advantages of this new age, what problems will they find that need to be addressed in public policy arenas?

The dominant challenge facing the private sector will be to balance stakeholders' interests in ways that allow business to be conducted profitably, productively, and responsibly with a minimum of interference from outside forces. To accomplish these ends, business leaders must demonstrate responsibility by action and increase the public's understanding of companies' needs and accomplishments. Issues managers must continue to overcome what, to many judicious critics, at least, appears to have been a half century of irresponsible actions that have severely damaged the reputation of the private sector. As it strives to meet this challenge, issues management will certainly benefit by increasing the skills needed to monitor issues, integrate the findings into planning and operations, and communicate with key publics. The prospect of issues managers can be enhanced by becoming increasingly capable of balancing the interests of competing stakeholders.

### Managerial Philosophy: Balancing Stakeholder Interests

An important conceptual change is occurring in management theory. The key ingredient in this change is the recognition that a company must respond to many stakeholders. The term *stakeholder* is often used in public relations literature to define a targeted audience, one with whom the company wants to communicate. But elsewhere the term is used with a broader meaning. Stakeholders are those persons and groups who have a vested interest in how a company performs. The media as a stakeholder, for instance, want to report about companies as well as sell advertising to them. Consumers are stakeholders, as are legislators, regulators, unions, neighbors, employees, and so on.

Effective management consists in balancing stakeholder interests, which often compete.

Emphasizing the problems of addressing stakeholder needs, Freeman (1984) observes, "First of all, we must understand, from a rational perspective, who are the stakeholders in the organization and what are the perceived stakes. Second, we must understand the organizational processes used to either implicitly or explicitly manage the organization's relationships with its stakeholders and whether these processes 'fit' with the rational 'stakeholder map' of the organization. Finally, we must understand the set of transactions or bargains among the organization and its stakeholders and deduce whether these negotiations 'fit' with the stakeholder map and the organizational processes for stakeholders" (p. 53).

Accurately identifying and being sensitive to the needs of a company's stakeholders is itself a large task. Balancing the competing interests is another matter. One stakeholder, the customer, wants a cheaper product of higher quality. At the same time, activist-group stakeholders press for operating changes (such as environmental protection or increased nutrition) by appealing to two other groups of stakeholders — legislators and regulators. The changes sought by the activist groups may increase the cost of the product (thereby hurting consumer stakeholders) and lower the profit, thereby lessening wages (employee stakeholders) and dividends (shareholder stakeholders). The employees of one company are the consumers of goods and services provided by other companies. All these groups are neighbors seeking the highest quality of life possible.

The challenge of balancing the interests of the company and its various stakeholders is requiring a new definition of the role of public relations and public affairs practitioners (Freeman, 1984, p. 222). Issues management will continue to expect corporate communication departments to identify key stakeholders, to calculate the stake each has in the company's activities, to estimate the degree of compatibility, and to communicate with each in an effort to foster understanding and appreciation of the company's position. In connection with this last activity, corporate communicators will be asked to help their managements ever more accurately determine which issues will yield to communication strategies and which will not. An even greater challenge of corporate communicators will be to partici- pate effectively in a dialogue to refine and affirm each stakeholder's conviction that business wants to achieve a mean- ingful partnership. Corporate communication often encoun- ters distrust because the messages are assumed to represent the company's vested interest, not the common interest of company and stakeholder.

To meet this challenge, new measurement techniques and unique criteria will be needed to guide the performance/ communication activities of businesses. One approach to this analysis can be drawn from Mitroff's (1983) argument that domi- nant archetypes can be used to evaluate the performance of managers. How managers typically perform, he says, can be translated into archetypes that themselves hold a stake in each manager's performance. Thus, to gauge a manager's effective- ness, he suggests that the person be classified according to the archetype he or she exemplifies. Each manager falls into one or more of a set of categories that includes Sherman tanks, com- plainers, wet blankets, and innovators. Once the manager is categorized, the person evaluating the behavior can determine whether that kind of behavior is appropriate to the task and situation.

By extrapolating from Mitroff's analysis, we might iden- tify archetypes to describe companies' performance: "Buyer be- ware," "Fly-by-night," "Read the fine print," "Check is in the mail," "Strip miner," "You can't make an omelet without breaking eggs," "We'll get back to you," "Planned obsolescence," and other simi- larly negative images. But there are also archetypes embodying positive images, such as "Customer knows best," "Customer is always right," "Your problem is our problem," "Service first," "Quality is job one," and "Superachiever." Issues management research can advance our understanding of what archetypes are stakeholders of corporate activities and how they can be used as yardsticks to measure performance. Techniques such as these can be used to define the public interest and see that it fits with an ideal of corporate behavior that does not waste the advantages society can accrue through the public sector.

### Performance Standards: What Is the Public Interest?

Corporate performance is the issue, but a related concern is the difficult challenge of defining the public interest. Conventional wisdom says that corporations must act in the public interest. Sethi (1977, p. 58) used this model to focus attention on the gap that can exist between corporate behavior and public expectation. When this gap occurs, activist groups and journalists broadcast their dissatisfaction. The primary assumption implicit in the formula is that when companies are at odds with approved standards of public expectation, they must change their operations to conform.

This model offers two challenges to issues management. The first is to constantly monitor prevailing standards of corporate responsibility and ensure that companies comply with them. This is a very realistic approach to issues management, but it grants supremacy to a hazy and often shallow understanding that outsiders have of company operations and obligations. This model assumes that the public interest is definable and reasonable.

Here is the crux of the second challenge facing issues managers in the next decade. Companies have a right and a responsibility to discuss with key constituencies the preferred standards of corporate performance. Public policy cannot be developed that is in the best interest of this country if it is founded on unwarranted indictments and faulty premises. Nor can public policy last if it unduly favors corporate interests. Corporate voices are beginning to address key issues with increased sophistication and greater sensitivity to public concern. Our national ideology has an unswerving commitment to support capitalism; but beyond that, the nation is far from consensus on broad public policy stances. Thus, a key challenge facing issues managers is to help sharpen the national sense of the fit between corporate and public interests.

The mood swings of the past fifteen years regarding energy issues supply ample evidence of the kind of problem that can arise when this consensus is lacking. For decades oil companies were allowed virtual free rein in the discovery, processing, and delivery of their products. Then groups protested the ravaging of the environment. Oil companies were charged with tax favoritism because of oil depletion allowances. The embargo brought a crisis of confidence that has softened only as gas pump prices have stabilized or dropped while the availability of product is sufficient so that the public is not waiting in line to top off automobile gasoline tanks. Now cries are heard calling for a national energy policy because states dependent on oil economies are in an economic depression and because the nation is becoming increasingly dependent on foreign oil sources. This single example demonstrates the need for informed and comprehensive public policy. Helping to formulate this kind of policy is a major challenge for issues managers.

These mood swings of policy are not constructive for company long-range planning. Nor are they appropriate for wise legislation, regulation, or planning by individual families. The concept of stakeholders has for the first time clearly delineated the variety of persons who shape and are affected by company practices and public policy formulations. Balancing these interests will test issues managers' intellect and skill. The challenge involves careful and insightful strategic planning that isolates variables that need to be considered for effective corporate operations. From this planning core, issues managers need to inform key stakeholders of what companies must have in order to provide goods and services and to serve public, as well as private, interests. The spirit of secrecy and combativeness that has sometimes characterized company relations with stakeholders must be reevaluated. Issues managers will be challenged to foster and reinforce management's commitment to the virtue of a constructive partnership with stakeholders.

## Big Brotherism—Ensuring Responsible Issues Management

The magnitude of these challenges, coupled with increasingly sophisticated tools, can lead to abuse by issues managers. The success of issues advocacy, grass-roots mobilization, and public policy clashes can be the undoing of issues management. This paradox results from the possibility that tactical sophistication and the ability to spend large sums of money on public policy battles can be so successful that a boomerang effect occurs. Companies, specifically issues managers, must submit their tactical efforts to scrupulous standards of ethics and must avoid tipping the scales so far that public outbursts call for increased public policy restraints, including controls on how companies participate in public policy campaigns.

In 1978, congressional hearings examined the problems of regulating issues communication. Regulatory machinery exists in the form of the Internal Revenue Service, the Federal Communications Commission, and the Federal Trade Commission. The first administers controls by prohibiting the tax-deductibility of certain campaign costs associated with public policy efforts. The FCC is in a position to influence corporate access to the electronic media, and the FTC can be authorized to scrutinize advertising content for fairness, deception, and accuracy. (For an extensive examination of this issue, see Heath and Nelson, 1986, chap. 4.) Critics abound who argue that deep-pocket spending so distorts the public policy agenda that the will of the people is denied. So far these accusations against deep-pocket spending lack much substance and are primarily rhetorical ploys. But this is a sensitive area worthy of constant monitoring.

This concern is likely to become more serious as companies acquire more tools to use in their public policy campaigns. These tools have grown up to serve product/service advertising and marketing campaigns as well as political campaigns. For the most part, these new methods have resulted from two convergent developments: creation of massive computer systems and sophisticated applications of social science research. Specialty agencies are now capable of providing companies with very narrow, targeted segmentation of populations who are sensitive to company public policy stances and who are willing to participate in grass-roots efforts. At least one agency can provide companies with computer-generated letters in slightly different versions printed with different type fonts on different kinds of stationery. These letters can be sent to carefully segmented, targeted populations who are likely to use the letters in mail campaigns to influence legislative and regulatory actions. The person need only sign the letter and drop it in the mailbox. Another technological innovation allows data-base computer systems to generate specially designed speeches to be delivered by speakers' bureaus. At least one statewide utility company has created a speakers' bureau that enables a speaker to select a speech from the computer by indicating the topic desired and the demographics of the intended audience. In minutes, the computer sorts through the available versions and segments of appropriate texts and arranges them into an address specifically designed for that audience.

Increasingly scholars and corporate behavioral researchers are delving into the cognitive processes related to effective issues advertising. Until recently very few studies were being conducted to determine how people receive and yield to issues advertising. Most of the advertising models being used in ad message design are derived from product/service advertising or standard public relations practices. Even the most casual observer knows that issues ads require quite different kinds of cognitive processes. To reach a targeted audience by breaking through advertising clutter is a major achievement. In addition, many people resist reading large amounts of ad copy devoted to public policy issues, often presented only from the company perspective. As research continues, its findings can be abused.

This kind of technology and research can assist companies in being more effective in getting their messages across to audiences, thereby decreasing the likelihood that unwise and ill-advised regulation will come about. Carried to an extreme and abused, however, such innovation will likely lead corporate critics to demand cessation of such tactics, thereby undoing a decade of hard work. The key: responsible, fair, and truthful issues campaigns. No one should be more capable of increasing the effectiveness of corporate communication than a well-educated, talented, and conscientious issues communicator who is willing to study the advances in behavioral research. Likewise, no one is better equipped to understand the necessity of responsible actions and to determine the latitudes of acceptable activities.

In the coming decades, issues managers will face many tests — including the ever-present battle to be a legitimate part of corporate planning and operations. This need to be effective must be held in check by a strong sense of the larger public good. The challenges are great, but the rewards can be increased understanding of and appreciation for the efforts of the private sector. Here is the foundation of a meaningful partnership among stakeholders as well as the challenge to issues management.

A recent advertisement by General Motors is evidence of the direction of the future. The ad acknowledges that the company has had to work hard to blend people and technology to produce better-built cars. The company proclaims an end to the old production method that "tends to exclude the creative and managerial skills of the people who work on the line." The company believes "that new technology must be integrated with new social systems in a human partnership. A partnership that gives people authority over machines and responsibility for their work." The benefits to the consumer are several: "We are already the leader in safety. The Insurance Institute for Highway Safety has rated GM cars best for nine consecutive years, based on overall injury claim experience. Now, in only the past few years, we've greatly improved the fit and finish of our cars. The driveability (that's the way the powertrain operates when it's in the car) of our cars has also improved significantly, according to our customer-oriented quality audit." The company has set its goal "to be the undisputed quality leader in every price class in which we compete." The company believes, "The vision is paying off." The theme is responsibility. Undoubtedly, General Motors has some distance to go to satisfy all its stakeholders. But by this public admission, it seems bent on managing its stakeholders in the best interest of all. That is the issues management goal of the future.

# References

Abell, D. F., and Hammond, J. S. *Strategic Market Planning: Problems and Analytical Approaches.* Englewood Cliffs, N.J.: Prentice-Hall, 1979.

Adams, D. "Effective School Business Partnerships." *School Business Affairs,* 1985, *51* (12), 24–25.

"Advantages of an Incumbent Seeking Re-election." *Americans for Democratic Action Special Report.* Washington, D.C.: Americans for Democratic Action, Dec. 1980.

Alexander, H. E. *The Case for PACs.* Washington, D.C.: Public Affairs Council, 1983.

Alexander, H. E., and Haggerty, B. A. *The Federal Election Campaign Act: After a Decade of Political Reform.* Los Angeles: Citizens' Research Foundation, 1981.

Alexander, H. E., and Haggerty, B. A. *PACs and Parties: Relationships and Interrelationships.* Los Angeles: Citizens' Research Foundation, 1984.

Alinsky, S. *Rules for Radicals—A Practical Primer for Realistic Radicals.* New York: Random House, 1971.

Anderson, J. E., Brady, D. W., and Bullock, C., III. *Public Policy and Politics in America.* North Scituate, Mass.: Duxbury Press, 1978.

Andrews, P. N. "Public Affairs Offices and Their Evaluation." Unpublished doctoral dissertation, School of Management, Boston University, 1987.

Ansoff, H. I., and others. "Does Planning Pay? The Effect of

Planning on Success of Acquisitions in American Firms." *Long Range Planning*, 1970, *3* (2), 2–7.

Arrington, C. B., Jr., and Sawaya, R. N. "Issues Management in an Uncertain Environment." *Long Range Planning*, 1984a, *17* (6), 17–24.

Arrington, C. B., Jr., and Sawaya, R. N. "Managing Public Affairs: Issues Management in an Uncertain Environment." *California Management Review*, 1984b, *26* (4), 148–160.

Ascher, W. *Forecasting: An Appraisal for Policy-Makers and Planners.* Baltimore: Johns Hopkins University Press, 1978.

Aupperle, K. E., Carroll, A. B., and Hatfield, J. D. "An Empirical Examination of the Relationship Between Corporate Social Responsibility and Profitability." *Academy of Management Journal*, 1985, *28* (2), 446–463.

Belitsos, B., and Misra, J. *Business Telematics: Corporate Networks for the Information Age.* Homewood, Ill.: Dow Jones–Irwin, 1986.

Beniger, J. R. *The Control Revolution: Technological and Economic Controls of the Information Society.* Cambridge, Mass.: Harvard University Press, 1986.

Bennett, J. T., and DiLorenzo, T. J. *Destroying Democracy: How Government Funds Partisan Politics.* Washington, D.C.: Cato Institute, 1985.

Berg, M., and others. "Factors Affecting Utilization of Technology Assessment Studies in Policy-Making." Institute report, Center for Research on Utilization of Scientific Knowledge, Institute for Social Research, University of Michigan, Ann Arbor, 1978.

Bergner, D. J. "The Maturing of Public Interest Groups." *Public Relations Quarterly*, 1986a, *31* (3), 14–16.

Bergner, D. J. (ed.). *Public Interest Profiles.* (5th ed.) Washington, D.C.: Foundation for Public Affairs, 1986b.

Bernays, E. L. *The Engineering of Consent.* Norman: University of Oklahoma Press, 1955.

Berry, J. M. *The Interest Group Society.* Boston: Little, Brown, 1984.

Block, P. *Flawless Consulting: A Guide to Getting Your Expertise Used.* La Jolla, Calif.: University Associates, 1981.

Boorstein, D. *The Republic of Technology.* New York: Harper & Row, 1978.

Boston University Public Affairs Research Group. *Public Affairs Offices and Their Functions: Summary of Survey Responses.* Boston: School of Management, Boston University, 1981.

Brenner, S. N. "Business and Politics — An Update." *Harvard Business Review,* 1979, *57* (6), 149–163.

Brodeur, P. *Outrageous Misconduct: The Asbestos Industry on Trial.* New York: Pantheon Books, 1985.

Brown, J. K. *This Business of Issues: Coping with the Company's Environments.* New York: Conference Board, 1979.

Buchholz, R. A. *Business Environment and Public Policy: Implications for Management.* Englewood Cliffs, N.J.: Prentice-Hall, 1982.

Buchholz, R. A. *The Essentials of Public Policy for Management.* Englewood Cliffs, N.J.: Prentice-Hall, 1985.

Buchholz, R. A., Evans, W. D., and Wagley, R. A. *Management Response to Public Issues: Concepts and Cases in Strategy Formulation.* Englewood Cliffs, N.J.: Prentice-Hall, 1985.

Burke, W. W. *Organization Development: Principles and Practices.* Boston: Little, Brown, 1982.

Chase, W. H. *Issue Management: Origins of the Future.* Stamford, Conn.: Issue Action Publications, 1984.

Coates, J. F., and Jarratt, J. "Issues Identification and Management: Developing a Research Agenda." Research report, Electric Power Research Institute, Palo Alto, Calif., 1986.

Coates, J. F., and others. *Issues Management: How You Can Plan, Organize, and Manage for the Future.* Mt. Airy, Md.: Lomond Publications, 1986.

Crable, R. E., and Vibbert, S. L. "Managing Issues and Influencing Public Policy." *Public Relations Review,* 1985, *11* (2), 3–16.

Davis, E. H. *But We Were Born Free.* Indianapolis: Bobbs-Merrill, 1954.

Democratic Study Group, U.S. House of Representatives. "Troubling Trends in Election Financing . . . Grassroots Money Shrinks as PAC Money Grows." *Special Report,* No. 99-22. Oct. 22, 1985.

Dizard, W. P., Jr. *The Coming Information Age.* New York: Longman, 1982.

Dominick, J. R. "Business Coverage in Network Newscasts." *Journalism Quarterly,* 1981, *58,* 179–185, 191.

Drew, E. *Politics and Money: The New Road to Corruption*. New York: Macmillan, 1983.

Drucker, P. F. "The New Meaning of Corporate Social Responsibility." *California Management Review*, 1984, *26* (2), 53–63.

Dunlop, J. T. "The Concerns: Business and Public Policy." *Harvard Business Review*, 1979, *57* (6), 86–87.

Ehling, W. P., and Hesse, M. B. "Use of 'Issue Management' in Public Relations." *Public Relations Review*, 1983, *9* (2), 18–35.

Electric Power Research Institute. "Issues Identification and Management: The Start of the Art of Methods and Techniques." Research report, Electric Power Research Institute, Palo Alto, Calif., 1985.

"Emergency Planning and the Right to Know." *ChemEcology* [Chemical Manufacturers Association, Washington, D.C.], Mar. 1987, entire issue.

Ettema, J. S., and Griswold, W. F., Jr. "Information Technology and Moral Vision: A Study of Enduring Social Values in the Information Age." In J. S. Salvaggio and J. Bryant (eds.), *Media Use in the Information Age*. Hillsdale, N.J.: Erlbaum, 1988.

Ewing, R. P. "Advocacy Advertising: The Voice of Business in Public Policy Debate." *Public Affairs Review*, 1982, *3*, 23–39.

Ewing, R. P. *Managing the New Bottom Line: Issues Management for Senior Executives*. Homewood, Ill.: Dow Jones–Irwin, 1987.

Eyestone, R. *From Social Issues to Public Policy*. New York: Wiley, 1978.

Faulhaber, G., and others (eds.). *Services in Transition: The Impact of Information Technology on the Service Sector*. Cambridge, Mass.: Ballinger, 1986.

Federal Election Commission. "FEC Final Report of '84 Elections Confirms Majority of PAC Money Went to Incumbents." News release, Federal Election Commission (Washington, D.C.), Dec. 1, 1985.

Federal Election Commission. "PAC Numbers Continue to Drop in 1985." News release, Federal Election Commission, Jan. 20, 1986.

Federal Election Commission. "1986 Congressional Spending Tops $450 Million." News release, Federal Election Commission, May 10, 1987.

Field, A. R., and Neff, R. "'Big Brother Inc.' May Be Closer than You Thought." *Business Week*, Feb. 9, 1987, pp. 84–86.

Finger, H. B. *Informing the Public About Nuclear Power: The Opportunities Ahead*. Washington, D.C.: U.S. Committee for Energy Awareness, 1986.

Frederick, W. C. "Toward CSR3: Why Ethical Analysis Is Indispensable and Unavoidable in Corporate Affairs." *California Management Review*, 1986, *28* (2), 126–141.

Freeman, R. E. *Strategic Management: A Stakeholder Approach*. Boston: Pitman, 1984.

Friedman, M. *Capitalism and Freedom*. Chicago: University of Chicago Press, 1962.

Friedman, M. "The Social Responsibility of Business Is to Increase Its Profits." *New York Times Magazine*, Sept. 1970, pp. 32–33, 122–125.

Galbraith, J. *Designing Complex Organizations*. Reading, Mass.: Addison-Wesley, 1973.

Gamson, W. A. *Power and Discontent*. Homewood, Ill.: Dorsey Press, 1968.

Gamson, W. A. *The Strategy of Social Protest*. Homewood, Ill.: Dorsey Press, 1975.

Gandy, O. H., Jr. *Beyond Agenda Setting: Information Subsidies and Public Policy*. Norwood, N.J.: Ablex, 1982.

Gluck, F., Kaufman, S., and Walleck, A. S. "The Four Phases of Strategic Management." *Journal of Business Strategy*, 1982, *2* (3), 9–21.

Goodman, S. E. "Why Few Corporations Monitor Social Issues." *Public Relations Journal*, 1983, *39* (4), 20.

Gray, D. H. "Uses and Misuses of Strategic Planning." *Harvard Business Review*, 1986, *86* (1), 89–97.

Hax, A. C., and Majluf, N. S. *Strategic Management: An Integrative Perspective*. Englewood Cliffs, N.J.: Prentice-Hall, 1984a.

Hax, A. C., and Majluf, N. S. "The Corporate Strategic Planning Process." *Interfaces*, 1984b, *14* (1), 47–60.

Heard, A. *The Costs of Democracy*. Chapel Hill: University of North Carolina Press, 1960.

Heath, R. L., and Douglas, W. "Issues Advertising and Its Effect on Public Opinion Recall." *Public Relations Review*, 1986, *12* (2), 47–56.

Heath, R. L., and Nelson, R. A. *Issues Management: Corporate Public Policymaking in an Information Society.* Beverly Hills, Calif.: Sage, 1986.

Heinz, L., and Coates, J. F. *Models for Issues Management: Superfund and RCRA as Test Cases.* Washington, D.C.: Edison Electric Institute, 1986.

Held, W. G. "Executive Skills: The Repertoire Needs Enlarging." *Columbia Journal of World Business*, 1967, *2* (2), 81–87.

Hersey, P. *The Situational Leader.* New York: Warner Books, 1985.

Hersey, P., Blanchard, K., and Natemeyer, W. *Situational Leadership, Perception, and the Impact of Power.* Escondido, Calif.: Center for Leadership Studies, 1979.

Hess, S. *The Government/Press Connection: Press Officers and Their Offices.* Washington, D.C.: Brookings Institution, 1984.

Hoffman, L. "Beyond Power and Control: Toward a 'Second Order' Family Systems Therapy." *Family Systems Medicine*, 1985, *3* (4), 381–396.

Hultman, K. *The Path of Least Resistance: Preparing Employees for Change.* La Jolla, Calif.: Learning Concepts/University Associates, 1979.

Jones, T. M. "Corporate Control and the Limits of Managerial Power." *Business Forum*, 1985, *10* (1), 16–21.

Karger, D. W., and Malik, Z. A. "Long Range Planning and Organizational Performance." *Long Range Planning*, 1975, *8* (6), 60–64.

Kiefer, C., and Senge, P. "Metanoic Organizations." In J. Adams (ed.), *Transforming Work: A Collection of Organization Transformation Readings.* Alexandria, Va.: Miles River Press, 1984.

Kiefer, C., and Stroh, P. "A New Paradigm for Developing Organizations." In J. Adams (ed.), *Transforming Work: A Collection of Organization Transformation Readings.* Alexandria, Va.: Miles River Press, 1984.

King, W. R., and Cleland, D. I. *Strategic Planning and Policy.* New York: Van Nostrand Reinhold, 1978.

Lang, K., and Lang, G. E. *Collective Dynamics.* New York: Crowell, 1961.

Lenin, V. I. "What Is to Be Done?" In V. I. Lenin, *Selected Works.* Vol. 2. New York: International Publishers, 1943. (Originally published 1902.)

Lerond, L. R. "Development of a Cost Model of Corporate Social Responsibility: Implications for Issues Management." Unpublished master's thesis, School of Communication, University of Houston, 1986.

Lesly, P. *Overcoming Opposition: A Survival Manual for Executives.* Englewood Cliffs, N.J.: Prentice-Hall, 1984.

Levy, A. "Second-Order Planned Change: Definition and Conceptualization." *Organizational Dynamics,* 1986, *15* (1), 5–20.

Lindblom, C. E. "The Science of 'Muddling Through.'" *Public Administration Review,* 1959, *19* (2), 79–88.

Lindblom, C. E. *Politics and Markets: The World's Political Economic Systems.* New York: Basic Books, 1977.

Linsky, M. *Impact: How the Press Affects Federal Policymaking.* New York: Norton, 1986.

Littlejohn, S. E. "Competition and Cooperation: New Trends in Corporate Public Issue Identification and Resolution." *California Management Review,* 1986, *19* (1), 109–123.

Lydenberg, S. D., and others. *Rating America's Corporate Conscience.* Reading, Mass.: Addison-Wesley, 1986.

McCloskey, D. N. *The Rhetoric of Economics.* Madison: University of Wisconsin Press, 1985.

Madison, J. "Topic 10: The Control of Majority Factions." In H. M. Bishop and S. Hendel (eds.), *Basic Issues of American Democracy: A Book of Readings.* East Norwalk, Conn.: Appleton-Century-Crofts, 1948. (Originally published 1787.)

Mahon, J. F. "The Corporate Public Affairs Office: Structure, Behavior and Impact." Unpublished doctoral dissertation, School of Management, Boston University, 1982.

Marrus, S. K. *Building the Strategic Plan: Find, Analyze, and Present the Right Information.* New York: Wiley, 1984.

Mason, K. "The Multinational Corporation: Central Institution of Our Age." In R. B. Dickie and L. Rounie (eds.), *Corporations and the Common Good.* Notre Dame, Ind.: University of Notre Dame Press, 1986.

Meadow, R. G. "The Political Dimensions of Nonproduct Advertising." *Journal of Communication*, 1981, *31* (3), 69–82.

Michael, D. N. *On Learning to Plan—and Planning to Learn: The Social Psychology of Changing Toward Future-Responsive Societal Learning*. San Francisco: Jossey-Bass, 1973.

Mintz, M. *At Any Cost: Corporate Greed, Women, and the Dalkon Shield*. New York: Pantheon Books, 1985.

Mitroff, I. I. *Stakeholders of the Organizational Mind: Toward a New View of Organizational Policy Making*. San Francisco: Jossey-Bass, 1983.

Morgan, G. "Cybernetics and Organization Theory: Epistemology or Technique?" *Human Relations*, 1982, *35* (7), 521–537.

Mutch, R. E. *Campaigns, Congress, and Courts*. New York: Praeger, forthcoming.

Nagelschmidt, J. S. (ed.). *The Public Affairs Handbook*. New York: AMACOM, 1982.

Nelson, R. A. "Entering a Brave New World: The Impact of the New Information and Telecommunications Technologies." *Journal of the University Film and Video Association*, 1983, *35* (4), 23–34.

Nolan, S. E., and Shayon, D. R. *Leveraging the Impact of Public Affairs: A Guidebook Based on Practical Experience for Corporate Affairs Executives*. Philadelphia: HRN, 1984.

Oberschall, A. *Social Conflict and Social Movements*. Englewood Cliffs, N.J.: Prentice-Hall, 1973.

O'Conner, R. *Planning Under Uncertainty: Multiple Scenarios and Contingency Planning*. New York: Conference Board, 1978.

Ogilvy, D. *Ogilvy on Advertising*. New York: Crown, 1983.

Ogura, K. "New Tasks and New Uncertainties: The Impact of Information Technologies." *Speaking of Japan*, 1987, *7* (75), 22–25.

O'Toole, J. E. "Advocacy Advertising Shows the Flag." *Public Relations Journal*, 1975, *31* (11), 14–15.

Pagan, R. D., Jr. "Issue Management: No Set Path." Remarks presented to the Issues Management Association, New York City, Nov. 7, 1983.

Parenti, M. *Inventing Reality: The Politics of the Mass Media.* New York: St. Martin's Press, 1986.

Paul, R. N., and Taylor, J. W. "The State of Strategic Planning." *Business,* 1986, *36* (1), 37–43.

Peck, M. S. *The Road Less Traveled.* New York: Simon & Schuster, 1978.

Pfeffer, J., and Salancik, G. R. *The External Control of Organizations: A Resource Dependence Perspective.* New York: Harper & Row, 1978.

Porat, M. U. *The Information Economy.* Washington, D.C.: U.S. Department of Commerce, 1977.

Post, J. E. *Corporate Behavior and Social Change.* Reston, Va.: Reston Publishing, 1978.

Preston, L. E., and Post, J. E. *Private Management and Public Policy: The Principle of Public Responsibility.* Englewood Cliffs, N.J.: Prentice-Hall, 1975.

Public Affairs Research Group, School of Management, Boston University. "Public Affairs Offices and Their Functions: Highlights of a National Survey." *Public Affairs Review,* 1981, *2,* 88–99.

Salvaggio, J. L. (ed.). *Telecommunications: Issues and Choices for Society.* New York: Longman, 1983.

Samuelson, R. J. "The Campaign Reform Failure." *New Republic,* Sept. 5, 1983, pp. 28–36.

Schmertz, H. *Good-bye to the Low Profile: The Art of Creative Confrontation.* Boston: Little, Brown, 1986.

Schwartz, P., Teige, P. J., and Harmon, W. W. *Assessment of Future National and International Problem Areas.* Report NSF/ STP76-02573. Menlo Park, Calif.: Stanford Research Institute, 1977. Summarized in P. Schwartz, P. J. Teige, and W. W. Harmon, "In Search of Tomorrow's Crises." *The Futurist,* 1977, *11* (10), 269–273.

Sethi, S. P. (ed.). *The Unstable Ground: Corporate Social Policy in a Dynamic Society.* Los Angeles: Melville, 1974.

Sethi, S. P. *Advocacy Advertising and Large Corporations: Social Conflict, Big Business Image, the News Media and Public Policy.* Lexington, Mass.: Heath, 1977.

Sethi, S. P. "Corporate Political Activism." *California Management Review*, 1982, *24* (3), 32–42.

Shapiro, I. S. *America's Third Revolution*. New York: Harper & Row, 1984.

Sinclair, W. "Consumer Activist Learns to Work with the 'Enemy.'" *Gannett Westchester Newspaper*, Sept. 23, 1986, p. D1.

Sorauf, F. J. "Caught in the Thicket: The Supreme Court and Campaign Finance." *Constitutional Commentary*, 1986, *3* (1), 97–121.

Stanley, G.D.D. *Managing External Issues: Theory and Practice*. Greenwich, Conn.: JAI Press, 1985.

Steiner, G. A. *Strategic Planning: What Every Manager Must Know*. New York: Free Press, 1979.

Stridsberg, A. B., in conjunction with the International Advertising Association. *Controversy Advertising: How Advertisers Present Points of View in Public Affairs*. New York: Hastings House, 1977.

Theberge, L. J., and Hazlett, T. W. (eds.). *TV Coverage of the Oil Crisis: How Well Was the Public Served?* 3 vols. Washington, D.C.: Media Institute, 1982.

Thompson, J. D. *Organizations in Action: Social Science Bases of Administrative Theory*. New York: McGraw-Hill, 1967.

Thune, S. S., and House, R. J. "Where Long-Range Planning Pays Off." *Business Horizons*, 1970, *13* (8), 81–87.

Tocqueville, A. de. *Democracy in America*. Vol. 1. New York: Vintage Books, 1945. (Originally published 1835.)

Turk, J.V.S. "Forecasting Tomorrow's Public Relations." *Public Relations Review*, 1986, *12* (3), 12–21.

Ungson, G. R., James, C., and Spicer, B. H. "The Effects of Regulatory Agencies on Organizations in Wood Products and High Technology/Electronics Industries." *Academy of Management Journal*, 1985, *28* (2), 426–445.

U.S. Department of Energy, Energy Information Administration. *Annual Outlook for U.S. Electric Power 1986*. Washington, D.C.: U.S. Department of Energy, 1986.

Varan, D. "An Analysis of Zaikai Influence in Japanese Telecommunication Liberalization." Unpublished master's thesis, School of Communication, University of Houston, 1987.

Votaw, D., and Sethi, S. P. *The Corporate Dilemma.* Englewood Cliffs, N.J.: Prentice-Hall, 1974.

Waddock, S. "Understanding Social Partnerships: An Evolutionary Model of Partnerships." Working paper, School of Management, Boston College, 1986.

Wartick, S. L., and Cochran, P. L. "The Evolution of the Corporate Social Performance Model." *Academy of Management Review,* 1985, *10* (4), 758–769.

Wartick, S. L., and Rude, R. E. "Issues Management: Corporate Fad or Corporate Function?" *California Management Review,* 1986, *29* (1), 124–140.

Weick, K. E. "Organizational Culture as a Source of High Reliability." *California Management Review,* 1987, *29* (2), 112–127.

Weisbord, M. "Organizational Diagnosis: Six Places to Look for Trouble With or Without a Theory." *Group & Organization Studies,* 1976, *1,* 430–447.

Wiebe, R. H. *The Search for Order: 1877–1920.* New York: Hill and Wang, 1967.

Williams, O. F., and Houck, J. W. (eds.). *The Judeo-Christian Vision and the Modern Corporation.* Notre Dame, Ind.: University of Notre Dame Press, 1982.

Wright, J. R. "PACs, Contributions and Roll Calls: An Organizational Perspective." *American Political Science Review,* 1985, *79* (2), 400–414.

Wygant, A., and Markley, O. W. *Information and the Future: A Handbook of Sources and Strategies.* Westport, Conn.: Greenwood Press, 1988.

Zuckerman, E. "Senate Looks Good in Deft Anti-PAC Vote." *PACs & Lobbies,* 1985, *6* (24), 1–10.

# Index

## A

A. H. Robins Company, 5, 174; and Dalkon Shield, 6–7
Abell, D. F., 149
Activist groups: coalitions with, 185–198; future of, 378–379; and issues management, 176
Adams, D., 370
Aduss, E. L., 284, 287
Advertising. *See* Issue advertising
Advertising agencies: in issues management, 41–42; and USCEA, 293–304
Advocacy advertising, 215. *See also* Issue advertising
Aerojet-General's Good Citizenship Campaign, 260
Aetna Insurance Company, 6, 377
Alcohol Tax Unit, 323, 324, 326
Alcoholic beverage industry: gray and parallel markets in, 329–332; legal counsel in, 321; need for uniformity in, 322–329
Alexander, H. E., 169, 258, 259, 265, 267, 273, 337
Alinsky, S., 336, 337
All-Saver Certificate plan, 273
American Association of Retired Persons (AARP), 189, 190, 306
American Association of University Women, 190

American Bankers Association (ABA), 285, 305; BANKPAC, 262; and repeal of TEFRA, 307–320
American Beverage Alcohol Association, 285
American Coalition of Citizens with Disabilities, 190
American Electric Power System, 175
American Home Product, 7
*American Lamb Company* v. *United States*, 330
American Lung Association, 10
American Medical Association, 11
American Petroleum Institute, 187
Anderson, J. E., 52, 54
Andrews, P. N., 361
Ansoff, H. I., 152
Apple Computers, 371
Arrington, C. B., Jr., 26–27, 49, 73, 82, 335
Asbestos, 7–10
Ascher, W., 148
Atlantic Richfield Company (ARCO), 26, 49, 187; strategic planning of, 82–85
Atomic Energy Commission (AEC), 290
Aupperle, K. E., 13

## B

Banking Advisory Program, 315
Bankruptcy. *See* Chapter 11

This is a continuation of the copyright page.

Figure 4, Chapter Five, reprinted with permission from: *Journal of Business Strategy*, Winter 1982, Vol. 2, No. 3. Copyright © 1982, Warren, Gorham & Lamont, Inc., 210 South Street, Boston, MA 02111. All Rights Reserved.

Chapter Eight, "Reaching the Opinion Makers," was first published in *Good-bye to the Low Profile: The Art of Creative Confrontation* by Herbert Schmertz, published by Little, Brown and Company. © 1986 by Herbert Schmertz. Reprinted, with modifications, by permission of the author and the publisher.

The author is grateful to Mobil Corporation for permission to reproduce the op-ed and "Observations" columns that appear in Chapter Eight. Copyright © 1970, 1971, 1972, 1973, 1974, 1976, 1980, 1981, 1984 by Mobil Corporation. Reprinted with permission of Mobil Corporation.